D1117358

HANDBOOK OF SPECIAL VOCATIONAL NEEDS EDUCATION

Edited by
Gary D. Meers, Ed.D.
Associate Professor
Special Vocational Needs
Teacher Education
University of Nebraska
Lincoln, Nebraska

AN ASPEN PUBLICATION®
Aspen Systems Corporation
Rockville, Maryland
London
1980

Library of Congress Cataloging in Publication Data

Meers, Gary A.
Handbook of special vocational needs education.

Bibliography: p. 323
Includes index.
1. Handicapped children—Education—United States—Addresses, essays, lectures. 2. Socially handicapped children—Education—United States—Addresses, essays, lectures. 3. Vocational education—United States—Addresses, essays, lectures. 4. Education, Cooperative—United States—Addresses, essays, lectures. 5. Vocational education—Law and legislation—United States—Addresses, essays, lectures.
I. Title.
LC4019.M43 371.9 80-17759
ISBN: 0-89443-288-5

Library of Congress Catalog Card Number: 80-17759
ISBN: 0-89443-288-5

Printed in the United States of America

1 2 3 4 5

To the Special Needs Students

Table of Contents

Contributors

Catherine Batsche, Ph.D.
Coordinator
The Illinois Network of Occupational Programs for Handicapped and Disadvantaged Students
Illinois State University
Normal, IL

John D. Bies, Ph.D.
Associate Professor
Vocational-Technical Education
University of Tennessee
Memphis, TN

George W. Fair, Ph.D.
Associate Professor
Special Education
University of Texas at Dallas
Dallas, TX

Jack Kaufman, Ed.D.
Associate Professor
Vocational Special Needs
University of Idaho
Moscow, ID

David Kingsbury, M.Ed.
Assistant Professor
Vocational Special Needs Education
Bemidji State University
Bemidji, MN

Gary D. Meers, Ed.D.
Associate Professor
Special Vocational Needs
Teacher Education
University of Nebraska
Lincoln, NE

Suzanne Merwick, M.Ed.
Survival Skills Specialist
Survival Skills Training Center
Lincoln, NE

Roger Sathre, M.Ed.
Supervisor
Special Needs Programs
Idaho State Board for Vocational Education
Boise, ID

Kathryn M. Shada, M.Ed.
Survival Skills Specialist
Survival Skills Training Center
Lincoln, NE

Allen L. Steckelberg, M.Ed.
Instructor
Special/Vocational Education
University of Nebraska
Lincoln, NE

Karen L. Stern-Otazo, Ed.D.
University of Northern Colorado
Greeley, CO

Stanley F. Vasa, Ed.D.
Associate Professor
Special Education
University of Nebraska
Lincoln, NE

Robert C. West, M.Ed.
Personnel Development Coordinator
Special Education Section
Idaho State Dept. of Education
Boise, ID

Jerry L. Wircenski, Ed.D.
Associate Professor
Vocational Education
Pennsylvania State University
University Park, PA

Preface

This volume was written for three reasons: (1) to fill the void that currently exists in the literature dealing with special needs programming, (2) to provide an information base from which teachers, administrators, parents, advocates, and any other involved individuals can make well-informed decisions concerning programming for special needs students, and (3) to assist special needs students in progressing along life's pathway by making career decisions that are meaningful and realistic.

This book is intended for anyone who comes in contact with or teaches disadvantaged or handicapped (special needs) students. It is designed for use with graduate and undergraduate students enrolled in teacher preparation courses dealing with special needs students in vocational and career settings. It is well suited for use in inservice settings due to the practical nature of the content. It is also very useable by researchers and consultants because of the historical perspectives and programmatic sections presented. Parents and advocates will find it useful in assisting special needs students in the selection of appropriate programs due to the foundational information it presents. School administrators will find the book helpful in the establishment of special vocational needs programs due to the program organizations and designs set forth.

The book is divided into three main sections, each building upon the chapters of the preceding section.

Section I deals with the foundation of special vocational needs programs. Chapter 1 compares the various educational delivery systems currently being used in public schools, gives a historical perspective, and introduces the area of special vocational needs programming. Chapter 2 outlines and describes the federal legislation that impacts upon special needs students, programs, and educational personnel. Chapters 3 and 4 describe the students that are being served.

Section II serves as the base for program development and implementation. Chapter 5 deals with program development for special needs youth. Chapter 6 contains curriculum modification techniques and strategies that are suitable for use with all types of students. Chapter 7 covers the critical area of work experience and cooperative placement programs. Chapter 8 focuses on the provision of support services for special needs youth. Chapter 9 deals with the counseling support needed by special needs students.

Section III contains information about program evaluation, administration, and personnel needed by special needs students. Chapter 10 outlines the personnel preparation needed to serve special needs students. Chapter 11 identifies the role of parents and advocates in supporting special needs students in vocational training. Chapter 12 discusses the administrator's role in the establishment and conduct of special needs programs. The last chapter outlines the procedures for conducting an evaluation of both students and programs in the area of vocational special needs.

This book, in short, provides a sequential flow of information that allows the reader to become familiar with the students to be served, where and how they can be served, and the support systems needed to ensure their success.

Gary D. Meers, Ed.D.
August 1980

Acknowledgments

Words seem inadequate to express the deeply felt thanks to the many individuals who made this book possible.

I would like first to thank the other authors who contributed their creativeness, professional expertise, and concern for special needs students to make each chapter come alive and be placed in print. Their willingness to work within tight deadlines and not to become disturbed with my insistance that we meet those deadlines is especially appreciated. Their ultimate reward for the sacrifices they made during the writing time will be in better programming for special needs students throughout the United States.

I would also like to thank Chris, Richard, Karen, Denise, Bill, Susan, and hundreds of other students who were in my special needs classes and who are the inspiration and reason this book was written. They helped me to grow and become experienced in this area because they had the patience and ability to train me to be a special needs teacher.

A special thanks goes to the team at Aspen Systems Corporation. Curt Whitesel, Darlene Como, Margot Raphael, Eileen Higgins, and Russ Pottle combined into a most effective team of author support, bookcrafting, and marketing. They backed this endeavor and assisted at each step so that a dream could become a reality.

Marian Green provided the valuable typing support that is necessary for the success of any writing effort, and for this I owe a deep debt of gratitude.

Lastly, the authors thank their families for their support and willingness to share their time so that the book might be completed.

Chapter 1

An Introduction to Special Vocational Needs Education

Gary D. Meers, Ed.D.

INTRODUCTION

Every fall, a human mass migration occurs that rivals any migration undertaken by animals. This migration occurs when the school doors open and the educational process gets underway for another year. Parents purchase new clothes, school supplies, and colorful lunchboxes to prepare their kindergarten son or daughter for the very important first day of school. Many times there are tears shed, pictures taken, and goodbyes as entrance is made into the large and oftentimes overwhelming structure called a school.

Going with that small child are the hopes, dreams, and fantasies of the parents because they want only the very best for their child. They base these feelings upon the fact that in the United States every child is entitled to a quality education. The first day in kindergarten is the beginning of an educational experience that will transform a scared child of 5 or 6 into an 18-year-old young adult with a high school diploma.

In an ideal setting, this educational experience would occur slowly and sequentially, so that the parents and students could see their hopes and dreams being realized. Provisions would be made by the school for the unique needs of the student, and every school day would provide for instructional growth. Both the school and the student would be aware of and receptive to their educational rights and responsibilities. The student would come every day to learn, and the school would be prepared every day to teach, and thus education would be grand for everyone.

The problem with this ideal setting is that life simply does not operate that way. Children that are sent off to school as kindergarteners do not always have two parents waving goodbye at the doorway, nor do they always have new clothes, school supplies, or fancy lunchboxes. In many cases, they are fortunate if they have enough to eat, coats to wear, or broken pencils to carry. They start the educational process with many factors working against them. As a result, many of those who start this educational trek never complete their journey. Presently 25 percent of the students who start school drop out before receiving a high school diploma.[1] Others have handicaps that require special services in order for them to participate successfully in the schooling process.

No matter what environmental background they might come from or disability they might possess, all children in the educational system of the United States have a right to a quality educational program that will meet their needs. To meet these individual needs, we need comprehensive and specific programming that will allow participation in programs that previously have been closed or nonexistent for special needs students.

The book as a whole focuses on the development of delivery systems for special needs students enrolled in vocational programs. In order to develop a comprehensive series of delivery systems, the reader must possess an adequate background in the terminology and purposes of special vocational needs programming. This chapter deals with profiles of students, a historical perspective, and definition of terms and describes programs designed to serve special needs students.

DESCRIPTION OF YOUTH TO BE SERVED

There are two major descriptors used to identify special needs students enrolled in vocational programs. These descriptors are disadvantaged and handicapped.

The Disadvantaged

The disadvantaged are persons (other than handicapped persons) who "(1) have academic or economic disadvantages, and (2) require special services, assistance, or programs in order to enable them to succeed in vocational education programs."[2]

The disadvantaged are divided into two major categories, academic and economic.

Academically disadvantaged means that a person

1. "lacks reading and writing skills;
2. "lacks mathematical skills; or
3. "performs below grade level."[3]

Economically disadvantaged means that

1. "family income is at or below national poverty level;
2. "participant or parent(s) or guardian of the participant is unemployed;

3. "participant or parent(s) of participant is recipient of public assistance; or
4. "participant is institutionalized or under state guardianship."[4]

The above legislative (Public Law 94-482) definition sets forth the technical aspects of defining the disadvantaged; but, from an educational perspective, there are many other influencing factors that must be noted when defining the term disadvantaged.

A disadvantaged student may have many personal problems that present themselves as barriers to successful completion of vocational training. The home situation may be such that the parents or guardian of the student have no expressed interest in the student's schooling. Whatever the student does at school is O.K.; if the student does not go to school, that would be O.K. too.

Another critical barrier to school success is the student's attitude. It has been said that 90 percent of success is in having the proper attitude. In many situations, this saying holds true. The disadvantaged student, after repeated failures at the elementary school level, moves to a junior high or middle school level only to encounter more of the same. By meeting this same situation over and over again, the student's attitude changes from one of hope to one of despair. To get to this position of nonsuccess, the student generally will have moved through four stages of failure. These stages are disinterest, disillusionment, disassociation, and disenfranchisement.

Disinterested youth are those who cannot see any subject, topic, or activity within the school setting that is of benefit to them. Social Studies is the study of a bygone era with no relevance to the present-day setting. English is a waste of time because everyone knows how to talk. Other school subjects have the same perceived nonrelevance, and disinterested students look for some other setting where their interests can be focused. These outside interests often bring the students into direct conflict with teachers and other school officials. The home settings, for one reason or another, are unable to capitalize on the students' interests, and, thus, the disinterest grows.

Out of this disinterest grows disillusionment. School is viewed only as a place where one can socialize with friends and where one can kill some time each day. Nothing of practical use occurs at school, and, thus, the groundwork is laid for the next stage: disassociation.

After repeated failures, conflicts with authority figures, and painful disappointments, troubled students disassociate themselves from the formal school setting. This disassociation may happen at any age, though it occurs most often between the ages of 14 and 16. In many states, the legal age for quitting school is 16, but it is a well-known fact that one can quit school at any time with minimal consequences. This knowledge enables students to work through the disassociation process more quickly because there are no real restrictions or impairments placed on their actions.

After the students have become disassociated from the formal school setting, they find themselves in a very uncomfortable position. They now have no identification with a school, yet they have not made a commitment in choosing a career. They are floating between youth and adulthood without the benefit of exercising the options available in either. They are seeking to be independent of their parents but do not have the resources available to make the complete break toward self-sufficiency. They are, in a sense, floating between levels of maturity; they are disenfranchised in that they have no identifiable place or person in whom they can place their confidence.

These young people develop profiles that display characteristics of irregular school attendance, poor grades, teacher conflicts, discipline problems (both at school and with the police), and difficult home situations. They are looking for some program, person, or reason for involving them in some kind of meaningful lifedirecting situation. Their negative attitudes reflect their life experiences.

Another barrier that disadvantaged students face is poor self-esteem. The negative image of themselves comes about as a result of some of the previously discussed experiences. Everyone loves a winner, and disadvantaged students who have little or no success in school are very much aware that everybody considers them losers. The loser image is compounded by more failure, and their self-esteem and self-image thus deteriorate further.

The above profile should serve to introduce the reader to some of the general characteristics of the disadvantaged student. Chapter three discusses the disadvantaged student in much greater detail.

The Handicapped

> The handicapped are those individuals who have been evaluated appropriately as being mentally retarded, hard of hearing, deaf, speech impaired, visually handicapped, seriously emotionally disturbed, orthopedically impaired, other health impaired, deaf, blind, multi-handicapped, or as having specific learning disabilities, who because of those impairments need special education and related services.[5]

The above legislative (Public Law 94-142) definition sets forth the technical categories of the formal definition of handicapped individuals who are to be served. In order to become familiar, on an introductory level, with the handicapped and the problems they have, one must explore the barriers they commonly face. The barriers that generally arise when the handicapped—or the disabled, as many individuals prefer to be called—seek specialized educational services are physical, psychological, and social.

The physical barriers are those barriers that stand in the way of a disabled person who seeks admittance to a particular location. Section 504 of the Rehabilitation

Act of 1973 (Public Law 93-112) specifies that the handicapped shall not be denied access to public-use facilities due to physical barriers. The American National Standards Institute provides accessibility standards both for new construction and for the remodeling of existing structures. At present, not all of the barriers faced by the physically disabled have been removed, nor will they be in the very near future. But major progress has been made. Some of the barriers that have been removed involve access to public transportation, such as travel by bus, plane, and train; curb cuts on major pedestrian thoroughfares; and building accessibility to public-use facilities. Much effort is being expended to ensure that the remaining physical barriers are removed as rapidly as possible so that the disabled will be able to participate in whatever activities they choose.

The removal of physical barriers is very important to those handicapped youth who seek access to vocational training. Many of the physical barriers, when viewed objectively, are not as insuperable as they appear to be; often, through minor modifications, laboratories and classrooms can be made accessible.

The psychological barrier is imposed by the handicapped persons themselves, in that they create a barrier of nonsuccess based upon previous experiences. They have had repeated failures in the past; and they feel in their minds that to engage in a new activity, such as vocational training, would only bring them failure again. Every new opportunity for involvement is met with an excuse—until finally the opportunities no longer appear. The psychological barrier is not created overnight but comes about as a result of many frustrating, often painful, experiences with another kind of obstacle: the social barrier.

The social barrier is imposed upon the handicapped person by society. Society, that is, human beings in general, have many misconceptions, biases, and fears regarding the handicapped and as a result impose restrictions upon them. Blind people should work in snack bars in government buildings; deaf people should work in printing shops; the mentally retarded should assemble hair curlers. And the list of restrictions goes on without anyone ever consulting the individuals involved as to what *they* would like to do. Society is quick to place a label on anyone who deviates from the norm. The norm however, exists only in the minds of particular members of society; since it never remains constant, it cannot be all-encompassing. Indeed, through increased information and training, progress is being made to condition society to accept the competence of an individual regardless of a handicapping condition.

Legislation can remove physical barriers, but it cannot remove societal barriers unless a massive educational effort is also undertaken. People fear the unknown, but with knowledge, appropriate decisions can be made. Though often not visible, such barriers pose a real threat to the opportunities for success available to the handicapped; and every effort must be made, through increased public awareness, to ensure that they are removed.

Chapter four explains in detail how each of the above disabilities is defined and the criteria by which students are diagnosed and determined to be eligible for special services.

HISTORICAL PERSPECTIVE

Early settlers came to the United States with the expressed purpose of pursuing their respective occupations, family interests, and religious beliefs without interference from the government. There were two common uniting beliefs that gave these people the strength and determination to survive in this harsh new land:

1. "An individual has much worth and the dignity of that individual must be preserved.
2. "Individuals should be free to earn their livelihoods in whatever way that proves most profitable."[6]

Many of the first settlers had special needs. These were the debtors, the misdemeanor criminals, or those who, in some manner, were perceived as being undesirable for residency in the mother country. These were the people who were sentenced by the courts to be exported to the colonies as potential settlers instead of being cast into prison.

Once they had made the difficult journey from the European continent to the colonies, they faced the immediate need to develop skills that would enable them to survive. This they did by transferring the European apprenticeship and indentured servant system to the colonies.

The apprenticeship system had the following objectives:

- To teach a particular trade; the apprentice would learn the skills and mysteries of the chosen trade.
- To give the apprentice a good general education.
- To give the apprentice good moral and social training.
- To pay off debts incurred by the father in apprenticing the son.
- To provide a system of poor relief by apprenticing poor, homeless, or orphaned boys.
- To eliminate idleness by forcing the idle into apprenticeship programs.

The chief advantages of the apprenticeship system for special needs youth (the disadvantaged) were that

- it was a good way to bring such youth into the new land,
- it allowed an opportunity for them to develop strong and close relationships with adults,

- it served to assist some special needs youth to get out of the ranks of poverty, and
- it involved the entire life of such youth, not just the working component.

Some of the problems with the apprenticeship system stemmed from the fact that many of the youth were exploited for purposes other than learning a trade. Also, their masters often failed to provide adequate food, clothing, shelter, and general education. Finally, the length of the apprenticeship (2 to 10 years) did much to kill the interest of many of the apprentices.

The other system used to involve special needs individuals in the new world settlements was indenture. Individuals could be indentured to ship captains by the courts. The captains in turn brought their charges to the colonies and sold the paper of indenture to eager employers. Indenture had the following characteristics:

- The master was not required to train the indentured servant in any area of skill or general education.
- The indentured servant had to do any work that was requested.
- The paper of indenture could be sold to another master at any time.
- Children and adults of both sexes could be indentured.
- The indenture paid the cost of transporting the servants to the colonies.
- The time of indenture ranged from one to seven years in length.

The apprenticeship system quickly became confused with the indenture system because of the common characteristic of serving a period of time. Masters soon wanted only indentured servants because they had only to work them, not train them. A very large illegal traffic in indentured servants quickly sprang up. The courts of England sentenced special needs individuals in great numbers to be deported to the colonies. Ship captains would buy the papers of indenture and then sell them at great profit upon arrival in America.

As the apprenticeship system declined into a form of indenture, many young special needs individuals were abused. They were beaten and starved and were left untutored in either a skill or in general education. Often such apprentices were forced to flee from their masters in order to survive. Many of these runaways were able to travel west and make a fresh start on the new frontier.

For young women, except for training in the home, the opportunities for skill training were practically nonexistent. Women were not involved in the apprenticeship system, only in the indentured system. They were not taught to read or write; if they did learn to do either, it was by accident rather than by design.

One large group of special needs individuals created during this period was the slaves. Much has been written about slavery in the United States; a summary comment would be to note that it is a tragedy that this segment of history occurred at all. Slaves were not perceived as having needs, wants, or desires when it came to planning their lives. Attention to this special needs group would not come until the late 1800s and early 1900s.

For the handicapped person, life was even more difficult. It was felt that such people should be removed from society so that normal people would not be contaminated by being exposed to their handicaps. The opportunities for vocational and academic training for such persons were virtually nonexistent.

From the earliest days of Jamestown until the 1830s, the conditions we have described remained pretty much the same. During the 1830s and 1840s, vocational training was introduced into orphanages and reform schools. This new thrust created a twofold set of attitudes that can still be seen today. First, it attached a stigma to vocational education in that it was perceived as being only for poor children, orphans, and delinquents. Thus, many young persons in need of vocational training would not enroll because they did not want to be associated with such "undesirable" students. Secondly, poor children, orphans, and delinquents were placed in vocational training programs with no consideration given to the individual student's preferred area of study. A vicious circle was created that did much to limit the opportunities of special needs students. Since vocational training was perceived as being only for special needs students, only special needs students would enroll in vocational education, and observers could then say, "See, I told you that vocational education was only for those kinds of people." The larger advantages of vocational training for all students were simply not appreciated. Beyond that, many educators feared that vocational education would contaminate general education.

With the coming of the Industrial Revolution in the 1860s, a great demand arose for labor of all types. The apprenticeship system was on its last legs, and the Industrial Revolution sealed its fate. Children, especially homeless or orphaned children, were soon working in factories 14 hours a day, 6 days a week. The conditions they worked under and the tasks they performed were very dangerous for their health and survival.

During the early 1900s, some societal and legislative changes were made that assisted children in general and special needs students in particular. These changes included a growing feeling on the part of the public at large that more assistance should be provided to special needs students. For the handicapped, there were isolated pieces of legislation that provided for particular disabilities, such as Public Law 58-171 which promoted the circulation of reading materials among the blind. Some teacher education institutions began to offer classes in special education for their students. States such as New York, Rhode Island, and Ohio began classes for children with various handicaps. But the vocational training of such children at this point was limited to isolated, specific, and repetitious tasks, such as broom making.

For the disadvantaged, there were child labor laws and compulsory school attendance laws that restricted the employment of 8-, 9-, and 10-year-olds. As a result, there was a growing feeling that these students should go into vocational training programs of some kind. There arose a common philosophy that the "whole boy" needed to be educated and that vocational training could help in this. Females, in contrast, could acquire their education in the home, because that is where they would spend their adult lives.

The Smith-Hughes Act (Public Law 64-347) was passed in 1917 as an emergency war measure. This act provided the basis for the vocational education movement. For the first time, there was money available for the promotion and development of vocational education in cooperation with the states. The total monies authorized under this piece of legislation was $7 million, with funds set aside at the secondary level in the areas of agriculture, trade and industry, and home economics. Of the $7 million, $1 million was set aside for teacher training.

Under another provision of the Smith-Hughes Act, a Federal Board for Vocational Education was established to administer the components of the act. The primary function of the Board was to supervise the expenditure of federal funds according to the provisions of the Act. An often overlooked additional function of the Board was to coordinate vocational rehabilitation programs for handicapped persons. This combination of duties was ideal for the purpose of serving special needs students, primarily the handicapped, in vocational programs. Unfortunately, this was not realized in the prevailing philosophy, as demonstrated by this excerpt from Policy Bulletin No. 1 which outlined who was to be served in vocational education.

> The Federal Board desires to emphasize the fact that vocational schools and classes are not fostered under the Smith-Hughes Act for the purpose of giving instruction to the backward, deficient, and incorrigible or otherwise subnormal individuals; but that such schools and classes are to be established and maintained for the clearly avowed purpose of giving thorough vocational instruction to healthy, normal individuals to the end that they might be prepared for profitable and efficient employment. Such education should command the best efforts of normal boys and girls.[7]

As can be seen from this statement, there has been a long dispute about who should receive vocational training. Though vocational training began in institutions of the 1830s to serve the special needs students, the clear policy statement in 1917 was that vocational education is not meant to serve special populations.

Chapter two explains in detail the various pieces of legislation that have been passed pertaining to serving special needs populations. A careful look must be taken at this legislation to gain a clear perspective of the social trends and of the way Congress has reacted to these trends in terms of further legislative acts. The majority of the legislation dealing with special populations has been reactive, not active, in the context of planning how to serve future citizens of the United States.

Since 1917, the United States has survived four major military conflicts (World War I, World War II, Korea, Viet Nam), a depression, several recessions, and numerous other tragic and sensitizing events. The decade of the sixties brought into full force the Civil Rights Movement. Emotions stemming from the Viet Nam conflict combined with the Civil Rights Movement to bring about a new awareness of the individual differences that exist in society and of how these differences contribute in their own unique way to make the United States function as it does. The theme that emerged during the sixties was *relevancy*. What was being taught, the work being done, and the programs being offered had to be relevant. These kinds of questions were asked: How are we serving the handicapped and disadvantaged? What are their rights when it comes to educational planning and program offerings?

The course of the decade of the 1970s was charted as a result of the experiences of the 1960s. The time was right for specific pieces of legislation (Public Laws 91-230, 93-112, 93-203, 94-142, 94-482, and 95-93) that would provide the mechanisms through which handicapped and disadvantaged persons could be served and trained. Because of these new social and educational commitments, the 1970s became known as the "total programming decade."

Deinstitutionalization and *mainstreaming* became two frequently used terms when concerns of the handicapped were addressed. Deinstitutionalization means moving handicapped individuals out of institutional settings into community settings where they can live and work successfully. The ultimate benefits resulting from this movement will probably never be fully measured because of the diversity of individuals involved, but there are certain benefits that have already been clearly realized. First, deinstitutionalized individuals are being recognized as human beings with rights and benefits. Secondly, such individuals are being allowed to work and thus to contribute to their own and society's well being. Thirdly, these persons are being given the opportunity to develop and mature as citizens in a democratic society. Through this movement, people in our society are, in a sense, looking at themselves and saying, "Yes, we are different, but through these differences we can grow, contribute, and love each other for who we are."

As noted earlier, the handicapped were for a long time isolated because they were unique and their uniqueness made them unacceptable in a "normal" society. As the trend of accepting individuals for who they are slowly gained momentum in the 1960s and 1970s, a new word was coined to describe this acceptance: mainstreaming. During the middle seventies especially, this term was used widely to describe programs for the handicapped. Mainstreaming can be defined as

> a belief which involves an educational placement procedure and process for exceptional children, based on the conviction that each such child should be educated in the least restrictive environment in which his educational and related needs can be satisfactorily provided. This con-

> cept recognizes that exceptional children have a wide range of special educational needs, varying greatly in intensity and duration; that there is a recognized continuum of educational settings which may, at a given time, be appropriate for an individual child's needs; that to the maximum extent appropriate, exceptional children should be educated with non-exceptional children; and that special classes, separate schooling, or other removal of an exceptional child from education with non-exceptional children should occur only when the intensity of the child's special education and related needs is such that they cannot be satisfied in an environment including non-exceptional children, even with the provision of supplementary aids and services.[8]

The basic premise of the mainstreaming concept is that exceptional and nonexceptional children have common needs. These common needs can serve as a basis for developing various instructional programs. By keeping these two types of students separated, each is being deprived of the opportunity to exchange experiences with and develop an appreciation of the other. It should be noted from the definition that mainstreaming does not eliminate special classes or programs for those exceptional students who need them in order to receive an appropriate education based upon their needs.

When the mainstreaming concept was first promoted, many school officials overreacted, both positively and negatively. The negative reactions focused on personal attitudes and fear. When people embark upon a new adventure, they often are frightened because they do not know what to expect. The same thing occurred when educators were exposed to the mainstreaming concept. The fear came from a lack of previous exposure to handicapped individuals. In their research education programs, only those educators who majored in special education received training in dealing with exceptional students. Also, since the majority of handicapped people were institutionalized or sheltered in homes, the average educator did not gain any experience with exceptional students. With uncertainty came fear, and with fear came the development of certain negative attitudes. For many teachers, it was easier to say, "Those people can't make it in my class," than it was to give the students a chance to try. Also, many teachers felt that these students were being unloaded on them, forcing them to act as babysitters for an hour or two. There were instances where teachers were not informed about the students they would be having; they only knew they had to take them. These kinds of situations created for both teachers and students real barriers that could have been avoided with adequate information and training.

The other side of the mainstreaming concept, however, was the positive approach that many school officials took. This approach tended toward the conclusion that "we will mainstream exceptional students into all our classes." Exceptional students were placed in advanced math classes, chemistry, or vocational agriculture because they had to be fitted into the entire school program. Many of these random placements resulted in dismal failures. This overreactive positive approach was unfair to both students and teachers because there was not a team effort made to allow the handicapped students to enter programs where they wanted to be, where they could succeed, and where the teacher could teach effectively. Placement was made only to illustrate that handicapped students could be entered in all programs throughout the school.

As educators became better informed and trained, however, the mainstream pendulum began to swing back toward the center. Educators, in cooperation with exceptional students and their parents or advocates, started to establish more effective systems for involving these students in school programs. The earlier mainstreaming concept had carried a connotation of "returning to" rather than "planning for," and new terms were now developed to reflect the new "planning-for" thrust. The new concept was *least restrictive environment*. This concept had been included in the original mainstreaming movement but had not really been explored or defined to the extent it should have been due to the newness of the entire handicapped movement.

The concept of a least restrictive environment means that individuals, whatever their exceptional characteristics might be, should have an opportunity to learn and function in an environment that is conducive to their success. Specifically, two things are legally required of public agencies:

1. "That to the maximum extent appropriate, handicapped children, including children in public or private institutions or other care facilities, are educated with children who are not handicapped; and
2. "that special classes, separate schooling or other removal of handicapped children from the regular educational environment occurs only when the nature or severity of the handicap is such that education in regular classes with the use of supplementary aids and services cannot be achieved satisfactorily."[9]

The Education for All Handicapped Children Act of 1975 (Public Law 94-142) led to the above guidelines for establishing least restrictive environments and for providing a device through which placement in nonrestrictive environments could be greatly facilitated. This device is the Individual Educational Plan (IEP.). The IEP in its simplest form is a written statement about a handicapped child that includes the following:

- "a statement of the child's present levels of educational performance;
- "a statement of annual goals, including short-term instructional objectives;
- "a statement of the specific special education and related services to be provided to the child, and the extent to which the child will be able to participate in regular educational programs;

- "the projected dates for initiation of services and the anticipated duration of the services; and
- "appropriate objective criteria and evaluation procedures and schedules for determining, on at least an annual basis, whether the short-term instructional objectives are being achieved."[10]

The IEP is a guide to help facilitate proper placement of and programming for handicapped students. Chapter five discusses the IEP and its components in greater detail.

Balancing the legislative and societal gains made by the handicapped during the 1970s was the new attention to the barriers facing the disadvantaged. The Civil Rights Act of 1964 and the growing societal acceptance of human differences throughout the seventies greatly aided the involvement of ethnic, cultural, and religious minorities in the educational process. Much, however, still needs to be done in this area in view of the fact that minority youth of ages 16 through 21 account for nearly one-half of all unemployed persons, even though they account for only one-fourth of the labor force.

Another large group of disadvantaged that requires services emerged during the 1970s. These are the structurally unemployed, those individuals who lack the educational background or skill levels to take advantage of traditional training programs. These are generally youth, ranging in age from 16 through 21, who have left school. To deal with this group, Congress in 1977 passed the Youth Employment and Demonstration Projects Act. This act provided funds to establish special training programs for youth both in school and out of school. The intent of these programs is to provide youth with the experiences that can enable them to make meaningful and realistic career choices, to secure training, and to enter successfully into the work world.

From a historical perspective, the sixties and seventies were an exciting time of social and human development. The eighties promise to be a decade of implementation. Legislation has been passed that enables all sectors of society to participate in school, work, recreation, and community activities. The challenge of the 1980s is to implement activities that will ensure that all our citizens will have opportunities to become involved in programs and employment based upon their needs, preferences, and desires without fear of exclusion or omission. If this can be accomplished, historians will look back at the 1980s as a time when the challenges and responsibilities of serving all citizens of the United States were met.

PROGRAM DESCRIPTIONS

As we have seen, our society has gone through a number of cycles in the delivery of educational services to special needs youth. As a result of some of these cycles, there has been a division of programs that requires a careful inspection of the roles that general, career, general literacy, special, practical arts, and vocational education play in the total delivery system.

General Education

General education has been defined as education through which one acquires the ability to cope with one's environment.[11] This definition assumes that general education is needed by all students and that specialized education will be offered to enable students to select training that they need to cope successfully with their environment.

Ideally, then, through successful integration of general and specialized training such as vocational education, students should be ready to cope with most problems that society or life might present. In order to understand why special needs youth do not fit within this educational framework and do not have its "ideal" skills to cope with life, one must look at the historical development of the objectives of education.

The major objective of public education in America has been to prepare individuals for living, not to prepare individuals to make a living.[12] Americans have long held to the notion that people who have developed their minds, bodies, and characters through formal exercises in cultural and intellectual disciplines will be better suited to enter occupations than those who have not so benefited.

Stemming from this view, a hierarchy of education has been created in our schools that allows special needs youth to slip through the cracks of the structure.

At the top of this hierarchical structure is the college preparatory curriculum, designed obviously for those students who will be going on to college. The problem that arises with the components of the hierarchy is that, in many cases, parents who "want something better" for their son or daughter insist that their child follow this curricular route. But students often have no desire to go on to college and would prefer to be in another program. They begin to have scholastic problems, and the situation snowballs until they become discipline problems or drop out of school.

The next layer of the hierarchy is the general curriculum. This curriculum is designed to provide opportunities for students to acquire the "basics:" reading, writing, and arithmetic. It is an inbetween curriculum that prepares the individual neither for college nor for employment after leaving school.

Vocational education is the training of individuals for gainful employment after completion of a specific training program. Vocational education finds itself at the bottom of the hierarchy due to the stigma it has carried as a dumping ground for noncapable students.

General education thus finds itself sandwiched between a college preparatory curriculum and vocational education, and, in many cases, there is uncertainty as to what should be done with it. Nevertheless, as a result of this sandwiching, general education finds itself with the challenging responsibility to provide quality educational opportunities to special needs youth so that these individuals can make meaningful and realistic lifedirecting decisions.

One important part of the general education delivery system should be the provision of career education to these youth.

Career Education

There have been many definitions of career education suggested by different individuals, agencies, and organizations. As a result of these different definitions, career education has been approached from many different presentation modes and concept positions. One widely accepted definition was proposed by Kenneth B. Hoyt, associate commissioner of education. He defines career education as "the totality of experiences through which one learns about and prepares to engage in work as part of her or his way of living."[13] By this definition, there are a wide variety of ways to interpret and develop programs that will provide opportunities for special needs youth to acquire the necessary information base from which they can make a career choice.

Career education is perceived as a flowthrough type of education whereby individuals acquire not only information concerning paid employment but information about other aspects of their lives as well. As the hours in a work week decrease, individuals now must look for ways to utilize the rest of their career opportunities.

People generally have three careers for which they need training: in the home, in the community, and in the work place. The career in the home is that of a homemaker. The word *homemaker* is used here as meaning someone who contributes in some manner to the successful operation of the home. This means that anyone can be a homemaker: a male or female, a boy or girl, a single or a married person, a son or a daughter. People need to have information and training in order to assume their roles in making a home, regardless of how typical or atypical their situation might be.

The community career also takes many forms. Participation in recreational, service, religious, or volunteer activities can contribute to a community career. Even if people are not involved in such activities, there is still one community career in which they hope to be successful: that of a consumer. No one can avoid or ignore this type of community career; everyone consumes, in one form or another, the community's services, goods, and activities. And a great deal of preparation is required to enable individuals to assume this critical career role.

The work world as a component of career education has received much attention but is still in need of much developmental work. This is because there are still many unknown variables in the selection, training, and placement of people in a paid employment setting. Vocational education has been the primary deliverer of training in this component of career education.

There are a number of career education models currently being used with special needs populations. The Clark (1979) model is presented in Figure 1-1.[14] This model provides not only for the employment component of career education but also for a systematic scheme to give students training opportunities in the other two careers of community and home. Clark's model focuses on the critical life development areas of (1) values, attitudes, and habits; (2) human relationships; (3) occupational information; and (4) the acquisition of job and daily living skills on the elementary (K-6) and junior high (7-9) levels. Instruction during these years would be on the awareness and orientation levels. Based upon this model, students, upon completion of elementary school, would have a career information base from which they could move readily into the junior high exploratory setting.

The junior high career component in the model provides more development in the four major areas as well as more time in actual career exploratory settings. The high school component includes the development of skills for entry into the semiskilled or skilled work setting or for preparation for further training.

As can be seen, Clark's model is not a form of tracking but a flowthrough system that allows students to branch off, based upon their individual needs, choices, and training requirements. This freedom-of-choice option is the real strength behind this type of model in developing programs for special needs populations.

The American Vocational Association's Task Force report pulls together the various thrusts of career education as the ingredients for career education program development. The task force concluded that career education should be designed to help individuals to develop:

- "Favorable attitudes toward the personal, psychological, social, and economic significance of work.
- "Appreciation for the worth of all types and levels of work.
- "Decision-making skills necessary for choosing career options and for changing career directions.
- "Capability of making considered choices of career goals, based on development of self in relation to the range of career options.
- "Capability of charting a course for realization of self-established career goals in keeping with individual desires, needs, and opportunities.
- "Knowledge, skill, and attitudes necessary for entry and success in a career."[15]

In order for special needs students to acquire these competencies, individuals who work in the areas that provide career education must understand the components that contribute to the universal concept of career education. These compo-

Figure 1-1 A School-Based Career Education Model for Special Needs Students (Dr. Gary Clark's Model)

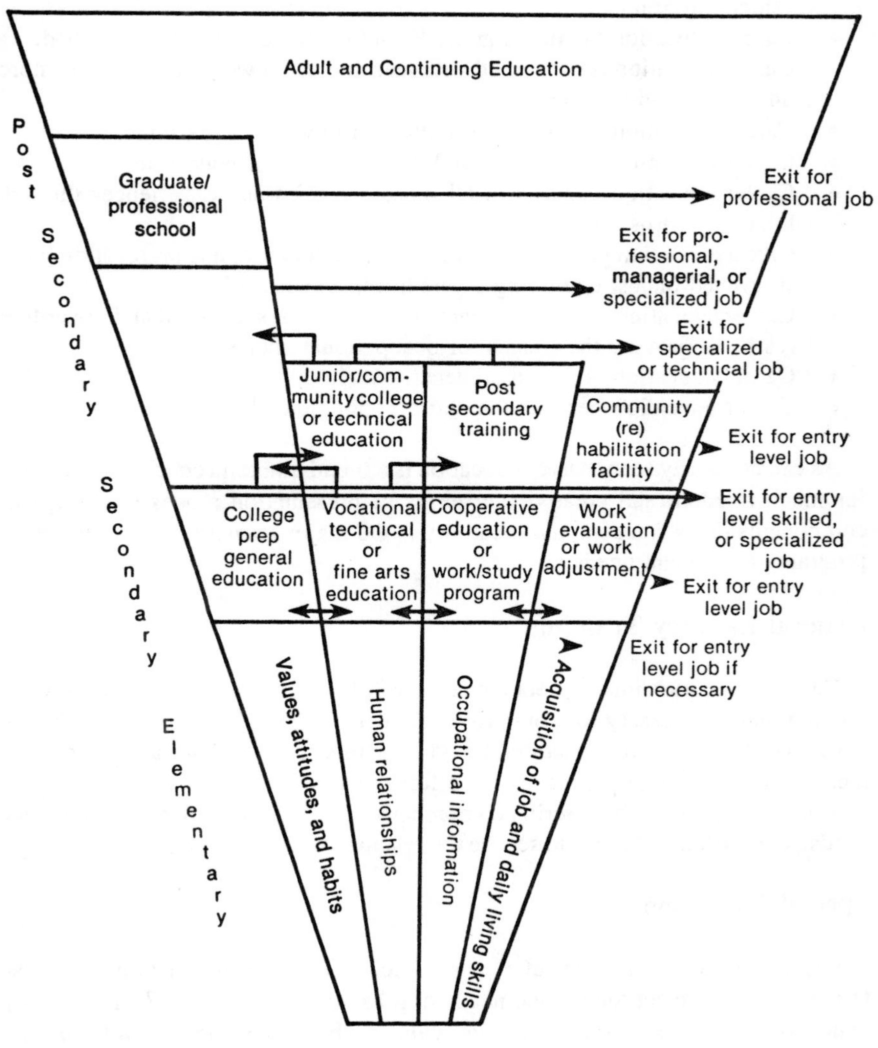

Source: Reprinted from *Career Education for the Handicapped Child in the Elementary Classroom* by Dr. Gary Clark by permission of Love Publishing Co., © 1979.

nents were identified by Curtis Finch and N. Alan Sheppard in 1974 as the following:

- "Career education is an educational philosophy rather than a physical entity or single program.
- "Career education begins at grade K and continues through adulthood.
- "Career education is concerned with learning about work and involves more than preparation for work.
- "Career education provides an orientation toward a work ethic.
- "Career education is encompassed in the totality of education.
- "Career education consists of all those activities and experiences through which one learns about work.
- "Career education provides an awareness, exploration, and preparation function instead of just equipping a person for a specific job.
- "Career education seeks to prepare all students for successful and rewarding lives by improving their basis for occupational choice.
- "Career education is for all students.
- "Career education benefits the entire population."[16]

As can be clearly seen, career education is a broad umbrella concept that allows for much freedom and creativity in terms of presentation modes and program components. This freedom and creativity is the major strength in the delivery of programs for special needs youth.

General Literacy Training

General education must accept the responsibility of providing the foundational training that is necessary for youth to function at a minimal literacy level. This is not to say that general education should bear this responsibility alone. Indeed, there should be a total programmatic effort made that encompasses a variety of school offerings. Only by offering comprehensive educational programs to special needs youth will they be able to see the total picture of what is being asked of them.

Special Education

Special education has been defined as "specially designed instruction, at no cost to the parent, to meet the unique needs of a handicapped child."[17] This type of education is intended to serve those individuals who have some type of handicapping condition that requires specialized educational assistance in order for them to develop and mature to the maximum degree possible. These specialized services can take on a variety of forms, but the basic premise is that these services must be offered in the least restrictive environment. This new thrust has been brought about as a result of federal legislation (Public Law 94-142) that has led to a new awareness of and attention to the serving of special needs students.

In the not-so-distant past, special needs students (disadvantaged and handicapped) were almost assured of placement in a special education class which often preceded haphazard placement in a vocational program. Many of these placements took place because the individuals in charge of placing students in specific programs did not have adequate information about either the students or the appropriate programs.

During the past few years, however, there has been a dramatic change in the quality of student placements. Special education is being recognized for the services it can provide rather than viewed merely as a "holding pen" until the student leaves school.

Special education is not by itself a total delivery system but is rather a part of the total educational delivery package. Careful placement must be based upon the individual needs of the student involved. Since special needs encompass both handicapped and disadvantaged students, care must be taken to ensure that an appropriate placement is made based upon a variety of informational sources, not made merely because a student fits into a particular category.

Special education's role is to serve the handicapped either as a primary deliverer or, if the student is in a regular school program, as a resource service. In addition, there are other special educational services available to classroom teachers. Special education has developed many strategies for working with students who have problems with the formal school setting. These strategies need to be utilized to their fullest and shared by all teachers for the benefit of their students.

Vocational teachers, as the result of least restrictive environmental programming, have in common with the special education teacher the same students. Since these teachers are working toward the development of a quality educational program for the student, it makes good sense for all those involved to share and care about what is being offered and the methodologies being used.

As stipulated in Public Law 94-142, arbitrary placement of individuals in special education programs is no longer acceptable without proper justification. Special education should be responsive to individual student needs. But it can only be a part of the total education picture. It cannot nor should it be asked to serve all special needs students. Total educational programming is a must.

Practical Arts

Practical arts, as defined by the American Vocational Association (AVA) in 1968 is "a type of functional education predominately manipulative in nature which provides learning experiences in leisure time interests, consumer knowledge, creative expression, family living, manual skills, technological development, and similar outcomes of value to all."[18]

Most practical arts courses are in the subject-matter areas of general agriculture, home economics, industrial arts, and general business. These courses are generally taught for one daily class period by teachers with degrees. The students enrolled in practical arts courses do not establish specific vocational goals for the training they receive. They explore these training experiences rather as a basis for making meaningful and realistic career decisions for the future.

As an educational area, practical arts can provide excellent programs for special needs students. The reasons are similar to those noted for vocational education. The students have an opportunity to create, to manipulate, and to possess—the three human expressions that are very important for developing students who are having only limited success in school. In addition, special needs students are afforded opportunities to gain new experiences from which they can make career choices that are consistent with their life goals.

Practical arts courses are offered in grades K-12, with the strongest delivery focused on the junior high level. The reason for this is that it is during the junior high years that students do much of the exploration that will shape the rest of their lives.

Much controversy has been created over the question whether practical arts is an area that stands by itself or is a prevocational or feeder program for vocational education. This controversy has stopped many students from taking practical arts, but it has persuaded others to turn to practical arts courses. Since each student is unique—based upon individual differences, family background, environment, etc.—the dispute should not be allowed to intrude into educational planning for students. Students should be enrolled in practical arts courses—or for that matter, in any other courses offered by the school—based upon their particular needs, interests, and desires, not because they are believed to be moving in this or that direction.

Because of their practical application approach, practical arts courses at the junior high level have meant in many cases the difference between a student leaving or remaining in school. If junior high students are aware of practical arts or vocational programs in a high school, that can often stimulate their interest in particular areas, bridge the gap between junior high and high school, and preclude their dropping out.

Vocational Education

Vocational education has been defined by the AVA as "education designed to develop skills, abilities, understandings, attitudes, work habits, and appreciations needed by workers to enter and make progress in employment on a useful and productive basis."[19]

Within this definitional framework, vocational education has the following basic characteristics:

- "Preparation for jobs requiring less than a baccalaureate degree.
- "Activities and experiences through which one learns to assume a primary work role.
- "An emphasis on skill development or specific job preparation.
- "A focus of attention at the upper-middle grades, senior high, and two-year college level.
- "A physical entity or program rather than an educational philosophy, with the major goal of gainful employment."[20]

The basic goal of vocational education is to take a nonskilled student through a series of training experiences so that at the end of a specified period of time the student will have the skills necessary to enter into and succeed in the work place. Vocational education is normally concerned with six major occupational areas: vocational agriculture, home economics, health occupations, trades and industries, business and office education, and distributive education.

Vocational training is generally offered by an instructor with a degree or suitable work experience who is vocationally certified according to state certification standards. Students enrolled in vocational programs set specific vocational goals in relation to the vocational program in which they are enrolled. The instructional time for vocational classes is normally three hours. This time can be divided up in many different ways, the most common being a combination of one hour of classroom instruction and two hours of laboratory experience.

Vocational education has long suffered from the hierarchical stigma noted earlier. Working with one's hands has commonly been misperceived as being less desirable than working with one's mind. This stigma, which can also be seen in the blue-collar vs. white-collar status controversy, is now changing for a variety of reasons:

- "Vocational education offers advantages to vocational graduates over non-vocational graduates.
- "Vocational education is training in occupational areas that are in demand and reflecting the needs of today's work setting.
- "Vocational education enrolls women in non-traditional occupation areas.
- "Vocational education enrolls minority students into programs leading to higher salaried and skilled occupational areas.
- "Vocational education is effective in working with existing employed workers to upgrade their competencies, increase their productivity, and enhance promotability.
- "Vocational education is effectively enrolling and working with handicapped students.
- "Vocational education graduates have a tendency to move into business ownership following their occupational training and work experience.

- "Comprehensive vocational education programs have an impact on the economic growth and development in communities."[21]

Vocational education has long been responsive to societal needs. This type of education enables the community to change, expand, or modify programs and training to meet emerging worker and employment demands.

Vocational education is faced with a real challenge and must assume a clearly defined responsibility to serve special needs students. Special needs students who are disinterested and disillusioned with school see no relevance of school to the world around them. Because of the training it offers and the methodology it employs in this training, vocational education is a logical deliverer of educational services to these troubled youth. It involves not only the cognitive aspects of learning but also the psychomotor and affective domains. Its basis is activity, which troublesome students frequently find lacking in day-to-day school life. Finally, through vocational education, students can see an immediate transference from the school setting to the world around them, whether their area of interest is automotive repair skills or consumer buying knowledge.

Special Vocational Needs Programs

Special vocational needs programs are a part of the general vocational education delivery system; because of our central concern with them, however, they deserve separate examination and analysis.

A special vocational needs program is a program that is designed to provide the necessary instruction or support service to enable a special needs student to succeed in a vocational or prevocational program.

Special vocational needs programs may take a variety of forms. Such a program may be

- a separate special vocational needs course such as vocational English or vocational mathematics,
- a regular vocational class with support or modified materials for use by special needs students,
- a regular vocational class with a resource teacher in the class to assist the vocational instructor, or
- a regular vocational class with a special needs resource center for use by special needs students.

There can be many modifications and variations of these examples, hence they should not be regarded as all-inclusive.

The key points to be remembered in developing a special vocational needs program are these:

- The inability to succeed in a regular vocational program should be the basis for identifying students for enrollment in such programs.
- These programs focus on individuals and their particular needs, not on generalized groups.
- The inability to succeed is the result, not the cause, of special needs conditions.

Special vocational needs programs or services should not duplicate nor dilute the offerings of other school programs. To avoid such overlapping, the following objectives of special vocational needs programs should be kept in mind:

- to develop the means to complete school
- to enable students to work toward their maximum potential
- to develop an attitude that the individual is a valued person
- to develop the self-confidence necessary to take advantage of employment opportunities
- to develop a desirable attitude toward the world of work
- to prepare students for a saleable skill

Clearly, special vocational needs programs deal with the skill development component of vocational education. Beyond that, however, much of the instruction focuses on human relations, self-development, and worker attitudes.

To qualify as a special needs program, a special vocational needs program must demonstrate that it

- can prepare the student for employment,
- is necessary to prepare individuals for successful completion of a special needs program, and
- is of significant assistance to individuals in making informed and meaningful occupational choices.

Whether these criteria have been met might be at times difficult to prove. The list does, however, provide some general directional indicators to establish program parameters.

DELIVERY OF SERVICES

None of the previously defined program areas can alone provide all the services required by the disadvantaged and handicapped. Each must cooperate with and assist the other to ensure maximum programming opportunities for such students. The process must include longitudinal educational assistance to the students; it is neither fair nor feasible to select a certain area in the process and then say, "These students are that area's responsibility." This is unfair to the programs involved, unfair to the teachers, and, most of all, unfair to the students.

To repeat, public education must develop a longitudinal system of services for special needs students. This would reduce the number of programs that have failed in the past because they were "too much, too late." It would also make it easier to treat the problems rather than merely deal with the symptoms.

Upon entrance into the public school system, a student should have a longitudinal plan that provides opportunities for growth and maturity. The opportunities in the plan should be clearly outlined in purpose and design.

Kindergarten students enter school with bright-eyed enthusiasm about learning and the world around them. This enthusiasm continues until about the third or fourth grade. Often at this point alienation begins, and the child continues on the educational journey by becoming more and more alienated until a strong pattern of failure emerges.

Through a strong career education program integrated into a strong academic program, general education can lay a solid foundation of interest and exploration for the child. The students study about careers in the classroom and then have an opportunity to see their newly acquired information applied in their community. They meet and visit with community helpers, view community businesses and industry, and participate in community projects. This career orientation can do much to keep education relevant for special needs students who are potentially failure-prone.

As students finish the elementary grades, a concentrated effort must be made by teachers to retain the enthusiasm they brought initially to the school setting and to make the transition from the elementary to junior high school as easy as possible. Disruption and alienation often occur when a student is faced with a new environment; for the student who is unsure and confused about what lies ahead, the potential for failure is greatly enhanced.

During the junior high years, general education should provide additional career education in the form of career exploration. The junior high years are a time of physical and mental growth that involves much activity by the student. A comprehensive career education program can offer many opportunities to utilize this activity. Practical arts classes enable special needs students to create, manipulate, and possess. In the academic areas, general education can give the student a tie between career exploration and the three Rs. The tie-in comes when, for example, career survival words are learned in an English class and then used in interviewing a worker within the community, or when math skills are used by the student in ordering lumber for a class project.

Another program that can be of great help in involving and retaining the special needs student is the work experience program. This program is known by a number of names, such as Experience Based Career Education (EBCE), Hands On Training (HOT), and Experience Programs in the Community (EPIC). Regardless of the name it goes by, its purpose is to involve the student in both the school and the world of work. Specifically, work experience programs

- help the student gain exploratory occupational experience,
- assist in keeping the student in school,
- provide in-school class and job support and personal development training,
- create a training base for cooperative occupational programs,
- provide, at times, programs to enable students to earn badly needed money, and
- allow students to develop close relationships with school staff members.

Since many students leave school between the ages of 14 and 16, the last point regarding close student-teacher relationships needs to be emphasized. The teacher can encourage and assist special needs students in making the transition from junior high to high school. The teacher may take students over to the high school and introduce them to their work experience or vocational teacher for the next year. This kind of visit is much different from the quick orientation tour conducted by high school students each spring for ninth grade junior highers. The transition must be made carefully because, in spite of their carefree and nonchalant attitudes, many students are psychologically fragile and need attentive treatment.

At the high school level, care must be taken in placing the special needs student. As noted earlier, there must be close cooperation and articulation between all segments of the student's education program. The general, special, and vocational education teachers must know and share each other's efforts. Each must call upon the other for assistance and strategies in serving special needs students.

CONCLUSION

Special needs students have historically been in need of assistance. In the past, various attempts have been made to serve those individuals who do not fit the expectations of the prevailing society. Many of these attempts have been feeble, to say the least, but at least they provided a base from which improvement could be made. Society has since become more informed, and people have learned to be more tolerant of human differences. This in turn has opened doors for the handicapped and disadvantaged that were previously closed.

Educators now face a real challenge in defining their role in the educational process for special needs students. Education is no longer the effort of a single person; it is a team effort. This allows everyone—the student, the teacher, the parent, and the school—to benefit from their joint efforts. Special needs students are unique individuals who need special teacher and school support to enable them to complete the schooling process successfully.

As a programming concept, special vocational needs education provides opportunities to train, support, and encourage disadvantaged and handicapped students in acquiring vocational skills. The services, talents, and human relationships of these students are needed; to deprive them of the opportunity to develop those services, talents, and relationships is to do a terrible injustice to both the students and society. Educators must renew their commitments to serve *all* the youth who enroll in their programs. They must renew their commitments to work with the uniqueness of each student. To do less is to cheat everyone involved of an opportunity to grow, develop, contribute, and live.

Will Rogers suggested the following recipe for success: "Mix knowing what you're doing, loving what you're doing, and believing in what you're doing."[22]

Teachers of special needs students have a unique opportunity to meet students where they are and to help them go places they never thought possible. If this can be accomplished, both students and teachers will have fulfilled the recipe of success.

NOTES

1. Department of Labor Statistics, *CETA Reader* 1, no. 9 (September 1979), p. 7.
2. U.S., *Federal Register,* vol. 42, no. 191, October 3, 1977, p. 53851.
3. U.S., *Federal Register,* vol. 42, no. 191, October 3, 1977, p. 53851.
4. U.S., *Federal Register,* vol. 42, no. 191, October 3, 1977, p. 53851.
5. U.S., *Federal Register,* vol. 42, no. 163, August 23, 1977, p. 42478.
6. Calfrey C. Calhoun and Alton V. Finch, *Vocational and Career Education Concepts and Operations* (Belmont, Calif.: Wadsworth Publishing Company, 1976), p. 31.
7. Federal Board for Vocational Education, *Statement of Policies, Bulletin No. 1* (Washington, D.C.: Government Printing Office, 1917), p. 17.
8. Council for Exceptional Children, Statement adopted by the 13th Delegate Assembly, *Delegate Assembly Final Report* (Chicago, Ill., April 1976), p. 6.
9. U.S., *Federal Register,* vol. 42, no. 163, August 23, 1977, p. 42497.
10. U.S., *Federal Register,* vol. 42, no. 163, August 23, 1977, p. 42491.
11. Rupert Evans, *Foundations of Vocational Education* (Columbus, Ohio: Charles Merrill Publication Co., 1971), p. 51.
12. Calhoun and Finch, *Vocational and Career Education Concepts and Operations,* p. 87.
13. K.B. Hoyt, *An Introduction to Career Education: A Policy Paper of the U.S. Office of Education.* DHEW Publications no. (OE) 75-00504 (Washington, D.C.: U.S. Government Printing Office, 1975), p. 4.
14. Gary Clark, *Career Education for the Handicapped Child in the Elementary Classroom* (Denver, Colo.: Love Publishing Co., 1979), p. 19.
15. American Vocational Association, "Task Force Report on Career Education," *American Vocational Journal* 47, no. 1 (January 1972): 12.
16. Curtis R. Finch and N. Alan Sheppard, "Career Education Is Not Vocational Education," *Journal of Career Education* 2, no. 1 (Summer 1975): 20.

17. U.S., *Federal Register,* vol. 42, no. 163, August 23, 1977, p. 42480.

18. American Vocational Association, *Definitions of Terms in Vocational, Technical, Practical Arts Education* (Washington, D.C.: AVA Committee on Publications, 1968), p. 16.

19. Ibid., p. 12.

20. Finch and Sheppard, "Career Education Is Not Vocational Education," p. 21.

21. American Vocational Association, *Effectiveness of Vocational Education* (Arlington, Va.: AVA Staff, 1979), p. 2.

22. The Innovative Educator (Stillwater, Oklahoma: Leadership Development Institute, 1979), pp. 3-15.

Chapter 2

The Impact of Federal Legislation on Special Vocational Needs Programming

John D. Bies, Ph.D.

INTRODUCTION

It is difficult to identify anything that has made a more profound impact upon the vocational education of special needs students than the federal legislation enacted by Congress. The process of federal contributions, regulations, and influences did not appear, however, overnight; it was a slow, evolving process that occurred over the history of our country. It must be remembered that the Constitution of the United States was so designed as to leave the responsibility of education to the individual states. Thus, the federal government's influences upon education have been slow in developing.

Funding for vocational education, specifically for both disadvantaged and handicapped students, was first made available with the passage in 1968 of amendments to the Vocational Education Act of 1963. In these amendments, Congress clearly identified the special needs population and authorized specific funding for that group. It should not be assumed, however, that vocational education funding for the special needs population began in 1968. In fact, the special needs group has been provided with federal government assistance and training for over 100 years. Until the 1968 amendments, however, no piece of vocational education legislation had so clearly defined and provided funding for the disadvantaged and handicapped.

Prior to discussing the legislative record (rehabilitation, social action, and educational legislation), a brief framework is needed to examine the federal government's evolving involvement in education per se. Thus, a brief analysis of this process will be presented first. This will be followed by an examination of specific enactments affecting the special needs population.

FOUNDATIONS FOR FEDERAL LEGISLATION

Under the Constitution of the United States, Congress and the federal government do not have responsibility for providing public education. By omitting such constitutional provision, education was left as a responsibility of the individual states (at times referred to as states' rights). Following the strictest interpretation of this delegation of power, Congress was reluctant to usurp the powers of the states in regulating educational services.

It was not until the Continental Congress adopted the Ordinance of 1785 that a cooperative relationship between the federal government and educational services at the state level was established. Under the ordinance, one section of land was to be set aside for the support of schools within each township. Though the ordinance did not give direct support to schools, it did establish the precedent-setting principle of assisting education at the state level. In 1802, Congress passed the Ohio Enabling Act that granted land to states for school support and set aside the 16th section of each township to the residents for educational purposes.

The next major piece of legislation affecting state public education was the Morril or Land Grant Act of 1862. Under the act, assistance was provided through the granting of public lands for the establishment and maintenance of agricultural and mechanical arts colleges and universities. It is interesting to note that this act was passed during the Civil War because of the lack of Southern opposition to the federal government's "interference with states rights." Once the Civil War ended, land grant institutions were also set up for blacks and were supported by the Supreme Court as being "separate, but equal"—again establishing a legal precedent that required many years to alter.

The last major assistance that Congress gave to public school education was provided by the Smith-Hughes Act of 1917 and other subsequent acts. The Smith-Hughes Act was the first to give direct funding to education at less than a collegiate level for the training and upgrading of students in agriculture, home economics, and trades and industries occupations. As vocational education funding was increased, so were the services areas included in the legislation (i.e., distributive education, health occupations, technical education, office education, and industrial arts). More recent federal legislation will be discussed later in this chapter.

REHABILITATION LEGISLATION

It has been noted that the passage of the Smith-Hughes Act of 1917 created a regulatory and funding precedent for subsequent legislation concerned with the job training and upgrading of other groups.[1] It was, therefore, not suprising when, a year later, Congress enacted the Smith-Sears Act (Public Law 179) of 1918. The purpose of this act was to provide for the vocational rehabilitation and return to civil employment of those disabled veterans discharged from the armed forces.

Though the Smith-Sears Act was the first legislated law that dealt solely with the rehabilitation of disabled veterans, concern for this population group can be traced back to the founding years of our country. Direct compensation for disabled veterans, however, was not provided until 1865, when the returning Civil War disabled veterans were provided with small stipends. Thus, Public Law 179 was truly a hallmark enactment in the rehabilitation field.

It should be noted that disabled civilians in need of rehabilitation were not covered in the first rehabilitation act. The rationale provided by a number of members of Congress was that such a show of concern and help for the civilian population would only coddle them and, in the long run, hurt their chances of returning to the mainstream of life.

The first vocational rehabilitation legislation was signed into law in 1920. The Vocational Rehabilitation Act, also known as the Smith-Fess Act (Public Law 236) provided rehabilitation services for civilians injured and disabled in industrial accidents during civil employment. However, the act provided only for vocational training. It was designed strictly for training services, guidance, and counseling; medical services were not provided for. Furthermore, only limited funding was made available for rehabilitation programs; $796,000 was appropriated during the first year of administration of the program, and only $1,000,000 was appropriated for the next three years. Not surprisingly, of the hundreds of thousands of disabled workers, only 5,600 disabled workers were rehabilitated by 1924. Thus, this piece of myopic legislation can be considered a practical failure.

Though the Smith-Fess Act failed to meet the needs of the disabled worker, it did provide two revolutionary incentives for future legislative actions. The first was the use of matching funds on a state-by-state basis. Prior to this time, all funding was based upon a population formula or some similar criterion. The Smith-Fess Act created a 50-50 matching funds formula, with additional funding to be determined by population. The second revolutionary aspect was that the administration of the act and its programs was made the responsibility of the Federal Board for Vocational Education.

No further legislation on this subject was passed by Congress until the early 1940s. This was due to a change in political philosophy during the 1920s and to the critical levels of unemployment during the Great Depression. Thus, while government reverted to a *laissez-faire* attitude during the twenties and gave top priority to providing work for unemployed, nondisabled laborers in the thirties, the physically disabled were all but forgotten and forced to fend for themselves.

When the United States became involved in World War II, Congress became aware of the critical shortage of industrial manpower caused by the Selective Service draft. To help alleviate this situation, the Bardon-LaFollette Act of 1943 (Public Law 113) was signed into law by President Franklin D. Roosevelt. The intent of the act was to take the cadré of disabled men classified as being unfit to serve in the armed forces and to provide them with the opportunity to receive vocational training.

Public Law 113 was unique in the annals of rehabilitation legislation in that it was the first such act to include medical services along with vocational training. Fifty percent of all funds were earmarked by the act for rehabilitation services in the areas of medical examinations, corrective surgery, hospitalization, transportation, occupational licenses, occupational tools and equipment, prosthetic devices, and so forth. The act also provided rehabilitation for the mentally impaired, but this program was limited by the fact that only a small number of mentally impaired individuals were willing or able to take advantage of the services. Rehabilitation services were also extended to the blind, who had previously participated only in programs sponsored by individual state agencies. L.H. Rivers, Jr. has noted that a key provision of the Bordon-LaFolette Act made it possible for states to develop plans that provided rehabilitation services for the blind by transferring operations from state administrations to other agencies serving the blind.[2] Today, there are approximately 30 states with separate agencies serving the blind.

In 1954, another significant piece of rehabilitation legislation was enacted. This was the Vocational Rehabilitation Act of 1954 (Public Law 565). The intent of this act was to relieve the existing shortages in rehabilitation personnel and facilities. Section 3 of the act provided for the extension and improvement of rehabilitation programs through a 75-25 matching funds appropriation system. Under this formula, the federal government provided 75 percent of the funding and the states contributed the remaining 25 percent for services and projects. This funding system applied only for a three-year period, but it is considered to have been quite successful in light of the added services provided for various groups of disabled personnel.

Two additional features of the 1954 Vocational Rehabilitation Act were in the areas of research and training. Funds were provided for research activities that contributed to the improvement and advancement of rehabilitation services, practices, and techniques. High priority was given to those research activities that encouraged the application of findings into practical, field-based rehabilitation services. The act also authorized funds for grants and fellowships for individuals seeking professional preparation in the various areas of vocational rehabilitation. This part of the act continues to provide professionally trained personnel in the rehabilitation services and medical and paramedical fields.

On October 3, 1967, President Lyndon B. Johnson signed the Vocational Rehabilitation Amendments (Public Law 90-99) into law. The amendments extended federal authorization of funds to provide for a total of $1 billion over fiscal years 1969 and 1970. The major objectives of the amendments were to provide grants for research and model projects for the rehabilitation of disabled migrant workers, to establish a national center for the deaf and blind, and to reallot funding for the District of Columbia to achieve a more equitable distribution of rehabilitation monies.

In 1968, Public Law 90-391 was enacted as the Vocational Rehabilitation Amendments of 1968. These amendments further extended the services and funding of rehabilitation programs and services. The major provisions:

- provided additional appropriations for grants for innovative rehabilitation and research and for demonstration and training projects,
- established funding programs for public and nonprofit agencies for the recruitment and training of manpower to provide services to rehabilitation programs,
- authorized up to 10 percent of the states' allotment for the construction of new rehabilitation facilities, and
- expanded rehabilitation services to include work by optometrists.

The Rehabilitation Act of 1973 (Public Law 93-112) was by far the most dramatic and significant piece of rehabilitation legislation ever passed. In effect, this act superseded all previous rehabilitation legislation. The main thrust of Public Law 93-112 was to provide services to individuals with severe handicapping disabilities.

One section of the 1973 act is just beginning to make profound changes in the rehabilitation and hiring of handicapped personnel. This is Section 504, which makes it illegal to discriminate against the hiring of or admission into a vocational education program of qualified individuals on the basis of their handicapping condition. The section provides that "no otherwise qualified handicapped individual . . . shall, solely by reason of his handicap, be excluded from the participation in, be denied the benefits of, or be subjected to discrimination under any program or activity receiving federal financial assistance."[3] Thus, it defines discrimination on basis of handicap as illegal under penalty of losing part or all of federally funded contracts, grants, or services.

Other objectives of the law are:

- to promote expanded employment opportunities for the handicapped in all areas of business and industry;
- to establish state plans for the purpose of providing vocational rehabilitation services to meet the needs of the handicapped;
- to conduct evaluations of the potential rehabilitation of handicapped clients and to expand services to them as well as to those who have not received any or received inadequate rehabilitation services; and
- to increase the number and competence of rehabilitation personnel through retraining and upgrading experiences.

Finally, the last significant pieces of rehabilitation legislation were the Rehabilitation Act Amendments of 1974 (Public Law 93-516). The intent of these amendments was to provide more equitable services and programming for the blind and those with impaired sight. The major provisions of the amendments established uniform treatment of the blind through agency coordination and cooperation, provided for the administration, in the "spirit of the law," of those provisions that allowed the blind to serve as vendors in public buildings, and authorized a White House Conference on Handicapped Individuals for the promotion and advancement of rehabilitation services and opportunities for handicapped persons.[4]

SOCIAL ACTION LEGISLATION

When they think of socialization, socialized government, or social or social action legislation in the United States, many people remember primarily Franklin D. Roosevelt's New Deal and its many legislative enactments. This is only logical, for that was the first governmental thrust, en masse, that created an all-out awareness of and a program of action aimed at solving the economic and social problems of Americans. Programs such as the Civilian Conservation Corps and the Public Works Administration typified the solutions offered to an economically deprived citizenry.

During the 1960s and 1970s, a new wave of social action legislation appeared. Unlike their predecessors of the 1930s, the new laws were more than "make work" legislation. The major weakness of the New Deal had been that it tended to relieve unemployment only through government supported projects and failed to provide any long-term solutions to the complex social and economic problems of the time. The new wave of legislation, in contrast, was aimed directly at eliminating and alleviating the problems of economic and social inadequacy.

After World War II, the Employment Act of 1946 (Public Law 304) was enacted to solve the unemployment problem. This was to be accomplished not by public funds but by a declaration of war against unemployment. The act stated that:

> The Congress hereby declares that it is the continuing policy and responsibility of the Federal government to use all practicable means consistent with its needs and obligations and other essential considerations of national policy, with the assistance and cooperation of industry, agriculture, labor and State and local governments, to coordinate and utilize all its plans, functions, and resources for the purpose of creating and maintaining, in a manner calculated to foster and promote free competitive enterprise and the general welfare, conditions under which there will be afforded useful employment opportunities, including self-employment, for those able, willing, and seeking to work, and to promote maximum employment, production, and purchasing power.[5]

Needless to say, Public Law 304 did not end unemployment. It did, however, provide two important incentives. The first required that the president prepare and present an annual economic report to the nation; the second established the President's Council of Economic Advisers. Thus, though the act did not eliminate unemployment in the United States, it did provide a means of developing an intellectual base and information source for identifying and developing policies to solve the country's economic problems.

The first act that signaled the oncoming wave of social action legislation of the 1960s was the Area Redevelopment Act of 1961 (Public Law 87-27). The main thrust of this act was to bring business and industry into areas of low economic development and chronic unemployment or underemployment. T.J. Hailstones and F.V. Mastriana note that the main function of the act was to provide financial aid to areas distressed or areas having a surplus of labor.[6] Some of the programs established under the act were aimed at the training of workers for jobs in newly established industries. These programs were later merged with those of the Manpower Development and Training Act of 1962 (Public Law 87-415).

The latter act, more commonly known as the MDTA, was perhaps the most significant piece of social action legislation of the 1960s. It was signed into law by President John F. Kennedy to create new programs and techniques to ensure to those who, for any reason, were unemployed or underemployed, an "environment guaranteeing employment."[7] Specifically, the MDTA set up training, retraining, and job-upgrading programs for individuals with no or outdated occupational skills. Title II of the act was specifically designed to retrain the unemployed who are otherwise unable to obtain full employment.

Under specifications set by the MDTA, four types of job preparation programs were established:

1. institutional training at either public or private institutions,
2. on-the-job training at the place of employment,
3. demonstration and experimental training programs, and
4. youth training programs for individuals 16 to 20 years of age who are out of school and out of work.

The 1963 amendments to the MDTA (Public Law 88-214) expanded job training for those unemployed individuals who lack basic education skills. It authorized training in minimum educational skills through specialized instruction in reading, writing, language skills, and arithmetic. It also expanded and designed programs for the disadvantaged and out-of-school youth between the ages of 16 and 21. These programs were limited, however, to youth from chronically impoverished environments that are conducive to academic or vocational handicaps, for example, cultural or language barriers, lack of motivation, lack of job skills, or emotional problems.

Training programs to meet the special needs of workers 45 years of age and older were not available until the enactment of the 1966 amendments to the MDTA (Public Law 89-792). These amendments also provided for physical examinations, minor treatment, and prescribing a prosthesis for trainees who are not capable of paying for health services. Finally, they authorized the establishment of experimental and institutional programs to provide job training to inmates of correctional institutions.

Like the MDTA, the Economic Opportunity Act of 1964 (Public Law 88-452) was designed to decrease the levels of unemployment among the disadvantaged and unskilled populations of the country. J.W. Rioux has noted that, though no general aid to education was provided for in the act, resources were made available for the upgrading of education.[8]

Public Law 88-452 established and funded seven major programs. These were:

1. the Job Corps
2. the Neighborhood Youth Corps
3. College Work Study Programs
4. Urban and Rural Community Action Programs
5. Adult Basic Education
6. Education of Migrant Children
7. Adult Work Experience Programs

Of the seven programs, three were specifically designed to reduce immediately the high rate of unemployment. A brief description of three of the law's more significant programs follows:

1. The *Job Corps* was developed for youth between the ages of 16 and 21 who had continuing records of school failure and displayed an inability to succeed in their communities. The corps provided residential training centers for young men and women in rural and urban areas and designed programs tailored to meet their occupational training needs. These programs were threefold: They provided (a) basic education, (b) skill training for the development of occupational competence, and (c) constructive work experience related to the training program.
2. The *Neighborhood Youth Corps* was designed for youth who indicated an intention to drop out of school prior to fulfillment of high school diploma requirements or who had left school and wanted to reenter. The program provided school and work experiences tailored to help students with weak academic interests and to relate their studies to the world of work.
3. *Adult Work Experience Programs* were designed to reeducate, train, or retrain the parents who were raising children in poverty and who were chronically unemployed and receiving public assistance.

Under the various programs established by Public Law 88-452, a number of special remedial and noncurricular services were provided to program participants. Two of these services were (1) the rehabilitation and retraining of the physically and mentally handicapped, and (2) the provision of health, rehabilitation, employment, educational, and related services to those not qualified for military service.

On December 28, 1973, the Comprehensive Employment and Training Act (Public Law 93-203) was signed into law. Commonly referred to as CETA, this act assumed many of the functions of the old MDTA programs. Indeed, with the passage of CETA, MDTA programs under the Manpower Administration were removed and placed under the supervision of the new act. Reflecting the high rates of unemployment in the early 1970s, CETA's primary purpose was to establish programs to provide comprehensive manpower services to the country. The act was aimed at the hardcore unemployed youth and adults who had no occupational skills and thus were not contributing to the development of the nation's economy.

Like most social action legislation, CETA was designed as a short-term, stop-gap attempt to alleviate the immediate unemployment problem. Job training was aimed at making adults and youth into productive members of society as soon as possible. Thus, training time was usually based upon how long it took trainees to secure a job.

Agencies sponsoring CETA programs can be from either public or private sectors, and the form of training may vary from on-the-job situations to formal in-class programs. CETA funds assure individual and family support for the trainees and provide monetary incentives for completing the programs. Support services and funds are also available for health and medical care, child care, residential support, transportation, counseling, and remedial instruction. In these ways, and by directing vocational educators to plan their programs in concert with CETA programs, Congress expressed its belief that CETA programming would be an extremely important means of curing the problems of the hardcore unemployed.

In 1977, The Youth Employment and Demonstration Projects (YEDPA) Act (Public Law 95-93) was signed into law. As an amendment to Public Law 93-203, the YEDPA set up two important programs—the Young Adult Conservation Corps and the Youth Employment Demonstration Program. In the Conservation Corps, economically depressed young adults between the ages of 16 and 23 were provided employment opportunities of a public nature. For example, the corps participated in field projects concerned with tree nurseries; wildlife habitat improvement; range management improvements; recreational development, rehabilitation, and maintenance; fish habitat and culture measures; forest insect and disease prevention and control; road and trail maintenance and improvement; general sanitation, cleanup, and maintenance; erosion control and protection from flood damage; and measures to prevent drought and other natural damage.

The act's Youth Employment Demonstration programs were designed to explore methods of dealing with chronic unemployment problems of youth. These programs attempted to address three types of employment situations for disadvantaged youth: (1) parttime employment during the school year, (2) fulltime employment during the summer months, and (3) work experiences on a cooperative basis for in-school youth. Authorized programs included outreach and assessment services, counseling, education for work transition, labor supply-demand information, literacy and bilingual training, high school equivalency certification, basic skill training, transportation assistance, child care services, job development and placement, and attempts to overcome sex stereotyping in job preparation and placement.

The most recent significant piece of social action legislation was the CETA Reauthorization Act of 1978 (Public Law 95-524). Its major contributions were twofold. First, it continued the funding of and support to existing CETA functions, such as the various youth programs, the Countercyclical Public Service Employment Programs, programs aimed at developing private sector opportunities for the economically disadvantaged, and the Young Adult Conservation Corps.

Second, as its most significant aspect, it attempted to maximize the coordination of the various plans, programs, and activities aimed at alleviating the unemployment problems of our country. Specifically, it required that programs involving vocational education, rehabilitation, public assistance, self-employment training, and social services work together to eliminate duplications and counterproductive competition. Thus, the 1978 act refocused the efforts of all relevant agencies toward the common goal of turning unproductive individuals into a productive force in the U.S. economy.

EDUCATIONAL LEGISLATION

The vocational education profession has traditionally been receptive to providing services to students with special needs. In fact, the Smith-Hughes Act of 1917 is said to have established the precedent for funding vocational preparation for the handicapped.[9]

The term *special needs* can be traced to its inception in the Vocational Education Act of 1963 (Public Law 88-210). This act was the first to define the term as meaning individuals with disadvantaged or handicapping conditions that would prevent them from succeeding in a traditional educational program. Specifically, the act stated that:

> It is the purpose of this part to authorize Federal grants to states to assist them to maintain, extend, and improve existing programs of vocational education, to develop new programs of vocational education, and to

> provide parttime employment to continue their vocational training on full-time basis, so that persons of all ages in all communities of the state—those in high school . . . and those with special education handicaps—will have ready access to vocational training or retraining which is of high quality, which is realistic in the light of actual or anticipated opportunitites for gainful employment, and which is suited to their needs, interests, and ability to benefit from such training.[10]

The act further stated that federal funds could be used for programs providing occupational training to individuals with academic, socioeconomic, and other handicapping conditions. Since it did not mandate or earmark the use of funds for the special needs population, little was done under the act to service this group. As a result, special needs programming was at best randomly funded and haphazardly organized.

Because the special needs population was not being properly serviced by vocational education, Congress, in the Vocational Education Amendments of 1968 (Public Law 90-576), decided to provide funds specifically for special needs students. These amendments identified two main categories in the special needs population: the disadvantaged and the handicapped. The disadvantaged were to receive 15 percent of all vocational education funding and the handicapped were to get 10 percent, for a total of 25 percent of all vocational education funds.

The 1968 amendments defined the disadvantaged as students with social, economic, academic, or cultural disadvantagements that prevented them from succeeding in the normal school environment. The handicapped were defined as students who were unable to learn successfully because they were mentally impaired; emotionally disturbed; orthopedically handicapped; visually handicapped; had hearing, speech, or other health impairments; or were multihandicapped.

The Educational Amendments of 1972 (Public Law 92-318) further expanded vocational programming and services to disadvantaged and handicapped students. These amendments provided funding and grants to institutions of higher education and to secondary school programs that extended career and occupational education services to students with special needs backgrounds.

The next major piece of vocational education legislation supporting the special needs population was the Vocational Education Amendments of 1976 (Public Law 94-482). The 1976 amendments, as signed into law by President Gerald Ford, expanded the funding formula for special needs programs and services. They increased the percentage of earmarked vocational education funds from 25 percent to 30 percent, with 10 percent going to the handicapped and 20 percent to the disadvantaged. The amendments further defined the disadvantaged as individuals with social, economic, or academic disadvantagements. Culturally disadvantaged students were dropped from this category because it was felt that an individual's cultural background and heritage should be viewed not as a disadvantagement but as something positive and necessary in developing a well-rounded individual.

The 1976 amendments contained two other major features. The first provided a means to ensure against sex discrimination in vocational education programs. To this end, the amendments were aimed at promoting vocational education programs for women and men in non-traditional occupations, for example, men in child care and health occupations and women in auto mechanics and work in machine shops. The antisex discrimination clause was included by Congress not only to eliminate sex discrimination practices in vocational education but also to help solve the skilled manpower shortage in numerous manufacturing and service businesses and industries.

The second major provision of the 1976 amendments was to establish a cooperative working relationship between vocational education and U.S. Department of Labor programs. Specifically, vocational education programs and CETA agencies were required to coordinate their efforts in an attempt to eliminate competitive duplication of programs and services. By requiring this sort of "cooperative venture," Congress hoped to stimulate a more concentrated effort on the elimination of unemployment among those lacking saleable skills.

It has long been the objective of our nation to provide an opportunity for all individuals to receive an education appropriate for securing employment and progressing in an occupation. Based on this concept and because of the rise in economic instability and unemployment in the early 1970s, many individuals outside the field of vocational education have also turned their attention toward the goal of solving our unemployment problems. Professionals in special education, for example, have always had an interest in the vocational preparation of handicapped students. As a result of such interest and of increased pressure from various special interest groups concerned with the establishment and maintenance of quality educational programs for the handicapped, the Education for All Handicapped Children Act of 1975 (Public Law 94-142) was signed into law on November 29, 1975, by President Gerald Ford.

The act states that:

> to assure that funds received by the state or any of its political subdivisions under any other Federal program including Section 121 of the Elementary and Secondary Education Act of 1965 . . . and Section 122(a)(4)(B) of the Vocational Education Act of 1963 . . . under which there is specific authority for the provision of assistance for the education of handicapped children, will be utilized by the State, or any of its political subdivisions, only in a manner consistent with the goal of providing a free appropriate public education for all handicapped children.[11]

Specifically, the Education for All Handicapped Children Act of 1975 requires every state to provide a free and appropriate education, including vocational education programs, for all handicapped children. However, if a local school district cannot provide such opportunities for their handicapped students, it is its responsibility to find these services, regardless of their geographic location and cost, and make them available. It is the clear intent of the law to "assure that all handicapped children have available to them . . . a free appropriate public education which emphasizes special education and related services designed to meet their unique needs . . . and to assess and assure the effectiveness of efforts to educate handicapped children."[12]

Thus, the 1975 act is considered to be a piece of civil rights legislation for the handicapped. Since it is still relatively new, its full impact is still not realized. But there is a possibility that the services required for the handicapped population will also be made available to the nonhandicapped.

The act, in essence, guarantees a number of rights to all handicapped children. These rights are specified in its major provisions:

- Services provided under the act are for handicapped children between the ages of 3 and 22, inclusive.
- State allocations will be made by a percentage formula. Allocations for the first fiscal year ending September 30, 1978, were determined by multiplying the number of handicapped children in the state by 5 percent. This amount is to be prorated upward to a maximum of 40 percent for the fiscal year ending September 20, 1982.
- States must identify and establish goals for providing a "full educational opportunity" to all handicapped children, a timetable detailing when these goals are to be accomplished, and a description of the services, facilities, and personnel needed to achieve the goals.
- An appropriate educational program must be made freely available to all handicapped children between the ages of 3 and 18 by September 1, 1978, and to all handicapped children between the ages of 3 and 21 by September 1, 1980.
- Where applicable, the state must provide a least restrictive environment (mainstreaming of the handicapped student into the regular school program) for handicapped children between the ages of 3 to 21 years.
- Each state must establish procedures to test and evaluate handicapped students so that they may be properly placed in an educational program. Steps must be taken to assure that these students will not be discriminated against due to testing procedures.
- The state must provide procedures for conducting annual evaluations of the effectiveness of various programs meeting the needs of handicapped students.

- Provisions must be made to "fully inform the parents" of the program or service in which the student is participating. Furthermore, the records diagnosing the status of the student's condition are to be made public to the parent or guardian.[13]

SUMMARY

The federal government has been a major force in providing financial and programmatic support for special needs students. This was not always the case, however. Since the Constitution of the United States left the responsibility of public education to the states, Congress was initially reluctant to give any financial or moral assistance to such students. Gradually, however, this situation changed, and Congress now provides help to the special needs population in three areas: rehabilitation, social action, and educational programming.

Rehabilitation legislation began with the passage of the Smith-Sears Act of 1918. Between 1918 and 1924, a significant number of rehabilitation programs was initiated for disabled workers. These, however, ceased with the rise of a *laissez-faire* attitude in the late 1920s and the unemployment problems of the 1930s. World War II created a manpower shortage and gave new life to the rehabilitation field. Since the end of the Second World War, there have been a number of rehabilitation legislative acts. The most significant of these was the Rehabilitation Act of 1973, which reorganized and consolidated all existing rehabilitation programs.

Social action legislation has its roots in the New Deal era of the 1930s. More recently, it emerged in the Area Redevelopment Act of 1961 and the Manpower Development and Training Act of 1962. The most important piece of social action legislation was the Comprehensive Employment and Training Act of 1973. This act provided millions of dollars of federal aid for the training and upgrading of hardcore unemployed and underemployed individuals who were not contributing to the U.S. economy.

Like the rehabilitation and socialization fields, the education sector has played a significant role in providing program aid for the special needs population. In the Vocational Education Act of 1963 and its amendments of 1968, the special needs group was defined and identified as a population in our schools needing more support. To back this up, Congress earmarked 25 percent of vocational education monies for this group. This was later increased to 30 percent in the Vocational Education Amendments of 1976. Perhaps the most far-reaching and significant piece of educational legislation in this area was the Education for All Handicapped Children Act of 1975. This law is the civil rights act for handicapped children, in that it guarantees all handicapped the right to a free and appropriate education.

NOTES

1. M.E. Switzer, "Legislative Contributions," in *Vocational Rehabilitation of the Disabled: An Overview,* ed. D. Malikin and H. Rusalen (New York: New York University Press, 1969).
2. L.H. Rivers, Jr., "History of Federal Vocational Rehabilitation As It Affects the Blind," in *Social and Rehabilitation Services for the Blind* (Springfield, Ill.: Charles C. Thomas Publications, 1972), pp. 69-87.
3. U.S., *Public Law 93-112* (Rehabilitation Act of 1973), Sec. 504.
4. U.S., *Public Law 93-516* (Rehabilitation Act Amendments of 1974), Title II, Sec. 206.
5. U.S., *Public Law 304* (Employment Act of 1946), Sec. 2.
6. T.J. Hailstones and F.V. Mastrianna, *Contemporary Economic Problems and Issues* (Cincinnati, Ohio: South-Western Publishing Company, 1976).
7. U.S., *Public Law 87-415* (Manpower Development and Training Act of 1962), Sec. 101.
8. J.W. Rioux, "Economic Opportunity Act and Elementary and Secondary Education Act of 1965," *Childhood Education* 42, no. 1 (1965): 9-11.
9. Switzer, "Legislative Contributions."
10. U.S., *Public Law 88-210* (Vocational Education Act of 1963).
11. U.S., *Public Law 94-142* (Education for All Handicapped Children Act of 1975), Sec. 613, (A)(2).
12. U.S., *Public Law 94-142,* Sec. 3 (C).
13. U.S., *Public Law 94-142,* Part B.

BIBLIOGRAPHY

Balino, A.C. *Manpower in the City*. Cambridge, Mass.: Schenkman Publishing Company, 1969.

Bies, J.D. "Serving Students with Special Needs." *Journal of Epsilon Pi Tau* 3 (1977): 39-46.

Blatt, B. "Public Policy and the Education of Children with Special Needs." *Exceptional Children* 38 (1972): 537-545.

Burkett, L.A. "Latest Word from Washington." *American Vocational Journal* 52 (1977): 9-10.

Conley, R.W. *The Economics of Vocational Rehabilitation.* Baltimore, Md.: The Johns Hopkins Press, 1965.

Hailstones, T.J., and Mastrianna, F.V. *Contemporary Economic Problems and Issues.* Cincinnati, Ohio: South-Western Publishing Company, 1976.

Kruger, D.H. "Manpower Planning and the Local Job Economy." *American Vocational Journal* 50 (1975): 32-35.

Lewis, J.W. "State Manpower Legislation: An Alternative Strategy." *American Vocational Journal* 50 (1975): 65-66.

Lund, D.R., and Tungman, R.J. "Linkages at the Council and Commission Levels." *American Vocational Journal* 52 (1977): 33-34.

Marburger, C.L. "The Economic Opportunity Act—and the Schools." *Educational Leadership* 22 (1965): 542-548.

Rioux J.W. "Economic Opportunity Act and Elementary and Secondary Education Act of 1965." *Childhood Education* 42 (1965): 9-11.

Rivers, L.H., Jr. "History of Federal Vocational Rehabilitation As It Affects the Blind." In *Social and Rehabilitation Services for the Blind,* edited by R. E. Hardy and J. G. Cull. Springfield, Ill.: Charles C. Thomas Publications, 1972.

Switzer, M.E. "Legislative Contributions." In *Vocational Rehabilitation of the Disabled: An Overview,* edited by D. Malikin and H. Rusalen. New York: New York University Press, 1969.

U.S., *Public Law 94-482* (Educational Amendments of 1976).

U.S., *Public Law 95-93* (Youth Employment and Development Projects Act of 1977).

U.S., *Public Law 95-524* (CETA Reauthorization Act of 1978).

U.S., *Public Law 178* (Vocational Rehabilitation Act of 1918).

U.S., *Public Law 11* (Vocational Rehabilitation Act of 1919).

U.S., *Public Law 236* (Vocational Rehabilitation Act of 1920).

U.S., *Public Law 113* (Vocational Rehabilitation Act of 1943).

U.S., *Public Law 304* (Employment Act of 1946).

U.S., *Public Law 565* (Vocational Rehabilitation Act of 1954).

U.S., *Public Law 937* (Vocational Rehabilitation Amendments of 1956).

U.S., *Public Law 85-198* (Vocational Rehabilitation Amendments of 1957).

U.S., *Public Law 85-213* (Vocational Rehabilitation Amendments of 1957).

U.S., *Public Law 87-27* (Area Redevelopment Act of 1961).

U.S., *Public Law 87-415* (Manpower Development and Training Act of 1962).

U.S., *Public Law 88-452* (Economic Opportunity Act of 1965).

U.S., *Public Law 88-210* (Vocational Education Act of 1963).

U.S., *Public Law 89-792* (Manpower Development and Training Act Amendments of 1966).

U.S., *Public Law 90-99* (Vocational Rehabilitation Amendments of 1967).

U.S., *Public Law 90-391* (Vocational Rehabilitation Amendments of 1968).

U.S., *Public Law 90-576* (Vocational Education Act Amendments of 1968).

U.S., *Public Law 92-318* (Educational Amendments of 1972).

U.S., *Public Law 93-112* (Rehabilitation Act of 1973).

U.S., *Public Law 93-156* (Rehabilitation Act Amendments of 1974).

U.S., *Public Law 94-142* (Education for All Handicapped Children Act of 1975).

Weebink, P. "Unemployment in the United States, 1930-1940." *American Economic Review* (1940).

Chapter 3

Identification and Characteristics of Disadvantaged Students

Jerry L. Wircenski, Ed.D.

CHARACTERISTICS OF THE DISADVANTAGED

Introduction

Who are the disadvantaged? This is perhaps one of the most difficult questions for educators and society in general to answer. When we label someone or some group as disadvantaged, we usually mean that they are disadvantaged in relationship to some criteria—educational level, economic standard, value system, cultural or social standard, or any other criteria individuals use as a yardstick to measure and make comparisons between people. The label disadvantaged is thus often based on personal judgments.

Mario D. Fantini and Gerold Weinstein state that the usual criterion for identifying the disadvantaged is an economic definition—poverty and low social status. But they note further that, "the meaning of disadvantaged must be broadened to include all those who are blocked in any way from fulfilling their human potential." They assert that this blocking can take place anywhere: in the inner-city ghetto or in the middle or upper-class suburbs. They state:

> The schools have failed the middle-class child as they have the child from low income families. The affluent child, who comes to the school prepared to succeed in a mediocre, outdated educational process is also being shortchanged, and thus, too, is disadvantaged. Simply because he does his homework, gets passing grades, and eventually graduates, is not necessarily a sign of advantaged.[1]

The professional literature abounds concerning the characteristics of the disadvantaged. Not surprisingly, there is widespread variation in the literature regarding those characteristics and the causes that produce them. Frank Riessman has described the culturally deprived as

- "relatively slow at cognitive tasks, but not stupid;
- "learning more readily from a concrete approach;
- "pragmatic rather than theoretical, often appearing anti-intellectual;
- "traditional, superstitious, and somewhat religious;
- "being from a male-centered culture, except for some major sections of the black subculture;
- "inflexible and not open to reason about many of their beliefs (i.e., morality, and educational practice);
- "feeling alienated from the larger social structure, with resultant frustration;
- "holding others to blame for their misfortune;
- "valuing masculinity and attendant action, viewing intellectual activities as unmasculine;
- "viewing knowledge for its practical, vocational ends;
- "not wishing to adopt a middle-class way of life but desiring a better quality of living, with personal comforts for themselves and their family;
- "lacking in auditory attention and interpretation skills;
- "deficient in reading and communication skills generally, and having wide areas of ignorance."[2]

Leon Eisenberg has stated that, psychologically, the disadvantaged do not have an individualistic, competitive orientation. Their values tend to be collective group values rather than individualistic, and they perceive advancement as coming from social group forces rather than from individual activity. They consistently require others to prove themselves in any situation and are generally unimpressed by middle-class prestige. They are often lacking in adequate verbal and experiential stimulation, and have not formed the learning sets that are necessary for formal learning.[3]

Ben Seligman has characterized the disadvantaged as lacking the goals and ambitions that characterize the middle class. They have a sense of alienation and isolation leading to fatalistic acceptance of the conditions of poverty.[4] These conclusions are supported by Francesco Cordasco and Eugene Bucchioni who characterize the disadvantaged as having feelings of fatalism, depending inferiority, and helplessness.[5] The manifested aggressive behavior of the disadvantaged is not channeled into constructive tasks but is directed to those tasks that provide immediate gratification.[6]

Disadvantaged learners are generally described as culturally, socially, educationally, and economically deprived.[7, 8, 9] They are normally below school grade level in achievement. Typically, by the end of the ninth grade, the reading levels of disadvantaged learners are from 2 to 3½ years below grade level, and their abilities in mathematics and other subjects are retarded. Conceptual and reasoning ability are, likewise, below that of nondisadvantaged learners of the same age. Also, typically, disadvantaged learners are apathetic toward school and structured learning situations in which their experience has been one of low achievement and failure.[10, 11]

Learning Traits

We should caution, however, that, in discussing characteristics, disadvantaged learners are not all alike. Cultural and socioeconomic factors, ethnic background, values, abilities, and other factors vary among students. Robert W. Walker has listed learning traits of disadvantaged persons that differentiate them from other learners, but not all of these traits apply to all disadvantaged learners. Walker's list includes the following traits:

- "Limited ability to use the basic scholastic skills,
- "limited perception of the value of an education,
- "lack of motivation to learn,
- "poor attitude toward the conventional school situation,
- "weak self-image,
- "lack of self-confidence,
- "dependent upon others,
- "low levels of aspiration,
- "short interest spans,
- "argumentative and hostile or passive and apathetic,
- "resentful of authority, and
- "feeling of 'not belonging'."[12]

J.M. Conte and G.H. Grimes have developed a similar list of 13 characteristics. Though similar to Walker's, this list is also presented here because it further delineates the learning characteristics of the disadvantaged. According to Conte and Grimes, the disadvantaged

- "seem to be oriented to the physical and visual rather than the aural;
- "show more interest in content rather than form;
- "are externally oriented rather than introspective;
- "exhibit problem-centered, as opposed to abstract-centered, learning characteristics;
- "use inductive rather than deductive reasoning;
- "are spatial rather than temporal oriented;
- "are slow, careful, patient, and perservering (in areas of importance to them) rather than quiet, clever, facile, and flexible;

- "are inclined to communicate through actions rather than words;
- "are found to be deficient in auditory attention and interpretation skills;
- "are very oriented toward concrete applications of learning;
- "have short attention spans, and experience difficulty in following orders;
- "are characterized by significant voids in knowledge and learning;
- "lack the experience of receiving approval for success."[13]

Environmental Characteristics

Much of the literature that has examined the disadvantaged has concentrated on elements other than personal characteristics. Describing the home life of the disadvantaged, Robert D. Strom noted that there is little opportunity for interaction among family members and little opportunity for language exchange.[14] The families of disadvantaged children normally do not have long-range goals. The focus of attention is on day-to-day survival.[15, 16] Leon Eisenberg found that children from disadvantaged families received infrequent attention from their parents and were often left to fend for themselves at a very early age.[17] Disadvantaged children do not receive the parental monitoring of daily activities that middle-class children typically receive. They are free to roam the streets and neighborhoods unsupervised at very early ages, whereas middle-class children of the same age are usually under strict parental supervision.[18]

Leonard M. Ridini and John E. Madden have provided a comprehensive description of the inner-city disadvantaged. They concluded that inner-city youth are generally troubled by the following eight problems:

1. "Possibility of being unemployed and underemployed.
2. "A tremendous amount of loud noise in their environment.
3. "High rates of illiteracy and undereducation.
5. "Discrimination.
6. "Inadequate health care.
7. "Negative self-concepts.
8. "A shortage of competent teachers to teach them effectively."[19]

Benjamin Bloom and Robert J. Havighurst describe the parent-child relationship of the disadvantaged family as nonexistent. They state that there is no time allocated for parent-children activities, no shopping trips, no visits to cultural sites, nor even trips to other neighborhoods. There are no joint activities through which the parent and child can communicate and get to know each other.[20, 21]

Herman P. Miller describes the home environment of the disadvantaged child as that of a single-parent. Over half of the homes are fatherless, and, in many of the homes where the father is present, he is often absent a good deal of the time. This is especially true of ghetto families.[22] Mario Fantini and Gerold Weinstein describe the family of a disadvantaged child as consisting of many brothers and sisters and many parents and parent substitutes, such as aunts, uncles, cousins, and grandparents, living together. They refer to this situation as an extended family.[23]

Based on the environmental characteristics of the disadvantaged, a number of basic needs become apparent. In review of the needs of disadvantaged youth, Vincent Feck has identified the following:

> (1) security and stability in their environment, (2) successful educational experiences, (3) recognition for achievement, (4) love and respect, (5) legal sources of finance, (6) financial management, (7) proper housing, (8) good health, (9) development of basic communication skills, (10) saleable work skills, (11) an appreciation of the meaning and importance of work, (12) successfully employed adult or peer work models, (13) positive self-concepts, (14) job opportunities and qualifications, and (15) socially acceptable attitudes and behavior.[24]

Comparisons of disadvantaged children with those of middle-class children on personal and homelife characteristics show wide discrepancies, as one would expect, knowing the plight of the disadvantaged in the United States. Yet some interesting commonalities have been found when studying disadvantaged children and middle-class children in terms of abilities. There is no evidence that disadvantaged children are inherently less intelligent than more privileged children. In discussing the abilities of disadvantaged children, Eisenberg notes that there is often confusion between differences and deficiencies.[25] Disadvantaged children are born into a familial environment that stems from a culture different from that of middle-class children. Disadvantaged children generally are not strong in verbal communication and cognitive skills because their survival in the subculture of the streets is dependent upon doing rather than talking. They thus assume responsibilities at a far earlier age than do middle-class children. Their skills enable them to survive an active, demanding environment, as opposed to the more formal learning environment of the schools. Martin Deutsch states that disadvantaged children simply enter the schooling situation less prepared and thereby are prone to failure at a very early age.[26] Arthur R. Jensen supports these findings, stating that it is generally conceded that comparing the I.Q. scores of one race, one ethnic group, or one socioeconomic group against those of another reveals little difference in intelligence between or among groups. Children reared in stimulating environments will have a higher intelligence quotient than those reared in a less stimulating environment, regardless of group.[27] Research conducted by Thomas F. Pettigrew, and by Clarke and Clarke, supports these findings. They state that it has been demonstrated that when any group moves from an unstimulating environment to a comparatively stimulating one, the intelligence quotient will be increased.[28, 29]

Research on the abilities of disadvantaged children seems to indicate that they are not unequal to those of more advantaged children. The disadvantaged have, however, accumulated a wealth of less desirable experiences that inhibits their success in the more formal school environment developed and fostered by the middle-class system of values. There is little doubt that the promise of American education has made little sense to a large segment of the population, including the disadvantaged. Contrary to historical myths, educational sociologists have produced strong evidence that schools serve the socioeconomic structure in which they exist. The schools have generally provided middle- and upper-income youth with the intellectual tools necessary for success in American society. But they have commonly failed to cope effectively with the task of educating the disadvantaged.[30]

In the 1960s, equality of educational opportunity was understood in simple terms. It meant that everyone in society or in education was to be treated equally: one standard, one set of books, one fiscal formula for children everywhere, regardless of race, creed, or color. Success went to the resourceful, the ambitious, the bright, the strong; failure was the responsibility of the individual, certainly not that of the school or society.

In this vein, the answer to the question, Who are the disadvantaged? was best answered by Fantini and Weinstein. They stated:

> The disadvantaged cannot be defined by the race, residence, jobs, or behavior alone. Although we tend to think first of such districts as Harlem, disadvantaged are to be found also in small towns, in the rural slums of back woods Appalachia, in the Spanish borough of El Paso, on American Indian reservations—or on the fashionable streets of Scarsdale. They are black, white, red, and yellow; with or without parents; hungry or overfed; they are the children of the jobless, the immigrant workers, or the unemployed. The only thing they have in common is that all are left out of the process which purports to carry all human kind, regardless of background: feelings of potency, self-worth, connection with others, and concern for the common good. *Anyone deprived of the means to reach out to these human goals is disadvantaged, for it is the purpose of our democratic social institution to advance the development of these human goals for all people* [emphasis added].
>
> Failure in human goal attainment is therefore a reflection of institutional failure and, until our social institutions in general, and the schools in particular, are equipped to satisfy these goals, full human development is thwarted. Until then we are disadvantaged. Our focus will, of necessity, be on the most obvious institutional casualties, but the implications for all should be recognized.[31]

Summary

There is a wealth of literature regarding the general characteristics of the disadvantaged. There is some disagreement, however, as to the personal characteristics, homelife, and abilities of the disadvantaged. What is evident from the review of the literature is that there is very often a tendency to overgeneralize, to almost stereotype the disadvantaged as being this or that. Thus, it is impossible to paint a composite picture of the "typical" disadvantaged person. When applying definitions or drawing implications from the literature, it is most important to remember that each disadvantaged youth or adult is *an individual*. Each disadvantaged person has certain unique characteristics, which, for purposes of delivering vocational education programs and services, can be drawn together into a composite profile, but only for purposes of implementation.

IDENTIFICATION OF THE DISADVANTAGED IN VOCATIONAL EDUCATION

Reacting to criticism about inequality of educational opportunity, Congress, in the 1960s, passed a series of acts designed to strengthen the public educational system. These acts called attention to students who found it difficult to succeed in traditional classes or courses, many of whom either were far behind in basic educational skills or had already been pushed out or dropped out of school.

The term disadvantaged came into widespread use following the passage of the Economic Opportunity Act of 1964. Disadvantaged persons were defined as individuals whose incomes were below minimum levels and who were included in the following categories: minority groups, school dropouts, under 22 years of age, 45 years of age or over, and handicapped.[32] At that time, the definition of disadvantaged used in connection with the antipoverty program identified "target groups." The Research and Policy Committee of the Committee for Economic Development stated: "The common meanings of 'disadvantaged' are vague and ambiguous. Frequently the terms 'disadvantaged' and 'poor' are used interchangeably, and the members of some minority ethnic groups are typically assumed to be disadvantaged."[33]

When applied in relation to poverty, the term disadvantaged failed to come to grips with the specific conditions suffered by individual members of the target group that required remedial treatment. The preceding chapter notes favorably the federal legislation regarding special needs learners. Here, it is important to highlight those federal acts that have defined the characteristics and clarified the identification of the disadvantaged. This legislation began with the Vocational Education Act of 1963, signed by President Lyndon B. Johnson on December 18, 1963. In this act, Congress directed vocational education toward the needs of people rather than into rigid categories and target groups. The act called for the vocational education of "persons who have academic, socioeconomic, or other handicaps that prevent them from succeeding in the regular programs of vocational education." The central theme of the act was "programs for people," rather than "people for programs." Although it was a first step in delivering vocational education services to the disadvantaged, the 1963 act ". . . merely recommended that students who have special needs related to disadvantaged or handicapping conditions be served by vocational education programs."[34]

The Vocational Education Amendments of 1968 went far beyond this by relating appropriations to objectives. The amendments mandated that portions of federal grants to the states be used to provide special programs or services to those who could not succeed in regular vocational education programs without such services. They required that individuals, rather than groups, be identified for special services. They also required that states spend at least 15 percent of their basic state grant funds to pay for services and programs for the academically and socioeconomically disadvantaged. According to Evelyn R. Kay, Barbara H. Kemp, and Frances G. Saunders, "the Vocational Education Amendments of 1968 present an unlimited challenge for states and their school districts to provide special programs and services to ensure vocational education success for the disadvantaged. . . ."[35]

The 1968 amendments also provided a definition for the term disadvantaged. The term was defined as meaning "persons . . . who have academic, socioeconomic, or other handicaps that prevent them from succeeding in the regular vocational education program. . . ."[36]

In 1970, a more inclusive definition appeared in the *Federal Register*. Kay, Kemp, and Saunders, quoting the *Federal Register,* Vol. 35, No. 9, May 9, 1970, stated:

> Disadvantaged persons . . . means persons who have academic, socioeconomic, cultural, or other handicaps that prevent them from succeeding in vocational education or consumer and homemaking programs designed for persons without such handicaps and who for that reason require specially designed educational programs or related services. The terms include persons whose needs for such programs or services result from poverty, neglect, delinquency, or cultural or linguistic isolation from the community at large, but does not include physically or mentally handicapped persons (as defined in paragraph 0 of this section) unless such persons who suffer from the handicap described in this paragraph.[37]

The charge to vocational education was clear; the amendments of 1968 focused on the needs of disadvantaged students, which were to be met through program development, services, and activities which meet the unique needs of the disadvantaged.

Title II of the Vocational Education Amendments of 1976 required that 30 percent of basic state grant funds be spent for necessary special services and programs—20 percent for the disadvantaged and 10 percent for the handicapped. The disadvantaged were defined as those persons who have academic or economic handicaps and who require special services and assistance to enable them to succeed in vocational programs. The Division of Vocational and Technical Education in the Department of Health, Education, and Welfare (HEW) provided, in the *Federal Register*, Vol. 42, No. 191, Section 104-804, a further interpretation by defining academic disadvantage to mean a person that "(1) lacks reading and writing skills, (2) lacks mathematical skills, or (3) performs below grade level."[38]

"Economically disadvantaged" was defined to mean "(1) family income is at or below national poverty level; (2) participant, or parents or guardian of the participant, is unemployed; (3) participant, or parent of participant, is recipient of public assistance; or (4) participant is institutionalized or under state guardianship."[39]

Under Title II, eligibility for participation in special programs for the disadvantaged (supported under the Title's Subpart 4, Section 104.801) is limited to the academically or economically disadvantaged who, as a result of their disadvantage "(1) do not have, at the time of entrance into a vocational education program, the prerequisites for success in the program; or (2) are enrolled in a vocational education program but require supportive services or special programs to enable them to meet the requirements for the program that are established by the state or the local educational agency."[40]

In order for persons to be eligible for special vocational programs, program modifications, and related services under the setaside and special funds for the disadvantaged, they must meet the following conditions:

1. "The individual is excluded from a regular vocational program because of the *effects* of a disadvantagement or
2. "The individual shows evidence of being unable to succeed in a regular vocational program because of the *effects* of a disadvantagement, *and*
3. "The effect of the disadvantagement is identified by a qualified professional person (teachers, counselors)."[41]

The Division of Vocational and Technical Education (HEW) has developed a classification system to simplify the task of identifying disadvantaged persons. The categories of the system can be used to report information to local and state administrators. The statements that follow each category below are only examples of the types of disadvantagement in that category. The identification categories are:

1. *Academically disadvantaged*

These individuals do not have adequate skills to succeed at the time of entrance into or while enrolled in a vocational program. Due to poor education preparation, they require supportive services or special programs to enable them to meet the requirements for entrance into the program or to continue and complete the program.

It is important that these prescribed skills be required for the occupational area in which the individual plans to be or is enrolled. In other words, the academic background for enrolling in an electrician program where mathematics is necessary is different from enrolling in a clerk-typist course where reading and writing are primary.

There are two cautions here. (i) A student may not be classified as disadvantaged because he/she does not have the prerequisites for a vocational program. For instance, a person who wishes to enter an electronics course but never took the science courses cannot be categorized as disadvantaged for this reason alone. (ii) If through testing and observation, a person shows little or no manual dexterity or other basic occupational requirements, a student should not be considered disadvantaged but should be counseled and encouraged to enroll in a program in which he/she has the demonstrated ability and interest.

1.1 *Limited English-speaking and comprehension ability*

Individuals in this group experience sufficient difficulty with the ability to communicate in English that their capacity to learn is reduced to the point that they do not substantially comprehend the course material.

1.2 *Reading and/or writing deficiency*

Individuals in this group experience sufficient difficulty with reading and writing in English to the extent that their capacity to learn the vocational education subject matter is reduced significantly to the point that they do not substantially comprehend the course material.

1.3 *Computational deficiency*

These individuals have an educational background in mathematics which is not adequate to perform computation activities at the level required by the vocational education program.

2.0 *Economically disadvantaged*

Individuals in this category are not succeeding or cannot succeed in a regular vocational education program for one or more reasons as described above pertaining to academic and vocational performance: the individual or his/her parents or guardian is a public assistance recipient, family income is at or below poverty level, unemployed, or the individual is institutionalized.

It is more difficult to pinpoint the effects of poverty which do not relate or affect the academic performance on a person's ability to succeed.

One effect may be on attitudes, motivation, or behavior which would reflect on a student's ability to succeed in a program, and therefore, reduce chances of subsequent employment. An expenditure for services of a special counselor to work with such students would be beneficial. Special pre-service and in-service training for teaching and support personnel could also help to enable the staff to cope with students whose economic circumstances have hindered their educational progress.

Obviously, the school system cannot solve the financial problems of those in a low income category. Circumstances do arise when students or potential students cannot attend class because they do not have proper clothing or food, or the means of transportation to get there. Several possibilities suggest themselves, such as contact with welfare and social agencies and special transportation arrangements.[42]

Groups of Individuals Most Likely To Show Effects of Disadvantagement

The Division of Vocational and Technical Education (HEW) has established the following guidelines to identify those groups of individuals who are most likely to show effects of disadvantagement:

> The only basis for identifying students as disadvantaged is their inability to succeed in a regular vocational education program without supportive services or special programs designed to meet their unique learning needs and who are not identified as being served as handicapped.
>
> *Further,* each should be identified as an *individual* who cannot succeed rather than as a member of a particular group of people. With this in mind, the following groups are listed only as guidance to identify the

individuals who are most likely to have some effect of academic or economic disadvantagement:

- Persons, regardless of age, with poor educational backgrounds
- Semiskilled and unskilled workers receiving less than poverty level incomes
- Persons in correctional institutions or in institutions for neglected children
- Members of groups which have been discriminated against because of race, color, sex, age, national origin
- Persons who have been isolated from cultural, educational, and/or employment experiences
- Persons who, because of a combination of environmental, cultural and historical factors, lack motivation or the necessary attitude for obtaining an education or a job skill
- Persons who are dependent upon social services to meet their basic needs
- Unwed mothers or teenage parents[43]

Disadvantaged persons can also be found in disproportionate numbers in certain geographical locations. Examples of such "target" areas include:

- "Economically depressed communities (low-income areas)
- "Areas of high youth unemployment
- "Public housing developments
- "Urban renewal areas
- "Rurally isolated poverty areas
- "Mexican-American barrios
- "Puerto Rican enclaves
- "American Indian reservations
- "Migrant streams
- "Communities of refugees; e.g., Vietnamese
- "Indo-Chinese, Russians"[44]

Demographic Characteristics of the Disadvantaged

The Division of Occupational and Technical Education (HEW) has stated that "in further delineating who the disadvantaged are for purposes of serving these individuals under the Vocational Education Act of 1976 [sic], it is essential to keep the *cause* of disadvantagement distinct from its *effect* in an educational context."[45] For example, students who are not succeeding in the regular vocational curriculum might trace their disadvantagement to the fact that they have a nonEnglish language background, which is the cause. Identifying such individuals simply as members of a minority group does not automatically classify them as disadvantaged. On the other hand, educational experiences and services must be designed to overcome effects, which might be limited to reading and comprehension disabilities or behavioral problems.

When working with disadvantaged persons, the Division of Vocational and Technical Education (HEW) has recommended that the following characteristics be identified for each individual:

1. "*English as a second language:* Students in this group come from home environments in which English is not the common language of communication, such as (a) Spanish, (b) Native American, (c) Eskimo/Aleutian, (d) French, (e) Pacific American, (f) Vietnamese and Indo-Chinese, (g) other.
2. "*Racial/ethnic groups:* (a) Black, (b) Native American, (c) Hispanic, (d) Pacific American, (e) other.
3. "*Adults* (persons beyond the age of compulsory school attendance):
   a. "*Functionally illiterate:* Persons who are unable to apply the basic communication, computational, and problem-solving skills in meeting the requirements for adequate performance in matters pertaining to jobs.
   b. "*Unemployed/underemployed:* The unemployed are those who are not working but are looking for a job. The underemployed are those who are not employed at their full potential.
   c. "*Offenders:* Persons who are incarcerated in, or on release status from, a correctional institution.
4. "*Dropouts or school leavers:*
   a. "*Actual:* Persons who have left school for any reason before graduating or completing a program of study and without transferring to another school.
   b. "*Potential:* Persons who may reasonably be expected to leave school for any reason before graduating or completing a program of study and without transferring to another school.
5. "*Migrant and seasonal worker family in fishing or agriculture:* Migratory agricultural workers or those in the fishing industry who have moved with their families from one school district to another during the past year to secure temporary or seasonal employment in agricultural related food-processing or fishing activities.
6. "*Dependent, neglected, and/or delinquent youth:* Dependent and neglected youth are those who have lost their homes through death or illness of parents or guardians. Neglected youth are those who are being abused by parent, guardian, or society in general as determined by the courts. *Delinquent youth* are those who are declared delinquent by a court of appropriate jurisdiction.

7. "*Families with income below poverty level:* The income of family or persons is below the national poverty level and is inadequate for basic living needs: (a) receiving public assistance, (b) unemployed parent or guardian, or the participants themselves, (c) family income is at or below the national poverty level.
8. "*Geographic-transportation-and-communication isolated:* Persons who have severely restricted access to communication and transportation resources and/or who have cultural traditions against modern or innovative technology that inhibit personal and occupational mobility, e.g., Appalachia Indian reservations.
9. "*Rural isolation:* Persons in sparsely settled areas inadequately served by highways or public transportation or communications and with a tradition of self-reliance and subsistence existence, with little access to cultural opportunities.
10. "*Urban location:* Persons in heavily populated areas whose mobility is restricted by economic circumstance, social pressures, or personal fears, and/or who are inadequately served by public transportation within their ability to pay."[46]

THE TASK OF IDENTIFYING DISADVANTAGED LEARNERS

Background

Given the learner characteristics of the disadvantaged and the target groups most likely to suffer disadvantagement as outlined above, one of the major tasks facing vocational and general education personnel is that of identifying individual learners who have certain disadvantages. As noted earlier, it is extremely important to think of each disadvantaged person as an *individual*. Each disadvantaged learner brings to the school environment certain strengths as well as weaknesses, and it is important for the educator to be aware of those unique strengths and weaknesses. Indeed, recognition of such unique learner characteristics is essential in the decision-making process concerning matters like instructional staffing, curriculum development and instructional strategies.

The importance of this identification task cannot be discounted. A study by John Walsh and Jan Totten of programs for disadvantaged students in the United States that covered 84 projects in 77 communities in 23 states indicated confusion about the meaning of the term disadvantaged. The investigators also found that the identification requirement set by the legislative acts for individuals rather than groups was not met. In fact, they found that there was little understanding of this concept at the state level; individual assessment was defined in terms of whether students met established criteria for enrollment in programs for the disadvantaged.

They concluded that "most states have devoted very little attention to the conceptualization of special vocational education services for the disadvantaged, based on specific criteria for the identification of disadvantaged students and individual assessment of students either eligible or potentially eligible for such services."[47]

Walsh and Totten found that the states generally used two major criteria, either separately or in combination, for identifying disadvantaged students: "(1) students who are behind one or more grades in academic achievement, or (2) students who reside in designated target areas (usually high youth unemployment areas, big cities, Title I areas, and areas of rural poverty)."[48] Very often, the criteria actually applied at the local level differed widely between states and between communities within states.[49] Jerry L. Wircenski found the discrepancy in the application of specific identification criteria was also evident in a study of national exemplary cooperative, self-contained, and mainstream programs.[50] One of the most disturbing findings of the Walsh and Totten assessment was that half of the 84 project directors interviewed in conjunction with the project level assessment said that they did not believe the students enrolled in their programs were disadvantaged.[51]

Three Basic Steps to Identification and Assessment

In the literature there is much confusion surrounding the identification process and the application of that process' information. Three basic steps to alleviate the confusion in the learner identification process are apparent in the literature. They are learner referral, learner assessment, and learner educational planning.

Learner Referral

The first step, learner referral, is usually made by academic teachers, counselors, administrators, parents, or support staff (i.e., psychologists, nurses, or community agency personnel). The learner referral is generally informal in that attention is called to a student who is having some academic, economic, or social problem. Once the student is identified by referral, most school systems have an established, more formal mechanism whereby the student's special needs can be more readily identified. During the informal referral process, many administrators prefer not to remove the referred student from the regular instructional program until an accurate assessment can be made of the unique problem.

L. Allen Phelps and Ronald J. Lutz have noted that "the referral identification process often removes the student and dangerously labels him or her among the peer group and the instructional staff.[52] Therefore, the current trend in providing special services for the disadvantaged is to reduce the number of referrals 'out' of regular programs."[52] In this way, the stigma of being labeled differently (by placement in programs where disadvantaged learners are segregated from the mainstream of regular classes) is minimized.

Phelps and Lutz make a number of suggestions to assist in-school and out-of-school personnel in the collection and reporting of student identification information:

1. "Initially, you should review and become familiar with any existing identification criteria, procedures, and/or forms used for the referral of special students in the district. It is important to be familiar with any existing process used in your school district so that the identification utilized here does not result in a duplication of effort. It may also be that some of the identification information has already been compiled on the special needs students in your class.
2. "A second activity involves deciding what specific identification information it is important and essential to collect. Most student identification information forms include the following:

   a. "Name, age, birthdate, sex, school, and grade placement of student
   b. "Name, address, and phone numbers of parents or guardians
   c. "Date on which the information is submitted for review
   d. "Name of referring teacher, teachers, or, in some instances, parents
   e. "Reason for the referral (usually a detailed description of the specific problems the student is encountering)
   f. "Special services the student is already receiving
   g. "Type of action the referring teacher or professional suggests as being appropriate
   h. "Name and title of the individual to whom the identification information is submitted. This is usually the building principal or director of special education.

3. "Careful consideration also has to be given to how the student identification information will be collected. Questions of who should compile the information and which information sources are to be used will also influence the identification-referral process. In some instances parents will point out the specific problems to individual teachers or counselors and request that a referral be initiated. In most cases, however, teachers or other school personnel will initiate the referral and utilize their written observation reports as an information base when compiling the necessary information. Parent and student interviews, school records, and numerous other references can and should be also consulted for background information.
4. "Once the basic student identification information is collected and summarized, it must be submitted to the appropriate person for action. Whoever this individual is, he or she must have the responsibility and authority for seeing that the referral-identification is acted upon.

5. "Depending upon the special services and personnel available and the nature of the student's special need, a variety of actions may then be undertaken by the principal or director of special services. In some cases it may be appropriate to call a meeting of the student's teachers to determine what special considerations or modifications are needed in the student's instructional program. In other cases it may be necessary to have the student's hearing or vision tested or to have some additional educational assessments done to determine more specifically the student's learning or behavioral problem(s).
6. "The identification-referral process can easily become bogged down in paperwork and exhaustive procedures. It is best to keep it as simple and as efficient as possible. Collect and report only the basic information needed to establish the student's eligibility to receive the special services he or she will need to succeed in an educational program."[53]

A number of forms have been developed to refer learners who might have some type of disadvantage. A sample referral form currently used for student referral purposes is shown in Exhibit 3-1. A similar learner referral form, developed by Thomas E. Hyde and Jerry L. Wircenski, is shown in Exhibit 3-2.[54]

Both forms are designed to solicit referral information from in-school and out-of-school personnel who suspect that a learner may have some type of disadvantage. Modifications can be made by the school district staff to accommodate local information or criteria. It is essential to keep in mind that merely because a learner is being referred does *not* mean one should conclude that the person is disadvantaged. The function of reaching such a conclusion is the concern of the second stage, the learner assessment process.

Learner Assessment

Following the initial identification process, the next step is to assess or diagnose the learner's strengths and weaknesses. The purpose of the learner assessment is to examine the effects, not the causes, of the academic or economic disadvantage. As mentioned earlier, it is essential to keep the cause of the disadvantage distinct from its effect. Special programs or services may not be required merely because a person is poor, a member of a minority group, or for other *causes*. On the other hand, such programs or services must be designed to overcome specific *effects*, such as limited reading ability, poor computation skills, or behavioral problems.

The purpose of learner assessment is to provide identification information that is useful for staffing, curriculum, and support service planning. The learner diagnosis can be made in any number of learner-assessor experiences. The most common is that of teacher assessment through the teaching-learning process. In this process, observations can be formulated and recorded. A similar diagnosis can

Exhibit 3-1 Disadvantaged Learner Referral Form A

Directions: Please complete as much information as possible.

Date ____________________
Student Name ________________________
Grade ____________________Subject ______________Sex ________________
Referred by ____
Relation to student ____
Referred to ____
Reason for referral ____
____
____
____
____
How long has this problem existed? ___________________________________
Describe action *already* taken
____
____
____
____
Have parents been contacted? __________yes __________no
Parents' names: Father ____
Mother ____
Parents' address ____
Home phone _____________________Work phone ______________________
Parents' reaction ____
____
____

be made as a result of a counselor's assessment, through the counseling process, of learner strengths and weaknesses. Likewise, community agency personnel and professionals can utilize the interaction process between student and advisor to diagnose individual problems.

In Exhibit 3-3, L. Allen Phelps presents a "learner profile" that focuses attention on those criteria that are applicable to adolescents and young adults interested in vocational education.[55] The left side of the learner profile identifies eight broad categories in which observable effects of disadvantages commonly occur. The center column provides a rating scale on which specific "special needs indicators" can be rated from learning difficulty to learning strength. The right side of the Phelps learner profile provides space for documentation. This documentation is especially important to have in order to substantiate accurately the learner's strengths and weaknesses. Classroom teachers, administrators, parents, counselors, and psychologists, as well as community resource agencies and school records, are some of the sources that can be utilized for documentation purposes.

Exhibit 3-2 Disadvantaged Learner Referral Form B

STUDENT NAME________________ REFERRING PERSON________________
DATE________________ SUBJECT AREA________________
GRADE________________ AGENCY________________
SEX________________ LENGTH OF TIME KNOWING STUDENT________________
AGE________________ REFERRED TO________________

The above named student, is in my professional judgement, having difficulties in the following areas: (Complete as many as apply). Provide examples where possible.

1. Attitude - Overall attitude toward school, adults, peers.
   Comments: Poor Fair Good Excellent
2. Social Skills - Ability to get along with peers, adults. Participation in soc., act. - clubs, sports.
   Comments: Poor Fair Good Excellent
3. Personal Hygiene - Overall general appearance, personal grooming.
   Comments: Poor Fair Good Excellent
4. Manual Dexterity - Coordination, ability to work with hands.
   Comments: Poor Fair Good Excellent
5. Reading/Writing Skills - Ability to express ideas in writing, ability to read and comprehend.
   Comments: Poor Fair Good Excellent
6. Verbal Communication Skills - Orally expresses ideas and opinions.
   Comments: Poor Fair Good Excellent
7. Mathematics Skills - Ability to perform basic computations - add., sub., mulitp., division.
   Comments: Poor Fair Good Excellent
8. Performing at grade level . . . . yes no
9. Potential school drop-out . . . . yes no maybe
10. Potential "social" drop out . . . . . . yes no maybe
11. Problems with:

	None	Few	Many
A. Discipline			
B. Acting Out Behavior			
C. Economic			
D. Law			
E. Drugs/Alcohol			
F. Home-Life			
G. Others - Specify			

Comments:

It is important that the documentation process be based on current objective data and facts and not on innuendoes, prejudices, or outdated information. Standardized, norm-referenced tests and criterion-referenced tests are possible sources for documentation, although caution must be exercised in evaluating the experiences of students who have not been in the social mainstream of the educational process. School personnel may wish to administer some individual testing to verify referral information or to observe the student directly during test administration.

Exhibit 3-3 Learner Analysis Profile

Learner: ____________________

School: ____________________

Date: ____________________

LEARNER ANALYSIS PROFILE

Assessment/Appraisal Team:

____

____

____

Special Needs Indicators	Learning Difficulty				Learning Strength	Documentation/Observed Behavior
QUANTITATIVE/NUMERICAL SKILLS						
Count and Record						
Add/Subtract						
Multiply/Divide						
Measure						
General Number Use						
Money						
Other Quantitative/Numerical Skills:						
VERBAL SKILLS						
Read						
Spell						
Record Information						
Verbal Communication						
Written Communication						
Other Verbal Skills:						
COGNITIVE SKILLS						
Retention						
Sequence						
Attentiveness						
Planning Ability						
Mechanical Aptitude						
Transfer						
Other Cognitive Skills:						

Special Need Indicators	Learning Difficulty				Learning Strength	Documentation/Observed Behavior
PERCEPTUAL SKILLS						
Auditory Discrimination						
Form Perception						
Form Discrimination						
Space Perception						
Color Perception						
Touch Discrimination						
Other Perceptual Skills:						
LANGUAGE SKILLS						
Listening						
Nonverbal Expression						
Technical Vocabulary						
Grammatical Expression						
Other Language Skills:						
PSYCHOMOTOR/PHYSICAL SKILLS						
Physical Strength						
Hand-Eye Coordination						
Manual Dexterity						
Mobility						
Other Physical Skills:						
SOCIAL SKILLS						
Sociability						
Cooperativeness						
Conformity						
Loyalty						
Safety						
Responsibility						
Sensitivity						
Other Social Skills:						

Exhibit 3-3 continued

Special Need Indicators	Learning Difficulty				Learning Strength	Documentation/Observed Behavior
OCCUPATIONAL INTERESTS						
Agriculture/Natural Resources						
Automotive and Power Services						
Construction/Manufacturing						
Graphics/Communications						
Food/Clothing/Child Care						
Health						
Office/Business						
Other or Specific Occupational Interests:						

Source: L. Allen Phelps, *Instructional Development for Special Needs Learners: An Inservice Resource Guide* (Urbana, Ill.; University of Illinois at Urbana-Champaign, 1976), pp. 47-49.

As noted, the purpose of the learner assessment step in the identification of disadvantaged learners is to pinpoint an individual learner's strengths and weaknesses. Based on the results of the learner assessment, special services or programs can be identified or designed to accommodate the disadvantaged learner. This may be sufficient in many school systems. It is suggested, however, that one additional task be performed before prescribing a plan of action. That task is to achieve an appropriate perspective.

A system of learner assessment developed by Hyde and Wircenski places a learner's assessment information in perspective with the learner's career choice as well as the career choices of the learner's peers (see Exhibit 3-4).[56] In this system, information is collected on every student who has been referred by school personnel, parents, or community resource agencies—a process similar to that in the Phelps "learner profile" or other identification-assessment systems. In the Hyde and Wircenski identification system, however, a student's profile is then compared with all other students who have expressed a similar career choice. Such a comparison may show that a student indeed can be identified as having some type of disadvantage, for example, poor reading skills. The student may still be able to succeed in a vocational program, however, because the skill deficiency may be acceptable when compared to the skill level of successful students already enrolled or satisfactorily placed on the job. Thus, in this instance, the label of disadvantaged is not accurate because the deficiency is *not* detrimental to success in the regular vocational program. In another case, however, the student's reading skills may *not* be adequate for a vocational program without special support services or remedial instruction. In short, educators often are too quick to label learners as disadvantaged without considering the possibility that the learner can succeed in the regular vocational curriculum. The comparison process must of course involve the vocational teacher for each program and must be based on sound data on both successful and unsuccessful program learners.

Learner Educational Planning

The last step in the learner identification process is to develop a learner educational plan. This plan focuses on the modifications or support services necessary to assist disadvantaged learners to overcome their disadvantages. The central purpose of the referral and assessment process is to inject some form of change into the teaching-learning process. Its most common impact is the utilization of individualized instruction. The delivery of services for the handicapped—those "individuals who are deaf, hard of hearing, mentally retarded, speech impaired, visually handicapped, seriously emotionally disturbed, orthopedically impaired, or have specific learning disabilities and who, because of these impairments, require special education and related services"[57]—through individualized instruction is much more clearly defined as a result of the Education for All

Exhibit 3-4 Learner Assessment Form

PROGRAM Carpentry

STUDENT NAME____________

GRADE____________

DATE____________

COMPLETED BY____________

General Directions: Complete the information in Part I for the above named student. Complete Part II for the typical student presently enrolled in this program or successfully completing this program.

CRITERIA	Part I Rating of the Above Named Student Based On Referral and Documentation	Part II Ratings of Students Presently Enrolled or Formally Enrolled in Program on This Criteria: Well Below Average	Below Average	Average	Above Average	Well Above Average
Attitude	Poor Fair Good Excellent (Rating)					
Social Skills	Poor Fair Good Excellent (Rating)					
Personal Hygiene	Poor Fair Good Excellent (Rating)					
Manual Dexterity	0 25 50 75 100 (Percentile)					
Reading Ability	0 3 6 9 12 (Grade Reading Level)					
Attendance	0 5 10 15 20+(Days Absent)					
Overall Grade Average	F D C B A (Grade Avg.)					
Math Ability	0 25 50 75 100 (Percentile)					
Average of Math Grades	F D C B A (Grade Avg.)					
Related Subject Grade i.e., I.A.	F D C B A (Grade Avg.)					

Comments:

Handicapped Children Act of 1975 (Public Law 94-142). This act states that each school system must establish a procedure whereby the educational needs of every single learner, rather than a group or class, are addressed through an Individual Educational Plan (IEP).

Although it is not our intent here to discuss handicapped learners, much can be gained from examining the IEP element for the handicapped stipulated in the 1975 act. The IEP must include:

1. "a statement of the student's present level of educational achievement in areas such as academic achievement, social adaptation, prevocational and vocational skills, psychomotor skills, and selfhelp skills

2. "a statement of annual goals that describes the educational performance to be achieved by the end of the school year under the child's individualized education program
3. "a statement of short-term instructional objectives, which must be measurable intermediate steps between the present level of educational performance and the annual goals
4. "a statement of specific educational services needed by the child, including a description of all special education and related services that are needed to meet the unique needs of the child, also including the type of physical education program in which the child will participate
5. "the date when those services will be initiated and terminated
6. "a description of the extent to which the child will participate in regular education programs
7. "objective criteria, evaluation procedures, and schedule for determining, on at least an annual basis, whether the short-term instructional objectives are being achieved"[58]

The 1975 act suggests that an IEP for the handicapped be developed on an annual basis through a planning conference consisting of special education teachers, classroom teachers, administrators, counselors, parents, and community service agency personnel.

There is no similar federal mandate for individualized education programs for the disadvantaged yet, but there has been much discussion about their need. In the absence of such legislative action, vocational educators and school personnel should assume the leadership in formulating similar learner educational plans for the disadvantaged. The purpose of the referral and identification process is to bring together individual strengths and weaknesses into a comprehensive and coordinated instructional program. Many forms are available for consolidating information into an individualized learner educational plan. Ann P. Turnbull, Bonnie Strickland, and John C. Brantley offer one of the more comprehensive learner educational plans.[59] Exhibit 3-5 presents their completed IEP for handicapped students that could be modified for disadvantaged learners. In Exhibits 3-6, L. Allen Phelps offers a much more simplified individualized learner educational plan.[60] Local school districts can adopt one of these two plans or they may design individualized learner education plans more appropriate for their own use. A number of suggestions for developing components of such plans are discussed in the following sections.

The initial referral and formal assessment forms discussed earlier contain essential information and documentation that are important for planning purposes. These forms therefore should become part of the learner educational plan.

Exhibit 3-5 Individual Education Plan

Checklist

9-1-77	Referral by Louise Borden
9-3-77	Parents informed of rights: permission obtained for evaluation
9-15-77	Evaluation compiled
9-16-77	Parents contacted
9-18-77	Legal committee meets and subcommittee assigned
9-28-77	**IEP developed by subcommittee**
9-30-77	**IEP approved by subcommittee**

Committee Members

Mrs. Louise Borden
Teacher
Mrs. John Thomas (Sp. Ed.)
Coordinators
Other IEA representative
Mrs. John Doe
Parents
Mrs. Mary Franks
Mrs. Joan Bambara
Mrs. Alice King
Date IEP initially approved
9-20-77

Yearly Class Schedule

Time	Subject	Teacher
8:30-9:20	math	Franks
9:30-10:20	language arts	Bambara (Resource)
10:30-11:20	social studies	Bambara
11:30-12:20	science	Franks
	lunch	
1:10-2:00	art	Shaw
2:10-3:00	P.E.	King
8:30-9:20	math	Franks
9:30-10:20	language arts	Bambara (Resource)
10:30-11:20	social studies	Bambara
11:30-12:20	science	Franks
	lunch	
1:10-2:00	art	Shaw
2:10-3:00	P.E.	King

Continuum of Services

	Hours per week
Regular class	20 hours
Resource teacher in regular classroom	6 hours
Resource room	4 hours
Reading specialist	
Speech language therapist	
Counselor	
Special class	
Transition class	

Others:

Identification Information

Name John Doe
School Beecher Sixth Grade Center
Birthdate 5-15-65 Grade 6
Parents:
Name Mr. and Mrs. John Doe
Address 1300 Johnson Street Raleigh, N.C.
Phone Home none Office 932-8161

Testing Information

Test Name	Date Admin.	Interpretation
PIAI	9-10-77	spell—1.7, math—5.7, read recog—1. read comp—N.A., gen. info—6.3
Test of initial consonants (CRT)	9-11-77	knows eight out of twenty-one initial consonant sounds total 20
CRT Reading Checklist	9-12-77	oral comprehension—6th grade reading skills—primary level
Carolina Arith. Inventory (Time)	9-2-77	Level IV
Carolina Arith. Inventory (Number concepts)	9-2-77	Level IV

Health Information

Vision: good
Hearing: excellent
Physical: good
Other:

Student's Name John Doe Subject Area Reading

Level of Performance primary reading recognition, 6th grade comprehension of oral material. Teacher Mrs. Bambara—resource teacher

ANNUAL GOALS: 1) John will successfully complete the primer level of the Bank Street Reading Series.

2) John will recognize and correctly say 90 new sight words.

3) John will master 14 initial consonants.

	SEPTEMBER	OCTOBER	NOVEMBER	DECEMBER	JANUARY
OBJECTIVES	Referred	1. Recognize and correctly state the sounds of the initial consonants *b* and *f* 100% of the time.	1. Recognize and correctly state the sounds of the initial consonants *s* and *m* 100% of the time.	1. Correctly recognize and state the sound of the initial consonant *g* 100% of the time.	1. Review and correctly state the sounds of the initial consonants *b,f,m,s,* and *g* 100% of the time.
		2. Recognize and correctly say ten new sight words 100% of the time.	2. Recognize and correctly say ten new sight words 100% of the time.	2. Recognize and correctly say five new sight words 100% of the time.	2. Recognize and correctly state the sound of the initial consonant *h* 100% of the time.
		3. Complete the first three stories of the primer, reading the material with 50% accuracy.	3. Complete the next three stories in the primer, reading the material with 50% accuracy.	3. Complete the next story in the primer, reading the material with 50% accuracy.	3. Review and correctly say 25 previously learned sight words 100% of the time.
					4. Recognize and correctly say five new sight words 100% of the time.
					5. Review the previously read stories in the primer, reading the material with 60% accuracy.

Exhibit 3-5 continued

	SEPTEMBER	OCTOBER	NOVEMBER	DECEMBER	JANUARY
MATERIALS		Bank Street Basal Reading Series, Hoffman Phonetic Reading Program, teacher-made materials	Bank Street Basal Reading Series, Hoffman Phonetic Reading Program, teacher-made materials	Bank Street Basal Reading Series, Hoffman Phonetic Reading Program, teacher-made materials	Bank Street Basal Reading Series, Hoffman Phonetic Reading Program, teacher-made materials
AGENT		regular teacher resource teacher	regular teacher resource teacher	regular teacher resource teacher	regular teacher resource teacher
EVALUATION		1. informal assessment 2. Criterion Referenced Test (CRT)	1. informal assessment 2. CRT	1. informal assessment 2. CRT	1. informal assessment 2. CRT

Source: A.P. Turnbull, Bonnie Strickland, and John C. Brantley, *Developing and Implementing Individualized Education Programs* (Columbus, Ohio: Charles E. Merrill Publishing Co., 1978.) Reprinted with permission.

Exhibit 3-6 Learner Educational Plan

LEARNING PRESCRIPTION

Learner: ______________________ Instructional Team: ______________
School: ______________________ ______________________
Date: ______________________ ______________________

A. Appropriate Learning Mode

Directions: Indicate by numbering, the three most appropriate learning modes for this student. Check others that may also be appropriate.

___Audio/visual presentation
___Observation of goal behavior
___Interview/conference with knowledgeable person
___Experiment/laboratory experience/project
___Programmed instruction
___Simulation/games
___Field experience(s)
___Role playing
___Reading
___Audio recording
___Other (specify):
____
____

B. Interaction Mode

Directions: Indicate below the situations in which the student will work most productively.

___Independently (alone)
___Peer/partner
___Small group
___Large group
___Individually with teacher or aide

C. Additional Learning Style Considerations: ______________________
____
____
____
____

Source: L. Allen Phelps, *Instructional Development for Special Needs Learners: An Inservice Resource Guide* (Urbana, Ill.: University of Illinois at Urbana-Champaign, 1976) p. 59.

Learning Style

The mode or channel of learning by disadvantaged students is receiving a great deal of attention. Some students learn better by visual than they do by auditory methods, and vice versa. The selected instructional experience or experiences should be applied only after careful examination of the learner assessment data. An analysis of the data from a learning style questionnaire can assist the teacher in the selection of the appropriate learning style, instructional strategies, and materials for each learner. Some disadvantaged learners will be capable of working in small groups, while others may prefer to work alone with appropriate instruction and learning aids.

Goals

It is important to establish both long-term and short-term goals for the disadvantaged learner. This will enable the teacher to focus attention on specific instructional experiences which, when fulfilled, will provide both the teacher and learner with some standard by which accomplishments can be measured. Some of the content areas that might be included in the formulation of long- and short-term goals are reading skills, vocational skills, language arts skills, computation skills, and social skills.

Evaluation

Consideration should be given to providing parents and the learner more detailed information in terms of the development of pupil skills than is normally available through the traditional A-B-C-D-F grading system. A second concern in the evaluation of a disadvantaged learner's progress should be to individualize the evaluation process so that an individual student's attainment and progress can be evaluated in terms of their starting points.[61]

SUMMARY

This chapter began with an examination of the literature in terms of the characteristics of disadvantaged learners. Personal and home-life characteristics and ability levels were reviewed. It is apparent from numerous studies that disadvantaged learners have been shut out of the mainstream of the average American's educational, economic, cultural, and social life. The life style of the disadvantaged learner typically has been one of mere existence.

Federal legislative acts concerning vocational education have served to identify and characterize the disadvantaged learner. It has been possible to identify certain groups that are most likely to show the effects of disadvantages. Similarly, the demographic characteristics of the disadvantaged have been explored.

We have noted the importance of identifying disadvantaged learners in vocational education and of applying the information from the identification process in the learner assessment and learner educational planning stages. Finally, we have shown how certain forms for the identification of disadvantaged learners can be usefully applied in this multiphased process.

Perhaps the staff of the Division of Vocational and Technical Education (HEW) summarized best the consensus regarding the delivery of services for disadvantaged learners in vocational education. They stated: "The effort and support of *all* educational personnel are required in identification and recruitment of disadvantaged and handicapped students and in coordinating the delivery of appropriate services to them. Cooperation and coordinated planning are essential among all segments of the educational community and the related agencies which serve disadvantaged and handicapped persons."[62]

In the preface of *Resurge '79* (1979), Daniel B. Dunham, deputy commissioner for occupational and adult education (HEW), stated: "Individuals must not be limited in their career objectives because of age, sex, race, or disability. Vocational Education must be provided in an equitable manner to all persons in all communities. That is why it is essential for all educators to know each of their students in terms of their interests and abilities to better meet their learning needs."[63]

NOTES

1. Mario D. Fantini and Gerold Weinstein, *The Disadvantaged: Challenge to Education* (New York: Harper & Row, Publishers, Inc., 1968), pp. 4-5.
2. Frank Reissman, "The Culturally Deprived Child," in John B. Bergeson and George S. Miller eds., *Learning Activities for Disadvantaged Children* (New York: The MacMillan Company, 1971), pp. 44-45.
3. Leon Eisenberg, "Strengths of the Inner City Child," in *Education of the Disadvantaged*, eds. M. Goldberg and A.J. Tennenbaum (New York: Holt, Rinehart and Winston, Inc., 1967), pp. 78-88.
4. Ben B. Seligman, *Permanent Poverty, An American Syndrome* (Chicago: Quadrangle Book, 1968), p. 95.
5. Francesco Cordasco and Eugene Bucchioni, *The Puerto Rican Community and Its Children on the Mainland* (Metuchen, N.J.: Scarecrow Press, Inc., 1972), pp. 15-465.
6. Seligman, *Poverty*, p. 95.
7. Charles Oaklief, *Review and Synthesis of Research on Vocational and Technical Education for the Rural Disadvantaged* (Columbus, Ohio: ERIC Clearinghouse on Vocational and Technical Education, August 1971), pp. 3-45.
8. W.F. White, *Tactics for Teaching the Disadvantaged* (New York: McGraw-Hill, Inc., 1971).
9. John Walsh and Jan L. Totten, *An Assessment of Vocational Education Programs for the Disadvantaged under Part B and Part A Section 102 (b) of the 1968 Amendments to the Vocational Education Act* (Salt Lake City, Utah: Olympus Research Centers, December 1976), p. 23.
10. Thomas C. Cook, "A Profile of Highly Successful Vocational Teachers of Disadvantaged Students" (Ph.D. dissertation, Pennsylvania State University, 1978), pp. 108-115.
11. Edgar I. Farmer, "Identifying Pedagogical Competencies Needed to Train Vocational Education Teachers to Teach the Socioeconomically and Educationally Disadvantaged Students in the Inner Cities of Pennsylvania" (Ph.D. dissertation, Pennsylvania State University, 1978), pp. 52-140.

12. Robert W. Walker, *What Vocational Education Teachers Should Know About Disadvantaged in Rural Areas* (Columbus, Ohio: ERIC Clearinghouse on Vocational and Technical Education, October 1971), p. 3.
13. J.M. Conte and G.H. Grimes, *Media and the Culturally Different Learner* (Washington, D.C.: National Education Association, 1969).
14. R.D. Strom, "Family Influence on School Failure," in *The Disadvantaged Child: Issues and Innovations*, eds. J.L. Frost and G.R. Hawkes (Boston: Houghton Mifflin Company, 1966), pp. 379-381.
15. Lawrence L. Le Shan, "Time Orientation and Social Class," *Journal of Abnormal and Social Psychology* 47 (1952): 589-592.
16. William E. Amos, "Disadvantaged Youth: Recognizing the Problem," in *The Disadvantaged and Potential Dropout*, ed. J.C. Gowan and G.D. Demos (Springfield, Ill.: Charles C. Thomas, 1966), pp. 9-16.
17. Eisenberg, "Strengths of the Inner City Child," pp. 78-88.
18. David P. Ausubel and Pearl Ausubel, "Ego Development Among Segregated Negro Children," in *Education in Depressed Areas*, ed. A.H. Passow (New York: Teachers College, Columbia University, 1963), pp. 109-141.
19. Leonard M. Ridini and John E. Madden, *Physical Education for Inner-City Secondary Schools* (New York: Harper and Row, 1975), p. 4.
20. Benjamin Bloom, *Stability and Change in Human Characteristics* (New York: John Wiley and Sons, Inc., 1964), p. 77.
21. Robert J. Havighurst, "Metropolitan Development and the Educational System," in *Education of the Disadvantaged*, eds. A.H. Passow, M. Goldberg, and A.J. Tannenbaum (New York: Holt, Rinehart and Winston, Inc., 1967), pp. 19-31.
22. Herman P. Miller, *Rich Man, Poor Man* (New York: Signet, 1964), pp. 59-80.
23. Fantini and Weinstein, *The Disadvantaged*, pp. 73-74.
24. Vincent Feck, *What Vocational Education Teachers and Counselors Should Know About Urban Disadvantaged Youth* (Columbus, Ohio: ERIC Clearinghouse on Vocational and Technical Education, October 1971), p. 21.
25. Eisenberg, "Strengths of the Inner City Child," pp. 78-88.
26. Martin Deutsch, "The Disadvantaged Child and the Learning Process," in *Education in Depressed Areas*, ed. A.H. Passow (New York: Teachers College, Columbia University, 1963), pp. 163-179.
27. Arthur R. Jensen, "How Much Can We Boost I.Q. and Scholastic Achievement?" *Harvard Educational Review* 39 (1969): 1-123.
28. Thomas F. Pettigrew, "Negro Intelligence: A New Look At an Old Controversy," in *The Disadvantaged Child: Issues and Innovations*, eds. J.L. Frost and G.R. Hawkes (Boston: Houghton Mifflin Company, 1966), pp. 96-116.
29. Clarke and Clarke.
30. Committee for Economic Development, *Education for the Urban Disadvantaged: From Preschool to Employment* (New York: The Research and Policy Committee of the Committee for Economic Development, 1971), p. 9.
31. Fantani and Weinstein, *The Disadvantaged*, p. 5.
32. Manpower Administrator, U.S. Department of Labor, *Definition of Term "Disadvantaged Individual,"* Order no. 1-69 (Washington, D.C.: *GPO*, January 16, 1969).
33. Research and Policy Committee of The Committee for Economic Development.

34. *Resurge '79: Manual for Identifying, Classifying and Serving the Disadvantaged and Handicapped under the Vocational Education Amendments of 1976 (P.L. 94-482)* (Washington, D.C.: U.S. Government Printing Office, September 1979), p. 1.
35. Evelyn R. Kay, Barbara H. Kemp, and Frances G. Saunders, *Guidelines for Identifying, Classifying, and Serving the Disadvantaged and Handicapped under the Vocational Education Amendments of 1968*, DHEW publication no. (OE) 73-11700 (Washington, D.C.: U.S. Government Printing Office, 1973), p. 1.
36. Ibid., p. 2.
37. Ibid.
38. *Resurge '79: Manual*, p. 5.
39. Ibid.
40. Ibid., p. 16.
41. Ibid.
42. Ibid., pp. 17-19.
43. Ibid., p. 20.
44. Ibid., pp. 20-21.
45. Ibid., p. 21.
46. Ibid., pp. 22-25.
47. Walsh and Totten, *An Assessment*, p. 35.
48. Ibid., pp. 28-29.
49. Ibid.
50. Jerry L. Wircenski, *Meeting the Needs of Teachers of Disadvantaged Programs in Pennsylvania*, Project no. 94-8032 (University Park, Pa.: Pennsylvania State University, Department of Vocational Education, September 1978), pp. 1-274.
51. Walsh and Totten, *An Assessment*.
52. L. Allen Phelps and Ronald J. Lutz, *Career Exploration and Preparation for the Special Needs Learner* (Boston: Allyn and Bacon, Inc., 1977), p. 110. Reprinted with permission.
53. Ibid., pp. 110-113.
54. Thomas E. Hyde and Jerry L. Wircenski, "Developing Career Counseling Instruments," mimeographed (University Park, Pa.: Pennsylvania State University, 1978), pp. 1-15.
55. L. Allen Phelps, *Instructional Development for Special Needs Learners: An Inservice Resource Guide* (Urbana, Ill.. University of Illinois at Urbana-Champaign, Department of Vocational and Technical Education, 1976), pp. 47-49.
56. Hyde and Wircenski, *Developing Career Counseling Instruments*, pp. 1-15.
57. William D. Halloran, "Handicapped Persons: Who Are They?" *American Vocational Journal* 53 (1978): 30-31.
58. S. Torres, ed., *A Primer on Individualized Education Programs for Handicapped Children* (Reston, Va.: Foundation for Exceptional Children, 1977), pp. 52-53.
59. A.P. Turnbull, Bonnie Strickland, and John C. Brantley, *Implementing Individualized Education Programs* (Columbus, Ohio: Merrill Publishing Co., 1978).
60. Phelps, *Instructional Development*, p. 59.
61. Ann P. Turnbull and Jan B. Schulz, *Mainstreaming Handicapped Students: A Guide for the Classroom Teacher* (Boston: Allyn and Bacon, Inc., 1979), pp. 80-97.
62. *Resurge '79: Manual*, p. i.
63. Ibid.

BIBLIOGRAPHY

Bergeson, John B., and Miller, George S. *Learning Activities for Disadvantaged Children.* New York: The Macmillan Company, 1971.

Black, M.H. "Characteristics of the Culturally Disadvantaged" in *Learning Activities for Disadvantaged Children,* ed. V.B. Bergeson and G.S. Miller. New York: The Macmillan Company, 1971.

Dunn, R., and Dunn, K. *Educator's Self-Teaching Guide to Individualizing Instructional Programs.* West Nyack, N.Y.: Parker Publishing Company, Inc., 1975.

U.S., *Federal Register,* vol. 35, no. 91, part II, sec. 102.3 (Definitions) May 9, 1970, p. 7335.

U.S., *Federal Register,* part XI (Rules and Regulations for Education Amendments of 1976, P.L. 94-482, Vocational Education, State Programs, and Commissioner's Discretionary Programs), October 3, 1977.

Chapter 4

Identification and Characteristics of Handicapped Students

Stanley F. Vasa, Ed.D., and
Allen L. Steckelberg, M.Ed.

INTRODUCTION

Recent legislation and judicial decisions have led to a dramatic change in the provision of educational opportunities for handicapped individuals in the United States. Judicial precedents have established and mandated free access to public educational opportunities for handicapped individuals. Legislative initiatives have come in the wake of judicial rulings. Passage of the Education for All Handicapped Children Act (Public Law 94-142) in 1975 made the right of the handicapped to have available to them a free, appropriate public education a nationwide, unambiguous declaration. This was further supported and extended by regulations implementing Section 504 of the Rehabilitation Act of 1973 which require, basically, that institutional recipients of federal financial assistance for education shall provide a "free appropriate public education" to each qualified handicapped person, regardless of the nature or severity of the person's handicap.[1]

Three pieces of legislation provide the definition of a handicapping condition. Public Law 94-142 provides a substantial answer to this question in defining handicapped children as "those children evaluated . . . as being mentally retarded, hard of hearing, deaf, speech impaired, visually handicapped, seriously emotionally disturbed, orthopedically impaired, other health impaired, deaf-blind multi-handicapped, or as having specific learning disabilities, who because of those impairments need special education and related services."[2]

The implementing regulations for Section 504 of the 1973 act appear to encompass the definition of Public Law 94-142 by defining a handicapped person as "any person who has a physical or mental impairment which substantially limits one or more major life activities, has a record of such impairment, or is regarded as having such an impairment."[3]

The Vocational Education Amendments of 1976 (Public Law 94-482) provide funding through vocational educational programs to serve handicapped students.

The rules and regulations for the amendments set forth a further delineation of the handicapping conditions and programming in vocational education:

> "Handicapped" means: a) a person who is: (1) mentally retarded; (2) hard of hearing; (3) deaf; (4) speech impaired; (5) visually handicapped; (6) seriously emotionally disturbed; (7) orthopedically impaired; or (8) other health impaired person, or persons with specific learning disabilities; and (b) who, by reason of the above: (1) requires special education and related services, and (2) cannot succeed in the regular vocational education program without special educational assistance; or (3) requires a modified vocational education program.[4]

In Table 4-1, the definitions of the handicapping conditions from Public Law 94-142 are presented. In later sections of this chapter, we will examine each of the major categories of handicapping conditions most frequently confronted by the vocational education teacher in the public schools. The conditions covered are deaf and hard of hearing, visually handicapped, orthopedically impaired, other health impaired, mentally retarded, seriously emotionally disturbed, specific learning disabilities, and speech impaired.

IDENTIFICATION OF THE HANDICAPPED

Under the Education for All Handicapped Children Act of 1975 (Public Law 94-142), 11 handicapping conditions are officially recognized. The act also provides specific guidelines for the assessment and placement of handicapped students. The evaluation procedures are explicit and require the following:

- "tests are provided and administered in the student's native language and validated for the purpose for which they are used;
- "tests are administered and selected to best ensure that the skills of a student with a sensory or physical impairment are reflected, rather than the student's sensory or physical limitations;
- "no single test shall be used as the sole criterion for placement;
- "a multidisciplinary team or group of persons including the classroom teacher(s) or other specialist with knowledge of the disability; and
- "student to be assessed in all areas related to the suspected disability including, when appropriate, health, vision, hearing, social and emotional status, general intelligence, academic performance, communicative status, and motor abilities."[5]

Table 4-1 Definitions of Handicapping Conditions Under Public Law 94-142

HANDICAPPING CONDITION	DEFINITION
Deaf	"Deaf" means a hearing impairment which is so severe that the child is impaired in processing linguistic information through hearing, with or without amplification, which adversely affects educational performance.
Deaf-Blind	"Deaf-blind" means concomitant hearing and visual impairments, the combination of which causes such severe communication and other developmental and educational problems that they cannot be accommodated in special education programs solely for deaf or blind children.
Hard of Hearing	"Hard of hearing" means a hearing impairment, whether permanent or fluctuating; which adversely affects a child's educational performance but which is not included under the definition of "deaf" in this section.
Mentally Retarded	"Mentally retarded" means significantly subaverage general intellectual functioning existing concurrently with deficits in adaptive behavior and manifested during the developmental period, which adversely affects a child's educational performance.
Multi-handicapped	"Multihandicapped" means concomitant impairments (such as mentally retarded-blind, mentally retarded-orthopedically impaired, etc.), the combination of which causes such severe educational problems that they cannot be accommodated in special education programs solely for one of the impairments. The term does not include deaf-blind children.
Orthopedically Impaired	"Orthopedically impaired" means a severe orthopedic impairment which adversely affects a child's educational performance. The term includes impairments caused by congenital anomaly (e.g., clubfoot, absence of some member, etc.), impairment from other causes (e.g., cerebral palsy, amputations, and fractures or burns which cause contractures).
Other Health Impaired	"Other health impaired" means limited strength, vitality or alertness, due to chronic or acute health problems such as a heart condition, tuberculosis, rheumatic fever, nephritis, asthma, sickle cell anemia, hemophilia, epilepsy, lead poisoning, leukemia, or diabetes, which adversely affects a child's educational performance.
Seriously Emotionally Disturbed	"Seriously emotionally disturbed" is defined as follows: The term means a condition exhibiting one or more of the following characteristics over a long period of time and to a marked degree, which adversely affects educational performance: (A) An inability to learn which cannot be explained by intellectual, sensory, or health factors; (B) An inability to build or maintain satisfactory interpersonal relationships with peers and teachers; (C) Inappropriate types of behavior or feelings under normal circumstances; (D) A general pervasive mood of unhappiness or depres-

	sion; or (E) A tendency to develop physical symptoms or fears associated with personal or school problems. The term includes children who are schizophrenic or autistic. The term does not include children who are socially maladjusted, unless it is determined that they are seriously emotionally disturbed.
Specific Learning Disabilities	"Specific learning disability" means a disorder in one or more of the basic psychological processes involved in understanding or in using language, spoken or written, which may manifest itself in an imperfect ability to listen, think, speak, read, write, spell, or to do mathematical calculations. The term includes such conditions as perceptual handicaps, brain injury, minimal brain disfunction, dyslexia, and developmental aphasia. The term does not include children who have learning problems which are primarily the result of visual, hearing, or motor handicaps, of mental retardation, or of environmental, cultural, or economic disadvantage.
Speech Impaired	"Speech impaired" means a communication disorder, such as stuttering, impaired articulation, a language impairment, or a voice impairment, which adversely affects a child's educational performance.
Visually Handicapped	"Visually handicapped" means a visual impairment which, even with correction, adversely affects a child's educational performance. The term includes both partially seeing and blind children.

Source: U.S., *Federal Register,* vol. 42, no. 163, Aug. 23, 1977, pp. 42478-42479.

Considerations in the placement of a handicapped student in a special program are included in the rules and regulations for the implementation of Public Law 94-142. Information from a variety of sources—including standardized tests, teacher observations, social and cultural background, and adaptive behavior—must be analyzed; and the placement decision must be made by a group of persons who are knowledgeable about the student, the meaning of the evaluation data, and the options available to the student.

The law requires that vocational educators are to provide input into the placement and programming of students into special programs. Data for the identification of the handicapped students are to be obtained from a variety of sources. Some of these sources are given in Table 4-2.

Decisions about placement should be made on the basis of what program would be most appropriate for the student in the least restrictive environment. The least restrictive environment is defined as:

> . . . procedures to assure that, to the maximum extent appropriate, handicapped children, including children in public or private institutions or other care facilities, are educated with children who are not handicapped, and that special classes, separate schooling, or other removal of

Table 4-2 Procedures Utilized in Obtaining Information About Handicapped Students

Source	*Use*
Standardized Achievement Tests	Comparative data with performance of other students
Individual Intelligence Tests	Indication of student's potential compared to other students
Observation in Classroom	Important to compare with student's performance on standardized tests Substantiate the need for intervention
Adaptive Behavior Scales	Comparative data with the social, emotional, and self-help skills of other students
Interviews	Indication of views of others toward the student and information about how student functions in other environments, e.g., home
Health Records	Information about the student's vision, hearing, and physical health
Parental Interview	Behavior and health history, developmental data, parents' views of student's problems
School Records	Status of students functioning in academic and vocational classes, attendance, educational history, etc.
Work Samples	Indication of students functioning in applied school/work placements

> handicapped children from the regular educational environment occurs only when the nature of severity of the handicap is such that education in regular classes with the use of supplementary aids and services cannot be achieved satisfactorily. . . .[6]

The important factor in the placement of handicapped students is that their best interests are taken into consideration. Administrative or instructional convenience in planning the individual education program for the specific student should not be a primary concern. An array of services to serve the handicapped student is available, based on the severity of the condition and the necessity for separate programming to meet the student's needs.

INCIDENCE OF HANDICAPPING CONDITIONS

Contrary to common misunderstandings and belief, vast numbers of handicapped students are not enrolled in the American schools. During the school year 1977-1978, 3,777,106 students were served in programs for school-age, handicapped children. This number encompasses 7.36 percent of the total enrollment in the public schools for the 1977-1978 school year. It is estimated that approximately 2.3 million potentially handicapped students were not receiving special education services during the same period. Table 4-3 provides a breakdown of the number of handicapped students (by handicapping condition) served and their percentage of the total school enrollment.[7]

Table 4-4 shows where handicapped students were served in the public schools in 1976-1977.[8] It is interesting to note that 67.9 percent of the identified handicapped students were served primarily within the regular classroom with only minimal time spent in special programs. The vast number of students being served in the regular classroom indicates the importance of vocational educators learning to work more effectively with the handicapped learner. A vast majority of the identified handicapped learners are mildly disabled and capable of functioning within the regular school environment with a minimum of outside support services.

In contrast, during the same period, 1976-1977, 24 percent of the handicapped students were educated exclusively in separate classes. This represents the small number of students too severely handicapped to be served in the regular classroom environment. Even smaller percentages of severely handicapped students were served in separate facilities and other educational environments.

The labeling of handicapped students in terms of rigorous categories is more important as an administrative-fiscal function than as an educational-planning endeavor. D.P. Hallahan and J.M. Kaufman point out the great similarities in learning characteristic behaviors and educational needs among the educable mentally retarded, emotionally disturbed, and learning disabled.[9] The labeling of a student as having a specific handicap generally will not provide the classroom vocational teacher with an appropriate teaching strategy. Classroom teachers have to do their own assessment of the specific needs of an identified handicapped student.

The remaining sections of this chapter are devoted to dealing with the handicapping conditions outlined in Public Law 94-142. Recognizing that there are more similarities than differences between categories of mildly handicapped students, the reader will note in these sections the many similarities that appear in the characteristic and vocational needs of students.

Table 4-3 Percentage and Number of School Age School Population by Handicapping Condition

Handicapping Condition	*Percentage of Total School Population*	*Number Served**
Speech impaired	2.39	1,226,957
Learning disabled	1.89	969,368
Mentally retarded	1.84	944,909
Emotionally disturbed	0.56	288,626
Other health impaired	0.27	136,164
Orthopedically handicapped	0.17	88,070
Deaf and hard of hearing	0.17	87,144
Visually handicapped	0.07	35,688
Total	7.36	3,777,106

*The figures are for the school year 1977-78.

Source: U.S. Department of Health, Education, and Welfare, Office of Education, *Progress Toward a Free Appropriate Public Education: A Report to Congress on the Implementation of Public Law 94-142: The Education for All Handicapped Children Act,* January, 1979.

Table 4-4 Environments in Which School-Aged Handicapped Children Were Served During the School Year 1976-1977 by Handicapping Condition

Handicapping Condition	*Regular Class*	*Separate Class*	*Separate Facilities*	*Other Educational Environment*	*Total*
Speech Impaired	1,135,377	100,417	12,123	1,772	1,249,689
Learning Disabled	729,984	153,358	16,011	4,185	903,538
Mentally Retarded	339,835	451,999	75,528	12,092	879,454
Emotionally Disturbed	117,333	103,524	37,903	11,158	269,918
Other Health Impaired	57,424	36,286	8,952	31,870	134,532
Orthopedically Impaired	38,893	23,895	8,215	22,090	93,093
Deaf	22,416	12,339	3,868	239	38,862
Deaf/Hard of Hearing	19,140	4,848	7,011	1,140	32,139
Hard of Hearing	3,384	9,770	11,247	426	24,827
Visually Handicapped	5,277	3,038	3,371	508	12,194
	2,469,063	899,474	184,229	85,480	3,638,246
Percentage of total	67.9	24.7	5.1	2.4	

Source: U.S. Department of Health, Education, and Welfare, Office of Education, *Progress Toward a Free Appropriate Public Education: A Report to Congress on the Implementation of Public Law 94-142: The Education for All Handicapped Children Act,* January, 1979.

DEAF AND HARD OF HEARING

The literature yields a number of definitions of deaf and hard of hearing. There appears to be no generally agreed-upon use of the two terms, partially because the implications of an auditory impairment vary with the person involved and the circumstances. Each professional field involved in the study of hearing impairments classifies according to its particular specialization and purposes. In general, several dimensions of classification have emerged.

Degree of Hearing Impairment

The degree of hearing impairment has implications for the educator and is, in fact, a major component of the present Public Law 94-142 definition. This dimension is measured in terms of decibel loss as measured by audiometric testing. Table 4-5 shows the estimated relationship of hearing loss to the ability to understand speech. From the table, an educator can infer that consideration of the severity of a hearing impairment is crucial for appropriate educational planning.

Age at Onset of Hearing Impairment

The consequences of a hearing impairment depend, in part, on the point in the individual's developmental sequence at which the loss occurs. A person born deaf, for example, faces difficulties in speech development usually not experienced by

Table 4-5 Estimated Relationship of Hearing Loss to the Ability to Understand Speech

Hearing Loss in Decibels	*Ability to Comprehend Speech*	*Degree of Handicap*
0-25	Normal range	Insignificant
25-40	Difficulty with whispers	Slight
41-55	Difficulty with loud and soft normal speech	Mild
56-70	Difficulty with loud speech	Moderate
71-90	Comprehends strongly amplified speech	Severe
91+	Speech not understood under amplification	Profound

individuals who become deaf in adulthood. Individuals who become deaf later in their development have greater speech and language capacity. In classifying the hearing impaired, those individuals born deaf are often referred to as *congenitally deaf* while those born with normal hearing but who later lose their hearing are called the *adventitiously deaf.*

Causal Factor

The causal factor (etiology of hearing impairment) has been divided into two types: exogenous and endogenous.[10] Exogenous refers to all causal factors other than heredity, while endogenous includes only heredity as an etiological agent.

Location of the Hearing Impairment

The origin of the hearing problem can be divided into two types of location used extensively in medical diagnosis and treatment.

Sensory-neural is used to designate hearing loss resulting from inner ear abnormalities. This is sometimes referred to as nerve deafness, because sound does get transmitted to the inner ear but goes no further. Hearing impairment results from the failure of the inner ear to generate the proper signal; the signal is not being transmitted through the auditory nerve pathway to the brain, or it is not being received by the brain. Causes of this type of damage include meningitis, Rh incompatibility between mother and fetus, pertussis, influenza, measles, trauma, and endogenous factors.

Conductive refers to hearing loss resulting from malfunction of the outer or middle ear, through which sound waves fail to be transmitted to the inner ear. The outer ear acts as a funnel for sound waves, while the middle ear's three tiny bones (hammer, anvil and stirrup) transmit these mechanical vibrations from the eardrum to the fluid of the inner ear. Congenital malformations, infections, fluid in the middle ear, and bony overgrowth in the middle ear can block vibrations before they are delivered to the inner ear. Two other common causes of conductive loss are otitis media (middle ear infection) and otosclerosis. In some instances, an individual may suffer a mixed loss of hearing, which is a combination of conductive and sensory-neural hearing loss.

Incidence

The incidence of deafness in the United States has been estimated through the National Census of the Deaf Population (NCDP) to be at 2 per 1,000 of the population for predeafness (deafness occurring at or before 19 years of age).[11] The information in Table 4-4 presented earlier indicates that approximately 1.7 per 1,000 school-aged students are being served in programs for the deaf and hard of hearing. During the school year 1977-1978, 87,144 students were being served in programs for the deaf and hard of hearing. J.D. Schein and T.D. Marcus report that impairment of hearing is the single most prevalent chronic physical disability in the United States.[12] More persons suffer a hearing defect than have visual impairments, heart disease, or other chronic disabilities.

Educational Provisions

The unique educational needs of the deaf and hard-of-hearing student have long been recognized. Simple educational modifications for assisting students with mild hearing losses include assigning the handicapped student to a front row seat, facing the child when speaking, outlining lectures on the blackboard, and making assignments in writing. The hearing-impaired students' most crucial need is for adequate communication between themselves and the teacher so as to facilitate learning. Since most deaf and hard-of-hearing students experience problems in acquiring expressive language, adequate communication involves both receptive and expressive language components.

The most common measure utilized to improve the deaf student's ability to acquire language skills is the provision of devices that amplify sound and educational programs that provide training in lipreading (also called speechreading) or manual sign language. Amplification is achieved through hearing aids prescribed and fitted by trained professionals. Children are now being fitted with hearing aids at very young ages to allow them to grow up in a "hearing world" and to experience the benefits of auditory learning. Education in speechreading and manual sign language is provided in most communities by colleges, vocational training centers, and universities.

The educator must be aware of the degree of hearing that a student possesses in order to make proper adjustments in the curriculum and learning environment. In cases where students have been identified as hearing impaired or deaf and Individual Educational Programs have been developed, professionals who are trained to work with the hard of hearing should be available to provide guidance. Services for the hearing-impaired and deaf students extend the full spectrum of the cascade of services for all special needs individuals presented earlier in this chapter.

Vocational Training and Employment

Based on data from the NCDP, it has been estimated that the proportion of prevocationally deaf people in the labor force is about the same as that for all other persons.[13] Approximately 80 percent of the general population of males and 44 percent of the general population of females are in the labor force, while approximately 83 percent of the NCDP's sample of deaf males and 49 percent of its sample of deaf females are in the labor force.

Schein makes the following statements about the employment of the deaf.

- "In terms of personal income, deafness strikes hard. Average earnings fall 16% below the general average.
- "Female deaf persons do less well than male. Deaf women have higher rates of unemployment than women in general.
- "In economic terms, deafness is more expensive. Additional expenditures of necessary appliances, extra travel because of inability to use telephone, and the inability to negotiate freely within the marketplace place a burden on the deaf."[14]

Many deaf people, however, may be working at jobs requiring far less education than they have and could be considered underemployed.

The vocational curriculum of the deaf and hard-of-hearing student in the high school need not be different from that designed for the hearing student. Individual differences in talents and intelligence exist among those suffering from hearing impairments, just as they do among those who have normal hearing. In providing for the vocational education of the hearing-impaired student, the instructor needs to make adjustments similar to those for other students, with emphasis on the teaching strategies previously cited.

VISUALLY HANDICAPPED

The definition of visual handicapped centers on the performance of the student within the educational environment. The definition of visual handicap is given in Table 4-1 presented earlier. The important factor is that the visual impairment limits the student's ability to function in the educational setting. A student who cannot use standard visual material in the classroom because of a lack of visual acuity would be classified as visually handicapped. In 1957, the National Society for the Prevention of Blindness defined a legally blind student as one who has a central visual acuity of 20/200 or less in the better eye after correction, or who has visual acuity of more than 20/200 if there is a field defect in which the widest diameter of the visual field subtends an angle distance no greater than 20°. The rating of 20/200 corresponds to the size of symbols on the Snellen Chart, each symbol relating to the standard distance at which a person with normal vision can comfortably read the symbol or letters. A legally blind student can, therefore, read comfortably no more at 20 feet than a normally sighted child reads at 200 feet.[15]

The major causes of blindness are:

- *Diabetic retinopathy* occurs when tiny blood vessels in the retina hemorrhage due to diabetes. The result is gradual visual acuity loss.

- *Cataracts* occur when the lens of the eye becomes cloudy or opaque. They may occur congenitally, due to senility or trauma, or as secondary effects of other diseases.
- *Retinitis pigmentosa* is a hereditary disease causing loss of night vision and side vision.
- *Macular degeneration* results when the macula, a small area of the retina, is damaged due to inadequate blood supply causing loss of central vision.

Blindness may be either congenital or adventitious. Congenital blindness is present at birth. The adventitiously blind person becomes blind due to disease, defective functioning and shape of the eye, or trauma to the eye later in life.

Incidence

Table 4-5 presented earlier showed that a total of 12,194 visually handicapped students were served in the public schools in 1976-1977, and that, of this number, nearly one-half were served in the regular classroom. The percentage of the total school population identified as being visually impaired in 1977-1978 was .07 percent. This figure contrasts with the more generally recognized incidence estimation of .50 percent of the population. The reason for this discrepancy may be the increase of visual impairments with the onset of aging.

Approximately 75 percent of the legally blind persons in the United States have some useable vision. Of the 1.7 million legally blind persons, 400,000 have no useable vision. In total, about 6.4 million persons in the United States have some degree of visual impairment after correction with eye glasses, contact lenses, etc.[16]

Educational and Vocational Provisions

Educational and vocational goals for the blind student are essentially the same as those for a normal student. One goal is to provide blind students with skills that will enable them to participate in life's opportunities to the fullest extent possible. Another goal is to provide the skills necessary for them to function at the highest possible level of remunerative employment. When these two goals are achieved, the blind person becomes a self-supporting member of society.

Barriers to achieving these goals lie in two major areas. In the first area are the physical limitations imposed by the student's blindness itself. Available alternatives to sight can enable the blind student to reduce these limitations. Educationally, the adjustments are minimal in most situations; among the available alternatives are talking books, employment of readers, braille textbooks, and recent technological developments in automatic reading machines that decipher the written word. Teachers can assist by giving good verbal instructions and explaining all written work placed on overhead projectors and the chalkboard.

The second area involves the attitudinal barriers established by sighted persons. These include discrimination in job opportunities, lowered expectations for the blind student, and misguided compassion. These attitudinal barriers restrict the goal of normalization by reducing opportunities and by lowering the self-image of the blind student. Blind persons are capable of a much higher level of functioning than that perceived by the general public. Education beyond the normal curriculum involves training the blind student to use techniques as alternatives to sight and to develop coping skills and a positive image.

During the past decade, the number of blind persons in competitive employment has doubled. H.J. Link has estimated that employment or openings in the professional category will, in spite of increased competition, remain high, due to the development of new occupational areas. The paraprofessional category is seen by Link as the area containing the greatest number of new opportunities.[17] Section 503 of the 1973 Rehabilitation Act, which requires businesses that provide contract work for the federal government to develop affirmative action plans for the employment of severely disabled persons, should also have an impact on the employment situation for the blind.

Link has noted the following needs in the vocational area:

- "more adequate training for job placement personnel
- "more adequate evaluation of clients for employment
- "reduction of employer resistance to the hiring of the blind
- "emphasis on the training of coping and related job skills for the blind client
- "use of vocational and technical schools in training blind clients."[18]

In summary, blindness holds connotations for the general public that cause the potential of blind persons in competitive employment to be underestimated. Attitudinal change is as important to the employment of the blind as is training of adequate skills.

ORTHOPEDICALLY HANDICAPPED AND OTHER HEALTH IMPAIRED

The categories of orthopedically handicapped and other health impaired are treated as two distinct groups in the classification proposed by Public Law 94-142. For our purposes, the two groups are placed in the same section, since many of the adaptations of the learning environment require similar considerations on the part of the teacher.

The definitions of orthopedically handicapped and other health impaired were provided earlier in Table 4-1. Some of the major categories included in the classification of orthopedically handicapped and other health impaired are discussed in greater detail in the following sections.

Orthopedic Impairment

Cerebral Palsy

Cerebral Palsy (CP) may result from brain damage that has occurred before, during, or after birth or from poor maternal nutrition and health, RH or A-B-O blood type incompatibility, anoxia, or birth trauma. CP refers to brain damage of the motor areas of the brain, either the cerebrum or the cerebellum, that affect motor control of certain groups of muscles.

CP has been divided into several categories depending on how it affects the child. The American Academy for Cerebral Palsy lists the various types as:

- "*Spasticity* (increase in muscle tone),
- "*Athetosis* (slow writhing movements which conflict with voluntary movement),
- "*Rigidity* (extreme stiffness and tenseness of extremities),
- "*Atoxia* (poor balance, coordination and difficulty with depth perception),
- '*Tremor* (regular and rhythmical involuntary shaking movements),
- "*Atonia* (lack of muscle tone, limpness and flaccidity), and
- "*Mixed* (combination of other forms)."[19]

Several other problems are often evidenced in combination with CP, including mental retardation, learning disabilities, emotional problems, seizures, visual impairments, auditory impairments, and speech impairments. Although these problems are of a high incidence in cerebral palsy, the affected child may have none of them.

The associated handicaps can make the CP child a less likely candidate for the regular classroom. However, it is possible that children with less severe CP involvement may be capable of functioning in the classroom. The spastic hemiplegic type, referred to above, usually manifests a higher level of intelligence but may have associated sensory impairments. The athetoid child also may have higher intelligence, while children of the rigidity type are usually severely retarded. It is evident that decisions and modifications of the educational program for the CP child must be based on the individual child's needs.

Congenital Anomaly

A congenital anomaly is a birth defect in which the child is without some body appendage or with a deformed appendage, such as a clubfoot or clubhand. The anomaly may also occur in joints or in the spine. The defect may be inherited from one or both parents or be environmentally caused.

Spina Bifida

Spina Bifida is a birth defect in which the bones of the spine fail to close. As a result, a sack containing spinal fluid forms in the area of the lower back and is present at birth. The condition is usually treated surgically immediately after birth. The extent to which a disability remains can vary from little or none, to paralysis of the legs, impaired autonomic nervous system functioning, difficulties with bowel and bladder control, to lack of any sensation in the lower body. These students are usually capable of profiting from regular classroom instruction with only minor adaptation.

Spinal Cord Injuries

Spinal cord injuries may result in paralysis. The area affected is determined by the level at which the spinal cord is injured. If the cord is severed between the fifth and eighth vertebra, a condition known as a quadraplegia results, in which control and sensation in the arms and everything below that point is lost. If the injury occurs below the eighth vertebra, control and sensation is lost in the legs and is referred to as paraplegia. In both of these conditions, there is usually loss of bowel and bladder control and often loss of sexual functioning. Other problems, such as physical deterioration of muscles and pressure sores from wheel chairs or braces, arise because of the paralysis and loss of sensation.

Rarely does the injury affect brain functioning. Therefore, victims of a spinal cord injury can be served in a regular classroom as soon as they have sufficient mobility to reach the classroom.

Amputation

Amputation is the surgical removal of a limb or a portion of a limb. It is usually performed when tissue has been injured beyond repair due to irreversible loss of blood supply to the limb; to infections, including bone tuberculosis, cancer, and osteomyelitis; or to the removal of congenital anomalies. Amputation is usually followed by the provision of a prosthetic device (artificial limb). When the prosthetic device has been fitted and the amputee has been trained to use it, the individual is capable of functioning well in the regular classroom, in most vocational training settings, and in job placement.

Contractures

A contracture is a permanent shortening of a muscle due to spasm or paralysis. This term also refers to a condition of high resistance to the passive stretch of a muscle, which may result from abnormal formation of tissue surrounding a joint. A student may suffer a permanent disability or deformity due to the shortening of a muscle caused by the shrinking of damaged tissue. Minimal modifications of the regular classroom, if any, are necessary to accommodate the student with a contracture.

Other Health Impaired

The category of other health impaired includes many medical conditions, both acute and chronic, that afflict students and adversely affect their educational progress. This section presents descriptions of several conditions with which the educator may wish to become more familiar. Not all of the health impairing conditions that the educator may encounter are included, due to the diverse nature of these conditions. However, those described will provide the educator with information that can be applied to the study and evaluation of other conditions.

Some health-impairing conditions are relatively rare and may not be encountered in the classroom with any frequency. Also, it is important to remember that not all health-impairing conditions are equally handicapping for the child. Some, like asthma, may involve occasions when breathing is difficult, yet for long periods between attacks there may be no obvious, observable symptoms. In contrast, other conditions, such as heart disease, may obviously affect the child at all times. The important point to remember is that the same impairing condition may vary in severity from student to student. Some students with heart conditions may participate in most classroom activities while others may exhibit marked diminution in their tolerance to the ordinary physical activities of the classroom. For children with health-impairing conditions, therefore, educators should provide educational programs that are planned in light of the students' unique behavioral assets as well as their medical classifications.

Heart Condition

To assist the educator in understanding medical classifications of heart disease patients, the American Heart Association Classification System is reproduced in Table 4-6.[20] The table provides a view of the functional and therapeutic capacity of patients with cardiac disease, together with estimates of what their hearts will allow them to do.

As suggested by the classifications of Table 4-6, children with heart disease can behave in different ways and can exhibit varying degrees of disability. Children with mild heart conditions may be therapeutically unrestricted but may be so anxious that they behave as if their disability were great. Those students whose tolerance is markedly diminished should be assisted in adjusting to their limits. G. McNutt suggests that individuals with surgically corrected, congenital heart disease should be able to function in normal vocational activities.[21] A good rule of thumb appears to be that the student with heart problems should not be pressed to the point of excessive fatigue.

Asthma

Asthma is an episodic, reversible, increased responsiveness of the smooth muscle walls of the lung's airways to various stimuli that results in a spasm of the

Table 4-6 Functional and Therapeutic Classifications of Heart Disease

	Functional Classifications
Class I	Patients with cardiac disease but without resulting limitations of physical activity. Ordinary physical activity does not cause undue fatigue, palpitation, dyspnea, or anginal pain.
Class II	Patients with cardiac disease resulting in a slight limitation of physical activity. They are comfortable at rest. Ordinary physical activity results in fatigue, palpitation, dyspnea, or anginal pain.
Class III	Patients with cardiac disease resulting in inability to carry on any physical activity without discomfort. Symptoms of cardiac insufficiency or of the original syndrome are present even at rest. If any physical activity is undertaken, discomfort is increased.
	Therapeutic Classifications
Class A	Patients with a cardiac disease whose ordinary physical activity need not be restricted.
Class B	Patients with cardiac disease whose ordinary physical activity need not be restricted, but who should be advised against severe or competitive physical effort.
Class C	Patients with cardiac disease whose ordinary physical activity should be marked restricted.
Class D	Patients with cardiac disease who should be at complete rest, confined to bed or chair.

Source: Adapted from American Heart Association Classification System, in *Interviewing Guides for Specific Disabilities: Heart Disease,* U.S. Department of Labor, 1969.

---

bronchial musculature and the production of an excessive amount of mucus. This produces the characteristic symptoms of recurrent attacks of labored breathing accompanied by wheezing and coughing.

Asthma is an allergic condition of the lungs. Along with the asthma, the afflicted individual is inclined to exhibit other allergic problems, such as eczema, hayfever, hives, and food intolerance.

An asthmatic attack may be a frightening experience for the teacher because of the struggle and gasping for every breath, the color change, and the obvious distress displayed by the child. The attack may be brought on by a specific sensitivity to an allergen, exposure to excessive physical activity, or possibly by an emotional reaction. It is believed that stress lowers the threshold of sensitivity to an attack.

Asthma, like other medical conditions, varies in severity from child to child. In general, asthmatic children should be encouraged to join in ordinary class activities and should be treated as normally as possible. The teacher should become aware of the factors that precipitate an asthmatic attack, have information concerning the proper course of action to follow should an attack occur, and should be aware of any possible side effects or behavioral changes that may be related to the prescribed drugs being used by the student. This information can be obtained from the student's parents and physician, and assistance can be obtained from the school nurse. Generally, afflicted students will regulate themselves, and no artificial restrictions need be placed upon them. However, efforts should be made to avoid exposing such students to the substances to which they are allergic or to cigarette smoke, dust, and other irritants which tend to promote broncho-spasm.

Epilepsy

Epilepsy is not a specific disease but is rather a symptom that can be produced by various diseases, tumors, or other injuries to the brain. These injuries result in recurrent, shortlived electrical discharges from the brain, commonly called seizures. These seizures take many forms, depending on what part and how much of the brain is involved. The common types of seizures are:

- *Grand mal.* The grand mal is probably the most dramatic type of seizure. All the neurons in the motor cortex discharge simultaneously and the person experiences violent convulsions and complete loss of consciousness. These episodes are often preceded by a warning (aura) which may be visual, auditory, olfactory, abdominal or by other sensations that the person recognizes. The attack itself results in (1) an abrupt loss of consciousness; (2) tightening of the muscles with the body rigidly extended (tonic spasm) for usually one to three minutes; (3) jerking movements of the head, arms and legs (chronic convulsion) lasting two to three minutes; (4) a period of recovery with or without confusion; and (5) a period of sleep. The frequency of attacks may vary from one per year to many a day.
- *Petit mal.* This is the second most common form of epilepsy. The person experiences a sudden fleeting loss of consciousness or a change in posture or muscle tone without warning. No confusion or aberration of consciousness follows the attack. Typically, there is nothing more than a momentary gap in the person's activities with a related gap in memory. Petit mal seizures are most likely to appear before or at puberty and tend to disappear with increasing age, but in some children they progress to grand mal.
- *Jacksonian.* These are localized seizures, beginning in one extremity or side of the face and progressing throughout the arm or leg of the same side, often without loss of consciousness. The convulsion may spread to the other side of

the body, in which case the attack becomes generalized, usually with loss of consciousness, as in grand mal.

- *Psychomotor*. In this type of seizure, the person exhibits behavior that is usually purposeful but not relevant to the situation. The attacks may last for a few minutes or may go on for more extended periods. While under the seizure, the person may act as if intoxicated, may be morose and irritable, and may engage in purposeless motor movements. Following the attack, the person has no memory of the incident.

An estimated .5 percent of the population is epileptic, but the condition is not apparent in these people except during seizures.[22] Epilepsy may occur at any age, in any race, and in both sexes. Approximately 75 percent of all epileptic seizures begin before the age of 25. Epilepsy occurs in one out of every 50 children.[23]

Special curricular modifications are not necessary for students with epilepsy, but the teacher should be aware of the disruption of concentration and the resultant learning problems that may be created by this disruption. The teacher should also be prepared for the possibility of a grand mal seizure. In this case, the Epilepsy Foundation of America suggests that the steps in Table 4-7 be followed.[24]

In general, the epileptic student can participate in nearly all school activities. However, the student's parents and physician should be consulted to determine if any activities should be avoided. Most children with epilepsy are well controlled on medication, have normal intelligence, and can be expected to lead normal lives.

Diabetes

Diabetes is a metabolic disorder in which the insulin produced in the body by the pancreas is insufficient to utilize properly sugar and starches. In the diabetic, carbohydrate metabolism breaks down, and conversion of sugar and starches into

---

Table 4-7 First Aid for Grand Mal Epilepsy Seizures

Teacher should:

- remain calm
- not try to restrain student
- clear area around student to prevent injury
- not force anything between student's teeth
- when seizure is over let the student rest
- inform the child's parents of the seizure
- turn the seizure into a learning experience for the rest of the class.

Source: Epilepsy Foundation of America, *Teacher Tips from the Epilepsy Foundation of America* (Washington, D.C., 1972).

energy or their storage for future use cannot be accomplished as in the nondiabetic. This condition may be due either to the inability of the pancreas to produce enough insulin or to the inability of the body to use properly the insulin produced. In either case, an excess of sugar accumulates in the blood (hyperglycemia) and may be excreted in the urine (glycosuria). In severe cases, the body can no longer obtain needed energy from carbohydrates and must draw upon protein and fat as a source of energy. This usually results in a loss of weight and strength. Other symptoms include excessive thirst, excessive hunger and appetite, and excessive urination.

Diabetes occurs at all ages and affects approximately 3 million people in the United States. Of these, about 4 percent have onset in childhood.[25]

Treatment of diabetes usually includes insulin injections, dietary regulation, or both. Additionally, the right amounts of exercise and rest are important components of most treatment plans. The most effective control of the disease is obtained when a balance of insulin, diet, and exercise is achieved.

The educator should be aware of symptoms of both high and low blood sugar to assist students with diabetes in the management of their condition and to provide their physicians with information about the students' management plans.

High blood sugar can result in a diabetic coma. This is fairly rare but can be serious if not treated immediately. This condition usually develops slowly and is characterized by dry skin, deep and labored breathing, dry tongue, thirst, excessive urination, a sweet or fruity odor to the breath, and finally coma. Treatment consists of keeping the child warm and resting after immediately notifying the parent, nurse, and physician.

Low blood sugar may result from anything that may increase the child's metabolism rate, such as too much exercise, too much insulin, not enough food, or nervous tension. This is called an insulin reaction. It usually develops rapidly and is characterized by any or all of the following: pale and moist skin, a sudden change in behavior, sweating, extreme hunger, restlessness, headache, and a tired feeling. Treatment of this condition consists of providing the child with a quick energy snack such as pop, a sugar cube, candy, or raisin. If no improvement is seen within five to ten minutes, the parents, nurse, and physician should be contacted. If there is doubt, the situation should be managed as a low blood sugar reaction, according to one authority, since the administration of sugars will cause no harm.[26] Each child has individual characteristic signs of low blood sugar; therefore, consultation with parents and physician may be necessary to know what to look for in that particular child.

The diabetic student can do everything the normal student does, and no restriction of activity is necessary unless specifically prescribed by a physician. Many children may need supplemental snacks, and a quick energy source should be available if a low blood sugar reaction develops.

The attitude toward employing diabetics is becoming increasingly liberal. The trend is to judge each applicant individually rather than generalize and reject all diabetic applicants. The present policy of the Civil Service Commission indicates that the commission believes that persons with *controlled* diabetes may be good employees and that it is good business to hire them.

Educational Provisions

The various orthopedic impairments outlined in this section affect the physical performance of children rather than their intellectual functioning. In most cases—with the possible exception of cerebral palsy, cerebrovascular accidents, and spina bifida—intellectual functioning remains normal. Recently, measures of intelligence that are less dependent upon language have shown that higher levels of intellectual functioning exist even in children with cerebral palsy. After an initial period of training in self-help skills, the child is capable of functioning in a normal classroom. Frequently, however, children with severe medical problems may be absent for extended periods of time. Special care should be taken to ensure that students have the basic tool skills necessary to do more complex tasks. The curriculum should include academic as well as career and vocational education.

Modifications may or may not be needed in the physical environment of the classroom, depending upon the particular student. For instance, if the student is using a wheel chair, doors must be wide enough to accommodate mobility. In some instances, instructional materials should be modified to facilitate handling by the student. In all but the most severe cases, or in cases of orthopedic handicaps accompanied by other handicapping conditions, the regular classroom provides the optimum setting for the orthopedically or other health-impaired student.

The two major barriers to the employment of the orthopedically or other health impaired are attitudinal barriers and architectural barriers. Removal of these two obstructions can greatly expand employment opportunities. Removal of architectural barriers is particularly important to orthopedically impaired persons, since they have limited mobility.

With increased technology, less emphasis is being placed on physical demands, and the number of suitable jobs has increased. Hopefully, under new affirmative action programs, attitudinal as well as architectural barriers will diminish.

MENTALLY RETARDED

Mental retardation refers to a general lack of intellectual and social ability in children and adults. The definition given earlier in Table 4-1 is the legal definition for purposes of funding special education programs for the retarded.

The definition of mentally retarded encompasses a wide variety of individuals and a vast range of etiologies and manifestations. Among the more than 200 identified causes are:

- Genetic irregularities—including those inherited and those caused during pregnancy by overexposure to x-rays, infections, and other causes
- Illness of the mother during pregnancy—including German measles, malnutrition, and glandular disorders
- Trauma during birth—including measles, meningitis, and encephalitis
- Glandular imbalance
- Malnutrition
- Accidents causing damage to brain tissue
- Anoxia (lack of oxygen)
- Poisons
- Understimulation (extreme environmental deprivation resulting in lack of development)

Individuals are considered retarded if their performance on separate measures of intelligence, academic achievement, and adaptive behavior are significantly below the norms of their agemates. The relationships between these three measures are clearly seen in Table 4-8, which outlines identification criteria for the school-age mildly retarded. To be considered mildly mentally retarded, a child must obtain scores which fall at least two standard deviations below the mean in all three areas. It is recognized that deficiencies in only one or two of these areas is insufficient evidence for the classification of mental retardation. Assessment in all three areas—providing measures of functioning on tests, functioning in school and in daily functioning within the natural environment—reduces errors in evaluation. Higher functioning in one area indicates abilities not shown in the other areas of measurement and precludes classification of the child as mentally retarded.

Table 4-8 Identification Criteria for School-Age Mildly Mentally Retarded

Measurement Area	*Measurement Tool*	*Performance*
Intelligence	Individual intelligence tests (e.g., WISC-R).	Full scale intelligence: 70 or less.
Adaptive Behavior	Adaptive behavior scales, observations, observation reports, developmental history, etc.	Significantly below average. Indications of slow or immature development.
Achievement	Standardized achievement scales. Classroom academic performance.	Ratings significantly below agemates (tests 2 standard deviations below mean). Failure or near failure academically.

Retardation manifests itself uniquely among different individuals, both in terms of severity and in terms of how individuals within the same measured range of ability function. Several systems have been developed in medical and educational disciplines to classify the severity of retardation. The popular classification systems use standardized intelligence test scores in part to describe ranges of ability. The systems are used concurrently to describe either programs or individuals.

Table 4-9 provides a summary of three popular classification systems: those of the American Association on Mental Deficiency, the American Psychiatric Association, and an educational system. It is important to note here that the functioning of specific individuals cannot be determined solely on the basis of their inclusion in one of these classifications. The child must be recognized as an individual with a unique set of abilities and preferences. As with normal children, development does not proceed along a linear continuum, and it displays considerable variability as a function of age.

The classification *profoundly retarded* usually implies severe impairment and the need for constant care. Many of the children who fall in this category require institutional care or constant care in the home; they are not capable of self-care. The classification *severely retarded* implies marked impairment in motor, speech, and language development, but the capacity for minimal independence is present. The *moderately retarded* or trainable individual is capable of learning self-care skills and of benefiting from training yet usually requires a sheltered environment. The vast majority of retarded persons fall in the *mildly retarded* or educable category. The mildly retarded person can usually be expected to obtain competitive employment and to function in daily community life.

Table 4-9 Three Classification Systems for Severity of Mentally Retarded

Classification System	*Level*	*Intelligence Rating*
American Association on Mental Deficiency	Profound	0-24
	Severe	24-39
	Moderate	40-54
	Mild	55-70
American Psychiatric Association	Severe	0-54
	Moderate	55-69
	Mild	70-84
Educational	Profound	0-24
	Severe	25-39
	Trainable	40-54
	Educable	55-75

Incidence

During the 1977-1978 school year, approximately 950,000 students or 2 percent of the school-age population were served in programs for the mentally retarded.[27] Table 4-4, presented earlier, showed that approximately 90 percent of the mentally retarded students were served in the regular classroom and separate classes, while only ten percent were enrolled in separate facilities and other educational environments.

A majority of the mentally retarded fall within the mildly retarded range of ability. This is demonstrated by the fact that, in 1976, approximately 40 percent of the identified mentally retarded were receiving a portion of their educational program in the regular classroom.[28] This supports the contention that vocational educators probably are already serving the mentally retarded in their classrooms.

Educational Provisions

Since mental retardation includes such a wide variety of etiologies and symptoms, an inclusive definition, by necessity, lacks specific reference to remediation or educational approaches. The standardized tests used to determine classification are used only for comparisons to normed populations and give no information pertaining to the child on a noncomparative basis. Use of classification should be limited to studies of incidence, prevalence, and so forth, and as a means of receiving appropriate special services for the child.

Educational services are typically provided through a continuum of levels of service. These levels range from little or no modification of the regular vocational classroom to basic self-care and occupational therapy in a hospital setting. Table 4-10 represents various alternatives in vocational education programming available to the mentally retarded student. Decisions about placement of students at various levels are based upon information gathered and evaluated for that particular student. The placement decision is based upon the individual needs of the particular student rather than on broad classifications of severity. Within this continuum, the regular classroom represents the least restrictive alternative and is chosen whenever possible.

As can be seen from the incidence figures in the previous section, the vast majority of mentally retarded students (90 percent) are served in a special class or less restrictive alternative. Educational modifications for these students may include additional emphasis on core components, opportunity for additional practice and overlearning, special materials for low reading ability and increased hands-on experience. The prevocational and vocational curriculum for the mildly mentally retarded student may also include greater emphasis on personal and social skills, daily living skills, and career information often acquired incidentally by nonhandicapped students.

Table 4-10 Alternatives in Vocational Programming for the Mentally Retarded

Restrictiveness	Alternative	Description
Least restrictive	Regular vocational program	Regular vocational programs may fit the needs of some mentally retarded students with little or no modification.
	Adapted vocational program	Regular programs are adapted to meet the special needs of students who cannot succeed in regular vocational programs. Adaptations may be in materials, course content, supervision, working style, etc.
	Adapted vocational programs plus remedial services	These programs provide remedial education in basic computational and quantitative skills, communication skills, work attitudes and habits, personal social skills, occupational information, and/or prevocational evaluation as a prerequisite to success in an adapted or regular vocational program.
	Special vocational education	Self-contained vocational programs offer services not possible in a regular vocational classroom and are open only to handicapped students.
	Special vocational schools	Schools may be established solely for the purpose of vocational education of the handicapped. Usually physically removed from the regular school setting. Basic emphasis on prevocational skills and entry level job skills.
	Sheltered workshop	These provide supervised work and training for those individuals not capable of engaging in competitive work experiences. Workshops may or may not be in conjunction with school programs.
Most restrictive	Vocational training in institutional settings	These vocational programs are offered as part of the total educational program in an institutionalized setting.

Since mildly retarded students generally do not go on to other education, work experience and placement have assumed growing importance as roles of vocational programs in secondary schools. These functions, as well as coordination with other services such as vocational rehabilitation, are designed to ease the transition from the school environment to the work environment.

In considering a mentally retarded person for employment, such factors as education, training, job experience, motivation, attitude, personality, and general health should be considered along with I.Q. scores. The sole use of I.Q. scores in determining placement may underestimate the potential of the student for employment. Many retarded persons are capable of obtaining jobs in the competitive employment market. With proper training, mentally retarded persons have been employed as general office clerks, messengers, office persons, mail carriers, stock clerks, sales clerks, domestics, dayworkers, housekeepers, nursemaids, nurses' aides, laborers, construction workers, welders, carpenters' helpers, filling station attendants, metal workers, upholsterers, and in many other responsible positions.[29] A positive approach to vocational education and job placement, which means concentrating on what the retarded person *can* do, greatly improves the chances of achieving competitive employment.

SERIOUSLY EMOTIONALLY DISTURBED

The seriously emotionally disturbed category of handicapping conditions can be seen to be one that, even in Public Law 94-142 form (Table 4-1), is composed of a complex and multifaceted array of symptoms. Use of the Public Law 94-142 definition reveals certain characteristics of the emotionally disturbed student that are associated with impaired educational performance. In many cases, such children exhibit maladaptive behaviors that interfere with learning. They may be unable to build or maintain satisfactory interpersonal relationships with others. Also, they may be generally depressed, possess physical symptoms or fears, exhibit inappropriate behaviors and feelings, or possess schizophrenic or autistic symptom patterns.

Behaviors which the emotionally disturbed child could display include:

- explosive temper outbursts
- hostile aggression toward others
- extreme withdrawal and lack of involvement with others
- depression and apathy in situations most students enjoy
- unreasonable beliefs about others, such as conspiring against someone
- loss of use of some bodily function (for example, sight or hearing) with no medical explanation
- extreme unrealistic fear of ordinary environmental objects

The above list is not exhaustive but rather representative of some of the presenting problems presented by the emotionally disturbed student. A number of variations in intensity and duration of the problems will be noted.

The identification of the emotionally disturbed child is usually the province of psychiatric and psychological specialists. Recommendations for treatment come from these specialists and from teams of educational specialists. In the screening process, the first step in identification of emotionally disturbed and behaviorally disturbed children is to determine if their behavior and actions in the classroom interfere with one or more of the following: (1) the learning of other students, (2) their own learning, or (3) the effectiveness of the teacher.

When one of the above three conditions occurs, the student has a behavioral problem significant enough to indicate a need for intervention on the part of the teacher. When the problem cannot be alleviated within the regular classroom by the teacher without assistance, a referral is made to the appropriate specialist designated in the school, often the special education resource specialist. Based upon data gathered from observations in the classroom, test data, and clinical data, the student would be judged either a simple discipline problem, behaviorally disturbed, or emotionally disturbed. The classification of emotionally disturbed is based primarily on the premise that the behavior noted has occurred over a period of time, that it is not a reaction to a specific stressful situation, and that it is of sufficient intensity to cause concern on the part of the staff. The decision for placement in a program for the emotionally disturbed would be based then on the duration and intensity of the behavior problem.

Incidence

Estimates of the incidence of emotional disturbance in the United States vary considerably because the definition used, the population sampled, and the identification methods employed differ from one investigator to the next. However, Table 4-4, presented earlier, suggests that .50 percent of the school age population needs intensive special education. Gearheart and Weishahn have utilized surveys conducted by several agencies to estimate the number of emotionally disturbed children in 1978 as 1,100,000, with 15 percent of this number currently receiving service and 85 percent remaining in need of service.[30]

Educational Provisions

In many cases, emotionally disturbed children can function in the regular class with certain behavioral adaptations. They can benefit from regular placement in situations where they are able to observe appropriate behaviors and see that they are regular members of society and that they are able to function in a milieu that fosters academic pursuits but is still safe and somewhat protected. Other students may receive special services in the school and participate in regular classes on a parttime basis; still others may receive psychiatric or psychological assistance while participating in regular classes. In all cases, however, the educational placement and programming should be consistent with least restrictive environment provisions of Public Law 94-142 and be appropriate for that child.

There are various approaches in working with emotionally disturbed students in the classroom, but none would be endorsed by most experts as the "correct" method. One system emphasizes the acceptance of inappropriate symptoms, followed by tolerance but not acceptance, and finally by limit-setting. Another approach involves acceptance of the child's behavior and reflection of the behavior back to the student. Still another stresses provision of understanding, acceptance, recognition, and clarification of feelings. In contrast to these acceptance philosophies, there is an approach that utilizes systematic procedures to change or modify inappropriate behaviors and to encourage appropriate behaviors. Regardless of the approach, there are many constructive steps that can be taken to provide a realistic, responsible environment for the emotionally disturbed student.

The educator should be cautioned about making generalizations about the emotionally disturbed student. The intensity of the presenting problem of individual students varies on a continuum of total withdrawal to extreme hostility. Since the presenting problems vary in symptomatology, intensity and duration, the intervention strategies, training programs, and employment potential must be based on knowledge of the particular student.

Vocational programs and especially vocational programs for the handicapped have traditionally included training in work habits and attitudes as well as in personal-social skills as components of training and job success. The Vocational Education Amendments of 1976 include training in personal-social skills as a component of their definition of vocational instruction. These areas are of primary importance to the emotionally disturbed student, both in vocational training and in future job success.

As in other handicapping conditions, one of the greatest barriers to employment is the attitude of the general public concerning emotional disturbance. Since emotional disturbance is not generally well understood, it often elicits unwarranted apprehension on the part of potential teachers and employers. Vocational educators have the job of preparing both the student and the potential employer to deal with this apprehension.

SPECIFIC LEARNING DISABILITIES

The present area of learning disabilities is an integration of three historically separate fields. Until the 1960s, disorders of spoken language, written language, and perceptual and motor processes were viewed as separate areas of interest.[31]

During the sixties, these disorders were integrated under the label *learning disabilities,* although the three theoretical approaches are still evident in the many definitions and remediation techniques. Because of the vast scope of the field, a behavioral working definition of the learning disabled (LD) student has not evolved.

Within the current definition of learning disabilities under Public Law 94-142 (see Table 4-1, presented earlier), the major characteristics of the learning disabled student are delineated:

- "a discrepancy between the student's intellectual level and his/her achievement in specific academic areas
- "does not originate from physical disabilities, such as, blindness, deafness, or physiological factors
- "student's intellectual ability is within the average to above average range of functioning
- "poor academic achievement resulting from mental retardation, emotional disturbance, or environmental, cultural or economic disadvantage are excluded."[32]

Various authors have attempted to further define the descriptive characteristics of LD children. One author, Thomas Jeschke, surveyed teachers working with LD students and identified the following ten characteristics that were frequently observed among such children: hyperactivity; perceptual disturbances; language difficulties; specific learning disorders in reading, arithmetic, writing, and spelling; coordination disorders; disorders of attention; impulsivity; memory problems; low frustration tolerance; and poor self-concept.[33]

Other authors have differentiated children by the area of disability[34] [35] and by learning channel defects.[36] The choice of classification system and the extent of its use is dependent upon the user's orientation and goals for the utilization of the classification system in remediation of the learning disability.

The procedures and criteria followed in the identification of the LD student are presented in Table 4-11. In the identification process, a multidisciplinary team composed of classroom teachers, local educational agency personnel, and individuals trained to administer individual tests seeks information in the following areas: physical, emotional, and environmental factors; intellectual ability; achievement; and observation of classroom behaviors to make decisions about whether the student is learning disabled.

Incidence

Since *learning disabilities* is an umbrella category and could encompass students with mild to severe difficulties, it is possible that a large percentage of the school-age population could be defined as belonging in this category. In general,

Table 4-11 Identification of Learning Disabled Students

Criteria	*Learning Disabled*	*Nonlearning Disabled*
Physical, emotional and/or environmental factors	Vision, hearing, physical abilities, emotional stability, cultural/economic conditions not primary factors in school failures	Sensory impairments, physical disability, emotional disturbance, environmental, cultural or economic disadvantage present
Intellectual ability	I.Q. greater than one standard deviation below the mean	I.Q. less than one standard deviation below the mean
Achievement	Elementary: Achievement test scores more than two years below present grade placement in: oral expression, listening comprehension, written expression, basic reading skills, reading comprehension, math calculations, and/or math reasoning Secondary: Scores two years below grade placement and below seventh grade in at least one of the seven areas listed above	Achievement test scores below present grade placement in all areas.
Observations	Observation data indicate lack of self-management skills; behavior which interferes with own or others learning primarily due to frustration in learning	Observation data reveal severe behavior problems and inability to manage self and surroundings
Classroom achievement	Data indicate sporadic or no progress toward goals	Data indicate steady progress toward goals
Meets above criteria	Identification of LD. Move toward placement in LD program	Alternative solution sought

two percent is an appropriate guideline. In fact, in the original legislative actions under Public Law 94-142, a temporary lid of two percent was placed on the number of students who could be labeled learning disabled for funding purposes. This temporary lid was removed after the publication of the identification procedures in November, 1975. In the school year 1977-1978, slightly less than two percent of the school-aged population in the United States was being served in programs for the learning disabled. It should be remembered, however, that the incidence figures vary from state to state depending on the rigorousness of the criteria used for identification.

Educational and Vocational Provisions

A number of models or methods of delivering services to the learning disabled adolescent are in existence. For the purpose of convenience in describing the various approaches, they have been grouped into five categories: (1) traditional special education, (2) tutorial, (3) survival skills, (4) career education, and (5) composite. The models are presented briefly in Table 4-12, along with authors' comments about the strengths or weaknesses of each. These models, all of which are used in one form or another in school systems in the United States, demonstrate the widely differing purposes, approaches, and philosophies involved in the education of the learning disabled.

SPEECH IMPAIRED

Speech impairment refers to those students who have difficulties with oral language. The educational/legal definition was given earlier in Table 4-1. Most students, especially in kindergarten and primary grades, at one time or another have difficulties with speech, particularly with articulation and syntax. These difficulties are not considered a speech impairment unless they deviate substantially from the speech patterns of the students' peers. The speech impaired student presents a picture that is not congruent with the predictable developmental patterns observed in the majority of students.

J. Eisenson and M. Ogilvie have pointed out several communication problems that are often confused with speech impairment. These include: (1) nonstandard pronunciations and language usage, (2) regional dialects, (3) poor oral reading, (4) immature articulation and fluency patterns, and (5) psychological disturbances that are manifested as speech symptoms.[37]

Speech impairment may be observed separately or in conjunction with other handicapping conditions. Several other conditions—such as deafness, cerebral palsy, and mental retardation—have a high incidence of related speech problems.

Table 4-12 Models for Delivery of Services to the Learning Disabled Adolescent

TRADITIONAL SPECIAL EDUCATION	*Description*	This model is an extension of the self-contained special classroom. The approach revolves around an emphasis on specific skill acquisition and remediation of academic or process deficits. The program can either be an integral part of the school program or can easily operate as a separate entity with little integration with the regular program.
	Comment	Frequently, the program lacks continuity with the total school curriculum, places insignificant emphasis on career-survival skills, and requires the LD student to be isolated from the mainstream of the school.
TUTORIAL	*Description*	This model is designed to permit the LD student to compete in the regular school program with assistance of support personnel. Alternative instructional procedures to master content are provided to the student. Major emphasis is one-to-one tutoring or small group instruction with the LD specialist. Regular liaison between the classroom teacher and the LD specialist or tutor is required to accommodate the LD student.
	Comment	Positive attributes include: continuity of the educational program for the LD student; opportunity for student to succeed in regular school program; opportunity for regular teaching staff to alter teaching procedures to accommodate the LD student. Weaknesses include: the students are obligated to adjust to the school curriculum, rather than the curriculum being adjusted to the unique needs of the students. The model can also be expensive to operate.
SURVIVAL SKILL	*Description*	This model is frequently used in conjunction with other models. The emphasis is on assisting the LD student to develop coping skills and response patterns to meet the demands of the instructional program. Activities could include: test-taking skills and teacher-pleasing behaviors. The goals are to teach self-management, assertiveness, and basic student skills. The program can be delivered on a tutorial or small group basis.
	Comment	When carried to an extreme, the model may be providing students short-term skills which have little value in later life. Students who have developed survival skills will be more likely to be successful in the public school.
CAREER EDUCATION	*Description*	The purpose is to permit realistic planning for the "world of work." The model is often organized in three areas: daily living skills; personal-social skills; and occupational and career guidance. The approach provides experiences for the student related to assumptions of adult roles. The instructional compo-

nents are generally delivered throughout the curriculum, with work experiences on either a simulated or actual placement basis as a culmination of the process.

	Comment	A career education component can be excellent as a part of the total program; however, caution is needed to insure that LD students are not prematurely directed to occupational choices that may not be commensurated with their potential. If emphasis is placed on career preparation, LD students may be encouraged to make occupational decisions based on their weaknesses rather than abilities.
COMPOSITE	*Description*	The model is composed of three parts: self-management instruction; basic academic skill instruction; and career-survival skill instruction. The model differs from the others in the amount of emphasis placed on each component. Basic academic instruction is provided on a tutorial or small group basis only to enable students to make progress. When little or no academic progress is noted, compensation skills are taught. Self-management instruction allows students to become responsible for their behaviors and their environments. Career-survival skills instruction extends through the first three stages of career education: awareness, exploration, and orientation. The emphasis is placed on skills that are important for success in the "world of work."
	Comment	This model has the advantages of each of the previous models and takes into consideration the whole student. The weakness of the model is the pressure placed on the LD specialist to provide the program. The teacher in the model has to have a broad base of training expertise as a teacher and consultant.

In general, speech problems fall into several categories based on the type of difficulty encountered. These include articulatory defects, stuttering, vocal defects, retarded language development, cleft palate speech, language impairment, cerebral palsy speech, and speech defects due to impaired hearing.[38]

Articulatory Defects

The most common types of speech problems are articulation defects. These may include errors of omission ("bo" for "boat"), errors of substitution ("wabbit" for "rabbit"), errors of distortion ("nother" for "mother") or errors of addition ("puhlease" for "please").

Stuttering

Stuttering is characterized by involuntary stopping, the rapid repetition of certain sounds, or the prolongation of a sound. Stuttering varies in its frequency of occurrence and in its debilitating effects.

Vocal Defects

Vocal defects are defects of pitch, intensity, quality, and/or flexibility. Pitch is important when it is inappropriate to the age or sex of the individual. Intensity may be too loud or too soft, in either case interfering with normal communication. Quality problems include breathiness, harshness and nasality. Flexibility problems are characterized by the monotone speaker.

Retarded Language Development

For most children, language development follows a predictable pattern. Some students who may have had a delay in language onset exhibit language more infantile than their peers. This may include limited vocabulary and simpler sentences, as well as speech omissions and infantile pronunciation of words. The important consideration here is that the lag in language development is outside that normally expected in similar children.

Language Impairment

Language impairment is usually associated with some type of brain damage. It includes students who have difficulties in the acquisition of language and also those who have difficulties from brain damage that has occurred after the acquisition of language. The first type is often included in the category of retarded language development.

Cleft Palate Speech

Cleft palate speech is caused by an opening in the hard or soft palate that allows air to pass between the nose and the mouth. This results in an impaired ability to reproduce consonants that require a buildup of air and gives speech a nasal quality.

Cerebral Palsy Speech

Defects in articulation and rhythm are caused by impaired motor functioning resulting from brain damage. Detailed information on aspects of cerebral palsy was provided earlier in the section on orthopedic and other health impairments.

Speech Defects Due to Impaired Hearing

Speech is largely learned and regulated through hearing and imitation. Impaired hearing is often accompanied by speech problems in articulation, voice, and intensity. Depending on the onset of hearing loss and compensation, the development of language itself may also be impaired.

Incidence

Usual estimates of the incidence of speech impairments range from 2.5 to 5.0 percent of the school age population. Table 4-1 indicated, however, that 2.39 percent of the school-age population were served as speech impaired during the 1977-1978 school year. Speech impairment as a handicapping condition affects the greatest number of students, comprising 35.2 percent of those served as handicapped. The American Speech and Hearing Association has reported that 75 percent of speech clinicians work at the kindergarten, first, and second grade levels and that only 2 percent work strictly at the high school level, indicating that the prevalence of speech problems is much higher in younger children.[39] Approximately 90 percent of the speech impaired students were served in regular classrooms; less than 2 percent were served outside the school system.

Educational Provisions

Remediation of speech impairment is usually the domain of the speech clinician (who is also known in some areas as the speech pathologist or the speech therapist), but the classroom teacher is often a valuable adjunct as a provider of services and a referral source. When the child is being seen by a speech clinician, the teacher should consult with the clinician to jointly design a classroom program that complements the clinician's therapy. An additional valuable service provided by the teacher is in the correct modeling of articulation and language usage. Referrals to speech clinicians are a teacher responsibility; such referrals may become necessary when the child has generally unintelligible speech, severely delayed speech, dramatic voice changes other than those ordinarily present during puberty, debilitating stuttering, or other speech impairments that adversely affect the child's educational performance.

NOTES

1. U.S., *Federal Register,* vol. 42, no. 86, May 4, 1977, p. 22682.
2. U.S., *Federal Register,* vol. 42, no. 163, August 23, 1977, p. 42478.
3. U.S., *Federal Register,* vol. 42, no. 86, May 4, 1977, p. 22678.
4. U.S., *Federal Register,* vol. 42, no. 191, October 3, 1977, p. 53864.
5. U.S., *Federal Register,* vol. 42, no. 86, May 4, 1977, p. 22682.

6. U.S. Code, Title XX, sec. 1412 (5)(6).
7. U.S. Department of Health, Education and Welfare, Office of Education, *Progress Toward a Free Appropriate Public Education: A Report to Congress on the Implementation of Public Law 94-142: The Education for All Handicapped Children Act* (Washington, D.C.: Government Printing Office, January, 1979).
8. Ibid.
9. D.P. Hallahan and J.M. Kaufman, "Labels, Categories, Behaviors: ED, LD, and EMR Reconsidered," *Journal of Special Education,* Summer 1977: 139, vol. II, no. 2.
10. H.R. Myklebust, *The Psychology of Deafness* (New York: Grune and Stratton, 1964).
11. J.D. Schein and T.D. Marcus, *The Deaf Population in the United States* (Silver Springs, Md.: National Association of the Deaf, 1974).
12. Ibid.
13. J.D. Schein, "Economic Factors in Deafness," *Yearbook of Special Education* (Chicago, Ill.: Marquis Academic Media, 1976).
14. Ibid.
15. National Society to Prevent Blindness, *Vocabulary of Terms Relating to the Eye,* publication no. 172 (New York: National Society to Prevent Blindness, 1957).
16. American Foundation for the Blind, Inc., *Facts About Blindness* (New York: American Foundation for the Blind).
17. H.J. Link, "Placement and Employment of the Visually Impaired: State of the Art and Identification and Unmet Needs," *Yearbook of Special Education* (Chicago, Ill.: Marquis Academic Media, 1976).
18. Ibid.
19. W.L. Mineas, "A Classification of Cerebral Palsy," *Pediatrics* 18:841-852.
20. U.S., Department of Labor, *Interviewing Guides for Specific Disabilities: Heart Disease* (Washington, D.C.: Government Printing Office).
21. G. McNutt, "Cardiovascular Disorders" *Workshop in Behavior Characteristics of Exceptional Children for Personnel Who Function in Vocational Preparation Programs,* ed. L.R. Kinnison and I.L. Land (Oklahoma State University).
22. R.H. Haslam, "Teacher Awareness of Some Pediatric Neurological Disorders," in *Medical Problems in the Classroom,* ed. R.A. Haslam and P.J. Valletutti (Baltimore, MD.: University Park Press, 1975).
23. G.R. Gearhart and M.W. Weishahan, *The Handicapped Child in the Regular Classroom* (St. Louis, Mo.: The C.V. Mosby Company, 1976), see footnote 31.
24. Epilepsy Foundation of America, *Teacher Tips From the Epilepsy Foundation of America* (Washington, D.C.: Epilepsy Foundation of America, 1972).
25. U.S. Department of Labor, *Interviewing Guides for Specific Disabilities: Diabetes* (Washington, D.C.: U.S. Government Printing Office, 1973).
26. H.P. Katz, "Important Endocrine Disorders of Childhood," in *Medical Problems in the Classroom,* ed. R.H. Haslam and P.J. Valletutti (Baltimore, MD.: University Park Press, 1975).
27. U.S. Department of Health Education and Welfare, Office of Education, *Progress Toward a Free Appropriate Public Education: A Report to Congress on the Implementation of Public Law 94-142: The Education of All Handicapped Children Act* (Washington, D.C.: U.S. Government Printing Office, January, 1979).
28. U.S. Department of Health Education and Welfare, Office of Education, Progress Toward a Free Appropriate Public Education: *A Report to Congress on the Implementation of Public Law 94-142:*

The Education of All Handicapped Children Act (Washington, D.C.: U.S. Government Printing Office, January 1979).

29. U.S., Department of Labor, Bureau of Employment Security, *Guide to Job Placement of Mentally Retarded Workers* (Washington, D.C.: President's Committee on Employment of the Handicapped in Cooperation with the National Association for Retarded Citizens and the U.S. Employment Service, 1975).
30. G.R. Gearheart and M.W. Weishahn, *The Handicapped Child in the Regular Classroom* (St. Louis, Mo.: The C.V. Mosby Company, 1976).
31. J. Lee Weiderholt, *Historical Perspectives on the Education of the Learning Disabled in the Second Review of Special Education* (Philadelphia, Pa.: Lester Mann, JSE Press, 1974).
32. U.S., *Federal Register,* vol. 42, no. 163, May 4, 1977.
33. T.A. Jeschke, *An Overview of Learning Disabilities for Classroom Teachers and Parents* (Iowa Department of Public Instruction, 1975).
34. H.D. Hammil and P.I. Myers, *Methods for Learning Disorders* (New York: John Wiley and Sons, Inc., 1969).
35. R. Valett, *Programming Learning Disabilities* (Belmont, Calif.: Fearon, 1969).
36. J. Stellern, S.F. Vasa, and J. Little, *Introduction to Diagnostic-Prescriptive Teaching and Programming* (Glen Ridge, N.J.: Exceptional Press, 1976).
37. J. Eisenson and M. Ogilvie, *Speech Correction in the Schools* (New York: The Macmillan Co., 1971).
38. Ibid.
39. American Speech and Hearing Association, "Public School Speech and Hearing Services," *Journal of Speech and Hearing Disorders,* Monograph Supplement 8 (July 1961).

Chapter 5

Program Development for Special Vocational Needs Youth

George W. Fair, Ph.D.

INTRODUCTION

This chapter is designed as a study guide. It presents a number of questions related to program development for special vocational needs youth. These questions provide important guidelines concerning the concept of program development. The questions that will be answered are:

- What is program development?
- Who should be involved in program development?
- What is the process of curriculum development?
- What is the appropriate content for program development?
- How can affective competencies be included in program development?
- How should teaching-learning activities be planned?
- How is evaluation used in program development?

WHAT IS PROGRAM DEVELOPMENT?

Program development as used here means the vocational education experiences that are provided for the student. Curriculum is a component of the program. Curriculum has been broadly defined as all the experiences that the student has, regardless of when or how they take place, including the experiences the student has under the guidance of the school. In the present context, program development is synonymous with this broad definition of curriculum. Program development means all the experiences that are related to the vocational instruction of the individual. The program for a student includes the curriculum for that student as well as other short- and long-term objectives.

Recent legislation that has encouraged vocational education personnel to make their programs more accessible to special needs youth is based essentially on the premise that special needs youth are not that much different from youth that are considered "normal". The following sections show the difference between a vocational education program for "normal" individuals and one for special needs individuals. They attempt to answer such questions as: Is this in fact the same program? Can these groups of students be included in the same program? How should programs for special needs youth be different? Program development, it will be seen, is not necessarily unique to special needs youth; it is appropriate for any student.

WHO SHOULD BE INVOLVED IN PROGRAM DEVELOPMENT?

Our approach to program development is a cooperative approach. This means that teachers, learners, parents, administrators, and consultants should be members of the team for program development.

Why a cooperative approach? Program development involves not only the stating, finding, or identifying of new content but also new ways of using old content, new teaching strategies, and new teaching techniques. Program development is an educational process. Broad participation in program development involves more people in the educational process; therefore, more people learn and grow as individuals. This is one of the objectives of program development for special vocational needs youth. Participation in such activities tends to generate a kind of psychological ownership of the resulting program. The persons included become involved and share responsibility for the resulting program. This involvement encourages individuals to become committed to the program and enables them to work for its success. In order to achieve successful program development, broad-based cooperation is essential.

Another important reason for including various types of persons in program development is that such a group can increase available information. Each of the individuals has something different to contribute to the program and views the student from a different perspective. The teacher is a professional educator who has had experiences with large numbers of students. Teachers in vocational education have competence in a vocational area and are dedicated to helping others learn the skills or abilities that they possess. The learner has a vested interest in the program. No one else can speak for the learners in the program, because no one knows the learners' feelings better than they themselves. The parent is an adult who sees the learner from a perspective that is different from that of other adults. The administrator has the supervisory responsibility for personnel who will implement the program and thus views it from that perspective. Consultants may be needed for a number of reasons. They may be helpful in providing information related to disabling conditions, specific data for content areas, and objective viewpoints that may not be available to those closer to the scene. Thus, each of the participants has a unique role to play in contributing to the program development process.

When we think of school administration, the principal is the person who comes most often to mind. The principal has a number of duties to facilitate program development, such as providing a time and place for program development groups to meet, recommending consultants to the groups, introducing curricula that have been developed, and arranging times for teachers to attend program development conferences and meetings. The principal is also in a position to coordinate various program development activities.

The principal can help to facilitate the social relationships necessary for good program development and can also provide a supportive atmosphere in which program development can take place. Good administrators will show teachers that they support program development and will encourage them to exercise their creative energy in the program development process. A principal should know and understand the kind of personality traits or relationships that exist among teachers. Thus, the principal will be able to select the teacher that is innovative, willing to initiate, and be active in program development, as compared to the teacher that has little interest in program development. In varying degrees both types of teachers need to be involved, and the principal can assist in distinguishing the two types in composing a group for program development.

The teacher has a very important role to play in program development. For some time, teachers have not contributed to program development as much as they probably should have. Yet, most teachers have good ideas and a great deal to contribute to program development. One important reason for including teachers in program development is that they are the ones that will actually have to implement the program. It goes back to the question of psychological ownership. If teachers are involved in developing the program, they will be committed to its implemention. This happens in a number of ways. One way is through talking with other teachers. If a program is developed without teacher input, teachers will be aware of that fact. A program that is developed with teacher input will obviously have a greater reception in the minds of teachers than a program that is developed without teacher input.

Another important aspect of program development for special vocational needs youth is the needs and concerns of the learners. There is probably no group better qualified to discuss and contribute information about these needs than teachers. The needs, concerns, and experiences that teachers have had with special vocational needs students in the past are vitally important to program development.

The inclusion of teachers in the program development process also aids in their own professional growth. They get an opportunity to examine other curriculum materials, materials that can be used in the future, and their own philosophies and goals for the program. Teachers are in a unique position to make judgments about what will and what will not work with students. They can contribute information on what is realistic for the classroom. Thus, teachers, because of their background, definitely have a unique contribution to make to program development.

The role of the students in program development is also unique. As noted, the participation of the students is important because no one knows the interests of the students better than the students themselves. How can student input be included? There are a number of ways. A program development committee can form a student advisory committee. That is, as the program is developed members of the program development committee can meet with an advisory committee of students, present key questions, and ask the advisory committee to respond to those questions. Similarly, inputs from student vocational education organizations can be obtained. For example, if the program development is in the area of agriculture, the Future Farmers of America (FFA) should be consulted. Student participation is important in the psychological ownership of the program. If students are aware that they have been involved in the construction and development of the program or curriculum, they will be more motivated to participate and achieve.

What is the role of parents in this program development process? Parents should be involved because they have seen their children develop over an extended period of time. Furthermore, they can communicate with other parents and laypersons concerning the development of the curriculum. This will encourage real community involvement and community ownership of the program.

Consultants are also important in the program development process. They may be drawn from a number of places. School district consultants may be responsible for a specific area or a specific age group of children. State education agency consultants are helpful because of their experience in program development for special vocational needs youth or in vocational program development in general. Consultants who have made themselves known for their expertise in specific areas can be helpful. It is important to have consultants from the business community who can contribute ideas and thoughts about what a student needs to be employed in certain industries. Consultants from the business community may also assist by identifying the latest developments in their areas. Finally, recent graduates of the vocational program should be included as consultants in the program development process. These graduates can identify the good and bad points of the program and thus be helpful in analyzing exactly what the program does to prepare students for their respective careers.

Clearly, cooperation is the key to program development for special vocational needs youth.

WHAT IS THE CURRICULUM DEVELOPMENT PROCESS?

The curriculum is the part of the program that is related to direct instruction. The curriculum includes the plan for instruction in skill competencies and knowledges. Counseling, though a program component, is not a specific element in the curriculum. However, precise definitions of these terms are difficult because of the overlapping connotations.

Authors have outlined a number of steps in the curriculum development process. In the present context, the process will be regarded as consisting of five steps:

1. Development of goals
2. Selection of instructional objectives
3. Selection and organization of content
4. Selection of instructional procedures
5. Evaluation plans

Development of Goals

The development of goals is the first step in the curriculum development process. It is particularly important to have a cooperative effort in designing the goals of a program for special vocational needs students. The five types of persons mentioned as participants in the program development process—teachers, learners, parents, administrators, and consultants—should also be included in the curriculum development process, thereby providing a broad base of input. Input data from other sources should also be included. One way of broadening this base is by utilizing surveys. Survey data concerning job availability should be gathered at both the state and local level. A survey of the graduates of the program is also important.

At the state level, surveys can help to determine the nature and number of businesses that may hire students who complete the program. Such surveys give the curriculum developers an indication of specific types of jobs that may be available. They are also helpful in estimating the kinds of barriers to employment that may exist for special vocational needs youth. Typical survey questions that might be asked of specific industries are:

- How many people are employed in the industry?
- How many handicapped or disadvantaged people are employed?
- What types of jobs are performed by the handicapped or disadvantaged employees?
- What types of jobs are performed by nonhandicapped or nondisadvantaged employees?

- For organizations that do not employ handicapped or disadvantaged persons: (1) Are there specific reasons for not employing such persons? (2) Do architectural barriers exist that inhibit employment of such persons? (3) Do you have reservations related to safety that concern the employment of such persons? (4) Do you plan to employ handicapped or disadvantaged persons in the future?

The local employment survey should include some of the same questions used in the state employment survey but can be much more specific. The curriculum development committee should have available to it more detailed information on local industries than can be obtained from the state survey. Thus, more specific questions should be asked on the local level, and, if possible, commitments to hire special vocational needs youth in the future should be obtained from the respondents.

Followup studies of graduates, as part of the program evaluation process in vocational and special education, are not unique. In fact, there are established guidelines for followup studies of graduates of vocational education programs. This is a very important source for data that can be useful in curriculum decision making. The graduates of a program have recent, detailed information on what it has taken to become employed or on the reasons they were not employed. Because this information is so important, an interview survey should be utilized. This is recommended because graduates may have difficulty communicating in written form, and individual interviews can provide more detailed information. A broad base of input is important to the making of decisions in the development of goals as a part of the curriculum development process.

Selection of Instructional Objectives

The second step in the curriculum development process is the selection of instructional objectives. The writing of these objectives helps to identify specific skills that can be used for individual students and also facilitates the organization and efficiency of the instructional process. The following is an example of a four-level process in the identification and development of instructional objectives for a vocational area.

Area: Furniture repair and upholstery

Subareas:
1. Orientation
2. Furniture repair
3. Reviving old finishes
4. Removing old finishes
5. Preparing for a new finish
6. Applying a new finish

7. Introduction to upholstery
8. Upholstery procedures

Skills and knowledges: In furniture repair, the student will:

1. identify tools and supplies
2. follow steps for gluing furniture
3. follow steps for fastening joints
4. patch dents and holes
5. repair cracks
6. repair broken corners and edges
7. remove dents and bruises
8. repair a joint
9. tighten round or square furniture joints
10. secure furniture tops to frame
11. repair drawers
12. make and install new parts
13. correct unbalanced furniture
14. install casters
15. patch surfaces
16. repair veneer

Objectives: The student will identify tools and supplies by naming, pointing to, and briefly stating the function of:

1. a spring bender
2. a cushion filler
3. fasteners
4. a band saw
5. a sander
6. a webbing stretcher
7. glue
8. dowels

The above type of strategy to identify instructional objectives in one vocational area is not new, but it is an important part of the curriculum development that is sometimes overlooked. The first level of analysis is the vocational area itself. The second level is concerned with the subareas of the vocational area, in other words, the components of the vocational area that will comprise the curriculum. At the third level of specification are the skills and knowledges that make up each of the component subareas. Finally, at the fourth level are the instructional objectives for each of the skills and knowledges. There are many different ways of breaking down knowledge and information for instructional purposes. This is one efficient way to organize information for the kind of instruction necessary for the special vocational needs youth.

Selection and Organization of Content

The third step in the curriculum development process has to do with the selection and organization of the content. If the second step, selection of instructional objectives, is thought of as the "what" of the curriculum, then the third step can be thought of as the "when" and "how long" of the curriculum. Two other terms, sequence and duration, are probably more appropriate.

These terms raise very difficult questions that begin to move the curriculum development process into a systems approach. The questions can be answered effectively only as one utilizes and evaluates the curriculum and continues to collect information concerning sequence and duration. This is especially important for programs in which individualization is necessary in the enrollment of special vocational needs youth. Suggestions for sequence and duration should be stated as a part of the curriculum development process, but the appropriate information can come only from the interaction of the curriculum with students.

There are a number of criteria that can be used in developing an appropriate sequence of instruction. One criterion is that of interest. That is, it can be decided that the most interesting material will be taught first and the least interesting last. Another often-used criterion is the chronological sequence of advancement in occupations that can be applied to instruction in a vocational area. The kind of job that is assigned upon entry into the industry receives instructional priority, and the other jobs follow in terms of their sequence over time. For example, the jobs that a carpenter's helper does would have instructional priority over jobs involving finishing work. Another way of examining sequence is in terms of basic logic. There are certain skills that are prerequisites to other skills. Thus, one learns how to use hand tools before learning how to use power tools. Another consideration is that of difficulty; in some circumstances, it is more appropriate for a person to learn the easier aspects before the more difficult aspects are considered.

The above four criteria—interest, chronological considerations, logic, and difficulty—can be used to determine the sequence of instructional objectives. It should be pointed out that, for any individual student, the actual sequence within the lesson plan may differ from that of other students. The curriculum development effort should indicate only a recommended sequence of activities, which should be modified as needed for individual students.

The question of duration or the "how long" of the curriculum is closely related to the sequence question. Most of the questions concerning duration relate to the importance of the material. Some material is extremely important and valuable and is therefore seen continually throughout the curriculum. On the other hand, some material is good to know but is not as important. These are decisions that should be made by the curriculum development team in a tentative manner until detailed information is collected.

Selection of Instructional Procedures

The fourth step in the curriculum development process is the selection of instructional procedures. As noted earlier, this is a complex step. The first point to be considered in the selection of instructional procedures are the instructional objectives. These objectives may imply a certain kind of instructional procedure that is dependent upon the philosophy of the curriculum or of the teacher. Is the philosophy of the teacher one of shared responsibility with the learner?

Another point to be considered in the selection of instructional procedures is the subject matter itself. Does the nature of the content suggest a certain approach? Instructional support also needs to be considered. What facilities are available for the instruction? What is the class size? What other support services or materials are needed for instruction? Evaluation is another important consideration. Has evaluation been included in the instructional plan? Are evaluation plans tied to the objectives?

Perhaps the most important consideration in thinking about the teaching-learning process is the nature of the learners. What are the interests of the learners? Who are the students that will participate? Are there specific learning styles, needs, or interests that should be considered in the selection of the teaching-learning procedures? These are some, but not all, of the important factors that influence the selection of instructional procedures.

Evaluation Plans

The fifth step in the curriculum development process is the planning for evaluation. There are two essential aspects of daily instructional evaluations:

1. *The evaluation of the learner.* What kind of achievement did the learner have as a result of the instruction that was presented?
2. *The evaluation of the instructional process itself.* Was the instruction presented in such a way that the learner benefited from it? Are there ways that the instruction could be improved so that the learner might benefit more?

Both types of evaluation should be completed on each lesson and objective. Evaluations should be conducted on a daily basis and planned for in curriculum development.

In summary, the curriculum development process encompasses the development of goals, the selection of instructional objectives, the selection and organization of content, the selection of instructional procedures, and the planning for evaluation.

WHAT IS APPROPRIATE CONTENT FOR PROGRAM DEVELOPMENT?

The content for program development cuts across several jobs and vocational areas. The occupational content, the major component of special vocational needs instruction, will not be examined here. Some examples of other kinds of content that cut across job categories are:

- Simple counting
- Simple reading
- Measuring
- Simple message writing
- Using the telephone for calling, answering, and taking messages
- Alphabetically arranging by letter
- Serially arranging by number

These skills are broad-based and thus can be used in many different kinds of job settings and situations. There are many other more specific kinds of skills, probably not as broadly based as the ones listed above, that are equally important. Some examples of these specific skills are:

- Tying knots and bows in string or rope
- Simple sorting by physical property (color, size, and so on)
- Simple cleaning on hard surfaces with simple equipment and supplies
- Reading simple dials, gauges, and thermometers
- Locating or identifying by number, word, or other symbol
- Using simple hand tools
- Making change and counting money
- Telling time

A very important skill that has not been mentioned above is job seeking. Instruction in this skill should include: how to fill out job applications, how to make job applications, and how to perform on a job interview. This whole set of job seeking skills is vitally important to the special vocational needs student.

The types of skills we have cited have not traditionally been a part of all vocational education programs. They represent, however, the kinds of content that must be included in programs for special vocational needs youths. Many educators make the erroneous assumption that these types of skills do not require specific instructional time. In fact, they must receive specific attention; they should be a part of the instructional plan for every student who is not competent in them. The instructional plan should designate the person who has the responsibility for instructing in these skills. The structure of the program may indicate that the person best able to do this is the occupational teacher, an academic teacher, a counselor, a teacher assistant, or a specially designated person. In any case, this kind of instruction should be included in programs for special vocational needs students, and some specific person should have the responsibility for it.

The newspaper is an important educational tool that can assist in the instruction of these kinds of skills. The newspaper is a particularly appropriate aid for special vocational needs students because it is readily accessible and fairly inexpensive. It has an important advantage over many other materials in that it is both relevant and interesting. Many programs that have difficulty securing educational materials should consider a subscription to the daily newspaper for some of their students.

As instruction is begun, it is essential to the students' success that they be thoroughly guided in a general introduction to the kinds of information available in the newspaper. The introduction should include a teacher-guided exploration of the front page and the index, followed by an orientation to the different sections of the newspaper and to the material contained in each section. Below is a detailed explanation, with specific examples, of how a newspaper can be used to assist with instruction in the seven skills mentioned at the beginning of this section.

Job Related Skills: Newspaper Activities

Objective: The student will learn a number of job-related activities by using the newspaper.

Skill Areas:

1. Simple counting
2. Simple reading
3. Measuring
4. Simple message writing
5. Using the telephone for calling, answering, and taking messages
6. Alphabetically arranging by letter
7. Serially arranging by number

Skill Area 1

Activity 1—Simple counting

Find the Classified Section.

a. Look under "cars for sale." Circle all the Cameros for sale. How many are there? Record.
b. Which Camero is the *most* expensive? Record.
   Which is the *least* expensive? Record.
c. Look under "want ads." How many ads are there for waitresses/waiters? Record.
d. Pick any job you want. How many ads are there for it? Record.

Skill Area 2

Activity 2—Simple reading

a. Look at the Comic Section.
b. Find your favorite comic strip character.
c. What does he or she have to say today? Record.

Skill Area 3

Activity 3—Measuring

a. Find the Food Section.
b. Cut out all ads for flour, sugar, potatoes, and onions.
c. Circle the amount of pounds each weighs. Compare.
d. Which one is the heaviest? Record.
e. Which one is the lightest? Record.
f. Now compare two ads of equal amounts of pounds.
   Example: five lbs. of sugar with five lbs. of potatoes.
   Which costs more? Record.

Activity 4—Measuring

a. How wide is a newspaper column? How wide are three columns together? Record.
b. Cut out three columns from the front section. Measure their lengths. Record.
c. Which one is the longest? Which is the shortest? Record.

Skill Area 4

Activity 5—Simple message writing

a. Find the Classified section. Look under "help wanted" and pick any job that interests you. With a partner, take turns role-playing the following model: Student (1) is an applicant who telephones. Student (2) answers.
   (1) Asks for manager or person in charge of applications.
   (2) Answers that he is not in. "May I take a message?"
   (1) Tells (2) his or her name and asks if manager could call back.
   (2) Writes down (1)'s name and asks for telephone number.
   (1) Answers with own number.
   (2) Asks, "May I ask what are you calling about?"
   (Why do you want the manager?)
   (1) Answers appropriately.
   (2) Records answers, which should include student (1)'s name, telephone number, and reason for calling. Then says, "Thank you, goodbye."
   (1) "Good-bye."

Skill Area 5

Activity 6—Telephone use and simple writing

a. Turn to Classified Section.

b. Write your own help wanted ad according to the form in that section. Be sure to state:
   - What kind of job it is
   - How much it pays per week
   - What the hours are

Activity 7—Telephone use

Pick a partner and role-play the following situation. You will be the employer. Using your ad, your partner will call in to respond. Then alternate roles using the other person's ad. Record your dialogue.

- Caller: "What kind of job is it?"
- Employer: Answers according to the ad.
- Caller: "How much does it pay?"
- Employer: Answers according to the ad.
- Caller: "What are the hours?"
- Employer: Responds according to the ad.

Skill Area 6

Activity 8—Alphabetically arranging by letter

a. Find the Classified Section.
b. Cut out ten ads for cars you would like to buy.
c. Arrange the names of the cars alphabetically.
d. Record.

Skill Area 7

Activity 9—Serially arranging by number

a. Find the Classified Section.
b. Cut out five help wanted ads and circle the wage amounts.
c. Arrange on your paper from the highest paying to the lowest.

HOW CAN AFFECTIVE COMPETENCIES BE INCLUDED IN PROGRAM DEVELOPMENT?

Many professional educators and other specialists agree that one of the most critical areas for the future employment of special vocational needs youth is the area of affective competencies, that is, social skills, affective skills, or personality factors. What do we mean by these terms? Affective competencies are shown by how individuals get along with their coworkers and supervisors, how they get along with customers and the public, how they indicate their interest in their jobs, and how they take responsibility for what they are doing. These factors often make the difference between success and failure in the world of work. Many followup studies in the field of mental retardation and other mildly handicapping conditions indicate that persons with such conditions lose their jobs more often because of a lack of social skills, of knowing how to get along with coworkers or supervisors, or because of so called personality factors than they do because they are unable to do the job. Skills in the affective domain are thus clearly of vital importance for the success of special vocational needs youths in employment situations.

In the past, affective skills were not always taught effectively in vocational programs. Some educators even doubted that good work habits and positive attitudes could be taught in instructional programs. Many people thought that these skills develop naturally, but, in any case, are difficult to identify. However, good work habits, positive attitudes, and positive social skills can in fact be taught effectively to most individuals.

A.G. Porreca and J.J. Stollard have identified 29 affective competencies that have been perceived as important for vocational education students. These competencies, listed in Table 5-1 are the kinds of affective skills that should be included in instructional programs for special vocational needs youth.

The instructional strategy that should be used for any of these affective or social skills is one in which the students are first assessed in relationship to the specific skills or competencies. Following the assessment, which should give an indication of the performance of the student, an appropriate training method or a combination of training methods must be chosen. Some examples of appropriate methods are behavioral modification, role-playing, and counseling. Once the skills and instructional strategies have been identified, it is important to recognize that the skills are not learned quickly. The practice of the skills must be reinforced on a day-to-day basis. Evaluation or behavioral data should be collected for each student. The purpose of the data is to monitor instruction and to record any changes that may occur. In these ways, social and affective competencies can and must be included in vocational programs for special needs students.

HOW SHOULD TEACHING-LEARNING ACTIVITIES BE PLANNED?

The basic premise of learning by students with any kind of learning difficulty is that each child learns differently; all pupils do not learn best through the same method or by the use of the same techniques. The ideal toward which programs should be striving is instruction that is modified for each pupil. Curricula should be flexible enough so that a variety of instructional approaches can be used. It is particularly important that new knowledge, ideas, or information be presented in a variety of ways so that the pupils' initial encounter with the new knowledge or information has meaning for them. As material is presented, opportunities should be made available for students to consolidate their learning and practice the skills they have learned. In vocational education, it is extremely important that students be given ample opportunity to reflect upon and apply their new skills.

Table 5-1 Common Affective Domain Competencies of Students in Vocational Areas

1. Develops some awareness of evaluating interests and abilities with realistic occupational goals.
2. Accepts need for accuracy in businesses, industry, and education.
3. Generates work independently without constant supervision.
4. Practices care of occupational possessions (tools).
5. Follows directions.
6. Displays promptness in work.
7. Practices safe work habits.
8. Practices a safetyminded and knowledgeable approach to work at all times.
9. Practices good health habits.
10. Practices care for good personal appearance, character traits, and attitudes.
11. Possesses a sense of responsibility for providing service.
12. Assumes responsibility for the property and safety of the customer.
13. Gains personal satisfaction from gainful employment.
14. Displays personal desire to get along with others.
15. Derives personal satisfaction in accomplishment of quality of work.
18. Accepts the need to verify work in business accuracy.
19. Prefers positive attitudes about work.
20. Accepts dignity of work.
21. Accepts and practices loyalty, honesty, and trustworthiness.
22. Maintains sound professional conduct.
23. Holds information confidential in his/her work.
24. Attempts to utilize effective decision-making processes.
25. Utilizes the ability to think through problems.
26. Displays realistic desire to work.
27. Develops resourcefulness in the work environment.
28. Understands the concept of work and the human satisfaction found in work.
29. Demonstrates perseverance in accomplishing a job.

Source: A.G. Porreca and J.J. Stollard, *Common Affective Domain Competencies of Students Among Vocational Areas,* final report, research series no. 47 (Nashville, Tenn.: Tennessee State Board of Education, Tennessee Research Coordinating Unit, University of Tennessee, College of Education, 1975), pp. 16-18.

The techniques of devising teaching-learning activities that provide multiple learning opportunities and multiple teaching techniques are difficult to develop. One recognized need is that for instructional support materials. Examples of such materials are simple information sheets and audio or video tapes that supplement instruction. These may include diagrams, definitions, names, or other important material that would not normally be provided to the students. For poor readers, audio tapes may be used in conjunction with information sheets. Video tapes can be used to demonstrate specific vocational skills.

A second, more elaborate technique is the development of a well-illustrated minitext that contains the most important information related to a particular vocational instructional area. Students working in that area will then be able to refer to this text. The same technique is applicable in the production of audio and video tapes. Often, such supplementary material can supply the more explicit information needed by students who have learning difficulties and can help them to understand difficult concepts. It can also help students to become more proficient in demonstrating the skills that are expected of them. Thus, such supplementary material makes it possible to integrate simple but important theory with hands-on experience.

There is no one correct method of instruction for all special vocational needs youth. The criterion for evaluation is whether or not the student has achieved the instructional objective. If the student has done so, the instruction can be evaluated as satisfactory. In other words, the best method of instruction is a failure if the student does not accomplish the objective.

An important concept that has recently been developed and implemented in the field of special education is the Individual Educational Program (IEP). The use of IEPs is mandated in Public Law 94-142 for handicapped students. The best way to understand the IEP concept is to examine its components. These are:

- A statement of the student's present level of educational performance. This includes academic achievement, social adaptation, prevocational and vocational skills, psychomotor skills and self-help skills.
- A statement of the annual goals that describe the educational performance to be achieved by the end of the school year.
- A statement of short-term instructional objectives.
- A statement of specific educational services needed by the student. This includes all special education and related services, any special instructional media or materials, and the vocational education program in which the student may participate.
- The date when the above services will begin and the length of time they will be provided.
- A description of the extent to which the student will participate in regular education programs.
- A justification for the type of educational placement that the student will experience.
- A list of individuals who are responsible for the implementation of the IEP.
- Objective criteria for evaluation and schedules for review of the IEP.

The IEP is legally required for all special education students. It is also a mechanism that can be used in developing teaching-learning activities. Vocational educators, special educators, and others must be involved in developing the IEP.

Vocational educators are thereby given an opportunity to formulate long-range goals and instructional objectives to meet those goals. An appropriate curriculum can be extremely helpful in writing IEPs.

Planning for teaching-learning activities may be summarized by reviewing three important factors.

1. The first factor is the instructional objectives. These objectives guide the whole instructional process. Teaching-learning activities must be consistent with the stated objectives. The activities should utilize various kinds of experiences and various arrangements for instruction.
2. A second important factor is the teacher. The curriculum and teaching-learning activities should not be entirely planned with one teacher in mind. Flexibility must be included to allow for differences in philosophies, preparation, and backgrounds of teachers.
3. The third factor, and perhaps the most important, is the nature of the individual learner. Regardless of the amount of planning that has gone into the teaching-learning activities, if they are not appropriate for the individual learners, they will be unsuccessful. It is not enough to design activities merely for a handicapping condition, such as visually handicapped or disadvantaged. Teaching-learning activities must rather be developed for the individual skills and competencies that the learners possess.

WHAT DOES EVALUATION HAVE TO DO WITH PROGRAM DEVELOPMENT?

Evaluation is the final component of program development. In evaluation, five simple questions must be answered: Why? Who? What? When? and How?

Why

Evaluation is a continuous and integral part of the program- and curriculum-planning process. This process must be a systems process. This means that we have to continually collect data, use that data to make decisions, and then implement those decisions in the program. This is particularly important in programs that involve special vocational needs youth, because the population is not uniform or homogeneous. Therefore, educators must continually develop procedures, processes, and objectives; implement those procedures, processes, and objectives; and then make decisions based on that implementation. In order to make those decisions, evaluation is necessary. Based thereon, changes in the procedures, processes, and objectives can be made whenever necessary. Evaluation must include a number of people, and it must be continuous. The people involved must be dedicated and believe that the results of the evaluation process are going to be used.

Evaluation is the only process that enables curriculum development to be ongoing. Typically, curricula are written and then put on bookshelves, in closets or into corners. This occurs because they have not been made a part of the instructional process, and data have not been gathered to change them periodically. Unless these steps are taken, the curricula will not be used or implemented. The ongoing process is also inhibited when curricula are printed in final form and bound in books whose pages cannot be changed easily. We recommend that curricula be printed on loose-leaf pages and placed in a loose-leaf binder so that the pages can be printed over and over again and replaced easily. In this way, dynamic curricula can be maintained. If the curriculum is not dynamic and cannot be changed, it will not be used, and the whole curriculum-development process will be a waste of time.

Who

The "who" part of the evaluation question involves everyone. Teachers, learners, parents, administrators, and consultants should be members of teams for program evaluation as well as for program development. Like the other aspects of program development, evaluation should be broad-based and cooperative.

Though it is seldom used, one technique for utilizing evaluation involves the evaluation of vocational teachers by their immediate administrators. Teacher evaluation should be a part of both program and curriculum evaluation. For example, a part of the teachers' evaluation should focus on their utilization of the curriculum and the amount of data they have collected regarding that curriculum. Teachers should also gather data on the instructional process and then use the information to revise their instructional techniques. This model of program development requires that the teacher collect daily data on content, techniques, and procedures. The teachers must be active in the total program evaluation process, and their evaluations should reflect the extent of their involvement.

The data to which teachers have access is necessary for program development. Assume, for example, that evaluations are made on the extent of student achievement on four objectives. The evaluations show that three of the objectives were mastered by 90 percent of the students and one was mastered by only 25 percent. From this data, it is clear that a change must be made. Supplemental information from the teachers is needed on student reactions and other factors. In a discussion with the teachers, based on notes they have made, the following comments might be contributed concerning the objective mastered by only 25 percent of the students:

- Not enough opportunities were given for practice.
- Materials were too difficult.

- The learning experiences were presented in the wrong order.
- The assessment materials were inappropriate.
- The meaning of the instructional objectives was not clear to the teacher.

This kind of data is absolutely necessary if the curriculum and program are to be revised in any systematic way. If the curriculum and program are not so revised, they will not be utilized as intended.

What

The next question concerns the "what" of the curriculum or program. In working with special vocational needs youth, more than academic achievement must be assessed. Thus, in the program development process, not only is academic achievement included, but also affective competencies and job related skills. Paper and pencil activities are a poor way of assessing most of the objectives of a program for special vocational needs students. But, as one moves away from the use of paper and pencil instruments, other instruments will have to be developed by the teachers, administrators, and implementers of the program. Because they will be teacher-prepared or locally prepared, such instruments will not have the sophistication of commercially prepared instruments. Nevertheless, they can be useful in providing the data necessary for the evaluation process.

As we have noted, pupil achievement is not the only element that should be assessed. Teachers, other personnel, materials, facilities, the educational environment, the process of the curriculum, and goals—all should be included in the assessment. This means a wide range of data that is continually collected and evaluated. A portion of the required data can be collected by the teacher merely sitting for five minutes at the end of each day and writing comments.

When

The key word for the "when" of evaluation is "always." Evaluation should be continuous; data should be continually collected, interpreted, and evaluated. Ongoing decision making should continuously upgrade the program and the curriculum.

There are three sophisticated sounding words that indicate when evaluations should be conducted: diagnostic, formative, and summative. Diagnostic evaluations are made before instruction or before the program is presented. Formative evaluation is made during instruction to assess both the progress and the problems. Summative evaluation occurs at the end of instruction or at the end of a unit to determine to what degree the objectives have been obtained.

How

The last question is the "how" of evaluation. One of the most important questions here is related to the interpretation of data. There are a number of ways of interpreting evaluative material. Three such methods are through norm-referenced, criterion-referenced and individual-referenced interpretation.

1. Norm-referenced interpretation compares the achievement of an individual with other individuals of similar age, background, or circumstances. This type of interpretation is not very appropriate when working with special vocational needs populations, because appropriate norms have not been developed and the populations are not homogeneous. All visually handicapped individuals are not the same, all disadvantaged individuals are not the same, and all mentally retarded individuals are not the same. In fact, all of these groups are clearly heterogeneous.
2. Criterion-referenced evaluation measures the individual's achievement of objectives. In a broad sense, a type of criterion-referenced evaluation is used when it is decided that certain competencies are necessary for an individual to be employed. For example, students might be required to do eight different kinds of activities before they are eligible for employment. In this case, they are evaluated in terms of the number and quality of the activities they accomplish. This type of evaluation is appropriate for special vocational needs students.
3. Another technique that can be used to evaluate vocational needs students is one that we call individual-referenced evaluation. In this type of evaluation the students are evaluated against themselves. The amount of progress that the students have made in the curriculum over a period of time can be determined by comparing the number of objectives they were able to achieve when they entered the program with the number of objectives they were able to achieve at the end of the program.

All three types of evaluation can be useful in special vocational needs programs. However, criterion-referenced evaluation *must* be used with the curriculum to assess the objectives. It must also be used, to some extent, to assess how well, when, or if the student is ready for employment. On the other hand, individual-referenced evaluation is helpful in assessing how well the student is learning.

An innovative concept that is sometimes used in vocational education—and hopefully will be used more in the future—is the concept of the open-entry/open-exit curriculum. This means that the student can enter or exit at any time during the school year. This is a necessity in many vocational special needs programs in which students are assessed throughout the school year and in which it is difficult to arrange that they be admitted or leave only at a certain time.

With an open-entry/open-exit concept, criterion-referenced evaluation assumes a greater importance. Individual-referenced evaluation also gains in importance, in that the number of competencies or objectives that the students were able to accomplish at the beginning of the program can be assessed and compared to their performance after various periods of time. For example, it might be determined that the students have accomplished an adequate number of competencies and that they should therefore be continued in the program. If the program is for one year, and the students have accomplished one-half of the program's objectives, then for those students the program should become a two-year program. In this way, progress that the students have made is compared to the initial objectives that they were able to accomplish.

SUMMARY

Program development includes curriculum development, job-related activities, affective competencies, and any other occupationally related experiences provided by the school program. The program for a special vocational needs student should include direct instruction as well as other learning opportunities that are experienced as a result of the school program. The development of such a program should require the participation of teachers, learners, parents, administrators, and consultants. Broad participation should be encouraged to make it an educational process for all involved. Such participation will increase the base of information for the process and produce a type of psychological ownership of the product that will be helpful when the program is implemented. A diagram of program development is presented in Figure 5-1.

As a part of the program, the curriculum includes the plan for instruction in the skill competencies and knowledges. The first step, development of goals, should include survey data from program graduates as well as from state and local industries. The second step, selection of instructional objectives, concerns a strategy of task analysis that is important for the specification of objectives. The third step, selection and organization of the content, has to do with decisions about the sequence and duration of activities. Appropriate information for such decisions can come only from the interaction of the curriculum with students. The fourth step is the selection of instructional procedures. The fifth step concerns planning for evaluation.

The content of a program should include the occupational content as well as the job-related skills and competencies that are a part of the affective domain. Simple reading and message writing are examples of this type of content that often are not included in programs because of the erroneous assumption that specific instructional time is not needed for teaching these skills. The daily newspaper is relevant here and can be used productively for instruction of many of these skills. The lack

Figure 5-1 Program Development

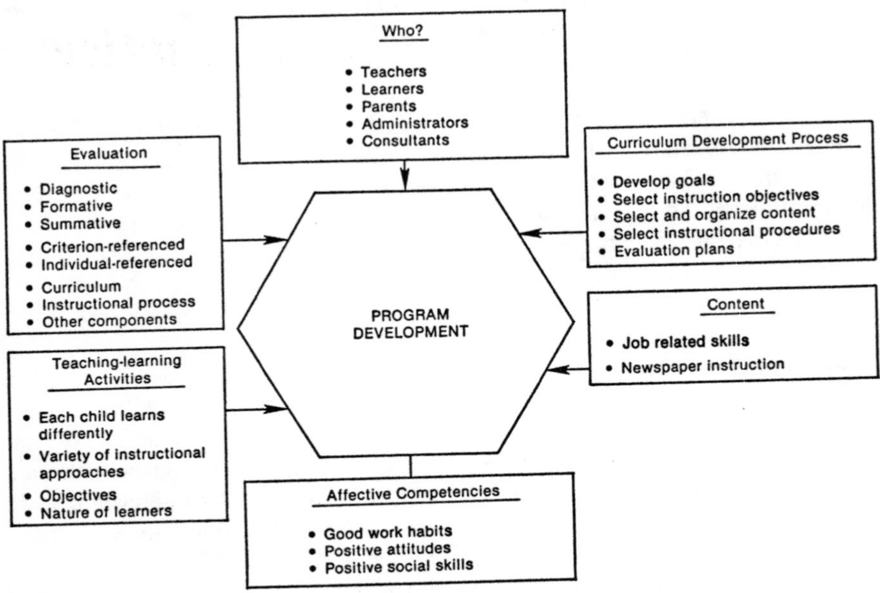

of social skills and of certain personality factors have often been cited as reasons why special vocational needs individuals lose their jobs. In our view, good work habits, positive attitudes, and positive social skills can in fact be taught effectively to most individuals.

Planning for teaching-learning activities and evaluation is based on the premise that each child learns differently. This requires that the curriculum be flexible in order to accommodate a variety of instructional approaches. The use of IEPs for handicapped students should provide a mechanism for planning and developing teaching-learning activities. The instructional objectives, the teacher, and the nature of the individual learners should receive the most attention when planning these activities. Evaluation should be continuous and enable the program to be implemented and constantly revised. The program is designed as a systems process that requires constant feedback, revision, and implementation. Criterion-referenced and individual-referenced interpretation should be used in the diagnostic, formative, and summative evaluations that are a part of the program for special vocational needs youth.

Chapter 6

Curriculum Modification and Instructional Practices

Karen L. Stern-Otazo, Ed.D.

INTRODUCTION

In this chapter we will examine some curricular and instructional ideas as they apply in working with students with special vocational needs. The purpose is to help develop a framework for the special needs teacher to meet some of the individual needs of students enrolled in vocational programs.

The thrust of the chapter is that special needs students should be accommodated in the regular classroom with minimal support. Although such students may need some individualized instruction, they are able to benefit from most of the day-to-day experiences in the regular setting.

The first section discusses the concept of curriculum and its relation to the instructional process. The following sections deal with instructional practices that can be applied when dealing with special needs youth. In this context, some selected solutions are offered to a few of the more common teaching problems faced by vocational educators as they respond to the very real and pressing daily learning needs of their students.

CRITERIA FOR SELECTION OF CURRICULUM

Curriculum is defined as the content of a vocational education course or program that is structured as a series of intended outcomes. More specifically, curriculum is defined as the organized content of a particular discipline that establishes parameters for instruction. Curriculum is thus concerned with ends. It is the content that the learner must master to reach desired occupational goals.

The needs of both the occupational world and the individual being served by the program must be considered in the selection of curriculum content. The following criteria are not all inclusive, but they represent important considerations for selection of curriculum:

1. Needs of the Job/Occupational Cluster:
   - Content is based on selected tasks of a given job or cluster of jobs whose commonalities are critical for successful employment.
   - Critical tasks are verified through local, state, or regional research matched against national task listings. These can be obtained from national curriculum centers.
   - The job(s)/occupation(s) selected for analysis must have a ten-year forecasted existence.
   - The resultant employment—after training—will sustain the individual above a poverty wage level.
   - There are sufficient placement opportunities within a geographic region.
   - The occupations or job(s) require initial education and training of not less than six weeks and not more than two years for the average student.
   - There is evidence of community support for the program.
   - There is evidence that the curriculum, when programmed, will be supported financially.
   - There is evidence that qualified personnel can be hired to facilitate the teaching-learning processes.
   - There is evidence that the state board for vocational education will approve the curriculum as part of a recognized service or program area.
2. Needs of the individual:
   - Content can be organized in terms of tasks and performance objectives and programmed as units to help the individual reach milestone objectives.
   - Content selected as three emphases for the individual: (a) need for occupational competencies, (b) level for personal interest/growth/development, (c) need for personal interest, growth, and development.
     a. Need for occupational competencies: The individual's need for occupational competencies is determined by the goals negotiated with an individual. The goals are dependent on the level or area that the individual wants or is capable of mastering and will continue to be negotiated as milestones or achievements are reached.
     b. Level of general education development: Several components of learning skills must exist before learning takes place. These prerequisites include general education development, which can be incorporated into the course curriculum by emphasizing the skill processes along with the vocational content.
     c. Need for personal interest, growth, and development: Vocational competencies do not exist in a box apart from the rest of the individual's life. While the students are being prepared to enter the world of

work, they are, at the same time, managing the rest of their lives. Daily living competencies, job seeking and keeping skills, consumer skills, and leisure time use are just some of the personal needs that can be incorporated into curriculum objectives to dovetail with traditional vocational objectives.

Curriculum Modification; Goals and Objectives

There is a sequence of events that leads to learning. First, there must be a curriculum in existence; even if there is no written curriculum, there is an unwritten one. Overwhelmingly, the goals and objectives of vocational curricula are based on the competencies needed for entry-level employment in the vocational areas:

- Goals are set with which the learner and the teacher can be comfortable.
- The teacher facilitates the learning process as the learner is exposed to and uses many instructional procedures and adaptations to reach the goal of learning necessary competencies.
- When a goal is reached, there are rewarding consequences for the learner in terms of grades and other rewards.
- When consequences are not satisfying, when goals are not met, several alternatives are possible: (1) There may be alternative ways to reach goals, perhaps with the aid of support personnel and other approaches. (2) The same material may be repeated. (3) Goals may be altered so that lower level competencies are substituted.

Curriculum modification takes place when goals and competencies are selected, met, and changed and when there are choices in the instructional practices that affect those goals and competencies. Table 6-1 presents some of the criteria used in curriculum modifications.[1]

When we learn, there are changes in the cognitive, psychomotor, and affective behaviors of an individual. The three types of behavior may be defined as follows:

- Cognitive: thinking, reasoning, solving problems, remembering, learning concepts or principles, and using these to understand new experiences.
- Psychomotor: all muscle activity, like walking, handwriting, talking and typewriting.
- Affective: attitudes, emotions, values, interests, and motives.

All of these behaviors are present whenever learning takes place. When, however, too many of them are incompatible with the individual's own learning situation, partial learning or no learning takes place.

Table 6-1 Adapting Curricula for Learner Differences

1. *Differences that must be considered when selecting and implementing choices among students of different ages:*

Younger students	Older students
Forced attendance	Voluntary attendance
Dependent self concept	More mature self concept
Fewer experiences	Higher expectations of school
Less willing to take chances	More life experiences
	More willing to take risks

2. *Physical abilities:*
   - Differences in physical strength, manual dexterity, balance, and endurance
   - Sensory disabilities in vision, hearing, smell, taste, and touch
   - Perceptual difficulties, that is, where there is not a sensory problem but rather a "short circuit" between the sense, like sight, and the information that goes to the brain, resulting in garbled information

3. *Intellectual abilities:*
   - Variations in the *rate* of learning
   - Variations in thė ultimate degree of competency within a reasonable length of time

3. *Other abilities:*
   - Communication skills
   - Social skills
   - Coping skills
   - Everyday living skills
   - Job-related skills

4. *Differences in cultural background:*
   - Societal differences
   - Differences among subcultures in the society:
     - racial minority groups
     - urban-rural differences
     - socioeconomic differences
     - different national heritages
     - differing customs, morals, attitudes, practices, and traditions
     - differences among the members of a subgroup

5. *Differences in family socioeconomic level:*
   - Individuals in the class will come from all socioeconomic levels
   - Socioeconomic backgrounds can affect needs, attitudes, and expectations
   - Middle-class expectations about jobs and vocational training may differ from those of lower socioeconomic groups
   - Students from lower-income families may have physical needs, such as hunger, that interfere with learning

Table 6-1 continued

6. *Differences in educational background:*
   - Vocational students differ in the amount and quality of previous formal education and experiential (at home or elsewhere) education
   - Students may have learning problems that have prevented them from learning what would be expected of them
   - Postsecondary students have widely varying educational backgrounds:
     - students may have dropped out of high school
     - some have graduated and others have an equivalent degree
     - some have been involved in community college courses, technical courses, graduate school, apprenticeship programs, military training, or training programs in business and industry
     - kind and amount of education greatly affect the length of course, examples to be used and understood, the vocabulary that can be used or taught, and the level of abstraction that might be meaningful

7. *Differences in motivation:*
   - Motivation and needs are closely related
   - Motivation is the combination of needs and desires that move the individual to do something that will satisfy those needs and desires
   - Motivation is within the individual
   - Environmental factors can be manipulated to help individuals develop their own motivation (contracts and rewards)
   - Generally, the more highly motivated the individual, the greater the learning that takes place; however, it is hard to climb mountains every day

8. *Differences in personalities:*
   - Individuals differ in traits like perseverance, curiosity, self-confidence, level of aspiration, and aggressiveness
   - These factors are similar to motivation in relation to learning
   - These traits occur spontaneously

9. *Differences in interests:*
   - Individuals differ in their interests
   - How much student interests should determine what is planned and taught is a controversial question

10. *Differences in aptitudes:*
    - An aptitude is an existing potential that, with practice and training, may result in good or superior performance
    - Aptitudes can be identified from standardized testing and by careful observation
    - Individuals may show aptitudes for varied areas; an individual may have no aptitude for English but may have an aptitude for mechanics

11. *Differences in self-concepts:*
    - What individuals do and how they behave are determined by their self-picture or concept

Table 6-1 continued

- Individuals will tend to start acting as others expect them to act (if you are told often enough that you are a failure, you will expect to fail)
- Individuals may have an idea, often conceived as an ideal self, of how they should be
- Problems arise when the self-concept and the ideal concept conflict

12. *Differences in vocational maturity:*
    - Individuals differ in their knowledge of vocations and career ladders and in how much planning and training they have done before enrolling in a vocational program

13. *Differences in learning styles:*
    - Prefers working alone or in groups
    - Is better able to learn by seeing, by hearing information, or by touching and working with something, or all three
    - Solves problems quickly or by carefully thinking them through
    - Desires to be competitive or to avoid competition
    - Cares about details or deals in generalities
    - Cares about approval and worries about being wrong
    - Has little tolerance for frustration and followthrough
    - Observes rules rigidly and needs constant supervision
    - Performs well on a variety of tasks and evaluates own performance

Source: Keller and Bennett, "Curriculum Modules: Planning Instructional Processes, Design, Development, Diffusion, Evaluation," 1978 (revised 1979).

The individual differences in learning mentioned above are important factors to be considered in selecting curriculum. Curriculum is not a series of information chunks to be fed to students; in vocational education, this too often leads to the view that the curriculum is merely the content or subject to be taught. When individual differences among learners are not considered, the impact of the curriculum on the special needs learner will not be as effective as it could be.

INSTRUCTIONAL PRACTICES

Instructional practices can be defined as the process of presenting and facilitating learning experiences for the student. As one works with special vocational needs (handicapped or disadvantaged) students, one automatically facilitates instruction. The role becomes increasingly that of a diagnostician and manager of learning. With experience, individual planning with individual attention can become easy.

With students who are aware of their own goals, their expectations and the quantity of instruction will naturally vary. The students' reading, writing, motor, or memorizing abilities will be displayed in varying degrees by the time they are encountered in a vocational setting. Thus, vocational teachers will have different expectations and goals for their students, defined according to the students' individual abilities.

Modifications of goals and materials are contingent upon an open student-teacher relationship. Goals should be negotiated and evaluated constantly to enable students to work at levels of which they are capable. At the same time, alternative levels and types of performance should be negotiated to prevent frustration and loss of motivation. Although negotiation is time-consuming, it helps to keep communication lines open and motivation high.

Many instructors who work with special needs students do not realize that their efforts and hard work now can result in substantial savings for everyone concerned in the long run. A student's sense of personal failure and the need for social rehabilitation will be far more costly than the time or energy it will take in advance to avoid such outcomes.

Many academic and vocational instructors unconsciously modify their teaching styles when dealing with students who have weak reading or writing skills. Some deliberate modifications that have been successful are outlined in the following sections.

Readability

In the classroom, the instructor will have students reading at many different grade levels. To help match their differing abilities with the instructional materials, some of the following suggestions might be considered:

- Evaluate the readability (reading level) of all chapters of a text, manual, pamphlet, or handout.
- Have materials available at many reading levels—from elementary to college level.
- Record lectures.
- Have recordings of texts available. These may be obtained commercially or students can record for extra credit.
- Request easier-to-read materials from publishing companies.
- Note that texts that are easier to read at any reading level usually have the following characteristics: (1) pages with enough blank space so as not to be confusing (this is especially true when there are pictures or diagrams involved); (2) bold print, capital letters, or different colored ink for important subject headings; (3) vocabulary in bold print or defined on the same page it is

used or at the end of the chapter; (4) a glossary and index (the glossary should include a guide to pronunciation).

There are several different methods by which you can determine the readability of instructional material. The instructor should check with the special needs personnel of the school, the vocational director, or the state department of education consultant. Readability is not at all difficult to determine and will save both the instructor and students hours of frustration and difficulty.

Support Services and Resources

Most school systems, depending on their size and economic capabilities, have some sort of support service available for students with special learning needs. Depending on the availability of talent and the needs of the student, one or more individuals might be called upon to help with the instruction of a particular student or group of students.

The instructor should explore the specific capabilities of the support staff, not only in terms of immediate needs, but also in terms of the students' broader interests. A speech clinician with whom the author has worked had an interest in electronics because of her involvement with electronic hearing devices. She was thus able to give an hour or two of instruction each week to a student in electronics.

There may also be available individuals who can be called upon from time to time to aid, without pay, specific students within the classroom or shop setting. If it is possible to pay these individuals with money or other incentives, all the better. Thus, student "buddies" who can help with directions or with notetaking may receive extra "As" for their work.

Some of the more common support services and resources are: reading, hearing, or vision specialists; resource room teachers; vocational and regular counselors; speech clinicians or therapists; psychologists; vocational evaluators; aides; interpreters (for those using sign languages or for nonEnglish speakers); community aides, including retired persons, Future Teachers of America, or other service groups; and other students in the class.

Learning Style

An important consideration in curriculum selection, learning style diagnosis is also vital in adapting instructional practices. The many factors that affect the learning process must be taken into consideration when planning instructional activities. These factors are elements within the student that can affect the rate and efficiency of learning. They may not all be important on any given day, and some may change with time and experience. However, all of them can and do affect learning and should not be discounted.[2]

Choosing What To Teach

Whether instructors are teaching specific vocabulary related to a vocational skill, the skill itself, or some related living skill that the special needs student may require to survive in the real world, they are constantly making decisions about what to teach. Often, it seems there will never be enough time to teach the students everything they need to succeed on the job. With some students, the instructor may be doubly frustrated because they need so much help.

Following are some suggested parameters for selecting and prioritizing what to teach.

Necessity

Is the particular skill, process, information, vocabulary, or concept necessary on a day-to-day basis for survival on the job and in the world? Of course, there are many gradations of necessity, depending on the student. For one student, understanding the pay stub and having a concept of time may be the skills most needed by that student to survive on the job. For another, maintaining accounting books in order to run a business successfully may be an important survival skill. Decisions on these questions should be made in conjunction with the student and others so that, when the "buck stops" at the end of the secondary or postsecondary school, the student can get along in the world.

Frequency

Though the particular skill, vocabulary, information, or concept may not be a necessity in the student's program, does it appear frequently enough in the program's operations to warrant teaching it just because it might be required when the student is out on the job? The consideration of frequency is especially important in teaching the spelling of words. How often will these words have to be spelled? If there will often be someone to help the student with a particular operation, is it necessary for the student to learn to do the operation in advance? If a student has to fill out a request for a Social Security card only once in a lifetime, is it necessary to teach that skill? Why not just have the student seek help with it? If filling out job applications is a difficult task for students, why not just give them a card with most of the relevant information and not force them to memorize it? Filling out applications may not be a frequently used, crucial skill, but filling out time cards may be. The skill to fill out loan applications may never be used, because most loan officers fill them out for you.

Relevance

Special needs students relate much more to classwork that has some direct relation to their daily lives. Bus and train schedules, menus, telephone directories, electric and other bills, all have more meaning if they are from the home town of the students. By including class members in stories about what is being studied that day or week, greater attention can be generated among the students. Having the students relate some of their in- and out-of-class experiences to include some of what the instructor is teaching can also make the lesson more relevant. It is important for students to see the connection between what they are learning and what they will have to be able to do on the job.

Presenting Information

The instructor can create an atmosphere in which students can ask questions by:

- allowing three minutes for questions whenever an assignment is given,
- allowing students to question one another whenever they are not sure of an assignment (the buddy system),
- making it a habit to ask one student to explain each assignment, and
- tape recording directions or lessons for students to listen to when necessary.

As instructors give directions or information, they can write symbols to represent the information on the board. It is best to have standard symbols every time that directions are given. Examples are:

Read:

Write: A B C D

Answer questions: ?

Study:

Those students who have trouble reading will benefit from graphics. Beyond that, graphics can make the whole class more attentive and aware of the directions or information from the instructor. For example:

- *Underlining*–to emphasize specific information, the action words in directions, or material to memorize.
- *Color code*—for memorizing, to show sequence of relationships.

- *"Hi–Lighting"*—with yellow, green, pink, or blue "hi-lighter" pen (ideal for pinpointing all the vital information in a chapter; the main ideas, important lists, vocabulary, and vital facts can be "hi-lighted" to help the students know what is important to study).
- *Lines and arrows*—to emphasize important information.
- *Index cards*—to cover material already read and to note key words and vocabulary so that the student is not tempted to continually look back while reading.
- *Masks*—to cover up part of the print on the page so that the important part stands out with no distractions.

Basic Mathematic Skills

All techniques that help with organizational learning carry over into the mathematical area. However, mathematics, like spelling, benefits from repetition. Here are some recommendations:

- If students are unable to complete an entire assignment, offer a choice of doing any 10 out of 20 problems or the top or bottom half of a page.
- Have a daily timed quiz (two or three minutes) at the beginning of the class. Each day have the students correct the quizzes themselves. Make the time allotment not quite enough for most of them to complete the quizzes. Give the same quiz four days in a row or give the same problems and only change the numbers. Grade on the last day.
- Concentrate on what the student is ready for.
- By the eleventh grade, bypass what the student is having trouble with by using calculators, tables, pocket charts, and so on.
- Check for the basics like: telling time, reading numbers up to six-place whole numbers and decimals to one-thousandths, knowing basic geometric shapes, reading and using the ruler to 1/32 of an inch, measuring temperature, and estimating time.
- Check for understanding of the math vocabulary. List the vocabulary and define at the beginning of class.
- Present materials in an organized, step-by-step way. List and number the steps.
- Make the symbols clear and understandable.
- If students reverse numbers or mislay them during operations, have them use graph paper or work the operation in a tic-tac-toe configuration.
- Have the student say the problem out loud and verbally indicate the steps.
- If the emphasis is on process and accuracy, allow extra time and the use of a calculator.
- Use oral tests in which students can explain process and pin point problems.

- Use practical and money-related problems, especially word problems.
- Talk through word problems; draw a chart to show the reasoning.
- Practice with formulas, and make the formulas understandable by putting them into common terms.

Testing

Students are not motivated to learn by failure, especially by frequent failure. Instructors can set up situations in which a test can be a learning situation. In such situations, alternatives should be allowed for credit. Below are some examples of such tests:

- On written work, lightly correct errors in pencil or erase the incorrect answer and allow the student to correct.
- Grade when the written work is handed in the second time.
- Grade all corrected parts with one-half the credits rather than no credit.
- Grade as quickly as possible, preferably with the student present.
- Do not permit a third student, who may not be flexible, to grade; either the instructor or the student who took the test should grade.
- If the submitted work seems hopeless, throw the work out and reteach the student; or have a replay with a videotape of your first presentation.
- At times, analyze what seems to have been missed and attack only that aspect (a rerun may only take a few minutes). Check out your perception of what was not understood with the student.
- As a standard technique, have separate tests for each student with individual names written on the test so that you can individualize and make the tests of more capable students longer.
- Involve the students in making up tests.
- Type tests and make sure that there is plenty of empty space around the questions so that they stand out.
- Make sure that directions are repeated each time there is a new section of the text, a new page, or more than ten questions.
- Underline the important verbs in your directions (e.g., <u>choose</u>).
- At the end of the term, give many smaller tests instead of one long one.
- Do not introduce new materials on the day of the test.
- Use clear and simple language that reflects vocabulary learned during the unit.
- Grade notebooks and folders rather than give occasional exams.
- Test for affective skills as well as cognitive skills (i.e., the important skills that go with a job, like being on time).
- Review before the test. Give a specific outline of concepts and terms to be tested.

- Give the test, or have it given, orally to students with low reading levels. Make sure that students understand exactly what the test questions are asking.
- Allow students to be responsible for only a portion of the test or allow them extended time.
- Make the choices short so that the reading problems don't hinder the student (multiple choice or matching may be easier than essay; recognition is easier than recall). Make sure the matching questions look similar to the following:

Computer Operation

1. Performs console operations	a. Copiers
2. Performs troubleshooting operations	b. Consoles
3. Performs peripheral operations	c. Emergency test
4. Performs storage functions	d. Card punches
5. Performs other data processing functions	e. Sorters

- Since we read from left to right in English, put the longer part of the matching test on the left so that the students do not have to read through long choices when they read through the choices on the right.
- Try to have tests that can be used later in an instructional manner.
- Make the first questions easier so that the student is not quickly discouraged.
- Discuss the area of test taking with the students. Allow them to tape the answers if that is their choice.
- Include bonus questions, especially for more able students.
- Use clear, understandable language that makes each section's direction very clear and specific.
- Type tests, if possible. Space questions so that the answers needed are obvious. Provide lined paper for essay tests.
- Give grades for long term projects, like notebooks, on which students can seek help to improve (grades can be a motivational factor, but they can also be scary).
- Give open notebook exams. These might approximate the real life ability to locate information in a manual.
- Use "contract" and independent assignments.

- To help the marginal student, contract for gradual improvements; ask for some low performance activity first, use positive reinforcement (no student wants to fail).
- Remember: "lazy," "indifferent," or "rebellious" students may just be afraid of failure.

An Alternative

Students who have handicapping or disadvantaging conditions that may prevent them from succeeding in the regular vocational education program may participate in an alternative student evaluation system. This includes students who receive special assistance or services but are still having difficulty succeeding in the program. Nevertheless, they need credit for their class time. This may include students in special education who are physically handicapped, mentally handicapped, learning disabled, severely emotionally disturbed, hearing impaired, or visually impaired. These are the students who have been previously identified by special education services and are enrolled in regular vocational education classes at a career education center. Credit for class time is granted on the basis of a number of minimum performance objectives met. Grades are not specifically related to performance objectives.[3]

Following are the major points of the evaluation system:

- Minimum performance objectives are established for each semester in vocational programs. These objectives represent entry-level performance for each job (using business and industry standards).
- Letter grades are used only to assess quality or job traits. Grades *A, B, C, D,* and *F* may be used by the instructor as appropriate in a particular occupational program. In another program, the instructor might use only an *A* or *F*. However, students may also be graded on the quality of their work or on job traits, such as attitude, persistence, creativity, independence, ability to work with others, accuracy, reliability, initiative, responsibility, promptness, and attendance.

ORGANIZATION AND PLANNING SKILLS

At times, everyone is faced with choices that may be conflicting or contradictory. The strong forces that affect our plans and choices might include habit; the demands of others; escapism; or spur-of-the-moment, default, or conscious decisions.[4] Most special needs students are familiar with all of the last-named types of choices except the last one. Like many of us, they are not in control of their choices or actions, although they may want to be.

Such students are not in the habit of attending to school work first, and they look to television and other ways of escaping and nonthinking to fill their time. Indeed, teenagers in general are not in the habit of making decisions on their own; they tend to rely on group opinions in reacting to the needs of the moment.

One of the best ways to help students help themselves is to give them an opportunity to plan and organize themselves. Most of them do school work only haphazardly and only when they feel forced to do so. An important spinoff from learning organization skills is that students can hopefully establish lifetime habits or organization and planning that will enable them to achieve and handle their time on the job. The following suggestions might help students to be aware of their futures and keep abreast of their school-related commitments.

General

- Prioritize tasks that you have to or want to do with letters of the alphabet. Give the most important task an *A* and so on. If there is more than one *A*, number them *1*, *2*, and so on.
- Very often, the *A* task may not be one that you want to do. It may be that necessary one, a "have to" one, that you do not want to tackle immediately. It is important that you do a small amount of the *A* task every day, however, even if it is only a small chunk.
- "Swiss-cheese" every task so that you make a small hole in it every day. Every time you think about it or notice it on your calendar, plan what you will do or what resources (like outside help) you will need to do it. Taking these small bites will cut down the overwhelming, large tasks into "doable" portions.

Organizing and Structuring

- Each student should have (1) loose-leaf paper of different colors or a spiral-bound notebook for each class; (2) a folder with a pocket in it to hold papers from each class. This can be hole-punched to fit in a notebook; (3) a paper calendar at the front of the loose-leaf notebook of approximately the same size as the notebook (banks are a good place to obtain multiple copies); (4) a plastic pouch for pens and pencils (always at least two) that has holes to match the notebook ring binders; and (5) a code reminder to indicate when an assignment is due and another code reminder for the week before it's due.
- When giving an assignment, have the members of the class mark their calendars immediately. To reinforce the calendar's use, have them refer to it daily.
- Set time and quantity goals for each student and grade all aspects of the assignment: quality, time usage, and quantity.
- Contract for behavior changes and have the contract go in the notebook.

Goal Setting

- Allow individual students to experience success based on their own ability and, when necessary, on modification of instruction.
- Tell the students precisely what you expect them to memorize or know. Example: "You must memorize this procedure," or, "You don't have to memorize this; you will have the table to consult."
- Tell the students precisely what you expect them to produce.
- See if they agree that they can meet your expectations.
- Tell the students each day or week that separate and discrete goals are expected.
- Set up contracts with students who are not producing.
- Establish short- and long-term goals for each student, based on the student's ability and continued progress.
- Decide whether it is memorization or understanding that is more important.
- Emphasize quality *or* quantity, not both.

Giving Directions

- Give only one or two directions at a time, and check to make sure that they are understood.
- Give very specific instructions; leave spaces for emphasis.
- Ask students to put your directions into their own words.
- When there are written directions, try to make sure that each section of an exercise has its own directions, even if this means that you must duplicate them.
- Read directions to the class.

Presenting Material

- If you cannot read a mimeographed handout of your own, think of the student who has troubles without this added frustration.
- Break down complex ideas and tasks into smaller component tasks.
- When presenting material, explain one phrase or a sentence at a time, then pause. Slow down to 55 words per minute (and save time).
- Decide what prerequisite skills the students need to handle successfully the material presented. Do your students have them?
- Write important phrases on the board as you say them. Seeing and hearing at the same time acts as a reinforcement.

Assisting Note Taking

- Print information on only one side of the board at a time, walk to the other side and continue, then come back to the first side and erase. Then, start all over. This gives the student a chance to copy as much information as possible. Make sure to print. Teach your groups how to outline, to scan for key information and to locate answers in the material.
- Leave blanks in a hand-out.
- Emphasize important material in some texts with a colored "hi-lighter." Let your weaker students use the texts that you have outlined.
- Use overhead projector. Keep notes.
- Decide what material the student really must know and what material must be memorized. If students understand a concept, they will retain it better than if it is simply memorized.

Vocabulary

- Define terms in words as simply as possible. If one word in a definition is not understood, the whole meaning can be lost.
- Use operational definitions. To say "This is what it is used for," can be most effective. Remember to evaluate on this basis, too.
- Use words in the context of the job or other related area so that specific examples stimulate interest and motivate the student to learn and remember. To help memorizing, make it funny or absurd. Example: "Quenching" treated steel makes it harder, "not less thirsty." Draw some "steel drinking."
- Deal with new vocabulary by relating it to words and terms that have already been learned.
- Always place vocabulary in the context of a sentence or paragraph.
- Have students put new vocabulary into their own words and give examples: "Tina drew on the metal with a *scriber.*"
- If applicable, show the language root of the word, and divide the syllables according to pronunciation. For example:

py-rom-et-er—an instrument for measuring very high degrees of heat, as in a furnace or molten metal.

"John measured the temperature of the furnace with a "*pyrometer.*"

Pyro = fire Meter = measuring device

Vocabulary Notebooks

When presenting vocabulary or having the students make or use a vocabulary notebook, it is helpful to have a format for learning. The format shown in Table 6-2 was taken from the "key word glossary" for distributive education in the *Vocational Reading Power Project*.[5] You will notice that each word has been divided into syllables, has two definitions (one complete and one put in simpler terms), and has been used in a sentence (put into context).

Table 6-2 Entries for a Vocabulary Notebook for Distributive Education

EMPLOYER
em-ploy-er

A. One who employs, especially for wages.

B. The person who hires for pay.

Ms. Brown is Jill's *employer.*

ENTERPRISE
en-ter-prise

A. The venture or project being undertaken in business.

B. A store where goods and services may be bought.

The carry-out pizza *enterprise* is doing a profitable business.

ENTREPRENEURS
en-tre-pre-neurs

A. Those engaged in the enterprise as owners or managers.

B. The people who invest or work in business.

Do you know any *entrepreneurs?*

EXCLUSIVE
ex-clu-sive

A. Not admitting of something else, incompatible.

B. Private.

This is an *exclusive* club for men.

FAD
fad

A. When a style catches the fancy of a sizable group of people, has a brief popularity, and dies out quickly.

B. Something new; everyone buys it then no one buys it.

"Hot pants" can be called a *fad.*

FASHION
fash-ion

A. Any style in merchandise, art, or activity that is generally accepted or practiced by a sizable group of people.

B. Newest style.

The paper shows the latest *fashions* from Paris.

Source: Roy Butz and Lynn Gunabal, rev. Eileen Ostergaard and Jon Kaiser, *Vocational Reading Power Project,* Pontrac, Oakland Schools, undated.

TEACHING COMPREHENSION

Comprehension may be broken into *understanding* and *memorizing*. In this section, the understanding aspect of comprehension will be approached from the point of view of the teacher. The teaching of understanding can be done with the written word in the form of textbooks, manuals, pamphlets and other written work or with the spoken word in the form of lectures, tapes, and explanations.

Memorization is a crucial aspect of comprehension. It is concerned with the question whether, after having learned, students will remember what they have learned. The two terms do not mean a division of effort; rather the techniques suggested below should be used concurrently while teaching.

The understanding aspect of comprehension embraces:

- organization of the text (or other written material)
- how the text will be used in the course
- how a chapter is organized
- a sample lesson using written materials
- vocabulary in the context of the lesson
- main ideas and subideas (topic sentences)
- details (facts)
- sequencing
- inference
- charts, graphs, tables
- a study guide (see rewriting and facilitating written materials)

Organization of the Course

In organizing the text or other written materials, it should be kept in mind that poor readers are weeded out very quickly when presented with reading tasks. Not only do they have reading problems, they also have not "psyched out" how the teacher has organized the work, the use of the textbook, and the giving of tests.

Everytime instructors start a new chapter or unit, they should go through the objectives for that unit and chapter. This is the "coming attractions" portion of the lesson, in which the student is given the highlights and main features of the coming lessons. In the movies, the high points are the exciting parts of the story. In the chapter, the high points are certain aspects that can serve as sign posts for the students to let them know *why* they are learning.

Understanding the Book

There are essential aspects of the book that need to be explained at the very beginning of the school year. These involve using a table of contents, using an index, and locating information. The last-named aspect involves a skill that is perhaps more vital than any other. After the school years, it becomes the prime reason for using written materials. The skill requires first locating the page, then locating the information on the page.

Understanding the Chapter

Most chapters in modern textbooks have a structure that includes:

- an introduction
- heavy, dark, or large-type headings
- lighter or smaller-type headings
- italics for important vocabulary or terminology
- boxed-in or highlighted information
- a summary or study questions at the end.[6]

The introduction gives an overview and a purpose for reading. Heavy, dark, or large-type headings indicate the main or important ideas. Lighter or smaller-type headings indicate the subordinate ideas. Italics make new and important vocabulary stand out. Often the word is defined by its usage or explained in a sentence. The summary and questions form a tidy review of the chapter. In fact, the study questions at the end can form a lesson in how to locate information.

The headings of an outline give the main ideas for study and notetaking purposes. These main ideas provide one of the best ways to understand and remember what one learns.

Following is the sequence for getting the main idea of a unit or paragraph:

- In one or two words, say what the paragraph is about.
- In a phrase, say what the paragraph is about.
- In a sentence, say what the paragraph is about.
- Make the sentence into a question.

The facts or details in the paragraph will answer the final question. These facts are usually what the student has to memorize. However, the main idea is what students can hang on to in order to remember the facts they need to know.

Using the preceding information, the instructor can help students make their own outline of the chapter and also help them pick out the important vocabulary. Every time a new unit is begun, part of the class period should be spent on:

- previewing the chapter
- having students put new vocabulary in a vocabulary notebook

- having students make questions out of headings and subheadings (if they have trouble doing this, they will need supportive help; if they keep coming up with answers that do not make sense, the instructor can tell where the student is having trouble).

The following format provides a means of organizing the chapter:

Chapter Organization

Questions (From main ideas)	Details (Facts in sections)
1. ____________	1. ____________
2. ____________	2. ____________
	3. ____________
	4. ____________

Technical Vocabulary

All important and new technical vocabulary can be pulled out of the text and included in a student vocabulary notebook. Each vocabulary word should be treated in the following manner:

- Each word should be written out ("Perpendicular").
- The word should be written in syllables ("Per-pen-dic-u-lar").
- The word should be used in a sentence ("Perpendicular lines form 90° angles.").
- The meaning of the word should be shown by a definition or by drawing a picture ("One line meeting another at right angles.").
- Where appropriate, a technically correct definition should be added ("A vertical line meeting a horizontal line.").

Locating Information Skills

Locating information is probably more important than any other reading or comprehension skill. Routinely, on a weekly basis, students should use the table of contents and the index of their text or of other written materials.

RUNNING YOUR CLASS LIKE A BUSINESS

The ultimate goal of the learning process is employment. In the real world of employment, there are vital aspects of the students' affective skills or behavior that will be as or more important than their specific vocational competencies. How can we teach cooperation, honesty, attendance, punctuality, and the many other important job-related behavioral skills to enable our students to get and keep employment?

Why not reward students with a point system in much the same way that they would be rewarded on the job? A point system has many variations. As in any business, the following rules apply:

- The point or "dollar" rewards for different types of jobs and behaviors must be known in advance. These may be fixed for the entire class for all jobs and behaviors or there may be a combination of fixed and variable rewards for individuals, depending on their individual needs and goals. For example:

A class reward system (Ways to earn money)

Completed miniassignment	$20	Cooperation w/teacher	up to $25
Completed final assignment	$40	Cooperation w/classmates	up to $25
Perfect weekly attendance	$25	Meeting personal goal for the week	up to $25
Perfect weekly punctuality	$25	Dependability and neatness	up to $25
Improved weekly personal effort	up to $20	Initiative, flexibility	up to $30

- Attendance and punctuality can be monitored with a time clock. It is important to make the rules dependent on fixed quantities and not only on the decision of the teacher. Personal effort can be a flexible item negotiated in terms of quantity and quality, with each student on a short contract. Cooperation is also subjective but can be easily quantified in terms of fighting, listening to the teacher, and so on.
- Students may receive dollar points for appropriate behavior that would also be rewarded on the job.
- Decisions as to how much an assignment or behavior is worth may depend on the judgment of the teacher about the difficulty of the task or behavior for the student.
- If behaviors are very bad, it may be necessary to reward students immediately for their effort or behavior.
- When a student is consistently performing well but is not performing as well as necessary to meet the vocational objectives, it may become necessary to decrease the dollars or points given for the same work.
- To make inappropriate behavior obvious, it may be necessary to have "withdrawal" or pink slips available to let students know immediately that they are acting inappropriately.
- The money received may be in the form of checks, play dollars, or bank deposit slips. Copies of checks or bank deposit and withdrawal slips (with carbon copies for the instructor) are all useful.

- Money is more useful when it can buy things other than grades. Points may be assigned for coveted assignments. "Loafing time" and points may be saved for better term grades and for special "treats" to be determined by contract.
- A convenient contract form to use when there is only one task for which there is a reward follows:

CONTRACT
Teacher's Stub

________ Name	I, ________ agree to complete ________
	by ________. I understand that I will receive
________ Date	$________ for completing the task and a bonus of
________ Amount	$________ if completed on or before time.
	________ Teacher / ________ Student

Contracting

Almost everything we do in life is based on a contract of some sort. Every time we are involved with another human being, there is a contract. Whether written or spoken, or unwritten and unspoken, the contract exists. Whether it is a contract to buy something, a marriage contract, or a classroom contract for completion of work or for a behavior change, the contract is an agreement with penalties for breaking it.

When contracting for behavior, it is important to look first at what is going on in the classroom. Questions about this aspect can establish "baseline data" on the specific ways the student is behaving in the learning situation. It can also be very helpful to have another adult come into the learning situation to observe what is happening. Here are the questions to be answered:[8]

- Where does the behavior occur most often?
- Where does it not occur?
- When does it occur most frequently?
- When does it not occur at all?
- What do other people do just before it occurs?
- What do people do just after it occurs?
- Who is present most often when it occurs?
- How often does it happen (per day, per week, per hour)?
- Can one identify one or two behaviors that can be counted?
- What would be appropriate substitute behavior(s)?

Contracts may allow the opportunity to make a poor choice and then to renegotiate for a new choice. Making choices and decisions are very important competencies to foster.

Here are some rules for contracting:

- Make sure that a mutually agreed-upon portion of the contract can be reached in a day or less, e.g., the layout of a job.
- Be systematic and do not suspend the contract for special reasons or circumstances. If the contract says five pages and both agree to it, offer a way to complete the contract, such as getting outside help. If you want to modify the terms, write a new contract.
- Be very specific about accomplishments, if possible, through the use of behavioral terms. For instance, "maintaining good eye contact" and "asking questions" are more effective than "paying better attention."
- Ask for high quality work, to the limits of the individual. It is better to sacrifice quantity for quality. Do not settle for poor, hasty, or sloppy work.
- Contract for active behavior. Allow the student to be rewarded for consulting with other students, finishing different parts of a project, checking against well-done work, and so on. It is not productive to indicate that the student should "stop doing sloppy work."
- Make sure the contract objectives and terms are clear and easily read by the student. If not, read them to the student.
- Treat partial success as success, even when objectives are not met in the negotiated time frame. Objectives include many variables, and partial success should not be regarded as failure.

Rewarding

Why should a dependent student want to achieve independence? What kind of inducements will change a comfortable, familiar pattern? Desirable rewards are powerful motivators for both large and small achievements. A person who is afraid of the water should be rewarded just for getting in. Besides the obvious reward of grades, the following can be strong motivators:

- social praise, compliments, smiles, approval
- material incentives: money, food, tools
- a point system convertible to free time (a pass to the cafeteria)
- time to work on one's own projects or in workshop areas
- being able to do a desirable job or task
- peer approval (having a special job)
- good reports to parents

Remember that, by granting rewards, you are creating a balance: On the one hand, you gain positive results as a reaction to your praise and attention; on the other hand, you want your students to develop their own good feelings about a job well done. Your job is to develop those feelings without losing sight of the desired end result of productivity.

A simple "thanks" or "that's a good job" always works to some extent. We like to benefit from our actions; our individual needs will dictate what kinds of rewards will be the most powerful and tempting motivators to reinforce the repetition of certain behaviors.

Basically, children want to do well, unless they have had so much failure and discouragement that they no longer get rewards for success, or they get such rewards so infrequently that the attempt to succeed is not worth the effort. Often, for such students, inappropriate behaviors, like acting up and disrupting or retreating into noninterest, may be what gets them the attention and rewards they crave. But children can change their behavior. Certain situations may induce them either to backslide or to improve. *You* can make the difference!

Consider the following situation:

John is not finishing his auto-related work. Of five assignments and one test each week, he finishes none of them. On the other hand, in his automotive shop, of eight to ten projects in one week, he finishes more than half of them.

When John is confronted with assignments involving written work, he often begins to cut up and to show off for his friends. He is a disruptive element in the classroom; sometimes it seems he is disrupting all the time.

But after observing John for awhile, a pattern of behavior becomes apparent. John is acting up whenever he is faced with an assignment that involves writing, written reports, or notations.

When confronted with the pattern of his behavior, John acknowledges that he is afraid of writing because his spelling and writing skills are so bad. Since he is in danger of failing school, he agrees to try a contracting system.

NEGOTIATING AND CONTRACTING

In a typical high school situation, the teacher presents the requirements for a term project to the students. One or two students wait until the deadline is near and then, acting helpless, approach the teacher. They claim they cannot do the project, or they say simply, "We don't know where to start."

There can be several different outcomes to this transaction. The teacher can essentially "do" the project for the students by gathering all the information and leading them through the whole project. For many teachers, this may be the "easy" way out of the situation. Conversely, the teacher can demand that the students who do not have the ability to do the project either work to meet the standards of the rest of the class or receive a failing grade.

In the first instance, the teacher loses respect for the lagging students. The teacher has been manipulated and may feel angry at the students, or may feel trapped in the situation because of a desire to be a good teacher. In the second instance, on the other hand, the teacher has denied responsibility for treating the student as an individual.

In this situation, with some help in asserting their capabilities, the students might eventually be able to present their problems in a positive and productive manner, and the teacher can then respond in kind. The result will be that both the students and the teacher will feel better about their involvement in the transaction.

Below is a dialogue between a teacher and a student that illustrates this kind of open interaction in a positive learning situation.

Student: I'm uncertain how to choose a term project.

Teacher: I'm willing to give you help on this. However, I am uncomfortable giving you all the help you want, when at this point you haven't done any work at all. If you would investigate three of the suggested projects on the list to see which looks the most interesting and then select one you can finish, I will help.

(after discussion)

Student: I now know which project is the most interesting to me. However, my reading and writing skills are very poor and I'm worried about my ability to give you a good project with an explanation.

Teacher: I appreciate your worries, and I know your skills may be poor, but I have to have a finished product on which to base your grade.

Student: Instead of the suggested five-page report, I would feel much more comfortable with a one- or two-page report with completed work. In that way, I can do a better job of writing the report while I do the project.

Teacher: If you want to do a shorter paper, I would expect a very careful job with good punctuation and spelling.

Student: Well, those aren't my strong points, but if it's o.k. with you, I'll have someone help me with that part.

Teacher: That's fine as long as they don't do the whole thing for you.

A sample contract that might be used following this type of teacher-student negotiation is shown in Exhibit 6-1.

Exhibit 6-1 Sample Student-Teacher Contract

SCHOOL CONTRACT

CLASS: ______________________ DATE: ______________
CONTRACTING PARTIES: 1. STUDENT ______________________
2. TEACHER ______________________

Contract to be filled out in duplicate with one copy to each party. Each week, the student and teacher will agree on the number and nature of assignments to be completed and the level of completion. For each completed assignment to the agreed on level of completion, the student will receive _____ points toward the weekly grade and for each assignment over _____ completed, the student will be able to decide on a class reward. The class will be told that the reward is the result of my effort.

ASSIGNMENT COMPLETED	DATE	LEVEL OF COMPLETION
1. ______________	__________	______________
2. ______________	__________	______________
3. ______________	__________	______________
4. ______________	__________	______________
5. ______________	__________	______________

Signature ______________________

Signature ______________________

Witnesses:
____
____

REINFORCERS AND MOTIVATORS

Why is it that some teachers spend all their energy trying to control the class and keep the students from misbehaving? Why is it that some students always have their heads down, never paying attention, never finishing their work, and seeming to talk only when they are out of class? What can turn them on? What can help to correct their inappropriate behaviors?

Fortunately, we are preparing students for a real world in which there are recognizable behaviors that can help them get and keep a job. Laurent Cormier and his associates have developed several techniques to help them in their efforts with special vocational needs students. These innovative individuals found that in their grass-roots, low-budget program, clear management techniques served as a motivational factor for their students. Their students were able to see their performance and progress and were able to work toward goals and rewards.[9]

We might hope that students would be satisfied with the intrinsic reward of a job well done. Unfortunately, that is not usually the case. For many of us, it is vital to have feedback and to know how well we have done.

Reinforcers and motivators may be controlled by others or they may be self-controlled. They may be tangible, like money, or intangible, like praise. Some examples of tangible rewards are:

- money (or the symbol thereof)
- grades (daily, short-term or long-term)
- time off or out of classroom
- extra time for a favorite task or project
- an errand
- games (scan, spill and spell, or card games)
- magazines, yearbooks, high-interest picture books (monster, cars/motorcycles, and sports) or other free reading
- food and candy
- other assignments
- talking times
- using multimedia equipment
- listening to tapes
- special films
- use of a radio with earphones

Here are some examples of intangible rewards:

- praise and encouragement
- respect for students' values and backgrounds
- acceptance
- success (in finishing)
- showing that you like the student
- peer approval
- approval of other adults (parents, administrators)
- public praise in front of the class or in front of adults

- freedom to make independent choices
- positive facial expressions

In summary, rewards can work to reinforce appropriate and desired behavior and to increase motivation. These are some rules to follow to help the teacher develop a reward system:[10]

- Reinforce immediately, that is, when you are first trying to improve performance or behavior.
- Tailor reinforcers to students' preferences and reward accordingly.
- Do not ignore a good performance; reward when children do a good job or behave appropriately.
- Be sure that you are reinforcing the thing you want to improve; wait until what you want occurs, then reward it when it happens.
- Reward improvement, but avoid giving predictable rewards for the same behavior.
- Try to ignore these kinds of inappropriate behavior:
    - talking
    - distracting others
    - leaving seat or work area
    - not completing assignments
    - messy work
    - complaining
    - commenting negatively
    - inappropriate questioning
    - dependency
    - constant need for attention
- Try to reinforce these kinds of behavior:
    - eye contact
    - paying attention
    - finishing work or project
    - staying in seat or at work station
    - remaining in work area
    - punctuality
    - proper hygiene
    - asking appropriate questions
    - seeking appropriate assistance
    - quality work
    - attendance

NOTES

1. Louise Keller and Lois Bennett, "Curriculum Modules: Planning Instructional Processes, Design, Development, Diffusion, Evaluation," mimeographed 1978, revised 1979.
2. Rita Dunn and Kenneth Dunn, Teaching Students Through Their Individual Learning Styles (Reston, Va.: Reston Publishing, 1978), p. 4.
3. Connie Zajac and Douglas Woolverton, "Proposal for Variable Credit: A Student Evaluation System," mimeographed, undated.
4. Alan Lakein, *How to Get Control of Your Time and Your Life* (New York: New American Library, 1973).
5. Roy Butz and Lynn Gunabalan, rev. Eileen Ostergaard and Jon Kaiser, *Vocational Reading Power Project* (Minneapolis Minn.: The Exchange, 1978), Butz et al., Keyword Glossaries, Vocational Reading Power Project, Pontrac, Oakland Schools, undated.
6. Patricia DiFranco, *Reading Ideas and Work Sheets,* mimeo., undated.
7. C. Brigley, "Pediatrics the Practical Nurse" (Delmar Publishers, 1965), p. 95.
8. Butz and Gunabalan, *Vocational Reading Power Project,* p. 18.
9. Laurent Cormier, "An On the Job Construction Program for Emotionally Disturbed and Disadvantaged Students," mimeographed, 1977.
10. Ron Carter, *Help! These Kids Are Driving Me Crazy* (Champaign, Ill.: Research Press, 1972).

BIBLIOGRAPHY

Chase, C.M. *Aid for High School Teachers*. Wellesley, Mass.: Massachusetts Association for Children with Learning Disabilities, Inc.

Crouse, William H. *The Auto Book*. McGraw-Hill Book Company, 1974.

Curriculum Associates, Inc., Woburn, Mass.

DiFranco, Patricia. "Reading Ideas and Work Sheets." Mimeographed, undated.

Educators Publishing Services, Inc. Cambridge, Mass.

Gustafson, Richard, and Goves, Patricia. *How New Hampshire Employers Evaluate Their Employees: Implications for Vocational Education*. Keene, N.H.: Keene State College, Spring 1977.

Hartley, Nancy; Otazo, Karen; and Cline, Connie. *Assessment of Basic Vocational Related Skills*. Greeley, Colo.: Colorado State Board for Community College and Occupational Education, University of Northern Colorado, 1979.

Kern High School District. *Career Training Center Project*. Bakersfield, Calif., undated.

Linari, Ronald, *The Evaluation Process: Principles and Practices for Vocational Technical Education*. Canton, Mass.: Blue Hills Regional Technical School, 1979.

Longo, Frank J. *Meeting the Needs of All Students*. Canton, Mass.: Blue Hills Regional Vocational School, 1978.

Vocational Education, Special Education Project *VESEP I and II*. Mt. Pleasant, Mich.: Central Michigan University, 1976.

Moran, Patrick J. "Commonsense Guidelines for Tutoring." *Journal of Reading,* February, 1976, pp. 370-372.

Reiter, Irene M. *Why Can't They Read It: How to Teach Reading in the Content Areas*. New York: Cambridge Book Co., 1974.

Special School District of St. Louis County. *Career Education Curriculum Guides: Career Alternatives for Handicapped Children Project,* Gregory Muenster, Program Director, undated.

Washburn, Winnifred Y. *Vocational Entry-Skills for Secondary Students*. San Rafael, Calif.: Academic Therapy Publications, 1975.

Chapter 7

Work Experience and Cooperative Placement Programs

David Kingsbury, M.Ed.

INTRODUCTION

In the development of work experience and cooperative placement programs, there are four points to be considered: (1) the different types of programs and the use of a cooperative approach in combination with them, (2) the placement of the student on the job, (3) the classroom-instruction portion of the cooperative work experience program, and (4) the followup or articulation of the students once they leave the work experience program.

TYPES OF WORK EXPERIENCE AND COOPERATIVE PLACEMENT PROGRAMS

A large variety of work experiences and cooperative placement programs is available. The structures of many of these programs are based upon the goals and resources available. Some common types of work programs are examined in this section.

The Work Experience and Career Exploration Program

The Work Experience and Career Exploration Program (WECEP) is a program for students who are 14 to 15 years old and are not finding success in the regular school program. WECEP allows students to participate in work stations in the community and also to explore different available job opportunities. It is a program that affords the students opportunities for earning wages and experiencing some success in a school-related program. Often, students enrolled in WECEP programs would be likely candidates for dropping out of school if it were not for the program.

Work Experience Handicapped Programs

The Work Experience Handicapped Programs (WEH) are special education work experience programs in which handicapped learners are given the opportunity to experience on-the-job work experience on a sheltered, semisheltered, or competitive employment basis. In these programs, the students are taught many of the basic prevocational survival skills that are necessary to seek and maintain employment.

Work Experience Disadvantaged Programs

In Work Experience Disadvantaged Programs (WED), students with special needs are placed in job sites that allow some direct instruction, along with a heavy component of remedial and basic survival skills that are related to the experience of the student on the job.

Cooperative Vocational Education Programs

Cooperative Vocational Education Programs include programs in Cooperative Distributive Education (DE), Cooperative Trade and Industry (TI), Cooperative Office Education (OE), and Occupational Home Economics (HE). The largest component of this type of program is the direct occupational skill training of students who may or may not have made some career path choice but would like to explore an occupational area in depth. There are a variety of components within this cooperative model that insures training that is up to date and relevant to the occupational field chosen. Students with special needs can often be placed in these programs if they receive the proper prevocational preparation and appropriate support services during the program involvement.

Certain program components must be considered when starting any type of work program or renovating a present program to accommodate students with a work-experience need. These components are most commonly found under the label of cooperative education. To develop a quality program, the following factors should be considered:

- Cooperative vocational education is a program that brings the resources of the school and community together in an individually integrated program for students.
- Cooperative vocational education combines learning on the job and learning in the classroom by utilizing a variety of approaches, including a training plan.

- Teacher-coordinators, using the cooperative method, act as supervisors and advocates for the students involved to ensure that all agreements and labor laws are being adhered to and that the educational needs of the students are being met.
- The students involved in a Cooperative Program have reasonable schedules, integrated by the cooperative work experience program, to allow them alternating periods of work and school.
- The students receive instruction in school that provides general survival skills and also relates specifically to their jobs in the community.
- The students receive experiences in class and on the job that relate to the students' career goals.
- The program coordinator organizes an advisory committee that ensures school and community input and that can serve as a sounding board for the teacher-coordinator.

Though work experience programs in the past have not shown aspects of Cooperative Education (see Table 7-1), this situation is changing. For example, in 1975, the Special Needs Division of the Minnesota State Department of Vocational Education awarded a contract to the study team of Peter Deanovic and William Lundell to ascertain the state of the art of the WECEP Program in 1975-1976. Some of the key findings of the team indicate that work experience programs are using more cooperative program approaches:

- Summaries of routine job site visits made by the teacher-coordinators showed that 88 percent of the coordinators visited the job site at least twice a month and 56 percent of them visited the site weekly.
- Sixty-eight percent of the WECEP Programs used an advisory committee in program operation.
- Eighty-eight percent of the coordinators used their positions to facilitate parent contacts in home visits.
- One major exception, however, was found in the area of student clubs. Though the Minnesota Vocational Guidelines stated in 1974 that the coordinator should "serve as advisor to youth group activities," 92 percent of the coordinators considered youth groups ineffective.[1]

While the sample of WECEP coordinators in Minnesota does not enable one to reach a general conclusion, other related research indicates that many components of the cooperative vocational education model can be and are being used presently with special needs learners in creating cooperative work experience programs.

Table 7-1 Comparison of Three Plans Using the Work Environment

Components or Characteristics	*Cooperative Education*	*Work-Study*	*Work Experience*
1. Established career objective by student	Yes, primary objective is entry employment training toward career	Sometimes yes, established in some vocational field. Program objective is usually earning power and motivation for student	No, but sometimes has general education values
2. Classroom instruction related to the career objective	Yes	Not necessarily	No
3. Established training station and close supervision by school	Yes	Not usually	No
4. On-the-job training plan	Yes	No	No
5. Paid employment	Yes, usually by profit-making business	Yes, (in some plans through government subsidy)	Not necessarily
6. An advisory committee used	Yes	No	No
7. Vocational youth group correlated with instruction	Yes	No	No
8. Certified teacher-coordinator in occupational field	Yes	No	No
9. Planned home visitations	Yes	No	No

Source: Ralph E. Mason, "The Effective Use of Cooperative Work Experience," Business Education Forum, © May 1970, p. 10. Reprinted by permission of the National Business Education Association.

THE ROLE OF THE TEACHER-COORDINATOR

The professional who makes the program come together is the teacher-coordinator. This is the person who makes or breaks the program.

Since the success of the program is the result of a variety of duties and responsibilities, it would be useful to take a closer view. In 1977, the Minnesota Department of Education issued a list of coordinator's responsibilities in *Vocational Education Work Experience Program for Handicapped Students, The Teacher-Coordinator's Handbook*. In the handbook, the following responsibilities were listed:

1. "Develop community and/or school work stations.
2. "Obtain an Employability Training Agreement between student and employer relative to role and responsibility (to be signed by parent).
3. "Insure that proper safety instructions are provided by coordinator and employer.
4. "Maintain a regular visitation schedule to observe students at work and to assist employers to fulfill their responsibilities to the students (half hour observations per week/per student).
5. "Develop a transportation system utilizing all available district and community resources.
6. "Act as team leader where possible in designing individual student plan utilizing such persons as rehabilitation counselors, psychologists, social workers, counselors, instructional staff, parents and others as individual cases warrant. This plan may include both paid sheltered and competitive work experience if agreed upon by participants in the student plan.
7. "Develop and maintain a realistic program designed to meet the individual needs of vocationally handicapped students.
8. "Develop procedures for evaluating each student's progress towards maximum level of employability.
9. "Coordinate the in-school educational program that may include assisting students who enroll in non-special education academic courses.
10. "Conduct employability skills seminar for a minimum of one school period per day for all assigned students except those who are receiving short-term rehabilitation services. Alternative teaching methods are essential to insure adequate understanding of the subject matter.
11. "Maintain records required by the State Department of Education and Department of Labor (State and Federal).
12. "Work with rehabilitation counselor to secure services available through Division of Vocational Rehabilitation both during and after high school.
13. "Utilize all available community resources for the students while they are in the program.

14. "Maintain and improve professional growth through involvement in continuing professional educational organizations and state and national conferences.
15. "Establish and utilize an Advisory Committee.
16. "Work with the student, the student's parents, school officials and other resource persons to develop concrete post high school vocational plans.
17. "Assist in the proper due process procedures.
18. "Promote advancement in an occupational area and/or exploration in varied occupations.
19. "Be informed of the school district's and employer's insurance policies.
20. "Develop medical history in cooperation with DVR, parents, family doctor, and student.
21. "Maintain open communication with principal, vocational director, and special education director to assure support.
22. "Provide students with the opportunity to be involved in student organizations such as VICA, FFA, etc."[2]

Aside from the responsibilities of a coordinator, there are some other human and rather subjective qualities that we have observed in coordinators across the United States. Coordinators should have some or all of the following qualities:

- They should have and show a genuine concern for students and be able to care for them even if the students' behavior is sometimes unacceptable. The ability to separate feelings and behavior is important, to be able to say, "I like you, but I don't like your behavior."
- They should have flexibility in thought and action. Successful coordinators are able to think on their feet and deal with new situations without losing their cool. An example of this is in the old story about how to greet an employer. The coordinator, coming in to check a student's progress, approaches the employer and says, "Hello, Mr. Employer, I am here to see about Student A." At this point, the employer will give one of the following responses: (1) "I haven't seen Student A in two weeks." (2) "I just fired Student A last week." (3) "Who is Student A?" (4) "Student A is doing just great, and I would like some more from your program." At this point, whatever the employer's statement, the flexible coordinator says, "I know, that's why I am here," and carries on with the duty of the day.
- They should have emotional stability and be able to operate for periods of time with no positive reinforcement from students or staff. The coordinator's job calls for periods of decision making about what is best for the student and program. Sometimes in making those decisions, friction can arise. At such times, coordinators may have to reevaluate their roles and proceed with the best alternative among the options.

- They should have the ability to give and receive feedback. Teacher-coordinators will often have access to information that can be difficult to deal with or hard to confront others with. Specific training techniques, such as the use of active listening and honest confronting, should be practical and be learned well enough so that the coordinators are able to understand the total message being sent to them.
- They should have the ability and willingness to use other resources. The hard truth is that you cannot be everything to everybody. A teacher-coordinator should be able to identify and utilize all of the resources within and outside the school to provide the best possible results for the students.
- They should have imagination, energy, good health, and enthusiasm. Students will find it difficult to understand why they should be excited about their jobs if the coordinators are not excited about their own. While all people go through times of stress and depression, students look to the teacher-coordinator as a model.
- They should have the ability to organize and individualize. A key ingredient of success for a coordinator is the ability to break out of the lock-step style of teaching and use a variety of teaching techniques and methods. If coordinators cannot organize their time and individualize their instructions, the results for their students are often disastrous.
- They should have the ability to give and receive affection and warmth. A teacher-coordinator must be able to play a variety of role models; not least, that of the "significant other." In this way, a teacher-coordinator can demonstrate appropriate caring and nurturant behavior.
- They should have the ability to "accentuate the positive and eliminate the negative." Teacher-coordinators must be positive people. They must believe in what they are doing and show positive feelings about the students, the school, and the program to employers, community agencies, and other appropriate people. They should not be afraid of positive enthusiasm, the mark of a winning program.

Teacher-coordinators are the key figures in making a cooperative work experience program function. They are the people who design the parts and make them function.

COMPONENTS OF A COOPERATIVE WORK EXPERIENCE PROGRAM

To understand better the situation in which the teacher-coordinator operates, it is essential to view the various parts and see how they fit into place. In Figure 7-1, an analysis of a work program is presented.

Figure 7-1 Analysis of a Work Program

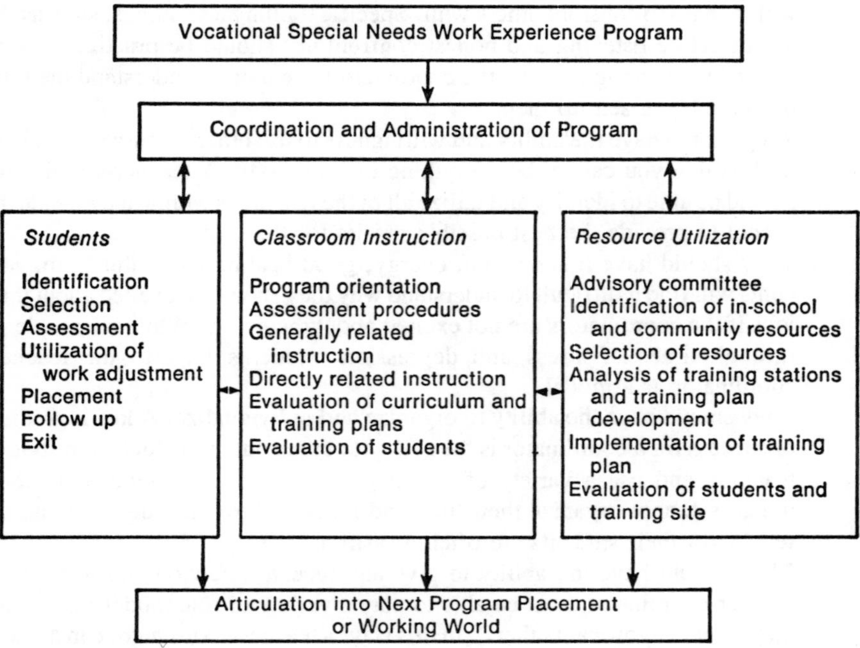

In this diagram it is possible to view the major components involved and to visualize the interaction between them.

PLACEMENT OF STUDENTS ON THE JOB

In examining the many crucial aspects of the placement part of the cooperative work experience program, it should be remembered that some of its structure is determined by the size of the community the program is located in and also by the emphasis placed upon job sites by the teacher-coordinator.

In the process of student placement, there are three main factors to consider: needs, abilities, and interests. In addition, the teacher-coordinator will find that each individual student has certain traits and other unique considerations that must be taken into account.

Informal and formal assessment of the learner is covered elsewhere in this volume. Some aspects of the assessment of students should be reviewed, however, in the context of their developmental level, as, for example, in the following items:

- Occupational interests. Have the students made any choices about the type of work that appeals to them, the kind of environment they like, and so on?
- Reliability. Does the student show responsibility in daily actions that could transfer to a training station?
- Physical skills. Does the student learner possess any physical strengths or weaknesses that will affect working on the job or that will require modifications?
- Language skills. Can the student shift gears in language and use appropriate communication at the job station?
- Personal appearance. Do the students know how to present themselves to the public; are they able to dress right for the job?
- Work readiness. Do the students want to work; are they ready to experience employment in an internship, or in a sheltered, semisheltered, or competitive setting?
- Student transportation. Can the student get to potential job sites?

While this list is by no means exhaustive, it presents the kind of information that should be collected before trying to place a student on the job.

After the students have been identified and their job-seeking readiness has been assessed, placement can be started by considering the kinds of job sites available. There are a variety of techniques that might be used to locate and select job sites. The real magic in the start of a program, however, is plain hard work. As one experienced coordinator said, "If you wear out the seat of your pants before the soles on your shoes, you're working on the wrong end."

Each program will have to take into account the geographic limitations or advantages of the area before a systematic search can be started. A new coordinator could begin by checking sources like the local chamber of commerce, the telephone book, or the city directory and listing the names, addresses and phone numbers of each location.

Some type of filing system, such as the use of three-by-five-inch cards, might aid in keeping track of each potential training station. A coordinator may want to categorize subsections of an industry together, such as grocery stores or automotive parts stores, or merely keep the list alphabetized in one master file.

The next step would be the analysis of a potential training station. A realistic rule is that good training stations are developed over time, not just picked out of the phone book. In analyzing different industries, the coordinator must first make an on-site visit. In this phase, coordinators should realize that they are not only trying to find training stations. They are also concerned with the public relations aspect of the program. This might involve spinoffs to other industries or the development of key contacts in the business world. If the result is the finding of a good situation, only then should the students be considered for possible placement on the job. A high degree of positive thinking is involved in this process. If asked, the coordinator must be able to explain the program fully in terms of its purpose, needs, and benefits to the student, the school, and the employer.

If it appears that a business has openings that match with the particular student's abilities, needs, and interests, then the coordinator is in a position to set up the job interview for the student worker. Some cautions are in order here, however. Some of the things that can cause difficulty are:

- Trying to force students on employers that are not ready to work with the program.
- Trying to force students to take jobs they do not want.
- Failing to check with parents about the job opportunities, the transportation, and the time elements involved.
- Assuming that one can always make a perfect match of a student to a job. Even if an employer wants only the "best" student to apply, send the best available selection. This forces the employer to make a responsible decision and to become more involved.
- Being unaware of the labor law restrictions that apply to the program.
- Failing to give each student who goes out on a job the safety training that applies to the situation, and failing to ensure that the employer does the same.

Here are some things that can be done to ensure a proper fit of students to training stations:

- Be positive about the students' chances for success and realistic about their abilities.
- Ensure a successful starting set of experiences for the student by use of a training plan and by close initial direction from the employer or supervisor.
- Stop by and see how the student is doing, or at least call frequently in the first week or two, to eliminate difficulties that might be avoided.
- Place the students at several stations; avoid the temptation to place too many on one job site. If there are several at one site, they will all seem to have problems at the same time, thereby providing a very negative experience for everyone involved.
- Make sure that all concerned know what is expected of them in the cooperative placement program. This can be done through the use of a training agreement that explains everyone's role and duties.
- Build a feedback system that allows supervision of the activities of all the students on a periodic basis.
- Never be afraid to tell the story about the cooperative work experience program. Though the coordinator might have had a rough day and be tired, the next person to be approached might become a tremendous asset to the program.

In conjunction with the provision of appropriate cooperative training, a coordinator must make everyone understand what is involved in the program and also ensure documentation and feedback of what is happening on the job. To do this, a series of documents and forms should be used in the placement process. Here are some sample forms from the Minnesota State Department of Vocational Education that can be used for this purpose:

- The Work Experience Employability Agreement (Exhibit 7-1) clarifies the role of the participants in the cooperative work experience program and ensures and documents their understanding with their signatures.
- The Training Plan (Table 7-2 and Exhibits 7-2 and 7-3) is used to schedule the work and school experiences of the student learners and to ensure vocational quality for the students. The Exhibit 7-2 form illustrates a training plan that is very unstructured to a specific job but that could be developed to meet individual student and employer needs. The Exhibit 7-3 form, used by the St. Paul public schools, includes an area for academic skills training as an in-school responsibility. (Training plans will be dealt with in greater detail in the section on classroom instruction.)
- Proper identification and due-process procedure forms are required if students are handicapped.
- Age verification forms are required if the student is not 18 and wishes to participate in a WECEP or other cooperative program.

A variety of other forms might be considered that would document certain functions and thus aid in coordinating the cooperative work experience program. For example:

- The Personal Data Sheet to provide vocational diagnostic information.
- The Student Agreement Form (Exhibit 7-4) which documents specific obligations of the student not covered under the training agreement.
- The Parent School Agreement Form (Exhibit 7-5), which records the responsibilities of the school and the parents and highlights activities not covered under the training agreement.
- A Rating Sheet for Student Evaluation (Exhibit 7-6), which can be used as a periodic device to help keep track of the student's progress on the job.
- Various forms to provide a transportation and coordination log to help the coordinator keep track of student visits, mileage, and dates of important upcoming events.

Exhibit 7-1 Work Experience Employability Agreement Form

4 Copies:
1-Training Sponsor
1-Student
1-Parent or Guardian
1-Teacher-Coordinator

EMPLOYABILITY AGREEMENT
WORK EXPERIENCE EDUCATION PROGRAM

Student's Name ______________________ Birth Date ______________

Student's Address ______________________ Social Security # __________
____

Parent's/Guardian's Name ______________ Phone ______________

School ______________________ Phone ______________

Training Station ______________________ Phone ______________

Training Station Address ______________ Date Completed __________
____

The major purpose of this program is to provide valuable work experience education for students. This agreement is made to show responsibilities of the participants: student (or trainee), parent, school, and employer.

STUDENT:

1. To be regular in attendance at school and on the job.
2. To work closely with the teacher-coordinator in building a valid educational program including work and work-related experience.
3. To maintain acceptable performance at school and on the job.
4. To maintain principles of integrity regarding school, job and community while a participant of the program.
5. To abide by the rules and regulations established by the school, training station, and governmental agencies regarding student employment.
6. To keep the teacher-coordinator informed of events or facts necessary to your progress in this program.

PARENT/GUARDIAN:

1. To grant permission for program participation by the student and encourage his/her effective performance.
2. To share with the teacher-coordinator information vital to the successful development and performance of the student.

TRAINING SPONSOR:

1. To adhere to all federal and state regulations regarding employment of students participating in job related programs.
2. To assist the teacher-coordinator in the evaluation of the student.
3. To consult with the teacher-coordinator regarding student performance.
4. To provide supportive supervision to the student.

TEACHER/COORDINATOR:

1. To establish a valid education and work-related program for student.
2. To assess the student's progress in the program and inform the parties involved.
3. To involve all personnel necessary in the development of the education, employability, and self-concept of the student.

____________________ ____________________
Student Parent

____________________ ____________________
Training Sponsor and Position Teacher-Coordinator

Source: The Work Experience Handbook: Vocational Education Work Experience Program for Handicapped Students, prepared through the Minnesota Instructional Materials Center (St. Paul, Minn.: Minnesota Department of Education, Vocational Technical Division, 1977) p. 41.

Table 7-2 Training Plan Form

TRAINING PLAN
GASOLINE SERVICE ATTENDANT

I. Title of Job: Service station attendant

II. Job Description: Cleans and maintains station and driveway, handles customer relations on the driveway, sells accessories, cleans and polishes cars, lubricates cars, and makes minor repairs. Learns some fundamental principles of management.

III. Career Objective: Service station manager

IV. Areas of experience and training:
A. Station care-housekeeping and maintenance
B. Driveway service
C. Carwash, clean-up, and polish
D. Lubrication
E. Tire, battery, and accessory sales
F. Minor repairs
G. Buying and ordering procedures
H. Principles of station management

V. Detail of areas of experience and training:

	In Class	Planned Learning At the Training Station
A. Instruction in station care		
1. Driveway housekeeping and maintenance	X	X
2. Rest-room cleaning		X
3. Lubrication department		X
4. Stockroom		X
B. Instruction in driveway service		
1. Six-step driveway service	X	X
2. Windshield, battery, tires	X	X
3. Underhood inspection and sales	X	X
4. Cash register operation and check-out	X	X
5. Making additional sales	X	X
a. radiator hose		
b. fan belt		

Table 7-2 continued

c. oil additive		
d. oil filter		
e. lubrication		
f. battery		
g. lights		
C. Instruction on car wash, clean-up, and polish		X
D. Lubrication		
1. Study and use of lubrication manual	X	X
2. Servicing of major parts	X	X
3. Wheel lubrication		X
E. Instruction on tire, battery and accessory sales		
1. Tire brands, sizes and selling points	X	X
2. Battery sizes and selling points	X	X
3. Other accessories	X	X
F. Instruction on minor repairs		
1. Tire change and repair		X
2. Muffler and tail pipe change		X
3. Brake adjustment and repair		X
4. Car tune-up procedure	X	X
5. Cleaning or steaming motor		X
G. Buying and ordering procedures		
1. Taking inventory	X	X
2. Determination of minimum number of items to keep on hand		
3. Ordering, so as not to order more than necessary	X	X
4. Display for maximum sales	X	X
H. Principles of station management		
1. Acquaintance with required records	X	X
2. Lease or rental arrangement with major oil company		X
3. Staffing and hiring personnel		X
4. Financing	X	X
5. Requirements		X
6. Importance of station location		X
7. Payroll		X

Source: Guide for Work Education in Manitoba's Public Schools (Winnepeg Manitoba, Canada: Ministry of Education, 1976), p. 63.

Exhibit 7-2 Training Plan Form

3 Copies:
1-Training sponsor
1-Student
1-Teacher-Coordinator

WORK-STUDY PROGRAM
TRAINING PLAN

Student-Learner ______________________ Birth Date __________
Social Security No. ________ Job Title ______________ O.E. No. __________
Training Station ______________________________
Address ______________________________
Supervisor(s) ______________________________
Job Definition: ______________________________
____

Description of Training Station Duties:
1. ______________________________
2. ______________________________
3. ______________________________
4. ______________________________
5. ______________________________
6. ______________________________
7. ______________________________
8. ______________________________

Career Objective(s): ______________________________
____
____

Training Experiences or Objectives	School Instruction Group or Individual	References and Evaluation	Time Schedule

Source: The Work Experience Handbook: Vocational Education Work Experience Program for Handicapped Students, prepared through the Minnesota Instructional Materials Center (St. Paul, Minn: Minnesota Dept. of Education, Vocational Technical Division, 1977) pp. 64-65.

Exhibit 7-3 Training Plan Form

TRAINING PLAN

Name of Student ______________ Employing Organization ______________

Job Title______________________ Job Supervisor______________________

CHECK OR LIST ALL AREAS OF INSTRUCTION

ON THE JOB	IN SCHOOL
Interpersonal Skills	
_____ Coordinate Tasks with Co-Workers _____ Develop Responsibility to Job _____ React Appropriately to Criticism _____ Deal with Public/Customers _____ Use Proper Procedures To Report Absences _____ Supervise Other Employees	_____ Job Application Skills _____ Job Maintenance Skills a. Interest and Aptitudes b. Responsibilities _____ Daily Living Skills a. Personal Appearance b. Social Contact _____ Job Safety Instruction
List of Training Station Tasks ______________________ ______________________ ______________________ ______________________ ______________________ Equipment Skills ______________________ ______________________ ______________________ Job Safety Instruction ______________________	Academic Skills _____ Reading _____ Writing _____ Spelling _____ Grammar _____ Alphabetizing _____ Number Identification _____ Basic Math Skills _____ Metric System _____ Problem Solving _____ Sequencing Tasks _____ Emergency Procedures _____ Preventative Safety/First Aid _____ Specific Safety Skills a. Machine Use b. Tool Use TO BE ATTACHED TO TRAINING AGREEMENT

(Continued on page 186.)

Exhibit 7-3 continued

TO BE ATTACHED TO TRAINING AGREEMENT

These are examples of tasks from different jobs which may be indicated on the Training Plan under "List of Training Station Tasks."

* *Dishwasher*
  Collect dirty dishes, pots, and utensils
  Empty bus pans
  Scrape food off pans, plates, etc.
  Arrange items in washer racks
  Sort silverware
  Read and adjust gauges on washer
  Stack clean items, arrange on shelves
  Wipe tables, mop floor

* *Cashier*
  Make change
  Write sales slips
  Credit card processing

* *Dining Room Attendant*
  Take food and drink orders
  Place orders with cooks
  Set tables
  Serve food and beverages
  Clear tables

* *Bus Person*
  Clear and wipe tables
  Carry bus pans to kitchen

* *Housekeeper*
  Change bed linens
  Clean tables, ashtrays, wastebaskets
  Clean bathroom, replace towels, etc.
  Vacuum floor

* *Office Worker*
  Filing
  Writing letters
  Addressing letters
  Use telephone book
  Keep records

* *Laundry Attendant*
  Place laundry in washer and dryer
  Sort, fold, and stack clean laundry
  Read labels and laundering directions

* *Gas Station Attendant*
  Pump gas
  Change, mount, and repair tires
  Clean windshields
  Check and add oil & transmission fluid
  Give directions
  Make change
  Credit card processing
  Take inventory
  Stock shelves

* *Sales Clerk*
  Make change
  Write sales slips
  Credit card processing
  Weighing/measuring
  Read labels
  Take inventory
  Fill orders
  Record keeping
  Clean and stock shelves

Directions: List appropriate items on Training Plan under "Equipment Skills"

EQUIPMENT LIST

Adding Machine	Elevator	Pipe Polisher
Cash Register	Film Slicer	Scales
Clothes Washer/Dryer	Garbage Disposal	Soft Drink
Coffeemaker	Gas Pump	Telephone
Deep Fryer	Grill/Oven	Typewriter
Dishwasher	Hydraulic Lift	Tire Changer
Electric Mixer/Blender	Iron	Vacuum Cleaner
Electric Slicer	Microwave	Welder

Source: Teacher Coordinator Handbook: Secondary Vocational Community Based Employment Programs Pub. 7879008 (St. Paul, Minn.: St. Paul Public Schools, 1978) pp. 117-118.

Exhibit 7-4 Student Agreement Form

STUDENT AGREEMENT

The Work-Study Program has been discussed with me by the teacher-coordinator and I understand that through enrolling in this program:

1. I am not quaranteed a job. My teacher-coordinator and I will work together to find a job which seems suitable for me and then it is up to the employer-coordinator and me to discuss the requirements and responsibilities of the job, and to decide if I am to be hired.
2. I am to be paid for my community work experience.
3. I am to have a combined school-work week which does not exceed 48 hours.
4. I understand that I will be required to take the Vocational Skills Class as a part of the Work-Study Program.
5. I understand that I will be present and on time each day, both in school and at work. I will report for my classes each school day that I work unless cleared through my teacher-coordinator.
6. I will notify my employer and teacher-coordinator as far in advance as possible if I am unable to report for work.
7. I will tell my teacher-coordinator about any problems that are giving me trouble in school or on the job.
8. I understand my school supervisor or employer will rate my work regularly and discuss my progress with my teacher-coordinator. The grade for my job training and class will be based on these ratings and interviews.
9. I understand the responsibilities connected with my job and am accepting this training of my own free will.
10. I will obey the rules and policies of my employer and the school.
11. I may be dropped from the program if I leave my job without the consent of the teacher-coordinator or if I do not live up to the terms of this agreement.
12. I will be given the first chance to be in the next year's Work-Study Program if I successfully live up to the terms of this Agreement.

Date ______________ Student ____________
Coordinator ____________

Source: The Work Experience Handbook: Vocational Education Work Experience Program for Handicapped Students, prepared through the Minnesota Instructional Materials Center (St. Paul, Minn.: Minnesota Department of Education, Vocational Technical Division, 1977) p. 59.

Exhibit 7-5 Parent-School Agreement Form

PARENT-SCHOOL AGREEMENT FORM
WORK-STUDY PROGRAM

The major objectives of this program are: (1) to help develop the student's basic educational skills, (2) to improve his knowledge and attitudes about the world of work, and (3) to develop social skills that will help the student to achieve "full employment" when he/she completes their schooling.

Your son or daughter will receive high school credits through participation in the work-study program. Because the Work-Study Program differs in many ways from most general high school programs, the following statements are made to aid your understanding of some of the important parts of the program.

1. This is a three-year program and each student is admitted to the first year on a trial basis.
2. Parents are responsible for the medical needs of the student when the student is not on school property.
3. Regular school and job attendance is a responsibility of parents or guardians.
4. Parents should not contact the employer without first consulting the teacher-coordinator.
5. The teacher-coordinator will attempt to place the student in a work-training experience that tries to develop his abilities to the highest possible level.
6. The student must maintain an average or better performance at school and on the job.
7. The student may be shifted from one job to another from time to time or he/she may be removed from a training experience as the teacher-coordinator and/or employer decides.
8. The student will remain with the original training station throughout the school year. Necessary changes must be cleared through the Coordinator.
9. Classes, while in school, will be used to develop the student's abilities.

We/I request and authorize Independent School District # ______ to release my son/daughter ________________ from school during the hours scheduled on his/her class schedule for individual on-the-job experience.

Dated ________________ ______________________________
(Parent or Guardian Signature)

Dated ________________ ______________________________
(Teacher-Coordinator)

Source: The Work Experience Handbook: Vocational Education Work Experience Program for Handicapped Students, prepared through the Minnesota Instructional Materials Center (St. Paul, Minn.: Minnesota Department of Education, Vocational, Technical Division, 1977) p. 61.

Exhibit 7-6 Rating Sheet Form

RATING SHEET FOR STUDENT-TRAINEE'S WORK EXPERIENCE

Marking Period ______________________ Date ____________
Name of Student-Trainee ______________________
Name of Employer ______________________

Instructions: Under each of the headings below, you will find numbered responses. Read carefully and then choose the response which most closely describes the student-trainee as the heading relates to him. Place the number of the response in the blank located at the left of each heading. Below the responses is a space titled "comments," which may be used if additional information seems necessary. The first heading "school level" is rated as an example:

______School level
1. Nursery
2. Elementary
3. Junior High
4. Senior High
5. College

Comments ______________________

______Punctuality - Does the student report to work on time and continue to work until quitting time?
1. Frequently arrives late and quits early.
2. Has seldom been late and rarely quits work early.
3. Always prompt and always works until quitting time.

Comments ______________________

______Personal Appearance - Does the student's clothing and grooming "fit" the job:
1. Has poor dress habits and needs to improve his grooming.
2. Has acceptable appearance, could make some improvement.
3. Usually is very careful of his appearance.
4. Always presents an appropriate well-groomed appearance.

Comments ______________________

______Cooperation - Does the student-trainee cooperate with his boss and co-workers?
1. Does not get along with his boss or co-workers.
2. Is indifferent or often ignores co-workers.
3. Is polite and friendly when working with others.
4. Is always friendly and courteous to others.

Comments ______________________

______Reliability - Can the student be depended upon to do a good job?
1. Cannot be depended on; requires constant supervision.
2. Often must be reminded of duties; generally has to be carefully supervised.
3. Generally performs all assigned duties; requires average supervision.
4. Is a good dependable worker; requires little supervision.

Comments ______________________

_____Care of equipment - Does the student take proper care of his/her tools and equipment?
1. Seldom uses or takes care of his tools and equipment properly.
2. Sometimes uses his tools and equipment improperly and/or without the proper care.
3. Usually uses his tools and equipment properly and gives them proper care.
4. Always uses his tools and equipment properly and gives them proper care.

Comments _______________

_____Poise - Does the student do his work with confidence and self-assurance?
1. Needs more confidence; tries to avoid or get out of difficult situations.
2. Usually confident; handles most situations satisfactorily.
3. Confident; usually handles difficult situations satisfactorily.

Comments _______________

_____Attitude Toward Work - Does the student seem to like his work and show interest in learning more about his job?
1. Seems to dislike the work; has no desire to learn.
2. Is willing to work but shows no interest or enthusiasm in his job.
3. Seems to enjoy his work but is willing to "stand still" and not advance.
4. Shows interest in his work and has a desire to learn.

Comments _______________

_____Job Skills - Does the student have the necessary skills and knowledge to be successful on his job?
1. Has a definite lack of skills and knowledge.
2. Has limited knowledge; is lacking in some essentials.
3. Has an average grasp of the essential skills and knowledge.
4. Possesses all of the essential skills and knowledge.

Comments _______________

_____Work Habits - Does the student have the necessary work habits to do a good job?
1. Has poor work habits and doesn't know how to organize his work.
2. Has fair work habits but sometimes doesn't see things that should be done.
3. Has good work habits and looks for extra work to do.

Comments _______________

_____Improvement and Progress - Does the student's quality of work show satisfactory progress or improvement?
1. Shows little or no improvement.
2. Is learning slowly and has shown only slight improvement.
3. Learns fairly quickly and remembers instructions; is making normal progress.
4. Learns fast; seldom forgets; is making good progress.

Comments _______________

THANK YOU FOR YOUR EXCELLENT COOPERATION.

Source: The Work Experience Handbook: Vocational Education Work Experience Program for Handicapped Students, prepared through the Minnesota Instructional Materials Center (St. Paul, Minn.: Minnesota Department of Education, Vocational Technical Division, 1977), pp. 68-69.

CLASSROOM INSTRUCTION IN A COOPERATIVE WORK EXPERIENCE PROGRAM

A common question asked by new coordinators is, "What do I teach?" The answer comes from two sources: (1) general related instruction that contains the curriculum applicable to the student who is entering a job, and (2) direct instruction in the world of work that the student is learning in common with others while in the program. In this section, we shall look at both components of the classroom curriculum.

General Related Instruction

The component of general related instruction stems from the assumption that there are common survival skills necessary for all persons who enter the world of work. It is important that these general curriculum areas fit into the career development and education of each individual. One way of viewing these general topics of instruction is in the context of a career development continuum, as shown in Figure 7-2.

The Division of Vocational Education in the Ohio State Department of Education has listed the steps of career development in terms of:

- Career motivation—from kindergarten through the sixth grade, forming ideas about work and gaining some sense of what work involves.
- Career orientation—the development of concepts involved in various kinds of work and in the lifestyles and environmental factors that are related to them.
- Career exploration—in which students experiment with a variety of job experiences to see if the job requirements match with their needs, abilities, and interests.
- Vocational education—in which the students begin, either through a classroom or cooperative approach, the specific job skill learning that makes them employable.
- Preprofessional education—in which the student has made some tentative choices calling for college instruction and hence has begun a college preparatory course of study.[3]

Some common units of instruction that teacher-coordinators have found useful are listed in the monograph *Work Experience Curriculum Outline and Bibliography*, issued by the Vocational-Technical Division of the Minnesota Department of Education in 1977.[4] These common units, to be taught by topical outline, are shown in Table 7-3.

Figure 7-2 Career Development Continuum

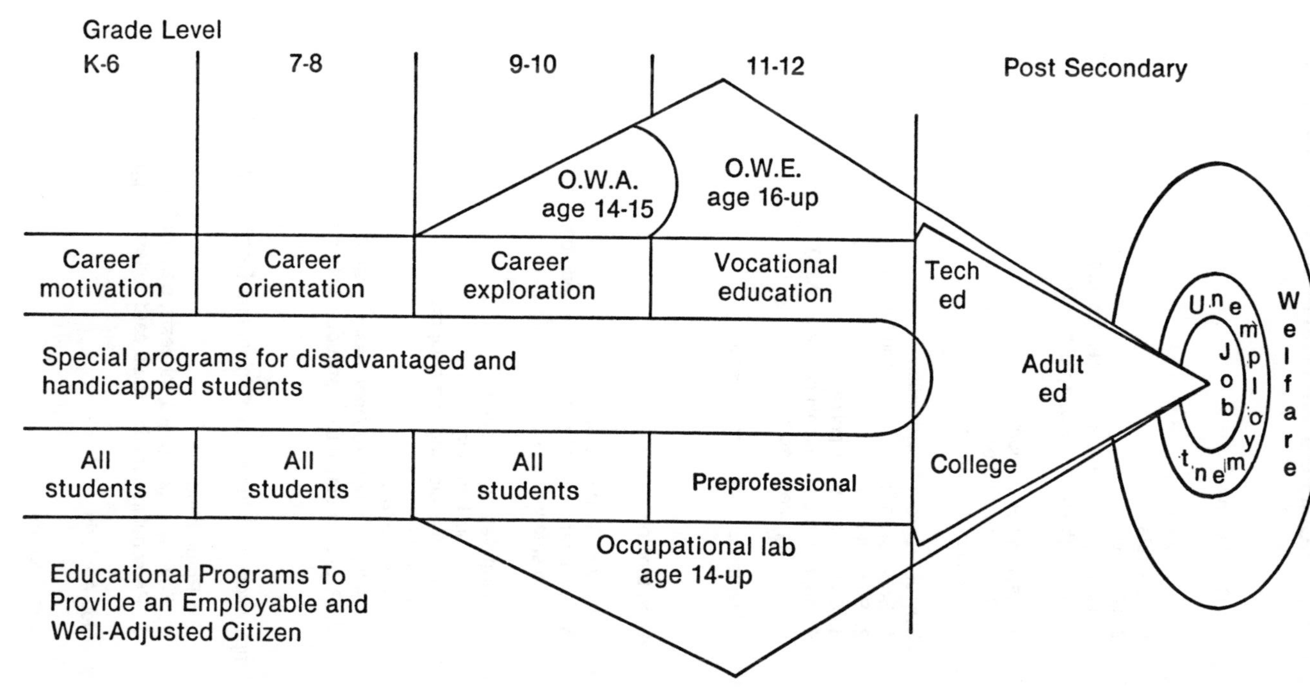

Source: Career Development Service, Division of Vocational Education, Ohio Department of Education, *Ohio's Career Development Continuum* (Columbus, Ohio).

Table 7-3 Common Units of Instruction in Career Development

I. Program Orientation

A. Intake Procedures
1. Referrals
2. Staffing
3. Home visits and conferences (parent involvement)
4. Forms (training plans, agreements)

B. Assessment Procedures
1. Goals and contract development
2. Vocational inventories

C. School Program Coordination
1. Scheduling (classes, transportation)
2. Support staff
3. School and work policies
4. Appropriate vocational courses (skills)
5. Training site selection

D. Advantages of Staying in School

II. Safety on the Job

A. Survey of Student Training Site
1. Emergency information and procedures
2. Job safety needs

B. General Safety Procedures
1. Materials handling
2. Protective clothing and equipment
3. First aid
4. Home safety
5. Self-protection (robbery, assault, rape)
6. Related safety topics (attitudes, safe driving)

III. Employment: Obtaining, Maintaining, and Terminating a Job

A. Job Preparation
1. Self-evaluation (skills, interests, personal hygiene)
2. Personal information (data card, letters of application)

B. Job Analysis

C. Job Sources

D. Job Seeking Techniques
   1. Using the telephone
   2. Reading maps
   3. Reading want ads
   4. Using the telephone directory and yellow pages

E. Job Application

F. Job Interview
   1. Interview preparation (manners, dress)
   2. Follow-up

G. Basic Job Performance
   1. Work habits
   2. Work attitudes

H. Job Termination

IV. Decision Making

A. Learning the Decision-Making Process

B. Applying the Decision-Making Process
   1. Peer problems and community problems
   2. Family problems
   3. Job problems
   4. School problems

C. Clarification of Values

D. Planning Careers

V. Basic Employment Skills

A. Communication (listening, writing, spelling)

B. Arithmetic (sales, commissions, weights, measures)

C. Business Machines (adding, cash register)

D. Transportation (bus scheduling, car pooling)

E. Timekeeping

VI. Significance of Work

A. Different Skill Levels

B. Dynamic Nature of Work

Table 7-3 continued

- C. Purpose of Work (lifestyles)
- D. Social Problem Solving
- E. Equal Opportunities and Work

VII. Development of Self-Awareness

- A. Personality
- B. Values and Goals
- C. Interests
- D. Skills and Abilities
- E. Physical Health and Grooming
- F. Character and Social Traits
- G. Personality and Job Success
- H. Development of Self-Concept
  1. Assertiveness
  2. Self-acceptance

VIII. Interpersonal Skills

- A. Employer-Employee
  1. Mutual expectations
  2. Need for rules
  3. Need for authority
  4. Fringe benefits
  5. Worker satisfaction
- B. Co-Worker
- C. Customer
- D. Family
- E. Group Dynamics (peer relationship)

IX. Career Exploration and Development

- A. Job Clusters
- B. Occupational Information

C. Career Self-Analysis

D. Training Programs

E. Future Trends

F. Vocational Planning

X. Money Management

A. Compensation for Work
1. Types of pay
2. Overtime
3. Common deductions
4. Fringe benefits

B. Budgets

C. Bank Services

D. Credit

E. Insurance Programs

F. Taxes

G. Consumerism
1. Housing
2. Clothing
3. Transportation
4. Food
5. Recreation
6. Legal problems

XI. Leisure in Your Life

A. Leisure Time Preparation

B. Personal and Social Growth

C. Avocational and Vocational Development

D. Job Selection and Leisure

XII. The Law and You

A. The Legal System

Table 7-3 continued

- B. Civil and Criminal Law
- C. Business Law (contracts)
- D. Labor Regulations

XIII. Employee Organizations

- A. Labor Organizations
- B. Role of the Union
  1. Negotiations
  2. Grievances
- C. Labor-Management Relations

XIV. Relevant Issues

- A. Chemical Dependency
- B. Family Living
- C. Economic Issues
- D. Current Events
- E. Minority Problems
- F. Futurism
- G. Business Ownership

Source: Vocational Education Work Experience Programs for Students with Special Needs Curriculum Outline and Bibliography, prepared through the Minnesota Instructional Materials Center (St. Paul, Minn.: Minnesota Department of Education, Vocational Technical Division, 1977) pp. 1-5.

The Table 7-3 outline could be modified to include more topics or to sequence topics according to the individual student's needs. In planning the instruction, the coordinator must use a curriculum plan. Such a plan might include the days of presentation, the method of delivery, and the evaluative method used to determine mastery. The units of the outline could be taught in an individualized approach or in a large group approach.

Direct Instruction

The second major area of instructional curriculum is direct instruction for the specific training station. This instruction is usually implemented with a tool called the training plan. A training plan is an outline of the major parts of instruction that are to be learned by the student for a specific job. The responsibility to learn these tasks is placed upon the student, and the responsibilities of implementation are delegated to the training station site or to the classroom site of instruction. Some training plans list only the tasks to be performed, with a check list for evaluating whether they will be learned in school or on the job. Other plans go into greater detail in the schedule of experiences that will be provided and what the time of completion will be.

Some coordinators discover that the full implemention of a training plan is a time-consuming and difficult task. Yet, it is the training plan that determines the quality of a work experience program. Like the Individual Educational Plan (IEP) outlined in Federal Legislation, the training plan can be a productive tool in implementing a work experience cooperative program.

Although coordinators may differ about the procedures for designing and implementing a training plan, the basic guidelines are these:

- The training plan should be individualized for each student's needs and should be based on specific job requirements.
- The training plan should take into account the student's career development needs (see Figure 7-2).
- The training plan should be developed cooperatively by the teacher-coordinator, student, and employer.
- The learning experiences listed should be observable by the teacher-coordinator, student, and employer.
- The training plan should emphasize the learning aspects of the program, not the program rules or regulations.
- The training plan should be simple, realistic, and flexible to meet both student and employer needs.
- The training plan should serve as a major part of the planning process for the direct instruction component of the program.
- Copies of the training plan should be open to review and distributed to the student, the employer and the coordinator.

IMPLEMENTING THE COOPERATIVE WORK EXPERIENCE PROGRAM

In the successful cooperative work experience program, the coordinator is able to blend the general related instruction with the direct instruction that specifies the student's individual needs for the job. In implementing the integrated program, the coordinator must know the proportion of each component that should be incorporated. Peter Haines and Ralph Mason have developed a cooperative distributive program that, when modified, would also be applicable to a cooperative work experience program (see Figure 7-3).[5]

The adaption of the Figure 7-3 concept to a cooperative work experience program would change the model of instruction to that shown in Figure 7-4. As can be seen, the teacher-directed general instruction is a heavy component at the beginning of the year. It then blends into a more individualized approach in the middle and end of the year, when the realities of classroom control dictate more teacher-directed instruction.

To understand more clearly this method of managing classroom instruction, assume that the person in charge of general-learning topics will be the teacher-coordinator, who will also have the major responsibility for setting the environment and motivation for learning. In this situation, the student learners are in the role of active receptors of the instruction as structured by the teacher-coordinator. In a graphic sense, a week of instruction might appear at the beginning of the year as in Figure 7-5.

Figure 7-3 Proportionate Allocation of Instruction for a Cooperative Program

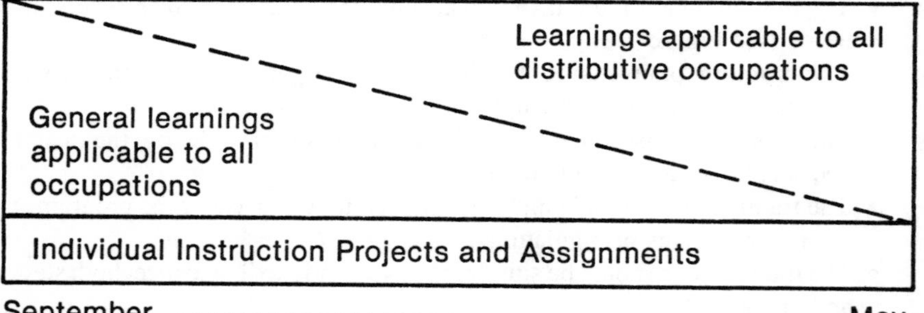

Source: Peter G. Haines and Ralph E. Mason, *Cooperative Occupational Education and Work Experience in the Curriculum* (Danville, Ill.: Interstate Printers and Publishers, Inc., © 1972) p. 20. Used by permission.

Figure 7-4 Proportionate Allocation of Instruction for Cooperative Work Experience Program

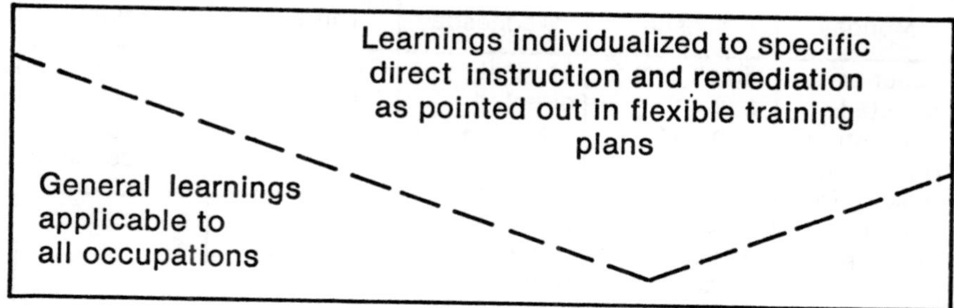

Source: Adapted from Peter G. Haines and Ralph E. Mason, *Cooperative Occupational Education and Work Experience in the Curriculum* (Danville, Ill.: Interstate Printers and Publishers, Inc., © 1972) p. 20. Used by permission.

Figure 7-5 A Week of Instruction: Beginning of Year

Monday	Tuesday	Wednesday	Thursday	Friday
Teacher directed lock-step lecture on safety on the job	Teacher directed individual activity for students on specific units	Teacher directed large group film on safety on the highway	Teacher directed small group instruction on safety rules in school and home	Teacher directed class meeting. Guest speaker on safety

Utilizing this schedule, the teacher-coordinator, assuming the major responsibility for instruction at the beginning of the year, begins individual instruction on Tuesday. On Thursday, some individual instruction occurs cooperatively in the small groups.

As the year progresses, however, the pattern of instruction changes gradually, as the students become familiar with the program. Through participation in small group instructional cooperative learning and individualized direct instruction, their skills increase; and the instruction plan begins to resemble the structure shown in Figure 7-6. Following this schedule of instructional management, the teacher-coordinator instructs the students on how to take responsibility and how to set up their own instructional methodology.

Figure 7-6 A Week of Instruction: Later in the Year

Monday	Tuesday	Wednesday	Thursday	Friday
Teacher directed instruction on decision making for career choices	Small group student directed instruction on exploring career choices, still somewhat structured through teacher coordinator	Student directed individualized instruction on specific remediation or job skill training	Student and teacher directed lab experiments on small job sample experiences	Teacher directed large group film selected by student committee

The advantages of such a system of instruction are:

- The students learn how to take responsibility for their own actions.
- The curriculum of the program can be individualized to allow students to receive proper, direct instruction and information about their specific job and career development.
- Once the structure is established, it allows students to transfer in and out of the program with a minimum of time loss. The teacher-coordinator can supplement lost instruction time with a particular student without necessarily hindering the progress of the other students.
- The system allows for a great deal of individual differences among students.
- Once the system is developed and field tested, it allows for development in any area but still has the continuity of the general learning that all students should have.
- The system is fun, effective, and efficient to teach; it permits a developmental approach that allows room for individual differences.

The disadvantages of such a system are:

- Teachers often feel the need continually to instruct and direct the student's activities and thus fail to let the system work.
- The system takes a lot of initial effort to organize and implement.
- It is sometimes difficult to monitor with so many activities going on.

In sum, to be effective, the teacher-coordinator will have to find and implement a delivery system of instruction that best suits the needs of the student.

FOLLOWUP OF THE SPECIAL NEEDS STUDENT

An important part of a cooperative work experience program for special needs students is the evaluation or followup on what happens to them after they leave the program. While specific procedures for followup are discussed elsewhere in this volume, there are some specific questions that teacher-coordinators should consider:

- Are the coordinator's work experience cooperative programs utilizing selection priority to ensure that there is a continuous flow of service and training throughout the student's training period?
- Do the students with special needs integrate into regular vocational training programs, cooperative or otherwise, after receiving the appropriate modified vocational instruction?
- Are the students able to participate in appropriate training or entry-level jobs in the community after graduation or program completion or after dropping out of school?
- Is there any type of program planning that utilizes all of the community resources available to ensure quality instruction, training, and service to students during and after program participation?
- Is there a program development and dissemination system that allows opportunities for program modification based upon the answers to the above questions?

By answering these followup questions, the coordinator will be able to develop the cooperative work experience program into one of the most exciting and effective types of modified vocational education for special needs students.

SUMMARY

The four basic aspects of cooperative work experience for students with special needs are:

1. The variety of available programs using the cooperative approach.
2. Placement of students on the job.
3. The classroom instructional component of cooperative work experience.
4. Followup of the special needs students.

Teacher-coordinators who are challenged by the ideas and procedures we have discussed in relation to these four aspects should pursue their particular interests by talking to other teacher-coordinators in the field and by communicating with teacher educators who have a background in cooperative vocational education. The results of such followup exploration could be very rewarding.

NOTES

1. Peter J. Deanovic and William Lundell, *A Report on the Effectiveness of the 1975-1976 Work Experience Career Exploration Programs in the State of Minnesota* (St. Paul, Minn.: State Department of Vocational Education, Special Needs Division, 1975), pp. 59-62.
2. Lyndon, Hagestuen et al., *Vocational Education Work Experience Handbook.* Prepared through the Minnesota Instructional Materials Center (St. Paul, Minn.: Minnesota Department of Education, Vocational-Technical Division, 1977).
3. Career Development Service, Division of Vocational Education, *Ohio's Career Development Continuum* (Columbus, Ohio: Ohio Department of Education, no date).
4. Curtis Engel et al., *Work Experience Curriculum Outline and Bibliography* prepared through the Minnesota Instructional Materials Center (St. Paul Minn.: Minnesota Department of Education, Vocational-Technical Division, 1977).
5. Peter G. Haines and Ralph E. Mason, *Cooperative Occupational Education and Work Experience in the Curriculum* (Danville, Ill.: Interstate Printers and Publishers, Inc., 1972), pp. 16, 20.

BIBLIOGRAPHY

American Vocational Association. The Advisory Committee and Vocational Education. Washington, D.C.: Publication Sales AVA, 1969.

Bichner, Jack; Brzinski, Leonard; Crewdson, Norma; Cronquist, George; Hoff, Vivian; Jenson, Dennis; Osland, Eugene, M.; and Shawbold, Dean. Teacher-coordinator handbook. Secondary Vocational Community-Based Employment Programs. St. Paul, Minn.: St. Paul Public Schools, 1978.

Brolin, Donn E. Vocational Preparation of Retarded Citizens. Columbus, Ohio: Charles E. Merrill Publishing Co., 1976.

Copa, George; Irvin, Donald E.; and Maurice, Clyde. Status of Former High School Students: Procedure for Local Assessment, summary report for a statewide sample of the class of 1974. Minneapolis, Minn.: University of Minnesota, February, 1976.

Crawford, Lucy C., and Meyer, Warren G. Organization and Administration of Distributive Education. Columbus, Ohio: Charles E. Merrill Publishing Co., 1972.

Engel, Curtis; Fields, Blaine; Noesen, Mike; Gorsky, Ken; Haskins, Cynthia; Henderlite, Marilou; and Kasma, Clint. Work Experience Curriculum Outline and Bibliography. St. Paul, Minn.: Minnesota Department of Education, 1977.

Hagestuen, Lyndon; Lane, Frank; Molick, Catherine; Rowland, Harland; Rud, Judy; Strom, J. Thomas; Wieger, Mark; and Zollar, Jack. Vocational Education Work Experience Program for Handicapped Students, Teacher-Coordinator Handbook. Minnesota Department of Education, Vocational-Technical Division, 1977.

Kenyon, Lawrence B. Job Placement Coordinators Manual. New Brunswick, N.J.: June 1976.

Mitchell, E.F. Cooperative Vocational Education—Principles, Methods, and Problems. Boston: Allyn & Bacon, Inc., 1977.

Phelps, L. Allen. Instructional Development for Special Needs Learners: An Inservice Resource Guide. Urbana, Ill.: University of Illinois, 1976.

Phelps, L. Allen, and Lutz, Ronald J. Career Exploration and Preparation for the Special Needs Learners. Boston: Allyn & Bacon, Inc., 1977.

Chapter 8

Identification and Utilization Support Services in Serving Special Vocational Needs Students

Suzanne Merwick, M.Ed.

> We need vehicles for understanding the interdependent roles that all citizens play in the education of our nation's youth. . . . Solving our educational problems is clearly a task for all sectors of the community. We are convinced that when schools and communities provide improved opportunities and a positive learning environment, students can be encouraged to accept responsibility as they become contributing members of our society.
>
> *Joseph A. Califano, Jr.*

INTRODUCTION

The purpose of this chapter is to explore the various special needs programs and to develop a model of inner-school and community support services that could help special needs programs improve the delivery of vocational training.

VOCATIONAL LEGISLATION

Between the Smith-Hughes Act and the legislation of the seventies, vocational legislation experienced a basic shift in philosophy.

Up until 1968, the thrust of vocational legislation often grew out of national manpower crises. More recent legislation, however, has redefined vocational education in terms of people, not manpower needs. In addition, the legislation has identified and focused on those handicapped and disadvantaged persons who cannot enter into or succeed in regular vocational programs.

The handicapped and disadvantaged are not appreciably different from other societal groups in their ambitions or potential. This has been evidenced repeatedly in success stories shared by special needs individuals. The handicapped and disadvantaged are far from unmotivated, untrainable, or uneducable. Usually, however, they do not succeed in regular vocational programs alone. They require conditions that demand a variety of methods for training success, and they need the support of a number of agencies and individuals.

MANPOWER LEGISLATION

Concurrent with the evolution of vocational legislation, there has been a similar move toward serving special needs populations through manpower legislation. Essentially, the shift from the Manpower Development and Training Act of the 1960s to the Comprehensive Employment and Training Act of the 1970s represents a change in philosophy similar to that which occurred in vocational legislation: a shift in a new direction, away from manpower crisis legislation toward training programs aimed at the employment of the structurally or hardcore unemployed populations.

The thrust of manpower programs is obviously employment. Over the years, however, many participants could not successfully complete training programs because of a lack of the basic social or educational skills necessary for effective and rewarding long-term employment.

It is interesting to note that the problems faced by the Department of Labor in serving the structurally unemployed are similar to the problems that special needs educators were asked to address by the 1968 and 1970 educational amendments. Apparently, what is needed, or has been identified by the Department of Labor as necessary, to remove the barriers of the structurally unemployed is what the educational system has been legislatively mandated to do: basic skills preparation and basic preparation in fundamental competencies.

Linkages

With education serving as the facilitator of the basic competencies and labor programs concerned with training and job preparation needs, a natural linkage seems to exist between labor and education. But money is scarce in both education and labor, and it is certainly scarce in human service agencies. If current levels of education, labor training programs, and human services are to be maintained, these three areas must cooperate. Only in that way can services be maintained at current levels for less money. By working together, duplication and fragmentation in all three areas can be avoided. By sharing administrative costs, facilities, resources, people, and services, we can help to ensure that the needs of special populations can be more effectively addressed at a time of reduced public financial support.

Economic and Social Factors Affecting Special Needs Programs

There are some prevailing conditions in our economy that make linkage between our schools and communities an imperative. Dissatisfaction with public education, reduced tax support for both schools and human service agencies, and a potential labor force deficiency in the 1980s and 1990s are all important factors that indicate that public schools will have to look toward increasing involvement and cooperation with support services in the community.

The American public is concerned about the education of their children. For the fifth consecutive year, the rating given to the public schools in the annual Gallup Poll of public attitudes toward public schools has declined. In 1979, only 34 percent of the American people gave their local public school a grade of *A* or *B*. In 1978, the figure was 36 percent; in 1977, it was 37 percent; in 1976, it was 52 percent.[1] This means that two-thirds of the American public now feel that their public schools are doing an average or failing job of educating their children. Not only is the American public upset over the role and function performed by their school system, a Gallup Poll conducted for the Charles F. Kettering foundation in 1978 indicated that students, too, are unhappy. In this poll, 1,115 teenagers, ages 13 to 18, were interviewed. When asked how much they enjoyed school, only 25 percent of those planning not to attend college reported that they liked school.[2]

What happens to public schools when two-thirds of the taxpayers and voters are dissatisfied with them? Tax levies are defeated, state legislators enact Proposition 13 initiatives, students are transferred to private schools; and the public schools, punished by the public in the only way it has of showing its displeasure, grow even weaker. Our system of public education may be becoming increasingly unable to do its job successfully, or even to define what that job is supposed to be. Perhaps the time has come when we must stop thinking of education as synonymous with schooling and take a good look at what functions will be needed and where in our society they should be performed. No longer can the school be everything to all students. Education is facing a decade in which it has to return to the community for cooperation in fulfilling its preparatory functions.

An additional significant factor for all educators and, more specifically, for special needs educators, is the possibility of a severe labor deficiency in the 1980s and 1990s. The factors shaping this potential labor shortage are already at work: lower birthrates, a slowdown in the participation rate of the female labor force, the lack of a sizable military force that can be reintegrated into the labor force, and lagging productivity. Projections indicate that the 1979 labor force cohort for

20-year-olds will be 90 percent by 1985, 85 percent by 1990, and will shrink to 75 percent by 1995.[3] This would mean projected unemployment in 1985 of 7 million, or a rate of less than 6 percent. By 1990, unemployment would amount to 5 million at a rate of less than 4 percent. Between 1990 and 2000, unemployment would virtually disappear; the labor force could be short by as much as 1 million or more workers by the year 2000.[4]

Cities throughout the country are already beginning to experience lower unemployment levels. When the unemployment rate is 10 or 12 percent, the quality of unemployed workers is much different than when the unemployment rate is only 3 percent. Increasingly, lower unemployment rates will force employers to tap the ranks of the unemployed and the underemployed. As a result, groups of people who have been previously ignored will have employers seeking their services. These sought-after employees will be people who, for many reasons, have been the hardest to train and the most sporadically employed. They will be the hardcore unemployed who often come into the employment world from the special needs classrooms of our schools.

If our educational system is to prepare students for participation in our society, then education in general, and special needs programs specifically, will have to assume even more responsibility for preparing viable workers for the 1980s and 1990s. The job of the special needs teacher must assume greater significance because no longer will we have the luxury of letting special needs students slip through the educational system poorly prepared for work and survival.

If the American public continues to be dissatisfied with the public schools, and if indeed there is a shortage of workers in the labor force of the 1980s and 1990s, vocational legislation may have to move away from meeting the humanistic needs of individuals back toward crisis legislation in order to meet the pressing economic and social need for workers.

SUPPORT SERVICES IN EDUCATIONAL PROGRAMS

Support agency cooperation can provide a major and effective link between education, training, and human services. If all those involved make a concerted effort to ensure that communication is open and ongoing, mutually beneficial relationships can be developed between schools and community support services. To understand these relationships, it is necessary first to look at the concept of support services.

Support services offer specialized assistance to individuals for the purposes of fulfilling needs. These services are diverse in nature; they project people-oriented goals to provide aid realistically to individuals who are in need. To best serve the interest of students, an educational program should interweave its proficiency in instruction and counseling with the expertise of other agencies, thereby creating a more complete program that will fill the students' needs at reduced costs to the school and, at the same time, utilize established expertise within both the school and the community.

To illustrate, consider the following: Though nationally the number of students has decreased over the last decade, the number of employed teachers has increased. Granted, reduction-in-force proposals have decreased the total number of teachers; nevertheless, the figures indicate that teachers are still being hired. The question is: what kind of teachers? The advent of mainstreaming has opened up a gap in the school systems: on the one hand, a need to teach the handicapped and disadvantaged; on the other, the fact that the school systems have not been equipped with teachers trained to fulfill this need. Thus, while the total number of employed teachers has decreased, the hiring of teachers in specialized fields has increased considerably. In some schools teachers of English are saying, "I can teach English, but I cannot teach a deaf, blind, or multihandicapped person. You must find three additional persons to serve these special populations." The irony is that the hiring of such teacher specialists tends to defeat the concept of least restrictive environmental programming. This is especially so if, in those specialized classrooms, you find only special student populations. Moreover, the cost of adding three other teachers comes at a time when the public is on record as favoring a curtailment of educational expenditures.

This could provide a tremendous opportunity for support services involvement. In the community there are already support agencies whose primary responsibility is to deal with the training and education of special populations. Though they, too, have begun to feel their existence threatened by reduced tax dollars, there they are, already in being, with the experience and expertise to fill an existing need and provide services for students. This, in turn, can help schools cut down on the rising costs of serving special populations. A final benefit accrues the students themselves in that they will be served both at home and in the community into which they will be moving. The support system does then, in fact, already exist. The question now is: when will it be used and who will initiate effective use of it within the educational system?

Interagency cooperation can stimulate positive relationships between the vocational system and community agencies and thus discourage duplication of services. A school program should not try to supply services which existing agencies can provide or can be modified to provide effectively. When students are referred to another agency, they do not end their association with the school; rather, the school, in cooperation with the support service, can provide them even better service.

Qualities learned in the school environment must find application in a wider social realm. This explains the special importance of community-centered learning situations and experiences. School personnel cannot afford to underemphasize the potential benefits of cooperation with the support services and the learning experiences in the community. These services and experiences can provide a unique combination of assets in the development of socially and educationally competent individuals.

Another good example of how the community and the school can work in conjunction with each other to achieve a fundamental goal of education is in the area of citizenship. Whether one is an academic or a special needs teacher, a basic goal of education is to foster good citizenship. There is no evidence to show that public schools are achieving this goal. In fact, the rates of crime, poverty, and deviant behavior have increased in step with each escalation of public school involvement. Public education has been unable to halt or even to slow the growth of these antisocial conditions. There is, in fact, almost total disagreement regarding the basic knowledge that should be presented in a class to prepare for citizenship. Indeed, surveys of student attitudes have shown repeatedly that social studies, where citizenship is traditionally taught, is frequently the most disliked class.[5]

In this situation, one might consider citizenship to be a community skill or value that is better learned in the community while, at the same time, it receives support at school. There is no difficulty getting students into the community; they are already there, in the courts and jails, in jobs, and in mental health agencies. When a student is faced with a problem, why then should not the school contact the many existing agencies to link their services with the school?

> Besides more pertinent topics and lessons, the school needs to respond with many more community-centered cooperative study and action programs. The disinclination of youths toward involvement in community affairs is a warning call for schools to institute community participation in their own procedures. Our high schools need to serve as workshops of civic experience. Far too many secondary schools fail to provide students with contact and services available to them in the communities in which they will eventually participate.[6]

The school benefits by not having to add additional staff to address the personal needs of students; at the same time it can upgrade its current staff by working jointly with support service agencies. The agencies benefit because a duplication of services is avoided and because they get the very people they are supposed to work with. The students benefit by getting school support while at the same time having their real needs addressed by people who are already experts and well acquainted with their problems. Moreover, they have an opportunity to learn that what is taught in school does indeed have something to do with their community. Such practical experiences and exposures can be invaluable in helping realistically to prepare special needs students for community participation.

Support Services in the Schools

Most educators are well aware of the support services offered in their own schools. The personnel in these services normally include administrative personnel, counselors, resource teachers, special needs personnel, and regular vocational and academic teachers. On a larger scale, school districts offer support services of psychologists, social workers, consultants, professional organizations, district workshops, and in-service days. Additional sources of information and support can be found in the programs of other schools in the district and in the advice and assistance of people in alternative school programs.

The most obvious and immediate source of support for special needs teachers and students, however, are the other teachers right around them. Often these other teachers have the same students in their classes and are acquainted with the problems. Thus, the relationship between teachers in the same school becomes an important source of support for the special needs teacher.

In this context, it should be remembered that for decades the American education system has supported a triple curriculum: general, college preparatory (academic), and vocational. The students in academic or college preparatory programs have progressed into professional positions, the general curriculum students have secured further training of some nature, while students in the vocational curriculum have obtained entry-level skills needed to enter the world of work. Recognizing the formal divisions between vocational, general, and academic programs, the 1968 amendments called for an important change of emphasis: "The educational experience should be devoid of the artificial barriers between academic, general and vocational curricula and be flexible for each individual."[7]

When working with special needs students, teachers have a real obligation to promote, within their own schools, good articulation between vocational and academic teachers. Schools have long recognized the need for vocational education, but, because society has valued the college education process, vocational education has often been viewed as merely producing "second class citizens." The primary criterion for certifying students has usually been the amount of time they have spent in school, rather than the skills that have been learned. The predicted labor deficiency of the 1980s and 1990s means that educators must begin to improve the public image of vocational education without destroying or attacking the merit of general education and widening the gap between the two systems. To waste human resources in such a shortage situation would be unconscionable.

In this connection, teachers themselves pose problems that can hinder the development of vocational education. Several authors have underlined the problem vocational educators have with their own images. Sidney Marland says it best: "The first attitude we, the educators must change is our own. We must purge ourselves of academic snobbery." [8]

When special needs programs first appeared, there was a tendency to water down the regular vocational curriculum. This, however, tended to alienate vocational, as well as academic, educators. Serious special needs educators must continue to resist this tendency. The legislation that gave birth to special needs programs clearly stressed that *what* is to be learned should not be changed, only *how* it is to be learned. The weakening of programs and services for special needs students will build a gap between special vocational education and regular vocational education similar to that already existing between vocational and academic education. If this is allowed to happen, special needs students will indeed become third class citizens, thereby reinforcing public criticism of vocational preparation and limiting even more the supply of workers who will be so badly needed in the future.

There are many definitional problems involved in the teaching of the disadvantaged and the handicapped. One author, in a 1970 article titled "Time to Start Teaching and Stop Labeling," called for a redefinition of the term disadvantaged, for the following reasons: (1) experts suspect the problems of disadvantagement lie not so much in the student as in the identification of the student's capacities and in the honesty of the identification system; (2) the term disadvantaged tends to group several problems into one prescription that may only cause the students to remain disadvantaged; and (3) the term overlooks such things as cultural and ethnic elements, thus leading to the generalization that to be a part of a subculture is to be automatically disadvantaged.

In the article, examples of English spoken by blacks were used to point up that this was the disabling element that posed a problem for the educational system, not the students who were labeled disadvantaged. Studies were cited, showing that students who spoke black English were tested and labeled disadvantaged because of their language. As a result of this label, they were given watered-down courses and ended up in the fifth grade reading less well than when they started school. Thus, the effect of the labeling was to foster permanent resistance to the category of disadvantaged. This article concludes that students labeled as disadvantaged need clear, supportive and consistent instruction from their teachers. In addition, they require teachers who really care.[9]

The point to be emphasized here is that teaching the disadvantaged student requires the best teachers, best materials, and the highest possible levels of expectation. Perhaps it would be better to redefine "disadvantaged students" as students who place the teacher at a disadvantage because they require more creativity, more effort, and more caring to teach.

Handicapped students have long encountered the same problem of labels. Their abilities have been limited because of the label attached to them as students. Fortunately, with the new programming thrusts in special education and special vocational needs, these restrictions are now being lifted.

Because special needs students are involved in the total school program, they will be involved in special needs programs, vocational programs, and academic classrooms. Special needs teachers must take the initiative to establish support services between vocational and academic teachers. All students, but especially special needs students, do not learn at the same rate or in the same way. Learning may vary greatly for students as they pass from area to area. It is important that academic and vocational teachers be flexible, have good broad backgrounds, and be willing to relinquish to someone else, when necessary, the instructional process in order to best serve the students. If one way of teaching does not work, an effective teacher must come up with another. The availability of these alternatives will help the student experience success. To this end, the special needs teacher may well be the one in the best position to provide support and suggestions for the special needs student who enters other classrooms.

Because teacher isolation can be dangerous, a support team within the school is very important. Teachers have different goals in their individual classrooms, and the student can become confused if teachers are isolated from the rest of the staff. A special needs teacher can do much to support other teachers in the school who also have special needs students. In return, the general education teacher can be an important support for the special needs program, thus creating an effective inner-school support system.

All teachers have the responsibility to consider both the academic and personal needs of students. With the support of other teachers, it is possible to create an environment in both academic and vocational classrooms that will help special needs students learn to work on their own, become more self-starting, learn about themselves, and learn from a wide variety of people.

The special needs teacher can create an additional support system within the school by helping with the curriculum modification that is necessary to serve special needs students. For the SVN student, learning may be different when being instructed via the regular methodologies and materials. Materials that are in logical sequence and given quick reinforcement usually help the special needs student to learn better. Flexibility in the use of all the media modes is essential with special needs students, but not all classes are prepared to offer these learning alternatives, and few teachers have the time to develop them. Here, special needs teachers have an excellent opportunity to lend their expertise and help the academic teachers who share the educational responsibilities for special needs students. (Chapter 6 deals extensively with relevant curriculum modification and program strategies.)

The National Committee on Employment of Youth has outlined some teacher qualities necessary for teaching the special needs student:

- "Ideally, a teacher of special needs students should have competence in subject areas, a familiarity with modern methods of instruction, and be able to communicate with the students. But, understanding and the ability to relate are more significant in dealing with the disadvantaged than either knowledge of the subjects or pedagogical training and teaching methods. Credentials, in fact, appear to be less important than commitment.

- "Teachers must understand the unique personal, family, community, social and economic conditions of the students.
- "Teachers must minimize cultural and ethnic differences by accepting the students for who they are, not what society expects them to be.
- "Teachers must communicate with special needs students without being patronizing, making genuine identification with the needs, avoiding sarcastic, judgmental or moralistic tones and making an optimistic, positive and encouraging approach.
- "Teachers must cooperate with other staff, counselors and professionals in dealing with the reluctance, fears and ambivalences of the disadvantaged. The goal of the teacher is to aid the student in gaining confidence in the ability to learn, achieve and experience success.
- "The teacher must adjust teaching approaches to the style and the rate of learning of the students by using step-by-step targets, stressing the concrete and literal rather than the theoretical and abstract, and pacing progress to the students' abilities while not underestimating their potential."[10]

Whatever form the delivery of education for special needs students takes, it must give freedom and structure at the same time; stress interdisciplinary and transference learning; provide multimedia exposure to oral, written, listening, and thinking skills; and, above all, be able to be delivered effectively and relevantly in a variety of ways. For example, educators are constantly searching for reading programs. They purchase system after system but have yet to find the one system that works for all purposes. Public education, at best, aims at what is best for the majority. A special needs program must avoid this approach and instead concentrate on what is best for the individual. Educational programs for the special needs student must evolve from an examination of all the delivery systems, then taking the best of each and putting together a unique creation for that student. As long as special needs students are involved in the total school program, special needs teachers must move toward providing a support system that will allow what has been learned about the teaching of special needs students to be transferred and shared by all involved.

The areas of counseling and testing are two other areas in the school system where support services can be modified and improved. A team approach, with the student as the central, most important factor, is imperative if counseling and teaching are to become integrated and ongoing throughout the duration of the student's affiliation with the school. Through a team, leadership becomes more group-centered, and, because there are several people involved in their program, the students benefit more.

In the vast majority of special needs cases, the assessment of educational potential has been left to the counselor or psychologist who usually administers a battery of tests. In most cases, the purpose of the tests is to find out what is wrong with the students in order to label them. Even in the case of a team approach (psychologist, doctor, counselor), the end result is still a label. What the educator needs, however, is not a label but a workable prescription for helping the student effectively. The traditional role of testing is to label or diagnose, but rarely to prescribe an effective teaching plan. Thus, specialists in special needs are currently recommending a team approach, using formal and informal assessments that involve far more than just testing. (See Chapter 7 for further information on assessment.)

Formal assessment involves the traditional assessment of the areas of mental function, such as intelligence, language, academic achievement, speech, perceptual-motor skills, and social-emotional development. One would expect that the formal assessment of students would yield information of value to the educator working with the student. However, this is not always the case. In practice, the psychologist usually collects the results of the tests and compiles them into a report for parents. This report can vary widely in educational relevance. At best, it can:

- eliminate or confirm the presence of mental deficiency;
- point out general areas and levels of failure in such subjects as reading, spelling, and arithmetic;
- indicate possible areas of language deficit;
- demonstrate modality strengths and weaknesses;
- identify patterns of disruptive and undesirable behavior;
- recommend areas for diagnostic teaching; and
- request feedback from the teacher.

Formal assessment can, however, also be instructionally useless. It can:

- demonstrate the obvious, that is, dwell at length on what is already vividly apparent to the teacher;
- stress excessively etiological factors, such as brain dysfunction, which are of no value to the teacher; or
- dwell at length on the interpretation of minimal and obvious evidence.

Other factors can cause the formal assessment to be less than helpful. Some of the inadequacies stem from:

- lack of test information,
- intrasubject variability,
- overgeneralization of findings,
- low test and subtest reliabilities,
- incorrect interpretation, or
- using normative tables with groups of differing populations.

The informal approach to assessment is characterized by the use of informal procedures administered by the educational diagnostician (the classroom teacher) and performed in a continuing educational setting. This kind of assessment is frequently called diagnostic teaching.

Generally, the informal approach is employed after formal assessment is completed. However, the two approaches will yield the best results if they are carried out simultaneously, making possible an unbroken, ongoing educational assessment of each student. Special needs educators have been using their own realistic informal assessments for years. Most teachers, however, would probably appreciate an opportunity to quit working alone and to get help by working with people far more qualified in the whole area of assessment. Through this type of sharing, teachers can get more assistance in prescription development for special needs students.

To provide the maximum potential service to special needs students, a team approach is an obvious choice. People learn in a variety of ways, from a variety of approaches and stimuli, and the more people that are involved in that learning process, the greater will be the chances of finding the most effective learning patterns for each unique student. An educator cannot realistically be expected to be able to meet all needs on his own. Thus, a team approach can increase the chances of optional learning in that there are several people ready to teach as well as to counsel. In this connection, the continuous nature of the teaching and the need to develop and modify materials are important considerations. A counselor or psychologist, for example, can assist in observing results and suggesting directions to take or to be abandoned before the student is turned off in an educational miscalculation.

Perhaps the strongest reason to encourage special needs teachers to move toward a support service that combines teaching and counseling is that such an approach is consonant with the entire thrust of a special needs program that stems from humanistic beliefs that the real importance of all education and learning is to produce an effective, functioning person. The assumption that teachers must have all the knowledge and responsibility for teaching and that the psychologists and counselors must stop their involvement after assessment is inconsistent with the goals of special needs programs. Clearly, support service teams must be created and implemented in order to maximumly serve the needs of special populations.

Support Services in the Community

In establishing a system to use community support services, the school should make an effort to become aware of the many service agencies and the types of service currently provided target groups. Often the community issues a directory of available services; this is an excellent place to begin, because such a directory can help the special needs teacher to become familiar with other agencies and to facilitate agency interaction. Initial contacts with other agencies can be made through various community meetings or through information-seeking phone calls. In a discussion about the purpose of a special needs program, it is possible, in turn, to find out what relevant services another agency has to offer. Counseling, consultation, and other services can thus be provided in an agency core and adapted for students. By merging the expertise of a special needs program with that of a support agency, the needs of students can be better addressed. Contact between support services can be related to a specific student's needs, or it can be a part of a process of interaction regarding a group of students. For example, if a special needs program has several students who are deaf, the teacher may want to identify the agencies in the community who work with that specific population and seek a contact person to whom referrals can be made or from whom advice can be sought.

There is a distinct advantage in establishing contact with other agencies even before the need to refer students arises. In such cases, when students need services from another agency, the contact will already have been made and cooperation is enhanced. The advance contact thus enables a special needs program to provide a smoother transition for students as well as a ready source of ideas and program planning for the teacher or counselor.

The developers of a special needs program should first determine the overall needs of a student and then decide what it can do to meet those needs. They should also determine which agencies could work with the student and in what capacity and thereby avoid duplication and ensure consistency. The existing gaps in the student's need for services could then be determined and the student referred to the appropriate agency. If there is no appropriate agency, a program could be developed jointly to meet the student's needs. If the students are visually impaired and have not been to the rehabilitation agency, a staff member in the special needs program could contact the agency to see if the student could get help there. Should the student fail to qualify, the teachers of the special needs program would be responsible for examining other alternatives, or they could seek advice from the rehabilitation agency in planning the school program for the student who did not qualify.

Initiating and developing contact with other agencies is vital for special needs programs. But ensuring continuous communication is even more important. The success of any program is determined by the success of the students. Ongoing communication between the special needs programs and those of the support agencies increases the chances of success for both types of programs. In cooperation with other agencies, the special needs program can better meet its goals for the students. In this way, the special needs program can issue a wide variety of services for students, one of the most valuable of which is to act as a referral and coordinating agent for the students.

Another advantage of continuous communication is that it helps to avoid the "shopper" syndrome. This is a process in which students go from agency to agency to receive maximum services without anyone ever addressing their fundamental problems. Many students in special needs programs have thus been allowed to continue in programs that have failed to deal with their underlying problems. With open communication, a student is less likely to be the recipient of duplicated services and be less likely to misuse available services, whether in the school or in the support agencies. If communication remains open, and an agency is not addressing the needs of the student, a special needs program may be able to intervene to clarify those needs and insist that the student deserves the agency's services.

A special needs program must accept the responsibility of maintaining and initiating communication with support agencies. It should continually seek and update information concerning changes and the status of students in other support agencies. Some agencies are responsive only to the extent that demands are imposed upon them. In such cases, the special needs program must assume responsibility to see that the agency either remains involved or becomes involved again with the students when necessary. Without other support agencies, a special needs program cannot be as effective as it should be. On the other hand, the services of the support agencies can certainly be enhanced by cooperation with the school system.

THE MANPOWER LINK WITH SPECIAL NEEDS

The Manpower Problem

The present problem of unemployed youth is not a new phenomenon; it has in fact developed over the past 30 years. Since 1948, the unemployment rate for 16- to 17-year-olds has doubled. For the last five years, young people of ages 16 to 24 have accounted for nearly one-half of all unemployed persons, even though they account for only one-fourth of the labor force.[11] Regular vocational programs long ago established supportive links with business and employers in the community through cooperative educational programs. Still, by 1978, many businesses surveyed by the Committee for Economic Development still felt that a great number of young people were coming out of school poorly prepared for the world of work.[12]

One of the major reasons for high youth unemployment can be traced to an inadequate transition between education and work. For a variety of reasons, including the greater complexity of the subjects to be learned, young people today often stay in school longer than their parents and grandparents, and they thus have less exposure to the real experiences they will face when they do enter regular employment.

There is also the problem of the time gap that exists between the age when young people complete their high school education (17 to 18 years) and the age at which employers generally begin to hire them for entry-level jobs. According to recent studies, for entry-level jobs, about 80 percent of employers start to hire personnel at ages 21 or 22.[13] For many youth, neither the experience gained in school nor exposure in searching for a job or working at the kinds of jobs usually open to teenagers is adequate preparation for an adult career. Many are unable to get a job because they lack the right kind of work experience, but they cannot get the experience without a suitable job.

The problem is not necessarily resolved once the youth reach the age at which firms are willing to offer them regular jobs. Many of them prove to be far less productive and adaptable than they would have been if the link between learning and work had been stronger. The problem may lie in the fact that most cooperative education programs have been aimed at traditional vocational students, with little involvement by special needs students. Many employers are trying to improve this situation by providing supplemental job training and by increasing their support for local school system programs that aid in the transition from school to work. Inadequate school preparation is proving extremely costly for the private sector, which often must make up for educational inadequacies through supplemental training.

In preparation for employment, special needs populations may need special counseling, partly because they have far less access to the informal job-search network of employed friends and relatives. Many of these young people face special problems in relating to the most basic elements and disciplines of the adult work place. They may need continuous counseling, starting early in school. Such counseling might have to focus on giving them opportunities to develop self-confidence and on teaching them how to pursue attainable goals step by step while at the same time helping them deal with practical problems after they have obtained their initial jobs.

Special needs educators may want to explore the possibility of establishing cooperative education programs specifically aimed at the needs of and the barriers facing special needs students. Although such cooperative educational programs could be modeled after existing cooperative programs in regular traditional vocational education, they would have to involve even more cooperation between schools, employers, and community support services if special needs youth are to successfully survive the transition from school to work.

The current high school drop out rate stands at 25 percent.[14] The reasons cited most often for quitting school are:

- I cannot afford to go to school.
- I am too far behind ever to catch up.
- I need money to help the family.

It is of course easier to get students back on the track if they have not been totally derailed. Special needs programs can assist in spotting potential dropouts and working to prevent them. A support system within a community can provide invaluable aid to schools that serve special needs youth who have previously dropped out but wish to return to finish their education.

It is possible to create better schools with the resources presently available if we use those resources wisely and in conjunction with community and manpower programs. Additional dollars are important, but schools in general, and special needs programs specifically, have a more fundamental problem: the competent and effective use of what resources we already have.

In testimony before Congress on March 1, 1979, Roman Pucinski, a member of the National Advisory Council on Vocational Education and a former Illinois congressman, said:

> You cannot assist the hard core unemployed simply by exposing them to minimal entry level schools, while ignoring other basic deficiencies in education, and expect them to hold a job. We must deal with the total person and provide basic communications skills when necessary to enhance job skills. We must not repeat the mistakes of the past and think that we are helping people by putting a rake or shovel in their hands; we must provide an educational component if we hope to do better than in the past.[15]

We have no real choice except to view our present circumstances as an opportunity to do more with less. But we cannot do it alone; we must link with others in the community. Walter F. Mondale, forty-fourth vice president of the United States, summarized it this way:

> We must join together to reduce unemployment among our nation's youth, especially the disadvantaged. Too many of our cities suffer from double-digit school dropout rates. Too many young people are leaving school without the skills they need to read, write, get a job and enjoy the full bounty of our society. We do not propose instant cures; there are none, but there must be a way to find out what works and what does not work. And to this end, President Carter has directed his administration to

conduct a major youth employment policy effort. This policy review will involve 18 agencies and it will draw upon the experience of state and local government, school systems, private employers, labor unions, and community organizations. It will provide the basis for legislation proposals for the next session of Congress to strengthen and improve those programs. Our goal is to find a joint public and private sector strategy to reduce youth employment in the 1980s. That means building stronger ties between education and work, and it also means boosting private sector participation in that effort. Four-fifths of the jobs in this country are private jobs. Simple arithmetic shows that we must enlist the total support of the private sector to solve this problem.[16]

Where Does the Individual Teacher Start?

Whether you are an academic, vocational, or special needs teacher, you can start to build a community support system very simply by locating within your immediate community, human service agencies from which you, your students, and your school can benefit.

The first and most serious barrier to establishing community support services for students is you yourself. Thinking about potential barriers before you even start can prevent you from ever starting or prevent progress when you do start.

Be practical, but do not approach a difficult situation by thinking that nothing can be done. Do not think about the barriers; instead, if you run into them, attack them one at a time. Be patient; many barriers are erected by impatient people who, if they had taken more time, would have avoided them.

Forget the past, start now and go from there. It is always worth one more effort. You may not always get what is needed, but chances are you can move closer, and even that is progress if the situation is better than when you started.

Share your frustrations with others. Do not be afraid to admit you do not know what to do. Another person, not as close to the situation, may be able to give you a creative idea you have not thought of or a perspective that may open up a whole new approach.

Although your school may do many things for your special needs students, you cannot possibly have the answer for everyone. In fact, there may be situations for which you do not even know the question. Situations will arise in which you cannot honestly be of much assistance to a student who enters your program or in which additional services are needed and you find yourself illequipped or unable to provide them. Still, you can—as an individual, a program, or even a school—set up a viable community interaction and referral system that can meet your specific needs.

Although we may not always think of junior and senior high school students as adults, it becomes quite apparent upon closer examination that these students do have definite adult-size problems that need attention above and beyond the services that are offered by the school itself.

Think about some of the special needs students you have worked with in the past and some of the problems they have faced that were not of an academic nature. If you ignore these problems, you may fragment the student and force a choice between school and addressing the problem at the time it needs attention. Ask yourself if you could have assisted the student in finding an appropriate source of help while at the same time reinforcing school concern and connections.

Think about students with whom you have worked, about the problems they brought to the classroom that had to be addressed within the school itself, such as difficulty with assignments, failing grades, or personality problems with other students or teachers. Are there support services—such as teacher advisors, social workers, counselors, or peer advocates—in your school to handle such problems? If not, you should be the one to take the initiative. First, address the problem and seek help either within the school or in the community. Secondly, learn from the experience and dedicate yourself to taking the necessary steps to develop both in-school and community assistance so that, when the next need arises, you and the school are better prepared to handle it.

When a void in support services appears, do not begin quickly to establish a new service in your school. Instead, explore what is already available in the community to avoid duplication and extra costs. If the support available in the community falls short of what is needed, rather than start a whole new service oriented only to the school, perhaps the school will have to assume responsibility for building a bridge between the service and the school. You, as a special needs educator, may have to help to show support services how what they have to offer can be modified and adapted to meet the needs of the students. Someone must take the initiative, and the results can be better school help, improved community services for all special populations, and more effective use of tax dollars.

If you work in a small community with very few community agencies, do not despair. Help may still be available. In such situations, one of the first places you might contact for assistance is the local churches. You might be surprised at the amount of assistance you will be able to obtain from such sources, such as emergency clothing or food, transportation help, even temporary housing, companionship, and tutoring.

If you find that you need legal assistance and your community does not have a public legal-aid office, contact your local county attorney, a local lawyer, or, if necessary, your local police. If health services are needed, contact local doctors, health clinics, or nearby hospitals. If you need employment services, examine the newspapers and periodicals, contact community business persons, and, by all means, contact your own colleagues for assistance. You might be surprised at how much support your community can provide, much of which you might not have been aware.

If you work or teach in a larger community, there are often some standard support services available. Here is a brief list of the types of support services your students might need:

Legal services
Legal advice, juvenile court personnel
Attorneys
Probation officers

Financial assistance
Welfare
Social Security

Employment
State job service
CETA youth programs

Health care
Visiting nurses
Planned parenthood
Red Cross
Vocational rehabilitation
Poison control
Open door health clinics

Counseling and personal crisis
Rape crisis line
Personal crises line
Big brother/sister
Local mental health centers
Alcoholics Anonymous
Chemical dependency programs
Child guidance and family counseling

Pregnancy
Parents without partners
Right to life
Adoption services
Birthright

Research

You can start by listing all obvious existing agencies in your community. You might simply take a telephone directory, find the list of community services in the Yellow Pages, and start from there. Most often these services are listed by categories, such as legal, financial, child care, employment, emergency, and so on. This will give you an initial overall structure to which you can add each time you come across a new service or agency. Also, the category list allows you to locate information more quickly because students usually identify their problems in terms of an immediate need. Following is a list of general need categories by need from which you might start:

Child day care
Counseling
Drugs and alcohol
Education
Handicapped assistance
Housing
Legal assistance
Medical assistance

Employment	Mental health assistance
Elderly	Mentally retarded assistance
Family support services	Personal support groups
Financial aid	Recreation
Food, clothing and furniture	Transportation

As you begin to place agencies in general categories, remember to cross reference. An agency such as your local office of mental retardation might offer many services that should be filed in several need categories. For example, you might list this one agency under all of these: transportation, medical assistance, mental retardation assistance, education, housing, and financial assistance. The point is to get to know *all* of the services covered. Make a file card for each agency and duplicate it so that you have one for each service category; then file the agency under all the headings that are relevant to your students' needs.

The result can become a quick reference for you to consult when needs arise. But you will have to keep addresses, phone numbers, and names of contacts up-to-date. Then you can make notes on the cards concerning what kind of financial or transportation services are offered, who to contact, and what the eligibility requirements are. You can even make personal notes on the cards to remind yourself of problems you have run into and how you can get around them. The reference cards thus can become a living list that is always growing and changing, unlike the published community services handbooks that so quickly become dated.

Telephone and Leg Work

As a way of adding to the list of services beyond the obvious ones in your community, pick up pamphlets wherever you go. In fact, call or write every relevant agency you can think of, and be constantly on the lookout for additional agencies you might want to contact.

Often, in conversations with an agency, you can find out about several related services they use that might be unknown to the average person but not to the specialist in that area. For example, until a need for emergency food arises, one might never discover that churches sometimes maintain a "pantry" program for just that purpose. Because such a program operates by word-of-mouth, it may never be listed in the phone book or in community directories.

Sometimes, simply by calling an agency you can discover quickly what services are offered that can be used to expand your basic list. You may, for example, never find out that a university has assessment and counseling services to offer to the community unless you just happen to call the psychology department and inquire about these specific kinds of support services. Similarly, you may discover that a neighborhood community center can assist someone in the area to arrange child care or transportation. The real point here is to call, explain the situation or need, and ask for any suggestions.

More leg work can be completed on a telephone than you can imagine. One real benefit in calling is that you have to explain who you are and what your program does, and you thus familiarize others with what your special needs program is all about.

Honesty

It is not always easy to be honest when attempting to arrange cooperative services for special needs students. This is because honesty requires that you clearly outline both the strengths and weaknesses of your program and admit that you need assistance with your students. For example, in helping a handicapped person get a part time job, it is often tempting to deny the person's handicap. This, however, is being dishonest with both the agency or employer and with the student. Yet, in too many cases, such a student is oversold and ends up failing on the job. Start by being honest: outline the student's capabilities, but also mention the student's disability. Then, if the employer or agency is willing to give the student a try, make suggestions and outline a system of support. One thing is certain, employers will be far more likely to try if they know you will follow through and not just dump the student upon them. Do not ever promise support you cannot provide or have no intention of providing. Misrepresenting a handicap or disadvantagement sets everyone up for failure—you, the agency, the employer, and, most importantly, the student, who does not need another failure.

Another way of being honest is to admit there might be other agencies that may be able to assist you or even meet a student's needs more completely than you can. Teachers cannot be all things to all people. When working with a blind student, for example, there are agencies that are far more effective than you can be in teaching needed coping skills to blind students, such as cane travel, braille, and independent living. Use such agencies, but complement what they do by keeping in touch sufficiently to reinforce in school what is learned through the agency. If blind students are working on cane travel, do not lead them around, rather let them be mobile throughout the school setting. Let them use their travel skills at school just as they do in the community. This kind of cooperation can help you appreciate what you can contribute while, at the same time, you utilize the expertise of the service agencies.

A final kind of honesty is honesty with the student. A special needs teacher who really cares will try to become part of the solution, not part of the problem. This will mean being honest even when it hurts. For example, students with epilepsy may want to learn to drive. State laws, however, often prohibit this until there has been a defined period of time free of seizures. If you really care, be honest: you cannot change the law, but you can help such students learn, with the aid of services in the community, how to take better care of themselves and work toward the goal of securing a driver's license while arranging viable transportation options during the interim.

Initiative

Initiative is really the key to effective school-community linkages. Be creative, be innovative, be an initiator whenever necessary in order to be a true advocate for the students that you work with. To do this, you must feel comfortable with the advocacy role.

Remember that many community agencies have never worked with youth, not because they cannot, but simply because they have never done so. In such situations, you may have to be a creative thinker. Because you are with the student daily, you may have a much better picture of what areas need to be addressed. If you are honest, you will know what the school can do and what help is needed beyond that. You must approach student situations with the attitude that it is worthwhile trying to get help. But you may need to convince other agencies to explore the possibilities of extending the needed services. Emotions Anonymous (EA) groups, now established in many cities, have traditionally geared their support to adults. Yet, many teenagers have emotional problems and need support outside of school. When teachers began to realize this, EA began to start groups specifically for young people. It was not easy to do, and it is especially hard to get such groups started today, yet the service does fill a gap in many cities across the country.

Initiative also means that the special needs teacher will at times take on a role of orchestrator. For example, a mentally retarded student who is nearing completion of school may have to address the problems of work, job training, and independent living. Agencies such as Goodwill, Vocational Rehabilitation, and the Office of Mental Retardation all may have relevant services to offer. The special needs teacher could contact these agencies, set up a meeting, and orchestrate how each could provide services that avoid duplication yet fit together to move the student toward being better prepared to live in the community.

An important operating philosophy for the special needs teacher who assumes the role of orchestrator is: never be afraid to ask or try. You must acknowledge that there are no easy answers to meeting the needs in question, and you may not even have any good suggestions; but by bringing together several minds, a way might be found to approach the task creatively. One thing is certain: there are no guarantees that the results will work. But there is always the possibility that they may, and, even if they do not, no one can be worse off than if nothing had been tried.

Too often we educators and those in service agencies try to fit students into the existing system. There is often real merit, however, in approaching our tasks from the back by laying out the needs first, then creatively thinking what can be done to make things better. This approach allows all involved to try new approaches, to determine if they work, to revise efforts, and to keep on thinking creatively. The end result may be to learn what not to do and to come closer to seeing what should be done.

Building up a viable network of community referrals and working in harmony with other community human service agencies may seem a monumental task. It is indeed time-consuming, but it is by no means impossible to achieve. And its value to the individuals you work with is beyond question.

CONCLUSION

At a time when the public is cutting funds for both education and human service agencies and also shows dissatisfaction with the preparation of students for the labor market, educators are faced with the problem of having to prepare populations considered as unemployable, yet to prepare them better than ever before.

The problem of getting more from less cannot be handled by the schools alone. Community support agencies must be prepared to cooperate if, in the future, there is to be a viable work force that uses the special needs population to its maximum potential.

NOTES

1. George H. Gallup, "The Eleventh Annual Gallup Poll of the Public's Attitudes Toward the Public Schools," *Phi Delta Kappan* 61, no. 1 (September 1979): 33.
2. "Newsnotes," *Phi Delta Kappan* 61, no. 1 (September 1979) 74.
3. Bureau of Labor Statistics, *Monthly Labor Review,* Table 1, December 1978, p. 87.
4. Donald E. Pursell, "The Emerging Labor Deficiencies in the United States," mimeographed (Lincoln, Neb.: University of Nebraska-Lincoln, Bureau of Business Research, August 1979).
5. Dwight Roper and Susan Roper, "The Accountable School: Elective Courses, Competition and Cost Effectiveness," *Phi Delta Kappan* 60, no. 7: 527.
6. Richard E. Gross, "Seven New Cardinal Principles," *Phi Delta Kappan* 80, no. 4 (December 1978): 291.
7. U.S. Office of Education, *Vocational Education Amendments of 1968,* Bureau of Adult, Vocational, and Library Programs (April 1969).
8. Sidney P. Marland, "Meeting Our Enemies: Carre Education and the Humanities," *English Journal* (April 1974): 901.
9. "Time to Start Teaching and Stop Labeling," *American Vocational Association Journal* (October 1975).
10. National Committee on Employment of Youth, *Teaching the Disadvantaged* (U.S. Office of Education).
11. Walter F. Mondale, "Joint Public and Private Sector Strategy Is Goal for the 1980's," *CETA Reader* 3, no. 9 (September 1979): 7.
12. Committee for Economic Development, *Jobs for the Hard-to-Employ: New Directions for a Public-Private Partnership* (New York: January 1978).
13. David Robinson, *Training and Jobs Programs in Action* (Committee for Economic Development, May 1978).
14. *CETA Reader* 3, no. 9 (September 1979): 6.

15. "Mind and CETA Working Together: The Education to Work Transition," Pamphlet #27 (Department of Labor: Government Printing Office, no date).
16. *CETA Reader* 3, no. 9 (September 1979): 6.

BIBLIOGRAPHY

Committee for Economic Development. *Jobs for the Hard-to-Employ: New Directions for a Public-Private Partnership*. New York: January 1978.

Ginzberg, Eli. *The Manpower Connection: Education and Work*. Cambridge, Mass.: Harvard University Press, 1976.

Kay, Evelyn; Kemp, Barbara; and Saunders, Frances. *Vocational Education: Guidelines for Identifying, Classifying, and Servicing the Disadvantaged and Handicapped Under the Vocational Education Amendments of 1968*. DHEW publication OE-73-117000. HEW: Government Printing Office, 1970.

Plumlugh, George. "Schools for the Eighties: 27.5 Miles Per Gallon." *Phi Delta Kappan*, vol. 61, no. 1 (September 1979) pp. 24-25.

U.S. Department of Health, Education, and Welfare. *Suggested Utilization of Resources and Guide for Expenditures*. U.S. Office of Education: Government Printing Office, February 1970.

Chapter 9

Teacher Strategies for Counseling Special Needs Students

Kathryn M. Shada, M.Ed.

INTRODUCTION

Counseling, as defined by Duane Brown and David Shebalus is "... an ongoing process between a professionally prepared counselor and a client or clients. In this process, a conversation develops around the concerns of the client, implicit or explicit goals develop, and the process terminates either when the goals are realized or the client ceases to seek their attainment."[1]

Eli Ginzberg, on the other hand, defines counseling as a "specialized function." He quotes Buford Stefflre as saying: "Counseling denotes a professional relationship between a trained counselor and a client which is designed to help the client understand and clarify his view of his life span so that he may make meaningful and informed choices consonant with his essential nature and his particular circumstances in those areas where choices are available to him."[2]

In *Counseling the Disadvantaged Youth,* William E. Amos and Jean Dresden Grambs explain that "to counsel is to foster self-understanding, self-acceptance, and self-direction on the part of the counselee by means of a carefully structured relationship." They go on to state that:

> to offer this unique relationship to others, a counselor must possess a number of firmly established attitudes toward human beings generally, and toward his clients particularly. He must view each counselee as a person of dignity and worth who is in no way required to demonstrate his claim to that dignity and worth. The attitudes of the counselor toward himself, toward others, and toward his purposes determine the kind of relationship that he will offer his clients.[3]

The above definitions of counseling are written in the professional context and directed toward counselors on a client basis. However, though written to assist professional counselors, their meaning can also be used to assist teachers in dealing with their students in the classroom. Counseling students in the classroom is no more than good teaching. Margaret Bennett describes group procedures in guidance as "good *functional* teaching," which means that teaching guides learners toward insight into the meaning of life about and within them and toward application of their growing understanding in their living. She goes on to say that "such teaching is inevitably concerned with the individual—his/her interests, needs, and welfare—and is therefore based on the personnel or guidance point of view."[4]

The integration of counseling and instruction allows the student and teacher to deal with areas of counseling through the more concrete areas of instruction. A teacher and student may discuss motivation or self-esteem with little success, but if a student can experience success in a subject area, the concept of self-esteem or motivation may take on new meaning.

Teachers working in the area of special vocational needs must consider many factors that influence the learning processes of this group of individuals. The key word in these considerations is *individuals*. Each student is a separate individual, thus having separate needs. All problems are not the same, all needs are not the same; therefore, all students are not the same. This philosophy applies to all students, but for the purposes of this chapter, it focuses particularly on special needs students.

As teachers of youth and adults, we must become increasingly aware of the problems and frustrations of disadvantaged and handicapped students. We should be, and should always remain, concerned with teacher education and what we teachers can do in our classroom to help make our students' lives more productive. Too often we "assume" that students are happy and doing fine—especially the student who says little, gets passing grades, appears adjusted, and who is not a whole lot of trouble in the classroom. But *are* these students doing fine? Do we really know how they are doing? In answering this question, we have to ask what we, as teachers, can do in our classrooms to assist these young people in setting and attaining goals for themselves.

STRATEGIES FOR EFFECTIVE TEACHER COUNSELING

Teachers do not claim to be professional counselors, but because of the many contact hours they have with their students, they often fulfill this role. To this end, it is time that we get away from behind our desks and become more involved with our students and their individual needs. In getting more involved in these critical tasks, however, we should begin by asking ourselves some key questions:

- What are the real needs of the individual students?
- Who can best help them meet their needs?

- How can I most effectively assist in this need-meeting process?
- How can I assist in goal setting and objective development?

Classroom teachers must develop a system of answering these four very important questions if they are going to serve effectively as counselor teachers for special needs students. In this chapter we will examine a series of six steps that will enable the teacher to develop this critical need-meeting system. These steps are:

1. Relating to students
2. Informal evaluation
3. Student motivation
4. Student self-esteem
5. Career guidance
6. Teacher involvement

Relating to Students

Relating may be defined as "establishing a relationship between two or more people in which each party finds meaning and benefit."[5] In teaching the disadvantaged and handicapped student, the teacher must be able to relate to individual problems, frustrations, and student differences. Charles Thompson and William Poppens state that:

> Much of the time, adolescents are meeting their needs in the best way they know how. If we are to help them, we must conclude that new learning or relearning must occur, especially if negative behavior is to be rejected in favor of positive or helpful behavior. We know that change is most easily facilitated when the distance between what the adolescent "wants" and what he/she "has" is greatest. Therefore, our major asset or strength in helping adolescents is being able to look *with* them, first, at the questions of what they now have and what they want and, second, at the questions of what they are now doing and how this is helping them to meet their goals.[6]

Many teachers make the mistake of trying to be a "buddy" when they are relating to special needs students. However, buddies are persons who run with their peers, and a teacher is not able to fulfill this role. A teacher should rather be a friend; the basis for friendship is trust, and this is the key to the relationship between the teacher and the student. Volumes of poetry have been written describing what a friend is, and it is not easy to define adequately here the basis of a true relating friendship. The key in relating to special needs students, however, must surely be to lay a foundation from which student-teacher friendship can grow.

Sincerity can probably do more to lay this foundation than any other trait. Teachers must genuinely care about their students; indeed, whether or not they do will become readily apparent to the students soon after they enter the classroom or laboratory.

Informal Evaluation

Special needs instructors must have some general idea about the educational background of the students they will be instructing and counseling. Many of the discipline problems that teachers have occur because of a lack of this kind of information. For example, the teacher may try to relate to the students, yet problems arise when there are reading or computational assignments. Such problems may well be due to the fact that the material is being written at a level that is higher than the literacy level of the students.

Diagnostic assessments, aptitude assessments, and learning-style inventories will help the teacher determine where the student "is at" upon entering the classroom. Teachers should want to know the educational background of their students in order to determine *what* the students know and where to start or continue the learning process of each student. For example, through use of a simple mathematics diagnostic assessment developed by the teacher, the teacher can see what math the student already knows, what areas of math might need to be reviewed, and what math the student does not know. In this way, the teacher will have a place to start, will know in what areas the student is proficient, and both the teacher and the student will feel more confident about what is to be learned.

Generally speaking, special needs students do not learn as well in the customary classroom setting as the average student. Therefore, it is important to discover the particular learning style that provides the student the best chance of success. The average student has a more diversified learning style, while the special needs student's range of learning is limited. Thus, it is especially important to pin point the particular learning style or styles that enable students to learn most successfully.

Learning style inventories and assessments are becoming more and more accessible, and also more research is being done to discover the various styles of learning by students. Types of learning styles have been categorized as follows:

- Pictoral—indicating the relative importance of actually seeing objects and activities in order for the student to learn.
- Printed material—indicating the relative importance of the written word in learning. "Visualization" denotes the extent an individual will get more detail of a certain incident by direct perception, as contrasted with reading a description of the event.

- Listening—indicating the degree to which the person is able to learn from the spoken language without recourse to some other learning mode.
- Activity—indicating the relative importance of kinesthetics in the learning process. When students score above the mean in this category, they will find it advantageous to become physically involved in some way in order to facilitate learning.

In administering a series of assessments to determine the styles of learning best suited for individual students, the following strategies might be used:

- Have the students listen to a passage being read and then answer questions or reiterate the passage back to the teacher.
- Have the students demonstrate sequencing ability by ascertaining audio and visual patterns in sequence and then responding by both writing the answers and responding to the patterns orally.
- Have the students watch and listen to a film or taped program, using audio, visual, and motor abilities, then write about what they have seen and heard.

Assessment of the student in the classroom will not only help the student but will also help teachers form their own opinions without referring back to the student's educational file. Such assessments may show that the student needs a more sophisticated form of assessment. In this case, the teacher will want to refer the student to professionals with expertise in assessment on a more sophisticated or formal evaluation level.

Through such informal evaluations, the teacher can attempt to identify the real educational needs of the special needs student, and thus better develop the relationship between the teacher counselor and the student. (Chapters 6 and 13 discuss student assessment and curriculum development in greater detail.)

Student Motivation

Self-motivation is the only true motivation. Teachers of special needs students cannot motivate a student, but they can set into place all the key components of an educational experience that will enable that motivation to develop.

Let us assume that the teacher as counselor has initiated the process of relating to the special needs student and through the informal evaluation process has developed a clear understanding of where the student is educationally. The teacher is now ready to set in motion educational opportunities that will allow the student to "catch fire" in terms of personal success. To do this, the student must see the relevancy of the area being studied. If, for example, the student can acquire a skill in the area of consumer education, such as comparison shopping, and then purchase a radio at a substantial savings, then the stage is set for self-motivation.

The teacher counselor can then display interest in this way of using the learned skill by inquiring about how the radio is being used, what accessories there are for the radio, what these accessories cost, and so on. Through this process, the teacher can informally discuss with the student how additional educational components might be utilized in real life settings.

Not all students will be motivated to learn at the rate teachers would like to see; but, by utilizing a number of teaching strategies based on teacher interest, the groundwork can be laid for student motivation.

Student Self-Esteem

If students are learning material that is in their preferred style and relevant to their needs, their motivational level increases along with their self-esteem. In other words, they begin to find some success in school, discover that they have the ability to learn, and they begin to feel good about both themselves and their new accomplishments.

It is difficult to distinguish the factors that influence special needs students. We tend to go "full circle" in this process—without one you cannot achieve the other. Students' self-concepts improve as they become more motivated to learn. To increase their motivation, however, we must discover what they need to know and what will be the best and most preferred styles of learning to attain the needed competencies.

Here is an example of how a teacher might destroy or at least greatly inhibit motivation or self-esteem in a special needs student:

> Doug was enrolled in a junior English class and was experiencing some problems. He had received a "down letter" from his teacher.
>
> Doug had developed a friendship with the Social Studies resource room teacher, and it was to her that he brought his problem. He was concerned about the "down letter" and his overall grade point average. He was on the wrestling team as well as being enrolled in a work-study program. Therefore, he had to keep his grades up or he would not be able to wrestle or participate in the work-study program.
>
> Doug's English teacher was intolerant of individuals different from herself, so that Doug, being from a disadvantaged home, was immediately disliked; and since she disliked the wrestling coach, Doug had another strike against him, being a wrestler.
>
> The resource room teacher and the wrestling coach worked on building Doug's confidence so that he might be able to successfully complete the English assignments. One assignment was to write a critique of the book *The Scarlet Letter*. The resource teacher and the coach, after several pep talks, were able to get Doug to complete the assignment in

good order. Three days after the assignment was completed, the English teacher cornered the resource teacher and the coach and in front of a large group of students and faculty proceeded to accuse the two educators of doing Doug's work for him because she "knew he wasn't capable of doing that quality of work."

Shortly after the confrontation, Doug found the two educators and told them how upset he was. He indicated he was going to quit school and get a job where people would take him for what he was. The two educators tried to calm him down and suggested he take a rough copy of his book critique to the English teacher so that she might see that he had completed the work himself. This Doug did after much coaxing.

The English teacher finally admitted that Doug might have done the work and gave him a C+ for his effort. Doug suffered for quite some time after the incident because of the severe blow his self-confidence had been dealt. He had been called upon to do good work and, when he had, he was accused of cheating. Doug recovered from the incident and went on to complete high school.

The English teacher is still carrying her biases and prejudices toward special needs students, and no one will ever know the number of lives she has altered as a result of her inability to assist in the development of self-esteem in students different from herself.

One can see from this example how a teacher with a prejudicial attitude can develop a relationship of distrust and suspicion with students. Often, teachers are not aware of attitudes, but students quickly sense any biases teachers have. Thus if they are going to be effective as counselors with special needs students, teachers must control any barrier-creating feelings they may have.

Career Guidance

Guidance activities that are conducted by school counselors and that can be incorporated into special needs classrooms involve such things as interest inventories, career awareness or exploration inventories, decision-making skills, and goal-setting exercises. Such guidance activities, through coordination between the counselor's office and the classroom, can do much to assist the special needs student to set life goals.

Too often students are put into career tracks that are not of their choosing. Often the career choices are made by the students' parents, teachers, or counselors without giving the students an opportunity to explore adequately the career options available to them. There are, however, many ways that the teacher can provide career information to students on both a formal and informal basis.

In the formal interest-inventory area, there are standardized assessments such as the Strong-Campbell or Kuder interest inventories. Also, a number of states are developing Career Needlesorts, in which the occupations available in the state are located in a needlesort stack. Students select careers in which they are interested. Then, by inserting a metal rod into the career cards, they can sort out those cards that contain information about the requested careers. A special needs teacher who is interested in identifying and administering these interest inventories can secure from the school counselor a listing of the devices and recommendations for their use.

Another helpful career informational source is the Dictionary of Occupational Titles (DOT) published by the Department of Labor. This document lists 20,000 occupations, together with their requirements and future outlook. The special needs teacher can have students look up the careers that they are interested in or have heard about or whose job descriptions have prompted their curiosity.

Most special needs students have very limited horizons in terms of the career options available to them. Often they will not spend time exploring the various career information sources in the counselor's office, but they might well become involved in these materials in a vocational laboratory or classroom. By capitalizing on the student-teacher relationship, the special needs teacher can involve such students in many activities that will assist them to see a much broader range of career options.

Television has done much to "occupationally misrepresent" certain careers. Police officers are portrayed as always being on the cutting edge of action and within sixty minutes of solving a major crime. Paramedics constantly save lives and deliver babies. Students, especially special needs students, are very susceptible to these portrayals and thus often do not go beyond what they see represented.

Kenneth Hoyt has identified the role of guidance in career development as helping students to:

- see themselves as worthy,
- experience success,
- find ways that school can make sense to them,
- consider and make decisions regarding the values of a work-oriented society,
- develop an understanding of their own talents, and
- make choices from a wide range of alternatives.[7]

In light of this list, the teacher clearly has to provide formal career guidance and then support the formal activities through informal counseling. The informal support can involve community participation. Guest speakers can be invited to come in and tell of their work, students can be sent out to observe community workers, or the students can work alongside individuals in whose careers they have displayed an interest.

E. Ginzberg and colleagues have identified occupational decision making as progressing through three distinct periods: (1) the fantasy choice, (2) the tentative choice, and (3) the realistic choice. The fantasy choice normally occurs from ages 6 through 11; the tentative choice, from ages 12 through 16; and the realistic choice, from ages 16 through 21.[8]

As noted earlier, the special needs student often is not able to move alone out of the fantasy stage. Based upon the individual needs and situation of the student, however, the teacher, as an adult role model, can assist in moving the student beyond the fantasy choice stage so that the student can make realistic and meaningful career decisions. This assistance requires the professional expertise of all the involved educators; only through a team effort can the student progress through the career selection process.

Another source of ideas to develop interest assessments for classroom use is the book *Test Your Vocational Aptitude* by Patricia Asta and Linda Bernbach. This volume contains a variety of assessments that can be used to test interest areas and aptitude.[9] A book of this type can also help teachers develop their own interest-assessment tools.

Defining areas of interest for students means nothing to them unless they can relate the areas to some form of occupation. If they are not shown occupational relationships, they will probably think, "Well, big deal! I know I have interests in music, so what does that prove?" The teacher and counselor cooperatively must provide the transition from interest to occupation.

Once the areas of interest are defined, the teacher can then explore with the student the various occupations that might be considered in the student's interest areas. Too often, we consider only the obvious choices, hence we emphasize the word *explore*. Our society is opening up more and more occupations for both males and females and/or the handicapped, disadvantaged, and minorities. We must therefore explore all the occupational alternatives available to our students, and we must assist them in the selection of realistic occupations of their choice. If persons are able to work in areas of interest or in something close to an area of interest, they are more likely to be happy with their work and to remain longer on the job.

Another popular method of career exploration is to develop a card catalog of the various jobs, about which particular teachers and administrators in the school have knowledge. Using this convenient card catalog as a reference, students interested in a particular occupation are then able to discuss the advantages and disadvantages with the teacher or administrator listed as a resource for that particular occupation. The card catalog may be maintained in the school's "career center," by the teacher involved with the work-study program, in the vocational director's office, or in the guidance counselor's office. This approach has the additional advantage of enabling the students to view their teachers more humanistically and realistically. The students see, possibly for the first time, that their teachers were once students themselves who can relate realistically to the students regarding work choices and not merely "give them a lot of junk to do in school."

Decision making and goal-setting skills are a "must" for everyone, but we usually learn them the hard way. We make decisions every day of our lives but are they the right ones? Or are we always retracing our steps? Do we know how to select alternatives to our problems?

Of course, making the choices for the students is easier than helping them learn how to make selections and decisions of their own. This is where "taking time" to listen and talk with the students becomes imperative. Yet teachers must also remember that, though they can guide and offer alternatives, the final choice must be the student's.

Teachers can assist students in researching the alternatives. What are the advantages? What are the disadvantages? How much more schooling is involved? What are the benefits? What options are there for the student? These and many other questions must be explored by the student. Having collected the pertinent information, they must now evaluate the options that would be best for them.

Again, teachers must assist, guide, and suggest alternatives, but they cannot make the selection for the student. If the alternative selected by the student does not work, the teacher should discuss with the student what went wrong and, also, what was learned in the process.

Many adults have little or no background and few skills in decision making. Almost everything that has happened in their lives has been by chance, and there have been few goals or decisions to make. Thus, knowing how to set goals is another goal that teachers should strive for in their classrooms. Here, the strategy should aim at ensuring that the students will not spend their adult years just floating.

In his book *If You Don't Know Where You're Going, You'll Probably End Up Somewhere Else,* David Campbell discusses goal setting, the various types of goals, and how we must plan to achieve them. He is thus concerned about "creating opportunities" in people.[10]

In our context, this means that teachers must start students thinking about setting goals. The students should decide what is important to them in terms of their values and what they have to do to obtain their goals. There are, of course, short-range and long-range goals, and educators will have to explain how the setting of short-range goals might help students reach long-range goals. Human beings have to have goals, whether it is buying a new car, renting an apartment, or buying a house. This is what keeps us striving to carry on and to achieve the values we have selected for our lives.

Teacher Involvement

Too often we hear, "Don't get involved, do only what you have to" to complete the requirements of a job. If one were packaging oranges, such advice might have some pertinence, but when one is dealing with human lives, it simply won't work. Teachers are hired to teach children first, and content second. Beyond that, however, effective teachers will also be effective counselors by becoming involved in the lives of their students.

At the same time, experience shows that teachers must keep their perspective when it comes to student involvement. Getting involved means taking time to listen to problems and offering specific solutions. Often, however, teachers, especially new teachers, dive in "feet first" and exhaust themselves trying to be all things to all people. Special needs students develop strong survival abilities, and they can quickly convert a teacher into a personal chauffeur or any other kind of personal servant they might need. Thus, the experienced teacher who offers counseling services will soon develop skills that require the student to make some kind of personal commitment for action and then to follow through with that action. If such commitments are not requested by teachers, they will soon find themselves being used as sponges into which the special needs students pour out their problems without any action on their part to resolve their problems.

Teachers must remember that they are there to guide, direct, and offer support but that it is up to the student to take the initiative to seek the assistance being offered. If students choose not to take the initiative, teachers should ask, Why not? Often, teachers will find that students are afraid to make a commitment and to go it alone. In such cases, teachers must make it known that they are willing to assist the students with their programs or commitments. If the students continue to reject the assistance, it may be best simply to wait until they indicate they are ready to make some progress.

Teachers must also remember, however, that, just because failure is the result in one case, they should not give up and refuse to become involved in the future. Each student's situation is different and requires careful consideration.

An example of teacher involvement is illustrated in the following case history of a ninth grader named Karen:

> Karen was 15 years old and enrolled in an alternative school. She had just returned to the formal school setting after spending 30 days at the girls' reformatory, where she had received psychiatric evaluations. She had been placed in the reformatory for evaluation as a result of her previous juvenile record of burglary charges.
>
> Karen came from a family of five children, three boys and two girls. Her father had been killed in a motorcycle accident when she was two years old. Her mother was a caring woman who, in order to support her

family, worked as a bartender from 6:00 P.M. until 1:00 or 2:00 A.M. This left the family unattended during the evening hours.

Karen had grown up on her own and, as a result of this experience, was very independent. This independence placed Karen in a role of not needing anyone for anything. The burglary charges came about because Karen was exercising her independence by simply taking what she wanted, no matter to whom it belonged.

Karen talked constantly of quitting school as soon as she was 16. The school year ended, and Karen floated through the summer, just marking time. She entered school in the fall as a sophomore and was counting the days until December, when she would be 16 and could quit school.

During the fall several things happened that started to change Karen's outlook on life. The learning center teacher started asking Karen about what she was going to do when she quit school, what plans did she have for her life, and what could she, as a teacher, do to help her in school. Karen really responded to this interest, and her grades started to improve dramatically. She was elected to the student council and started displaying real leadership potential.

Every fall the Armed Forces Aptitude Tests were given to sophomores. Karen took the test and scored in the ninetieth percentile in all of the test categories. All of these pluses were just the boost that Karen needed, because December came and went with never a mention of quitting school.

In March, a real tragedy overtook Karen and threatened to destroy everything she had accomplished. Karen had been involved in a burglary before she had gotten off of probation, and it had taken almost a year for the charges to catch up with her. On the charges, Karen would be sentenced to two years in the reformatory.

The learning center teacher, who had befriended Karen, could not stand by and let Karen be destroyed by these long-ago incidents. The teacher, not sure about how much or how little she should become involved, decided to do anything she could to help Karen. She made an appointment with the juvenile judge and went to see him and explain about Karen. She told of Karen's progress, about her attitude change, grade improvements, and her remaining in school. The teacher also volunteered to take personal custody of Karen. The judge thanked the teacher for her concern and said he would take the case under advisement after he did some investigating of his own.

The teacher in the meantime went and secured for Karen a parttime job so she could pay for the stolen merchandise.

In thirty days Karen's case came up, and the judge gave her two years' probation, allowed her to drive only to and from work, and ordered that she had to complete high school. Based upon the progress Karen had made to that point, the restrictions of her probation were not at all severe. The judge indicated that he was granting Karen probation only because of the faith that her teacher had in her.

Karen completed high school with mostly *As* and *Bs,* paid off her debts, and matured into a poised, confident woman. She remains grateful to her teacher who became involved by simply making a few phone calls, taking a little time, and showing a real interest in a special needs student who needed help.

INCORPORATING THE STRATEGIES INTO THE CLASSROOM

Earlier in this chapter, we raised four questions relating to the unique and individual counseling needs of special needs students. By emphasizing teacher and student interaction, teachers should be able to answer the four questions and apply the results successfully in their relationships with special needs students.

Often the biggest difficulty that teachers face when using their counseling skills stems from being so close to the problem that it is difficult to perceive it objectively. When assisting their students to make major life-directing decisions, special needs teachers must learn to achieve objectivity and still display genuine concern.

The following eight points can assist teachers in incorporating counseling strategies into their classrooms:[11]

1. Take time. Make sure that *all* of your students receive a fair share of your time.
2. Listen to your students. "The teacher who really listens to students may be the first adult outside their home that has listened to them as one adult to another. A teacher's advice, given appropriately, can be of great benefit to a student throughout his or her life."[12]
3. Show your concern for your students. This is the only way they know that you do care.
4. Be concerned about the field in which you work. Get involved in professional and school activities. This shows others that you do care.
5. Meet individual student needs. Assist the students to find alternatives to problems through their separate needs.
6. Be a model. By dress, attitude, and action, teachers create the model that they want to portray. Remember that students are looking for someone they can identify with and confide in.
7. Remember you are only human and will not always meet with success. Teaching and counseling is a never-ending process of learning—learning

from our setbacks and moving forward professionally to be an even better teacher than before.

8. Never be satisfied with your performance as a teacher. Always strive to do better. Upgrade yourself by trying new methods, attending workshops, or classes. This constant striving will serve you and others well.

SUMMARY

Because of the time they spend with students, teachers are looked to for advice and counsel. By the same token, they should never forget the impact they can have on their students' lives.

Our intent in this chapter was not to advocate that teachers assume the school counselor's role but simply to offer strategies whereby teachers can complement the efforts of counselors. Students need someone they can look to for assistance in making life-directing decisions. Special needs students are in particular need of that "someone." The special needs teacher must have the skills to meet this need whenever it arises.

NOTES

1. Duane Brown and David J. Shebalus, *Contemporary Guidance Concepts and Practices* (Dubuque, Iowa: William C. Brown Company Publishers, 1972), p. 103.
2. Eli Ginzberg, *Career Guidance: Who Needs It, Who Provides It, Who Can Improve It* (New York: McGraw-Hill Book Company, 1971), p. 6.
3. William E. Amos and Jean Dresden Grambs, *Counseling the Disadvantaged Youth* (Englewood Cliffs, N.J.: Prentice-Hall, Inc., 1968), p. 336.
4. Margaret E. Bennett, *Guidance and Counseling in Groups* (New York: McGraw-Hill Book Co., Inc., 1963), p. 34.
5. Charles L. Thompson and William A. Poppen, *For Those Who Care: Ways of Relating to Youth* (Columbus, Ohio: Charles E. Merrill Publishing Company, 1972), p. 12.
6. Ibid.
7. Kenneth B. Hoyt, "Role, Function, and Approach for Guidance in Career Development of Youth from Junior High through Senior High" (Paper presented at the Vocational Development Seminar, West Georgia College, Carrollton, Georgia, available from Division of Guidance and Testing, Ohio State Department of Education), pp. 1-12.
8. E. Ginzberg et al., *Occupational Choice: An Approach to a General Theory* (New York: Columbia University Press, 1951), p. 10.
9. Patricia Asta and Linda Bernbach, *Test Your Vocational Aptitude* (New York: Arco Publishing Co., 1978).
10. David Campbell, *If You Don't Know Where You're Going, You'll Probably End Up Somewhere Else*.
11. Gary D. Meers, "Moving Beyond Cynicism," *Vocational Educational Journal* (March 1979): 22-24.
12. Ibid.

BIBLIOGRAPHY

Glasser, William. *Schools Without Failure*. New York: Perennial Library, Harper and Row Publishers, 1969.

Harms, Ernest, and Schrieber, Paul, eds. *Handbook of Counseling Techniques*. New York: The MacMillan Co., 1963.

Chapter 10

Personnel Preparation for Serving Special Vocational Needs Populations

Catherine Batsche, Ph.D.

An inservice sounds like an efficient way to disseminate information: a presentation of materials, methods, and theories to the teachers en masse. In reality, it is usually a mandatory, two hour lecture at the end of the day, when specialists or guest speakers discourse in educational abstractions . . . to teachers . . . who still have to correct, lesson plan, and prepare materials for the next instructional day. One specialist was elated when three (out of twenty) teachers actually used materials provided at an inservice. If my response rate was only 15 percent, I'd seriously reexamine my presentations.

John P. O'Dwyer

INTRODUCTION

Educators have generally been disillusioned with personnel preparation efforts—at both the preservice and the inservice levels. Although this dissatisfaction is not a new phenomenon, it has received renewed emphasis in recent years. Rapid social and technological changes have increased the demands that teachers acquire new competencies in order to implement educational reform. It is no longer assumed that teachers can acquire all the skills they will need in their professional career solely from an undergraduate or graduate training program. Teacher educators now acknowledge that they are preparing entry-level teachers, counselors, and administrators and that continuous, coordinated staff development should be a life long process complementing on-the-job experience.[1]

Expectations for staff development are especially high in the area of vocational education for special needs students. Vocational educators find it necessary to upgrade continuously their expertise in order to stay current with the new and emerging developments in their occupational fields. At the same time, they are asked to increase their capacity to teach these occupational skills to a wider range of clientele: the handicapped, the disadvantaged, the limited English-speaking, the displaced homemaker, and high-risk youth, to name a few. It is imperative that personnel training programs be expanded to respond to the continually demanding challenges faced by vocational teachers. It is equally imperative that these efforts avoid the mistakes that have plagued inservice and preservice in the past.

LEGISLATIVE PROVISIONS

When the vocational education of special needs students became a national priority, the Congress of the United States recognized the accompanying need to expand opportunities for personnel preparation. As a result, the Personnel Training section of the Vocational Education Act of 1976 (Public Law 94-482) included special needs learners as a priority for training programs. According to this law, the purpose of vocational education personnel training is " . . . to improve the States' vocational education programs by improving the qualifications of persons serving or preparing to serve in vocational educational programs."[2] The regulations provided that the funds available for this purpose could be used for training that was designed to improve the quality of instruction, guidance, supervision, and administration of programs for persons with special needs.

The Education for All Handicapped Children Act (Public Law 94-142) required states to establish, in addition, a comprehensive system of personnel development. The regulations of the act specified that the annual state plan must include a personnel development plan that provided a structure for personnel planning and that focused on preservice and inservice education needs.[3] The plan was to ensure that the ongoing inservice training programs were made available to all personnel engaged in the education of handicapped children. These programs were to include the use of incentives to ensure participation by teachers (such as released time, payment for participation, options for academic credit, salary step credit, certification renewal, and updating professional skills). The inservice programs were to involve local staff and the use of innovative practices that had been found to be effective. Furthermore, personnel development programs were to be based on the assessed needs of statewide significance.

In 1977, the Council for Exceptional Children (CEC) translated the requirements of the federal legislation into an administrative policy guide for the vocational education of handicapped students. Because of the shortage of teachers prepared to work with handicapped students in vocational education, it was recognized that inservice education would have to be emphasized. The resulting policy development guidelines recommended that the inservice training plan should include:

- "Identification of the areas in which training is needed (such as individualized education programs, modifying vocational programs for handicapped students, teaching methods to use with handicapped students, least restrictive vocational environment).
- "Specification of the groups requiring training (e.g. special teachers, regular vocational teachers, administrators, supportive services staff).
- "Description of the content and nature of training for each area of training need.
- "Description of the training to be provided.
- "Specification of funding sources and time frame for the training.
- "Specification of procedures of evaluating the extent to which program objectives are met."[4]

With regard to certification of staff, the CEC noted that special educators had traditionally been allowed to teach prevocational and work experience programs without any specific vocational education preparation. Likewise, vocational educators had been relatively free to teach handicapped students without any specific vocational education preparation. Therefore, the CEC policy guidelines recommended that local education agencies require special education teachers to gain occupational experience and that vocational teachers be required to obtain experience working with special needs individuals. These guidelines were intended to ensure that competent personnel were employed to provide vocational programming for students with special education needs.

THE STATE OF THE ART

What has been the impact of federal legislation on personnel preparation programs? There is no doubt that the quantity of inservice and preservice options has increased. A 1979 report by the Department of Health, Education, and Welfare to Congress indicated that the states had launched a major training and dissemination effort to ensure that the least restrictive environment concept becomes a reality.[5] Data in the report supported the fact that vocational educators were being included in inservice programs. But the report also indicated that the personnel training programs now underway, even though significant, may still be inadequate to meet the needs in the field.

It is difficult to assess the quality of the programs that have been developed. Nationwide evaluation data are difficult to obtain. From the information that is available, however, two conclusions might be drawn:

1. Exemplary inservice/preservice program models and practices have been developed.

2. Unfortunately, these "best" practices have not yet been incorporated into the major delivery systems and much of the teacher education efforts have continued to be "a kind of massive spectator sport."[6]

A study report of the National Education Association (NEA) has noted that current teacher training programs are "entirely inadequate to prepare classroom teachers to work effectively with handicapped children and to prepare both special and regular teachers to relate effectively and supportively to each other."[7] The NEA panel was convinced that no single factor was of greater importance to the successful implementation of Public Law 94-142 than the appropriate education of the staff members. But little effective inservice was found by the NEA review panel. The type of inservice most prevalent was the type teachers considered least helpful: the fragmented one-shot meetings with little continuity and with a low level of involvement by teachers. There was apparently very little coordination between universities and the public schools in the planning and delivery of inservice and preservice programs.

Similarly, it has been suggested that comprehensive inservice education activities and university preparation programs should be expanded to better prepare vocational teachers to work with handicapped. According to Gary Meers and Charlotte Conoway, the vocational teachers' lack of preparation has possibly been the major contributing factor in the low priority given to including handicapped students in vocational education programs. Meers and Conoway do not expect vocational teachers to develop all of the skills and expertise required of special educators. However they do expect that teacher preparation efforts should give priority to assisting vocational teachers actively participate in the educational planning team and should prepare them to identify and locate necessary resources and support services.[8]

It would be misleading to infer that all preservice and inservice education programs have been totally ineffective. As stated earlier, many exemplary practices do exist. These programs have done much to dissipate the fears of educators who are working with special needs students. For example, a systematic approach to inservice has been developed by L. Allen Phelps. His manual, *Instructional Development for Special Needs Learners: An Inservice Resource Guide,* consists of seven modules designed to acquaint occupational and special educators with a systematic process of providing cooperative instructional arrangements for special needs learners. Each of the modules contains inservice activities that relate to the student's individualized education program. A self-directed needs assessment is included so that teachers may select the modules or the activities that are appropriate to their needs. Ideally, the inservice activities are completed by a special educator and a vocational educator team so that professionals can communicate their particular expertise and concerns.[9]

Another example of an inservice program that might be helpful to special needs teachers is *An Inservice Program for Vocational Teachers of the Disadvantaged.* This manual, developed by Norman Ehresman, John Hanel, and Betty Robertson, contains six inservice supplements that provide suggestions for improving teacher interactions with disadvantaged learners.[10]

In addition to these activities at the inservice level, there has been an affirmative response by institutions of higher education to the need for expanded preservice programs. As a result of a series of projects funded by the Bureau of Education for the Handicapped, a wide range of teacher training alternatives has been developed.

> A dramatic example of the kinds of changes that have occurred is provided by a project at the University of Vermont, Burlington. There, the College of Education has eliminated all its departments, so that faculty in various disciplines can work closely together to develop a mainstream training program that views all teachers as 'human service educators.' In another project—at Indiana University, Bloomington—the School of Education has been reorganized into new divisions, including one in which all disciplines work together to develop programming for regular and special education teachers as well as for the students interested in alternative education and multicultural education. Thus, regular education teachers receive training from special education teachers and curriculum specialists, while special education teachers are exposed to new and differing roles they may play. [11]

These programs are only a few of the many alternative practices that are currently operational. But widespread usage of systematic, cooperative personnel development programs is still uncommon. In the following sections we will discuss some of the processes that have been found to be effective in responding to personnel preparation needs.

PERSONNEL PREPARATION PROGRAM PLANNING

There are several approaches that can be taken when planning staff development programs. Most methods that have been found to be effective support a systematic program process based on needs assessment, program development, program delivery, and evaluation. Each of these components will be examined in detail.

Needs Assessment

A frequent complaint directed at personnel preparation programs is that they are irrelevant, impractical, and divorced from actual teacher needs. To overcome this criticism, it is essential that systematic planning be based on the assessed needs of the participants. There are several methods of assessing personnel needs, including the use of formal needs assessment instruments, open-ended interviews, and group process techniques. Whichever technique is used, the information obtained must be interpreted and utilized to design training strategies. Too often needs assessment information is collected and then ignored in the planning process. If used effectively, the needs assessment data will increase the participants' involvement in and ownership of the training program. The following are some specific assessment techniques that have been found to be effective.

Survey Instruments

Several instruments have been designed to assess the needs and interests of teachers who work with special needs students. A list of some of these instruments is presented in Exhibit 10-1.[12] A sample of one of the instruments, the Self-Directed Needs Assessment, is shown in Exhibit 10-2.[13] The Self-Directed Needs Assessment has been used by the author both on a statewide basis and at the local inservice level. In both cases, the instrument provided feedback that was useful in increasing the validity of the training activities that were offered. Because of the design of the instrument, it was possible to assess those activities that were already being implemented in local educational settings as well as those activities in which participants needed to know more in order to improve special needs services.

Group Process Techniques

An extremely effective assessment technique is one that provides for group interaction in the priority-setting process. The Nominal Group Technique (NGT) is one method of identifying group needs through a structured interaction process.[14] The NGT is so named because it assumes that a group of persons is a group in name only until it has a commonly determined set of goals. The process is designed to assess needs systematically and to establish group priorities that are representative of the group consensus. The process begins with a clearly worded question or statement that is given to the group to respond to in a designed sequence of stages. For example, one question might be, What barriers have you encountered in "mainstreaming" handicapped students in your vocational classes? The participants would then be asked to respond to the question by using the following steps:

- *Silent Generation of Needed Actions:* Participants are asked to identify individually and briefly describe, in writing, those barriers that they have encountered in mainstreaming special needs students in vocational education classes.
- *Listing of Needed Actions:* During the allotted time period, each group's facilitator lists the participants' responses on newsprint. Responses are verbalized in a round-robin fashion until all needed actions are listed.

Exhibit 10-1 List of Needs Assessment Instruments

NEEDS ASSESSMENT INSTRUMENTS

1. Self-Directed Needs Assessment. (Source: Phelps, L. Allen. *Inservice Resource Guide*. Urbana: University of Illinois, 1976.)
2. Vocational Education and the Special Needs Student: A Faculty Survey. (Source: McKinney, Steve and Winkelman, Eric. Penn State University, Division of Occupational and Vocational Studies, University Park, PA.)
3. Iowa Vocational Education/Special Needs Assessment Project. (Source: *Summary Report*. Iowa Department of Public Instruction, Special Needs Section and Drake University, 1977.)
4. A Questionnaire for Vocational Teachers. (Source: Selig, Risa W. and Schriber, Peter E. *Summary of Needs Analysis and Recommendations for Module Content*. Amherst, Massachusetts: National Evaluation Systems, Inc., 1978.)
5. Teacher Competency Survey. (Source: Albright, Leonard; Nichols, Charles; and Pinchak, James. *Identification of Professional Competencies Necessary for Teachers of Disadvantaged and Handicapped Youth*. Kent, Ohio: Kent State University, Department of Vocational Education, 1975.)
6. Special Vocational Needs Attitude Scale. (Source: Meers, Gary D. Development and Implementation of Program Models for Assisting Vocational Teachers in Dealing with the Educationally Disadvantaged, Handicapped, and Minorities. Lincoln: Special Vocational Needs, University of Nebraska, 1977.)
7. Inventory of Services Provided Vocational Education Students Classified as Handicapped or Disadvantaged. (Source: Kay, Evelyn R., Kemp, Barbara H., and Saunders, Frances G. *Guidelines for Identifying, Classifying, and Serving the Disadvantaged and Handicapped Under the Vocational Education Amendments of 1968*. Washington, DC: Department of Health, Education, and Welfare, 1973.)
8. Assessment Checklist: Physical Environment. (Source: Smith, Robert, Neisworth, John T., and Greer, John G. *Evaluating Educational Environments*. Columbus, Ohio: Charles E. Merrill Publishing Company, 1978.)
9. Assessment Checklist: Community Services. (Source: Smith, Robert, Neisworth, John T., and Greer, John G. *Evaluating Educational Environments*. Columbus, Ohio: Charles E. Merrill Publishing Company, 1978.)
10. Assessment Checklist: Social Environment. (Source: Smith, Robert, Neisworth, John T., and Greer, John G. *Evaluating Educational Environments*. Columbus, Ohio: Charles E. Merrill Publishing Company, 1978.)
11. Interview Schedule: Vocational Administrator. (Source: Phelps, L. Allen. Competency-Based Inservice Education for Secondary School Personnel Serving Special Needs Students: A Formative Field Test Evaluation. Unpublished Ph.D. dissertation, University of Illinois, Urbana, Illinois, 1976.)

Source: Phelps, *Technical Assistance and Staff Development Handbook*, Unpublished document (developed through a contract with the Illinois State Board of Education, Department of Adult Vocational and Technical Education, Springfield, Ill., 1978).

Exhibit 10-2 The Self-Directed Needs Assessment

Listed below are tasks which might be performed in working with special needs students. Please respond by circling one number for each task.	To what degree has this activity been implemented in your educational setting:					As a local educator working with special needs students, do you feel you need to know more about this task?				
	Not at all		some		A great deal	No		yes a bit more		yes much more
Program Planning and Evaluation										
1. Develop goals, and/philosophy for a special needs program.	1	2	3	4	5	1	2	3	4	5
2. Analyze local or regional job market and/employment trends.	1	2	3	4	5	1	2	3	4	5
3. Identify and use community resources in planning programs and services.	1	2	3	4	5	1	2	3	4	5
4. Establish and/or use program advisory committees.	1	2	3	4	5	1	2	3	4	5
5. Identify occupations and clusters of occupations to determine instructional content.	1	2	3	4	5	1	2	3	4	5
6. Conduct a Needs Assessment of teachers and students.	1	2	3	4	5	1	2	3	4	5
7. Conduct inservice activities for staff development.	1	2	3	4	5	1	2	3	4	5
8. Design and implement a system for monitoring student progress and achievement on a regular basis.	1	2	3	4	5	1	2	3	4	5
9. Obtain follow-up information on special needs students leaving or graduating from school program.	1	2	3	4	5	1	2	3	4	5
10. Conduct a comprehensive evaluation of the total special needs program.	1	2	3	4	5	1	2	3	4	5
Student Assessment										
1. Develop and use screening and referral processes for identification of students.	1	2	3	4	5	1	2	3	4	5
2. Analyze students occupational interests and aptitudes.	1	2	3	4	5	1	2	3	4	5
3. Develop appropriate assessment methods.	1	2	3	4	5	1	2	3	4	5
4. Collaborate with other educators, specialists, parents, and students in developing an individualized educational plan.	1	2	3	4	5	1	2	3	4	5
5. Provide support services to meet identified students needs.	1	2	3	4	5	1	2	3	4	5

Listed below are tasks which might be performed in working with special needs students. Please respond by circling one number for each task.	To what degree has this activity been implemented in your educational setting:					As a local educator working with special needs students, do you feel you need to know more about this task?				
	Not at all		some		A great deal	No		yes a bit more		yes much more
Implementing Programs										
1. Coordinate vocational planning with academic areas (reading, math, and other academic areas required for graduation.)	1	2	3	4		1	2	3	4	5
2. Use diagnostic and prescriptive assessment techniques for planning instruction.	1	2	3	4	5	1	2	3	4	5
3. Develop individual student performance goals and objectives.	1	2	3	4	5	1	2	3	4	5
4. Use instructional techniques that individualize instruction (e.g., peer instruction, small group instruction, or programmed instruction.)	1	2	3	4	5	1	2	3	4	5
5. Select or modify instructional materials appropriate for different special needs learners.	1	2	3	4	5	1	2	3	4	5
6. Modify when necessary the tools, equipment, facilities, or conditions in the learning environment.	1	2	3	4	5	1	2	3	4	5
7. Plan and coordinate off-campus work (on-the-job) instruction.	1	2	3	4	5	1	2	3	4	5
8. Plan and coordinate on-campus work (on-the-job) instruction.	1	2	3	4	5	1	2	3	4	5
Guidance/Placement										
1. Provide career counseling and guidance.	1	2	3	4	5	1	2	3	4	5
2. Provide personal counseling.	1	2	3	4	5	1	2	3	4	5
3. Provide work adjustment counseling.	1	2	3	4	5	1	2	3	4	5
4. Develop and use simulated job application and interview procedures.	1	2	3	4	5	1	2	3	4	5
5. Provide and/or coordinate job placement services for special needs learners.	1	2	3	4	5	1	2	3	4	5
6. Train employers and supervisors to work effectively with special needs learners on the job.	1	2	3	4	5	1	2	3	4	5
Other										
1. ____________________	1	2	3	4	5	1	2	3	4	5
2. ____________________	1	2	3	4	5	1	2	3	4	5

Source: Phelps, *Instructional Development for Special Needs Learners: An Inservice Resource Guide* (Urbana, Ill.: University of Illinois, 1975).

- *Serial Discussions:* The proposed actions listed on the newsprint are discussed and clarified within each group.
- *First Vote:* Each group votes on its list of needed actions to collectively determine the five most important items. The voting is done by having each participant select five actions among those cited by the group and rank them in order of personal priority. Group priorities are established by tallying the individual votes and by listing those items that received the highest number of votes.
- *Discussion of Voting:* The participants discuss the results of the voting, during which time members of the group are given the opportunity to reconsider their positions. This is a period for lobbying and advocacy.
- *Second Group Voting:* After discussion, group members once again vote on the total list of needed actions to determine the five most important actions and their final priority.

Once the priorities for the group have been identified and agreed upon, the participants can be asked to volunteer to work on an action team that will address possible actions to ameliorate each priority barrier. The progress made by each action team should be shared periodically with the entire group to ensure continued group commitment and support of the actions suggested by the team.

Professional Growth Plan

The *Monticello Model for Inservice Staff Development* contains another alternative for individualization of the needs assessment process.[15] Following the administration of a staff opinionnaire instrument, staff members are asked to design an individualized plan based on each member's professional goals. The first step in the process is the identification of five personal needs or interests for professional growth. The needs are listed in priority order, and the steps that will be taken to meet the needs are listed for the first two or three concerns on the list. A decision is then made as to which of the priorities will be addressed by the teacher during the upcoming year. This decision can be made jointly by the teacher and administrator or training coordinator. A simple progress report is maintained by the teacher to indicate the accomplishments made throughout the year toward personally identified goals. If a copy of the professional growth plan is given to the personnel training coordinator, known resources can be shared and individualized consultation can be provided.

Program Development

In addition to data on the training needs of participants, information should be collected on the types and numbers of special needs learners who need vocational programming in the area being served and on the adequacy of the services being provided. This information can then be used as the basis for designing the training program to be delivered. A critical strategy in the planning process is the collaboration of representatives of both vocational education and special education. M. Naumann-Etienne and W. Todd found that the success or failure of training efforts is "directly related to the commitment of those it is designed to affect; the more a staff is involved in planning the events and procedures, the more likely it will want to carry on self-improvement throughout the year, beyond the days specifically designed for staff development."[16] It has been found to be particularly effective to form an inservice steering committee that consists of representatives from administration, special education, vocational education, guidance and counseling, and other related support service areas, such as remedial reading, bilingual education, and so on. Because this interdisciplinary approach is strongly advocated, it is important for the steering committee to develop a formal plan for coordination of the training program among the participating disciplines. The plan should specify methods of coordinating activities, such as joint staff meetings, multidisciplinary case conferences, team teaching of courses or workshops, and joint supervision of practicum experiences.

The following findings should be taken into consideration when planning training programs:

- When participants are involved in both the planning and conduct of inservice activities, programs tend to have greater success than when they are planned and conducted by college or outside personnel without teacher assistance.
- Programs in which supervisors or administrators participate in any of several roles tend to be more successful in accomplishing their objectives.
- College-based programs tend to be more directed toward changing the teacher's store of information or cognitive behavior than school-based programs.
- Inservice education programs that place the teacher in an active role (constructing and generating materials, ideas, and behaviors) are more likely to accomplish their objectives than are programs that place the teacher in the receptive role.
- Programs that emphasize demonstrations, supervised trials, and feedback are more likely to accomplish their goals than are programs in which the teacher is expected to store up ideas and behavior prescriptions for a future time.
- Personnel training programs that have differentiated training experiences for different teachers (i.e. "individualized") are more likely to accomplish their objectives than are programs that have common activities for all participants.
- Inservice education programs in which participants share and provide mutual assistance to each other are more likely to accomplish their objectives than are programs in which each teacher does separate work.[17]

The Content of Personnel Training Programs for Special Needs Learners

Several topics have emerged as necessary components of the personnel training program in special needs vocational education. For example, in a survey of vocational educators in Iowa, "most instructors felt techniques for identifying and assessing student needs, strategies for individualizing instruction, and procedures for acquiring up-to-date knowledge of available resources and support services" were needed inservice topics.[18] In addition to inservice education, the instructors indicated that additional staff resources (aides, tutors, resource teachers, and counselors) and additional planning time were needed for program improvement and implementation.

Additional topics that should be included in the content of preservice and inservice programs include: attitude development of staff and students; techniques designed to maximize student behavior in the classroom and on the job; procedures for articulating and coordinating in-school and out-of-school resources; procedures for modifying curriculum, equipment and teaching materials; and services to enhance job placement, school-to-work transition, and job maintenance.

Incentive Assessment

Public Law 94-142 specifies that professional development activities should include the use of incentives that ensure participation by teachers. The incentive options available within an institution should be determined by the steering committee. Then, a survey can be conducted to ascertain those incentives which are most desired by participants. The *Monticello Inservice Model* includes the incentive assessment questions in a program needs assessment instrument (sample questions are shown in Exhibit 10-3).[19] It is also possible to assess incentive needs in a followup to the program needs survey. In either case, it is important to assess the incentives that are desired by participants and to ensure that the top three or four priorities are made available. A result of such a survey at one school district indicated the four highest incentive priorities were: (1) money, (2) university credit, (3) refreshments at inservice sessions, and (4) support services to enable teachers to implement in their classrooms what they learned in inservice.

The district responded to the first priority by offering a mini-grant program for teachers who wished to develop a project based on the inservice training activities. Teachers submitted to the steering committee a two-page proposal that included a statement of the need for the project; a listing of objectives, activities, and evaluation strategies; a timeline for completion of the project; and a project budget. The proposals were reviewed against predetermined criteria, and the projects were funded (typically from $50 to $250 per project). Resource assistance was made available to the teachers throughout the project development. As a result of the mini-grant procedure, several special needs curriculum projects were developed by the district staff.

Exhibit 10-3 Monticello Inservice Model: Sample Incentive Assessment Questions

PARTICIPANT INCENTIVE ASSESSMENT SURVEY
(Sample)

Incentives. In this section incentives or rewards for actively participating in inservice education activities are listed. Please respond to each incentive according to your perception of its desirablity.

Being released from some routine work responsibilities.	1	2	3	4	5
Receiving higher salary.	1	2	3	4	5
Receiving special recognition.	1	2	3	4	5
Being more directly involved in policy and decision making.	1	2	3	4	5
Receiving extra pay for special assignments.	1	2	3	4	5
Receiving more time for travel to professional meetings.	1	2	3	4	5
Sharing teaching assignments with faculty from other areas.	1	2	3	4	5
Receiving written notes of appreciation from administration.	1	2	3	4	5
Exchanging evaluations of teaching with peers.	1	2	3	4	5
Having nearby opportunity for professional development.	1	2	3	4	5
Being more satisfied with my job.	1	2	3	4	5
Receiving tuition rebate for taking credit courses when credit on salary schedule is not applicable.	1	2	3	4	5
Using school day for staff development activities.	1	2	3	4	5
Having additional assistance when desired (student aides, clerical help, teacher aides.)	1	2	3	4	5
Other ________________	1	2	3	4	5

Source: Maquet, *Monticello Model for Inservice Staff Development* (Springfield, Ill.: Illinois, 1976).

In response to the second incentive priority, arrangements were made with a local university to offer special education or vocational education credit for the inservice program. The assigned professor was an active participant throughout the planning and delivery process and served as a consultant to teachers on an individual basis.

The third priority was met through a simple, but important, provision of refreshments at inservice sessions. And the fourth priority was met by providing paraprofessional assistance, substitute teachers, audio-visual assistance, and clerical assistance to teachers during the development of the mini-grant projects.

Resource Identification

Once incentive and program content needs have been identified, internal and external resources should be identified. The expertise existing among the participants can be a potential source of assistance that can simultaneously increase both participant involvement and the individualization of the program delivery. One method of identifying resources is to post the list of program needs in the teacher lounge and to ask for volunteers. Another alternative is to survey the in-house staff to determine potential resource personnel. A sample survey for internal resources identification, developed by the Illinois Office of Education, is shown in Exhibit 10-4.[20]

After the internal resources have been identified, a search for external resources should be conducted. Potential sources are staff from the state office of education, universities, local community agencies, professional organizations, business clubs, and other governmental agencies. Plans should be made to coordinate preservice and inservice activities so that available resources are used as an effective part of the staff development system. The available resources should be matched with the identified needs. The need should be clearly specified to the resource person assigned to the training activity so that this person can plan an appropriate method of responding to the identified need. A breakdown in communication at this point could result in the destruction of the best planning efforts.

Program Delivery

Although personnel training can employ a variety of delivery modes, the workshop presentation format continues to be the single most frequently reported strategy (alternatives to the workshop delivery strategy will be discussed in a later section).

According to Alonzo Myers, the first regularly organized educational workshop was conducted at Ohio State University in 1936.[21] John Moffitt has cited several characteristics of the workshop that makes it a valuable and popular delivery strategy:

Exhibit 10-4 Sample Survey for Internal Resources Identification

SURVEY FOR INTERNAL RESOURCE IDENTIFICATION

MEMO

TO: All Staff
FROM: Inservice Committee
RE: Your Help

We want and need **you.** We have listed the priority training needs indentified by our staff. Now we need your resources. If **YOU** can help, please let us know. If you yourself can't be a resource, maybe you can suggest other resources in the district or from your experience. Please respond before Friday.

Topic	Sorry, I Need Help	I Know Some Books	I Have Skills To Share	I Can Do A Workshop
Classroom Management				
Legal Implications 94-142				
IEP				
Communication Skills				

Other names I'd suggest:

Name: **Phone:**

____

____

____

____
Signature

Source: Illinois State Board of Education, *Educational Personnel Development Through Inservice Training: Planning and Implementation* (Springfield, Ill.: State Board of Education, 1979).

- "It emerges to meet the existing needs of the participants.
- "It provides expert assistance (commonly from higher institutions).
- "It is flexible and consequently can be adapted to many diverse groups and situations.
- "It provides for the pooling of information and sharing of experiences.
- "It motivates participants to change their behavior where and when such changes may be helpful.
- "It gives added support to a changing program by assuring approval of the group.
- "It develops both individual and group skills in attacking new problems.
- "It adds morale to a faculty or a school system.
- "It strengthens working relations with others in different status assignments.
- "It develops knowhow in utilizing democratic procedures in other situations (such as teachers working with students).
- "It redefines and refines the objectives of education.
- "It evaluates both the results of the effort and the process by which results are attained."[22]

Although the workshop holds much potential for serving as a change agent, many workshops fail to accomplish their goals. Such failures can be minimized by using the planning strategies we have discussed. However, these planning efforts can be futile if the delivery strategies are boring, if the physical conditions of the meeting room are inappropriate, and if followup activities are not well-planned and implemented.

The National Academy for Vocational Education has prepared *A Guide For Planning, Conducting, and Evaluating Workshops, Seminars, and Conferences.* This document provides a systematic approach for workshop planners. A sequence of activities is included for each of five phases of workshop delivery: staffing, planning, arranging, conducting, and evaluating. The reader is referred to this guide for a comprehensive coverage of the numerous details that can result in effective workshop delivery. Some of the guidelines discussed in the guide are:

- "The objectives should be developed so that participants can think or do after the workshop what they could not think or do before attending the workshop.
- "The program must have a well designed flow which provides opportunities for the participants to identify what is expected of them as well as what options they might have.
- "The planners must determine if the workshop flow will provide the same input for all participants or if multiple options will be made available. Planners are encouraged to show alternatives which can be used to meet the individual needs of participants."[23]

The delivery mode of the workshop will depend upon the audience and the goals established by the planners. The guidelines discussed in this chapter should be remembered when selecting the delivery mode. The author has found that well-designed activities in which the audience can actively participate tend to be more effective and motivating than straight lecture programs. The use of simulations has been particularly beneficial in promoting attitude change and growth. However, there are certain groups and programs for which the lecture presentation continues to be the best alternative for delivery. Thus the lecture approach should not be totally dismissed. It should be remembered that the more direct an experience is, the more interesting it tends to be for participants. "Telling" delivery strategies provide fewer direct experiences than do "showing" strategies (films, exhibits) or "doing" strategies (simulations, direct practicum experiences, role playing experiences).[24] Some of the "doing" activities that have been beneficial in working with vocational educators are simulations of handicapping conditions (hearing, visual, and motor impairments), simulations of learning-style differentiations and their matching teaching techniques, and demonstrations of behavior management strategies. The use of films has also been found to be helpful in contributing to the awareness and sensitivity for vocational educators. The brochure *Focus On Films* contains several unique films that relate to handicapped and disadvantaged persons in vocational and employment settings.[25]

In summary, the delivery of successful personnel training programs should include a balanced combination of the following practices. They should:

- involve skilled practitioners in the presentation of inservice content,
- emphasize how-to-do-it approaches,
- encourage participant "doing" activities,
- provide the participants with an opportunity to view successful programs and practices, and
- point out the existing services and resources available in the school and community to help instructors better serve special needs students.[26]

Followup activities are essential to maximize the results of an inservice workshop. A danger with many inservice programs is the tendency to utilize a "one-shot" delivery approach. While some of these programs may be very helpful in promoting short-term enthusiasm, they tend to be ineffective in achieving long-term change and impact. A simple technique, the Action Plan, can be used as a followup activity that may increase the long-term impact of an inservice workshop. At the conclusion of a workshop session, the one-page Action Plan can be distributed and completed by individuals or teams of participants (Exhibit 10-5).[27] A carbon copy can be made of the plan and left with the workshop presenter. Phone calls can be made periodically to the participants to inquire about their progress on the plan and to determine if additional resources or assistance are needed. This

Exhibit 10-5 The Action Plan

PLAN OF ACTION

I. Identify one idea or material discussed today that you would like to utilize in your work setting?

II. What actions will you take to implement this idea or material in your setting? What steps need to be taken?

1.

2.

3.

III. When is the earliest date you think it is possible to begin to implement your idea?

What is the latest date you think your idea should be implemented?

IV. How will you determine if the idea (material) is helping reach the goal of better serving special needs students in vocational classes?

V. What additional services/resources can the presenters provide to help you implement your Action Plan?

____
NAME

____
INSTITUTION

____
PHONE

c.c. Inservice Coordinator/Workshop Presenter

simple technique often rekindles the enthusiasm that may have been started at the workshop and provides some encouragement to the participants to continue with the self-determined changes.

A more sophisticated approach was designed by Charles Greenwood and Raymond Morley.[28] Following a summer workshop held at Drake University, interdisciplinary teams from local school districts developed an action plan that included a statement of local program needs, a list of long-term goals and short-term objectives, strategies for attaining stated objectives, resources needed, anticipated outcomes, and anticipated followup support needed during the first year. Throughout the year, technical assistance to the teams was made available by Drake University and the Iowa State Department of Education.

Evaluation

Evaluation of staff development activities is essential for the continued refinement of the program plan to meet changing participant needs. Unfortunately, evaluation is often not accomplished because it is seen as threatening, time-consuming, or unimportant. Evaluation and assessment provide valuable information for the development of future program activities. A plan should be devised for continuous evaluation that encompasses feedback from all of those involved in the activities: the steering committee, the deliverer, the participants, the school administration, and so on. The assessment strategies could include pretests of attitudes and competencies of participants and then followup posttests immediately after program completion. Of greater importance is the long-term change that may have occurred as a result of the inservice. It is expected that, in the future, increased emphasis will be given to the assessment of long-term impact. The results of assessment information can be used to improve the quality of decisions made about future activities, to provide accountability, to assess effectiveness, to make comparisons of delivery styles, and to redefine the needs and goals of participants.

Increasing Impact

To increase the effect of teacher training efforts, a long-range plan of resource assistance should be developed. One promising method of increasing impact is through the use of a resource teacher. The resource teacher can be available to assist vocational teachers implement the strategies learned during inservice. If the resource teacher is trained in special education, the expertise gained by that teacher through university training and classroom experience can be shared with vocational instructors. The role of the resource teacher can take many directions. Some of the activities that could be performed by the resource teacher are:

- Coordinate the inservice training program.
- Provide individual consultation with vocational teachers following inservice activities.
- Coordinate inservice needs of staff with community resources (business, social services, governmental agencies, universities, and so on).
- Assist vocational teachers with the identification of student needs.
- Assist vocational teachers to understand the content of student diagnostic data (achievement scores, interest inventories, vocational assessments).
- Assist vocational teachers with the development of Individualized Education Programs (IEPs) for handicapped students.
- Coordinate resources needed for implementation of IEPs.
- Periodically monitor student progress on the IEP through consultation with vocational teachers, special education teachers, and other personnel.
- Coordinate communications with parents, schools, and other community service agencies.
- Assist with curriculum adaptations, alternative teaching strategies, equipment modifications, and job redesign.
- Provide direct support services to students who need particular assistance.

Alternative Modes of Delivery

The workshop presentation mode is only one method of personnel preparation delivery. Other methods include practicum experiences, observation of exemplary practices and programs, newsletters, materials review, student case conferences, professional journal article review, media presentations, individual consultation, and team teaching. It is not possible, in the present context, to present an exhaustive list of professional development activities. Suffice it to say that the common belief that personnel development is equivalent to a 2-hour inservice session or to a 16-week university lecture course is a narrow view. The concept of personnel development should be more broadly considered to be a continuum of preservice and inservice activities that utilizes a variety of resources and alternative strategies to improve staff capacity to respond to student needs.

It is unfortunate that the latter concept of personnel development remains underutilized. There is a growing competition for control of staff development functions among the primary providers: professional organizations, state education agencies, colleges and universities, private consulting firms, and local school districts. It is doubtful that many of these agencies recognize or would admit to such competition. However, the fragmented, duplicative attempts at staff development by each of these agencies implies a lack of coordinated, communicated effort. According to Gary Adamson, Judy Smith, and Paul Renz, this fragmentation appears to stem from issues of territoriality, power politics, and resistance to change. These authors suggest effective inservice education "will depend on the capacity of education agencies, colleges, universities, and professional organizations to collaborate in this area of potentially mutual enterprise."[29] Significant changes must be made in the ways the providers interact with one another and with the community.

A collaborative approach to special needs vocational education has been undertaken by the state of Illinois. The approach is a complex design that interfaces the resources of state agencies, universities, local education agencies, and professional organizations. The system is not yet complete and weaknesses still exist. However, the overall design has the potential to link the multiple providers of personnel development in a unified coordinated approach. The system, called the Technical Assistance and Dissemination System for Special Needs Populations, consists of:

- A management team appointed by the state director of vocational education. The team consists of members of the state education office management staff who are responsible for the provision of special needs vocational education. The management team sets policies and guidelines for the system.
- An advisory staff consisting of state office consultants, university teacher educators, and implementers of local exemplary projects (for example, bilingual education).
- Six special needs consultants who provide technical assistance and inservice to local education agencies based upon assessed local needs. Local education staffs are utilized for program design and delivery of inservice. These consultants also provide feedback to the state office and universities concerning the local needs for research, curriculum development, and preservice training.
- Four university externs who are graduate students in a special needs vocational education doctoral program. Funded through a project with the state education agency, these externs assist the special needs consultants and develop special projects that correspond to locally identified needs and to their doctoral program goals.
- A university-based dissemination center that provides state level inservice to professional organizations and local educators, identifies and disseminates teacher-made and university-developed materials, and conducts research related to program improvement activities.
- An interagency coordination task force consisting of state agency personnel (special education, vocational education and division of rehabilitation services), professional organization representatives, parent organization representatives, and university and local education service providers.[30]

The Illinois system is a multifaceted approach that grew out of an exemplary local-level program network. The system requires strong leadership at the state education agency level, supported by a coordinated delivery approach among all participants. The impact of the system is yet to be determined. However, its design has the capability of responding to personnel development needs through a collaborative unified system.

SUGGESTIONS AND FUTURE DIRECTIONS

Well-designed teacher training programs can be the critical factor leading to successful implementation of the intent of federal legislation for the vocational education of special needs students. The coordinated preservice-inservice approach to personnel preparation has the capability of delivering a systematic training program that can continue to be responsive to the needs of teachers in the field. Because of the particularized needs of vocational teachers who work with handicapped and disadvantaged students, a well-designed personnel program should be developed and implemented at the state and local levels. This coordinated plan should include education of vocational and special educators, administrators, paraprofessionals, and volunteers. Following are ten specific recommendations:

1. Educational agencies (state offices, universities, local school districts, and intermediate agencies) should examine personnel preparation efforts to ascertain their compliance with the intent of Public Law 94-142 and Public Law 94-482 and the possibilities for collaborative delivery strategies.
2. Educational agencies should determine the need and potential for increased coordination of the delivery of systematic, long range, and continuous personnel training programs.
3. Personnel training activities should not be limited to academic theory but should include opportunities for practicum experiences that are related to the theory base.
4. Personnel preparation activities should begin with an assessment of participant attitudes and concerns. Strategies should be developed to encourage those attitudes that are favorable to working with handicapped and disadvantaged students.
5. Inservice efforts should be based on assessed needs of staff and should allow for the personal growth of individual staff members as well as for the development of the staff as a whole.
6. Teacher certification requirements should be examined to determine their potential for (a) encouraging special education coursework for vocational certification and (b) vocational education coursework for special education certification.
7. Specific plans for the provision of continuous inservice and followup consultation should be investigated, possibly through the utilization of the resource teacher and team-teaching arrangements.

8. Nonhandicapped students and employers should be provided with inservice to help them learn to interact with handicapped individuals in a realistic manner.
9. Boards of education should be provided with assistance in understanding the intent of federal legislation; the social, personal, and economic benefits of complying with the legislation; and the programmatic designs that are needed to serve adequately special needs students in vocational education.
10. Teacher education programs should consider the following options that encourage cross appointment of faculty in vocational education: special education, cross majors who take courses in both programs, cross listed courses in both departments, and joint departmental resource centers.[31]

NOTES

1. Gary Leske and Steve Frederickson, *Needs Assessment For Vocational Education Administrators: An Evolving System for Staff Development Decision Making* (Minneapolis, Minn.: University of Minnesota, Department of Vocational and Technical Education, 1979), p. 1.
2. U.S., *Federal Register,* vol. 42, no. 191, October 3, 1977, p. 53850.
3. U.S., *Federal Register,* vol. 42, no. 163, August 23, 1977, p. 42492.
4. Sharon Davis and Michael Ward, *Vocational Education of Handicapped Students: A Guide for Policy Development* (Reston, Va.: Council for Exceptional Children, no date), p. 71.
5. U.S. Department of Health, Education, and Welfare, *Progress Toward a Free Appropriate Public Education: A Report to Congress on the Implementation of P.L. 94-142,* HEW Publication No. (OE) 79-05003 (January 1979), p. 65.
6. R.M. Brandt et al., *Inservice Teacher Education: Cultural Pluralism and Social Change* (Palo Alto, Calif.: National Center for Educational Statistics and Teacher Corp. 1976), p. 125.
7. National Education Association, *Education for All Handicapped Children: Consensus, Conflict, and Challenge* (Washington, D.C.: National Education Association, 1978), p. 27.
8. Gary D. Meers and Charlotte Conoway, "Vocational Education's Role in Career Education for Handicapped Students," *Journal of Career Education,* Winter 1977.
9. L. Allen Phelps, *Instructional Development for Special Needs Learners: An Inservice Resource Guide* (Urbana, Ill.: University of Illinois, 1975), p. 11.
10. Norman D. Ehresman, John F. Hanel, and Betty V. Robertson, *An Inservice Program for Vocational Teachers of the Disadvantaged* (Bowling Green, Ky.: Western Kentucky University, 1976).
11. U.S. Department of Health, Education, and Welfare, *Progress Toward a Free Appropriate Public Education,* p. 58.
12. L. Allen Phelps, *Technical Assistance and Staff Development Handbook* (State College, Pa.: Occupational Research and Evaluation) pp. 1-17.
13. Phelps, *Instructional Development,* p. 13.
14. D. Ford and Paul M. Nemiroff, "Applied Group Problem Solving: The Nominal Group Technique," *1975 Annual Handbook for Group Facilitators* (Iowa City, Iowa: University Associates, 1975), pp. 179-182.
15. Martin Maquet, *Monticello Model for Inservice Staff Development* (Springfield, Ill.: Illinois Office of Education), p. 39.

16. M. Naumann-Etienne and W. Todd, "Applying Organizational Development Techniques to Inservice Education" (Paper presented at the annual meeting of the American Educational Research Association, San Francisco, California, April, 1976), p. 2.
17. G. Lawrence et al., "Patterns of Effective Inservice Education," *Inservice,* February 1977, p. 7.
18. Charles Greenwood and Raymond Morley, "How to Operate an Inservice Activity," *Industrial Education Magazine,* April 1978, pp. 26-29.
19. Maquet, *Monticello Model,* p. 34.
20. Illinois State Board of Education, *Educational Personnel Development Through Inservice Training: Planning and Implementation* (Springfield, Ill.: State Board of Education, 1979), p. 16.
21. Alonzo F. Myers, "Workshops," *Journal of Educational Sociology* 24, no. 5 (1951): 249.
22. John C. Moffitt, *Inservice Education for Teachers* (New York: Center for Applied Research in Education, 1968), p. 26.
23. National Center for Research in Vocational Education, *A Guide for Planning, Conducting, and Evaluating Workshops, Seminars, and Conferences* (Columbus, Ohio: 1979), p. 8-2.
24. Raymond S. Ross, *Essentials of Speech Communication* (Englewood Cliffs, N.J.: Prentice-Hall, Inc.), p. 146.
25. Illinois Network of Exemplary Occupational Education Programs for Handicapped and Disadvantaged Students, *Focus On Films* (Ill.: Illinois Office of Education, 1978). (Available upon request from the author, Turner Hall, Illinois State University, Normal, Illinois 61761.)
26. Greenwood and Morley, "How to Operate an Inservice Activity," p. 27.
27. The Illinois Network of Exemplary Occupational Education Programs for Handicapped and Disadvantaged Students, a project funded through the Department of Adult, Vocational, and Technical Education, Illinois State Board of Education.
28. Greenwood and Morley, "How to Operate an Inservice Activity," p. 28.
29. Gary Adamson, Judy Smith, and Paul Renz, "Inservice and the University: Innovation Without Change," *Forum: Issues In Special Education* 1, no. 1 (September 1977), pp. 1-4.
30. Catherine Batsche, ed., *Network News,* Newsletter for the Technical Assistance and Dissemination Network. (Published by the Illinois Special Needs Populations, an activity funded with the Department of Adult, Vocational, and Technical Education, Illinois State Board of Education, Fall 1979.)
31. James A. Sullivan, "Who Are The Special Needs Students and How Can Special Education and Industrial Teacher Education Work Together and Help Them?" (Paper presented at the 64th Mississippi Valley Industrial Arts Teacher Education Conference, Chicago, November 1977), p. 7.

Chapter 11

Parents' Roles in the Education of Special Vocational Needs Youth

Stanley Vasa, Ed.D.
Allen Steckelberg, M.Ed.

INTRODUCTION

Within the past decade, the perceived relationship between the home and the school has undergone a major transformation. Whereas, in the past, parents have not been regarded as particularly useful in contributing to the educational process, their more extensive involvement in the school is now increasingly viewed by educators as essential. This change in attitude about parent involvement has been brought about by an awareness of several factors: (1) passage of legislation, specifically Public Law 94-142 and Public Law 94-482, which delegates certain responsibilities to parents in their children's education; (2) increasing realization that parents play a key role in the education of their children; and (3) knowledge that parents also play an important role in the vocational choices of their children.

The effectiveness of the parent involvement in vocational programs will be determined by the ability of the school and, more specifically, of the vocational educator to coordinate communication between the home and the school. The effectiveness of the parent-school relationship will rest to a great extent on the planning and implementing of a meaningful parent education program. In this chapter, we examine some assumptions regarding the parent role in education, the purposes of parent education programs, program delivery models, and the importance of program evaluation.

ASSUMPTIONS ABOUT PARENTS

Three important assumptions about parents and their role in education serve as an important basis and rationale for the development of parent-school communications:

1. Parents care more about their children than the school does.
2. Parents have the right to know about and be involved in their child's educational programs.
3. Parents can be effective teachers.

The first assumption simply means that parents have a greater personal and emotional interest in their child than the school has. This assumption is often misunderstood by educators who conclude that parents' nonparticipation in school-related activities is tantamount to not caring about their child's education. In reality, parents may choose noninvolvement for any of a number of reasons, such as fears of inadequacy in discussions with educators; the irrelevance of past contacts with the school; and failing to understand the role the school expects of them.

That parents have a right to know is documented in the laws governing the education of the handicapped. Parents are afforded, for example, the right of access to school records as stipulated in the rules and regulations governing Public Law 94-142:

> . . . shall permit parents to inspect and review any education records relating to their children which are collected, maintained, or used by the agency. . . . The agency shall comply with a request without unnecessary delay and before any meeting regarding the individualized educational program or hearing relating to the identification, evaluation, or placement of the child, and in no case more than 45 days after the request has been made.[1]

Parents play a key role in three segments of the handicapped child's vocational education. First, they participate in and approve their child's placement; secondly, they participate in the development of the Individual Educational Program (IEP); and, thirdly, they monitor their child's progress and the school's performance of services outlined in the IEP. The Family Educational Rights and Privacy Act further documents the rights of parents to access and to monitor the contents of the individual student's records maintained by the school.

The literature supports the contention that parents are effective teachers.[2,3,4,5,6] We must also recognize that parents of exceptional children have probably invested more of their personal time in the education of their children than have parents of students enrolled in regular education. Parents can and do play a key role in the education of their children; it is impossible for them to delegate totally the teaching responsibility to the school. Indeed, parents have universally assumed the responsibility of teaching their children basic self-care skills, such as dressing and speaking.

Parents are thus effective support personnel in the education of their children. For example, in the area of career education, parents are regarded as key individuals in the occupational choices of students. Handicapped students are likely to receive considerable support from their parents in such choices. Parents are in a particularly advantageous position to use outside opportunities to expand their children's education. S.F. Vasa and A.L. Steckelberg have pointed out that "with the aid of good teaching skills, such as establishing behavioral goals, utilizing systematic reinforcement and identifying successful and unsuccessful teaching techniques, parents can provide home and community experiences which contribute to their child's learning."[7]

PURPOSES OF PARENT EDUCATIONAL PROGRAMS

Specific Goals

The first step in establishing a meaningful parent education program is to determine the specific purpose of the program. In a generalized way, one can immediately conclude that improved parent-school communications can be helpful in the establishment of strong vocational educational programs in the community. However, to rest the importance of parents' education programs solely on the vague concept of communications can be potentially disastrous. Meaningless communication and disorganized conferences can quickly alienate an otherwise interested parent. To avoid the pitfall of purposeless and meaningless parent interaction with the school, vocational educators must quickly assess what the potential goals of communication can be to both the parent and to the education of the handicapped student. For the parents of handicapped students, the potential goals of parent education programs include a better understanding of:

- what to expect from the school vocational program
- the scope of the vocational education program
- the program's safety standards and provisions
- the ways the parents can support the acquisition of specific skills
- the grading and evaluation procedures utilized by the school system
- the content and rationale of the career education program
- the acquisition of skills by their child
- the needs of the vocational program for future growth and development
- the performance of their respective children in the vocational program

But parents are not the only beneficiaries of parent-school communication. Vocational educators can also benefit by:

- obtaining information about the individual student's progress
- obtaining information about the students' experiences and expectations from the perspective of their parents
- increasing the opportunities for individual students by involving parents in the educational process
- transmitting information about parents' rights and responsibilities under the law
- obtaining support from groups of parents for the expansion and alteration of present vocational programs to better accommodate the handicapped

Needs Assessment

The needs assessment is the second essential component of a viable parent education program. This assessment should help the vocational educator define more precisely the program's priorities. Priorities may be based upon a need to identify particular areas where knowledge is lacking or to highlight the importance of a topic expressed by either the parents or the vocational educator. Some examples of needs commonly resolved through parent education programs are information about the parents' goals for their children, experiences outside the school, purposes of the school program, and the expectations of the school.

The needs assessment can be conducted in a variety of ways. Parents can be polled by telephone, written questionnaire, or personally. The major consideration for the teacher is to make sure that the choices offered to the parents are those that the teacher can reasonably deliver in a parent education program. In addition to obtaining information about what the parents want to learn, the needs assessment instrument can be used to determine how the parents wish to receive the information, for example, through individual conferences or large group orientation sessions. Only through careful analysis and use of the information from needs assessment can a successful parent education program be planned and implemented.

PROGRAM DELIVERY MODELS

Vocational educators must be aware of the many ways of communicating with parents and the many forms of parent education programs. Some of the modes of communication available to vocational educators are:

- individual parent conferences
- telephone conferences with parents
- correspondence with parents by mail or as transmitted through students

- small group parent meetings
- large group parent orientation meetings
- home visitations

Each of these means of interacting with parents is designed for a specific purpose. But all parent contacts are potentially valuable in the education of the student. The harvesting of this information is the responsibility of the teacher.

Individual Parent Conferences

One of the most important communication delivery systems available is the parent conference. This is the single most commonly used mode of transmitting information to and receiving information from the parents. An interesting phenomenon is apparent in parent education programs: parent participation in conferences tends to decrease as the age of the student increases. The cause for this appears to be twofold: (1) parents have become turned off by parent conferences for a variety of reasons or (2), as students mature in age and development, parents become more and more removed from direct participation in their lives.

The first cause is often avoidable if sufficient preplanning and attention is given to the conduct of the conference. The educator is responsible for establishing a purpose for each conference and expressing this purpose to the parent, either prior to or at the beginning of the conference. Conversely, parents who want a conference with the educator should declare their purpose prior to the meeting. The declaration of purpose should allow both the parent and the teacher time to prepare for the conference and to determine the issues to be discussed. In Exhibit 11-1, a set of guidelines is presented as a checklist and a gentle reminder to the vocational teacher of the importance of preparing for parent-teacher conferences.

Telephone Conferences

It is important that the teacher be acquainted with both the potential values and the dangers of telephone conferences. On the one hand, telephone conversations are valuable as a means of relaying information to the parents and announcing the availability of other forms of communication. On the phone, teachers can give positive feedback to the parents about a student and also information about the general needs of the student. The weaknesses of the telephone conversation, on the other hand, lie in the inability to restrict and guarantee the confidentiality of the message. The content of the conversation must be of such a nature that potentially sensitive information cannot be obtained by an unwanted listener. The best policy is to use the telephone judiciously in conversing with parents. When it is utilized, teachers should try to follow up on sensitive issues through an individual conference.

Exhibit 11-1 A Checklist of Parent Conference Guidelines for Educators

Educators should:

- plan for all student conferences in advance
- have a clear purpose in mind for each conference, for example, to report student progress
- inform parents of the purpose of the conference
- have all student records available for review prior to the conference
- consider the parent conference as an important event and not merely routine
- allow enough time to discuss the issues thoroughly; the parent should not feel rushed during the conference
- conduct the conference privately in a place free from distractions and interruptions
- have prior knowledge of the conference for purposes of self-briefing
- invite others to the conference only if they will contribute to resolving an issue or problem
- invite the student to attend, unless the conference covers emotionally laden subjects that might adversely affect the student
- hold the conference at a time convenient to the parent
- be aware of parent transportation needs and child care needs
- deal honestly with parents
- listen to the parents and respect their confidence
- avoid using educational jargon in conversing with the parent
- try to put themselves in the parent's role during the conference
- not jump to conclusions based on statements made by parents
- back the school administration and other teachers during the conference
- be cautious of the content of written communications
- keep a record of the conference
- keep the parent informed of change following the conference
- establish a means of communication between the parent and teacher
- evaluate the effectiveness of the conference
- attempt to answer all questions raised by the parent
- realize that the responsibility for the success of the conference lies with the teacher
- not argue with the parent
- avoid giving direct advice to the parents on parenting

Correspondence

When mailed correspondence is used to communicate with parents, the composition of the letter requires careful consideration. The correspondence must be carefully monitored to ensure that the parent does not misinterpret the content and that factual information is provided. Parents often read such letters very carefully to determine the accuracy of the grammatic construction and the spelling of words.

Written communications are most frequently used to do one or more of the following:

- announce a parent meeting or conference
- announce a meeting or conference that may be of interest to parents
- provide descriptive information about the vocational program
- solicit the parents' involvement in the evaluation or development of the vocational program
- provide parents with positive feedback on the achievements of their children
- solicit parents' approval for student involvement in field trips and other activities
- provide parents with evaluation data about each student's achievement in the program

Small Group Meetings

Small group meetings are frequently used to transmit information or to seek support from parents who have common interests. Such meetings are generally limited to no more than ten parents. The small number is necessary to permit maximum interaction and to guarantee commonality of concerns. The meetings could be conducted for the purpose of discussing a specific problem or to solicit parent input on the organization of a specific component of the vocational training program.

Small group meetings offer the advantages of being more intimate and personal. They permit a more careful delineation of specific topics for discussion based on the interest of the group. The disadvantages of such meetings are the time-consuming burdens they impose on the busy schedules of both the vocational educator and the parents.

In planning a small group meeting, a number of considerations should be kept in mind:

- Each session should last no longer than two hours.
- The educator and the parents should not meet more often than once a week.
- The time between meetings should be less than 10 weeks.
- The meeting group should be no larger than ten persons.
- Parents should play an active role in determining meeting content.

Large Group Orientation Meetings

Largely overlooked at the secondary level of vocational education is the large group orientation meeting. This type of meeting has the advantage of allowing the vocational educators to present information needed by a large number of parents in a relatively short period of time and in one session, such as a summary of the curriculum of the program, the amount and degree of involvement requested of parents, and the unique or specific requirements of the course of study. Parents often prefer to attend fewer larger sessions when learning about the vocational program rather than receive this general information at an individual conference. Vocational teachers can save considerable instructional and personal time by clearly delineating the most frequently requested information from parents and developing a general orientation session to provide such information.

A successful orientation session is based on the accuracy of the vocational educator in assessing the parents' need for information. The parents' satisfaction with the session will depend on the accuracy of the information announcing the purpose of the session and their comfort level in receiving the information.

Exhibit 11-2 presents a checklist of characteristics of parents that are important to remember in the planning of parent education programs. This checklist should be reviewed prior to developing the content of any group activity with parents. The points listed underscore the fact that parents are adults who have their own interests and priorities. Careful adherence to this checklist of needs will enhance the probability of success for group education programs for parents.

Exhibit 11-2 A Checklist of Parent Characteristics That Are Important in Planning Parent Education Programs

Parents:

- are individuals who have pride
- have other interests and responsibilities besides their children and the school
- have creative ideas and a wealth of experience
- have established childrearing philosophies
- have a limited amount of free time for school programs
- can assimilate a limited amount of information that is contrary to their individual philosophies and beliefs
- are individuals who have developed behavior patterns consistent with their values, attitudes, and beliefs
- have decisions to make and problems to solve
- have, if parents of handicapped children, developed a certain amount of resistance to suggestions from specialists and school personnel
- are often bewildered and confused by all of the options available to them
- have frustrations and concerns about the services previously rendered to their children
- are suspicious of the school and its functions
- are secretly afraid of failing in the rearing of their children
- do not like to be talked down to or belittled for their failures
- can *change*

Home Visitations

Home visitations have been an important part of a number of vocational programs, especially in the area of vocational agriculture where the instructor is monitoring the progress of students in the establishment and maintenance of projects in conjunction with their school programs. Home visits can provide important information to the vocational educator about the family environment of the student and economic conditions under which the student lives. However, this information may also prejudice the educator's expectations for the student.

Home visitation should be made only when a specific reason for it has been ascertained. Having the parents visit the school program is potentially more valuable than the educator visiting the home. Parents should be encouraged to visit and participate in the educational program for their children. Generally, home visits provide the parent with little useable information about the school.

Following are four guidelines for home visitations:

1. Home visitations should be made only on the request of the parent or when the parent refuses to visit the school.
2. Home visits should be made when a specific tangible value to the student's educational program from the visit can be anticipated.
3. Home visitations should be made only with the approval of the student or at the student's request unless mitigating circumstances exist.
4. Home visits should occur only when parents are informed of their time and purpose in advance.

Home visitations are potentially valuable if utilized properly. If used indiscriminately, however, they can add a burden of extended working hours on the teacher, invade the privacy of the parents, and possibly humiliate the student.

PROGRAM EVALUATION

Program evaluation is the final component of a successful parent education program. Evaluation is undertaken for two reasons. First, it can determine the effectiveness of the program in meeting stated objectives. Secondly, the information obtained through the evaluation can provide helpful information for future planning decisions.

The goal of any educational program is to bring about a positive change in the parents' knowledge, performance, and attitudes or behavior (for example, concerning school or child rearing). The evaluation, therefore, must be designed to determine the effectiveness of the program in changing:

- the parents' attitudes
- the parents' knowledge
- the parents' behavior
- the students' behavior

A wide variety of dependent measures and measurement devices can be used in collecting such information. Table 11-1 lists a number of alternatives for data gathering in each of the four areas mentioned above. Selection of a specific means of collecting information should be based on several factors, including cost, the feasibility of carrying out the procedures, and the value of the data collected.

Table 11-1 Evaluation of the Parent Education Program

Parameters	*Dependent Measures*	*Data Gathering Techniques*
Parent increase in knowledge	Attainment of knowledge objectives, i.e., what is covered, parents' school relationships, parents' role in the home, etc.	Pre-post assessments Observations Self-assessment scales Interviews Questionnaires
Parents' change in attitudes	Change in attitudes toward child rearing; change in attitude toward career; change in attitude toward school, etc.	Questionnaires Opinionnaires Rating scales Interviews
Parents' behavior	Involvement in the education process, i.e., cooperation with the school, parent/child involvement	Attendance rosters Teacher observations Interaction analyses Anecdotal records Records of parents School contacts
Child's behavior	Increase in knowledge or performance in related areas, i.e., career options, values, attitudes, habits, decision making, etc.	School attendance Test data IEP objectives Sociometrics Observations Teacher records

NOTES

1. U.S., *Federal Register*, vol. 42, no. 163, August 23, 1977, p. 42498.
2. B.P. Berkowitz and A.M. Graziano, "Training Parents as Behavior Therapists: A Review," *Behavior Research and Therapy* 10 (1972): 297-317.
3. Eric Denhoff, "The Impact of Parents on the Growth of Exceptional Children," *Exceptional Children* (January 26, 1960): 271-274.
4. E. Kelly, "Parental Roles in Special Education Programming: A Brief for Involvement," *Journal of Special Education* 7 (Winter 1973): 357-364.
5. D. MacDonald, "Parents: A New Resource," *Teaching Exceptional Children* 3 (1971): 81.
6. L.O. Walder et al. "Teaching Behavioral Principles to Parents of Disturbed Children," in *Behavior Therapy with Children*, ed. A.M. Graziano (Chicago, Ill.: Aldine-Atherton, 1971).
7. S.F. Vasa and A.L. Steckelberg, "Career Education, Parent's Role and the Choices for the Handicapped," *Proceedings of the Barkley Memorial Conference* (Lincoln, Neb.: University of Nebraska-Lincoln, 1979).

Chapter 12

Administrative and Supervisory Functions in Special Vocational Needs Programs

Roger Sathre, M.Ed. and
Robert C. West, M.Ed.

INTRODUCTION

It is fitting that administration and supervision of special needs programs be considered in this penultimate chapter. That is because administrators and supervisors must be aware of all of the preceding aspects of the programs and services in their charge. They must be able to determine needs, write an acceptable proposal, seek out and develop good staff, perform evaluations, and provide followup data.

We believe that a program must have the following elements if it is to provide successfully more than the minimal services to special needs students: a warm, caring, concerned, and firm staff, adequate facilities and time blocks for instruction, and suitable equipment based on the curriculum guide. The job of the program administrator or supervisor is to develop or obtain these elements and mold them to provide maximum benefit to the students.

PROGRAM MODELS

Vocational special needs programs cover a broad range of activities, depending upon the needs of the community. Those suggested here are not meant to be definitive but rather to be used as models that can be shaped to the administrators' desires, the teachers' skills, the schools' facilities, and the students' abilities. They include prevocational and occupational skill training, the mainstream model, separate facilities, in-school programs, work experience and cooperative programs, tutoring, and alternative schools. In short, any vocational and special education model, from junior high to postsecondary and adult, can be adapted to best serve special needs students.

Prevocational and Occupational Skill Training

Prevocational training includes skills and attitudes gained prior to enrollment in a vocational program. It is usually offered at the junior high school. The curriculum consists of high-interest, hands-on activities that are basic to independent living or to vocational programs offered at the high school. Another purpose of a prevocational class is to serve as an assessment laboratory by allowing students to explore for a limited time several occupational fields. Some examples of hands-on activities are: small-engine disassembly and reassembly, horticulture, carpentry, welding, food service, masonry, upholstery, body and fender repair, bicycle repair, plumbing, electrical wiring, and sewing. The life skills taught include budgeting, apartment hunting and furnishing, basic nutrition and meal planning, planned parenthood, and job finding and leaving.

The Mainstream Model

The mainstream model is to be encouraged wherever possible. Many handicapped students can succeed in a mainstream setting if instructional staff is made available for tutoring, safety, or other reasons. It is unrealistic to expect shop teachers to deal adequately and effectively with several handicapped students in addition to their regular classes. Without aides or other staff members, such arrangements benefit nobody.

Separate Facilities

Separate facilities are the logical answer for students who demonstrate they cannot tolerate or cope with a regular setting. It is also an ideal solution to a school that has few or full classes where special needs students have little chance of enrolling. Frequently, after a year in a separate program, a student will be able to succeed in a regular mainstream vocational setting.

If traditional shops are not available in the school building, it may be possible to rent or purchase nearby buildings that are acceptable. Many "storefront schools" operate successfully. In any case, adequate facilities are a must for a successful program, and every effort should be made to secure them.

In-School Programs

In-school programs may have either regular or modified curriculums. Many special needs students cannot complete an entire vocational course without assistance. They need extra time or instruction to be able to achieve their objectives. These extra services can be provided by special needs funding for tutorial help or aides. When special needs students demonstrate that they cannot succeed in a regular school setting, their programs have to be modified. Lowering the student teacher ratio, having specially trained teachers, using aides, rewriting texts to lower reading levels, and group counseling can all be used as modifiers of programs to make them successful.

Work Experience and Cooperative Programs

Work experience and cooperative programs permit the student to be employed in a participating business and to learn on the job. A teacher-coordinator is involved in the process and works with the employer to be sure there is a strong educational component at the job site. The student is paid for his work. (Detailed information on work placement is presented in Chapter 7.)

Tutoring

The program model most widely used with disadvantaged students is tutoring. Most disadvantaged students are poor readers and need remedial help to read texts and other necessary material. A widely used approach is individualized prescriptive education. Basically, this approach determines the student's problems by testing, observation, or other means and then prescribes a solution. A tutor then works with the student to meet the individual's needs.

Alternative Schools

Alternative schools are surfacing across the country to serve youth with special needs. Most focus on a particular group or characteristic of the student and develop the curriculum accordingly.

A typical alternative school that provides vocational special needs may enroll only dropouts or those identified as potential dropouts. Depending on the enrollment and funding, it may include only a few vocational offerings or it may develop into a complete vocational high school with many offerings. One such school is Vocational Village in Portland, Oregon. This school started in 1970 with disadvantaged funding from the state department of education. Three programs with 40 students were run the first year. In the 1978-1979 school year, 236 students were enrolled in 8 programs. In addition to the vocational faculty, there were many academic and related faculty and counselors.

The curriculum of Vocational Village is based on individual competencies; when these competencies are achieved, credits are awarded. Attendance is encouraged but varies greatly among the students. Absences are followed up by the faculty and counselors. Personal characteristics, such as smoking and dress, are given little attention as long as they do not infringe upon the rights of other students.

The average school day consists of three hours in a shop or lab setting and three in academic classes slanted toward the particular trade in which the student is enrolled. About 30 students graduate each year. This is low in relation to the number enrolled, but many students spin off into jobs as their skills and available jobs match to provide job opportunities. Followup studies cannot track all students because they are a very mobile population. But those who have been contacted mention repeatedly the modified program, the heavy shoptime, and the concerned and caring staff as positive points of the school.

Vocational Village has thus proven to be successful over the years. Presently funded almost completely by the Portland School District, it is an example of an idea that worked and solved a problem, and it has become an integral part of the district's offerings.

PROGRAM MANAGEMENT

Effective program management is essential if students are to make maximum progress. The local educational agency should designate an individual to be responsible for vocational special needs programming. The agency should also develop a job description which specifies the functions of the position in coordinating and providing services.

In a large district, this position may have the title of director of vocational special needs; in smaller districts, the title might be director of special or vocational education; and in the smallest, it may be principal, superintendent, or lead teacher.

Program coordinators work with special needs and vocational staffs to ensure a smooth operation and with the advisory committee to keep the program on target with community needs and also to provide accountability as requested by state officials. They must be aware of all state and federal regulations and policies that apply.

Program coordinators also handle program expansion, modification, funding and inservice. Credibility with both the state department and the school board are essential in carrying out the assigned duties.

Administrators set the tone for instruction and learning not so much by their formal policy statements as by their attitudes and activities. Some of the activities in which they can indicate a positive attitude include:

- planning for the future in terms of numbers, space, materials or processes, and staff
- developing, presenting and coordinating inservice programs for all concerned
- working in the programs as time permits so as to be continuously aware of students and staff needs and abilities

- promoting the benefits of the program through an ongoing public relations campaign.

Administrators of special needs programs also must:

- establish priorities for services, first, with respect to exceptional children not enrolled in any educational program and, second, for those children with the most critical learning problems who are receiving an inadequate education.
- develop plans for the continuum of levels to be served from early childhood through age 21, emphasizing career education prior to secondary program models.
- review annually the special arrangements developed to augment district services through interagency agreements and special contracts with public or private agencies.
- maintain an ongoing child find program to locate the unserved, to program adequately for the underserved, and to provide for the previously served who have returned to school and continue to be eligible.
- maintain an ongoing data collection and program review process to monitor the quality and quantity of the services delivered.
- monitor budgets and fiscal records relative to local, state, and federal accounting requirements.
- coordinate with agency administrators to assure integration of handicapped students into the total school program and to develop appropriate eligibility criteria for placement options.
- assist principals and teachers in the development and scheduling of classes and programs.
- organize an effective, flexible child study team whose operation should encompass: (1) uniform procedures for referral; (2) comprehensive, multifaceted student assessment; (3) the development of the required components of an IEP; (4) establishment of placement procedures; (5) change of placement procedures; (6) annual review of the students' needs, strengths, and programming; (7) substantial parental involvement; and (8) procedural steps mandated by state and federal laws.
- assist or provide for the selection of personnel to provide special education, related services, and surrogate parent assistance.
- submit applications, proposals, reports, and forms as necessary for the operation of an approved program.
- assist instructional and support personnel in selecting and securing needed materials, equipment, and ancillary services.
- maintain administrative and student records in accord with applicable state and federal laws.
- ensure the participation of handicapped students attending private schools.

- provide for appropriate graduation requirements, avoiding discrimination of students because of their handicapping conditions.
- provide for personnel development programs based on sound planning and staff input.

Table 12-1 presents a list of possible services and the agencies under which the services may be provided in the areas of vocational rehabilitation, vocational education, and special education.[1]

Table 12-1 Services Provided by Selected Agencies

Service		*Agency**	
	DVR	*DVE*	*SP.ED.*
Information, consultation	X	X	X
Evaluation of potential, when critical to development of individual plan	X		X
Counseling client/student	X		X
Medical restoration	X		
Vocational training	X	X	X
Maintenance of client	X		
Placement of client/student	X	X	X
Transportation of client/student	X		X
Telecommunications	X		
Salaries of selected personnel involved in delivering special program		X	X
Supplies and instructional materials over and above standard school resources		X	X
Instructional staff travel needed for workshops, prevocational meetings, or work placement coordination		X	
Staff development	X	X	X
Specialized support services contingent on student/client condition, program circumstances, and problem	X	X	X

*DVR—vocational rehabilitation
DVE—vocational education
SP.ED.—special education

Source: Schrag and West, *Interagency Planning: Special Education and Related Services for Idaho's Handicapped/Exceptional Students* (Boise, Idaho: Idaho State Department of Education, 1978).

PROGRAM PROPOSAL DEVELOPMENT

The development of a new program to serve special needs students can move in several directions. Whatever the avenue chosen, however, the time given to anticipating the needs of each step and to planning in general will help smooth out any wrinkles in the program. Procedures may vary among states and districts, but in general the following functions must be considered:

- determine program need
- develop objectives
- develop new or modify existing curriculum
- identify funding sources
- establish policies
- develop and implement policies
- adhere to established mandates
- provide for program planning timeline

Determine Program Need

Frequently one or more people in the school or community will be concerned about a group not being served effectively and will begin to advocate for them. A possible solution might be discussed informally, heard at a workshop or conference, or read about in a newspaper or journal. Eventually, a school leader will approve further study and serious investigation will begin.

At this point, a quick call to the state department of education should be made to determine if the proposed program is worth pursuing. In this context, general topics, like available funds, matching requirements, time lines, teacher certification and availability, and proposal development workshops, can be discussed.

Some basis in fact is needed to justify a Vocational Special Needs (VSN) program, and this usually is determined by a needs assessment or community survey (a detailed explanation of the needs assessment procedure is given in Chapter 8). Most occupational vocational programs are justified by a community survey that determines how many jobs there are in the area in the general category and how many new workers are needed annually. This data can be collected by visits to the local state employment office, talking with managers of local industries, tabulating want ads for a period of time, and surveying business and luncheon groups. Because VSN students are in specific categories, the counselors or directors of special and vocational education can help identify them.

Develop Objectives

Objectives must be spelled out so that all concerned are aware of what is to be accomplished in the program. Wherever possible, the objectives should be in measurable terms so that they can be evaluated. Well-written objectives form the skeleton that teachers or curriculum writers will use to give direction and purpose to the program. Without them, it will be difficult to get a handle on what the program will provide to the students.

Develop New or Modify Existing Curriculum

Special needs programs are based on the assumption that the students might not succeed in a regular program of instruction without modifications in the program. Often, such students do not have the mental or physical capabilities or basic education necessary to succeed without assistance. The corollary is that, with reasonable assistance and modification, special needs students can succeed to some level of employability. Indeed thousands of these students successfully complete school and go to work each year.

In Figure 12-1, Larry Barber presents varying degrees of program modification for handicapped youth.[2] A similar classification can be applied to disadvantaged students. The classifications include:

- Regular vocational education—developed and designed for all students in the regular continuum of secondary education. Handicapped students or students receiving support services (that is, speech, counseling, social work, or therapy) might be placed in this program if it is determined that they can benefit from its offerings.
- Adapted vocational education—regular vocational education programs that are altered to accommodate handicapped students through the provision of special materials, equipment, and personnel. Special education students eligible for this program are usually those participating in resource room programs.
- Special vocational education—programs designed solely for students placed in special education classes. Such programs are for handicapped persons whose disability precludes integration into a regular vocational education program.
- Individual vocational training—offered on an individual basis to the handicapped to match a specific training program to a person's exhibited vocational interests and needs. Specific programs, such as apprenticeships, manpower development, training placement, or identified training stations, are used to train the student in a particular job. The program includes individual vocational training that is community-based or included in a school vocational or industrial arts class.

Figure 12-1 Degrees of Program Modification for Handicapped Youth

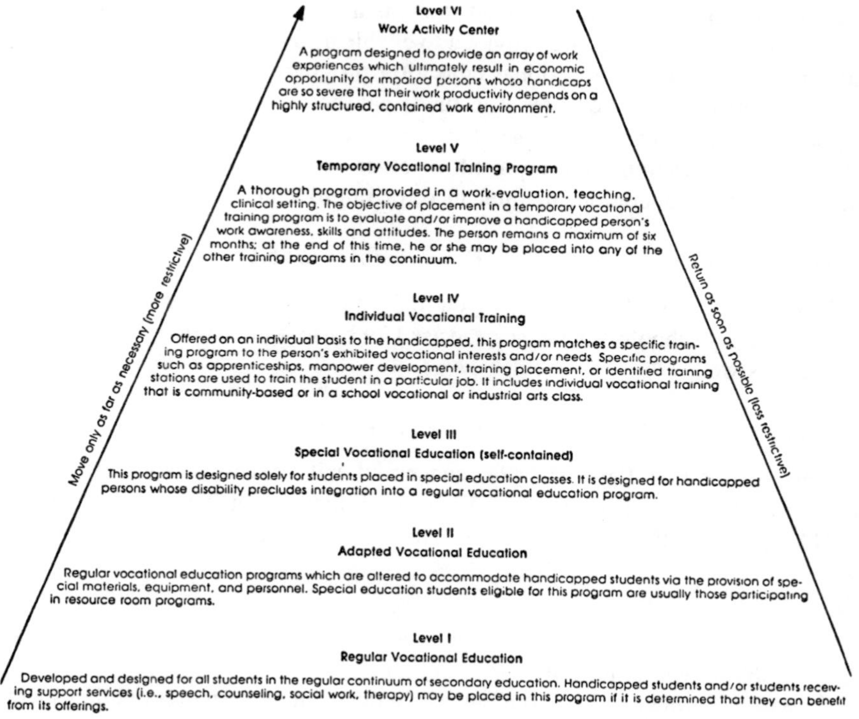

Source: Jean J. Moore and Vance S. Engleman (Eds.), *Administrators Manual* (Salt Lake City, Utah: University of Utah, 1977) p. 22.

Facilities, special and modified equipment, and services must be considered in terms of the handicaps of the students. Space in nearby vacant stores or industrial sites may have to be rented until campus space can be made available. Go/no-go gauges, guards, rails, jigs, and other devices may have to be purchased or made.

Identify Funding Sources

Several potential funding sources are available for special needs programs. Because laws and rules change from time to time, the state department of education should be contacted for specific information on how to tap these funds.

Vocational Amendments of 1976

The 1976 vocational amendments (Public Law 94-482) set aside 10 percent of the basic grant to serve handicapped students and 20 percent to serve disadvantaged students. The funds are provided to enable disadvantaged and handicapped students to succeed in vocational education programs. All funds require a 50 percent match within the state. The funds can be used for any of the program models described earlier, to pay for personnel, equipment, supplies, travel, evaluations, curriculum development, or other costs directly related to program implementation, operation, maintenance, or improvement.

Title I Elementary and Secondary Education Act (ESEA)

Title I funds serve disadvantaged youth. Frequently these funds are used only in the elementary schools, but they can be used for basic skill instruction in secondary schools as well.

Education for All Handicapped Children Act of 1975

This act (Public Law 94-142), concerned with excess costs, significantly amends previous portions of Title VI of the Education of the Handicapped Act (EHA), particularly Part B of that title. The four major purposes of the 1975 act are to:

1. guarantee the availability of special education programming to handicapped children who require it,
2. assure fairness and appropriateness in decision making in providing special education,
3. establish clear management and auditing requirements and procedures, and
4. financially assist state and local governments through federal funding.

The fourth purpose given above concerns the extra effort necessary to implement the requirements spelled out in the law and accompanying regulations. This has been termed the "excess cost" feature of funding under this law. In order for a local educational agency to receive these Part B funds, the local education agency must submit an application to the state education agency. The local education agency may use these funds only to cover, above a minimal level, costs of providing a free appropriate education. Rules and regulations implementing the law provide a statutory formula to figure the minimum amount to be funded by a variety of resources. (See 121a.184 of the regulations dated August 23, 1977, for assistance in computing the formula.) Records must be kept to show that excess-cost funds were spent for services above a minimum local effort in order to avoid supplanting state and local financial responsibility with federal funds. Part B funds may not displace state and local monies for a given type of expenditure or on an aggregate basis.

For example, if a special education or special needs teacher's salary were to be switched from local or state funding to Part B funding to provide the same service, that would be supplanting. It would not be supplanting if a new program were added to the system to be taught by the teacher. In this case, Part B funds could be used, as this would increase services not previously provided. School administrators should be cautious about "loading" their budgets with Part B-funded teachers and other professionals. In the evolution of a solidly based service delivery system, a strong local- and state-funded program for essential services has greater long-term advantages than reliance on federal funds.

If a district spent $250,000 of non-Part B monies for special education in the fiscal year previous to the one for which an application is being developed, the district must spend the same amount the next fiscal year to avoid supplanting. However, allowance may be made for decreases in enrollment of handicapped students and unusually large expenditures in the previous year for long-term purposes involving such things as equipment or construction.

Because this act is applicable to all public agencies receiving federal funds to assist state and local governments educate handicapped children, the impact and requirements will continue to have far-reaching implications yet to be completely defined.

CETA

The purpose of CETA is to provide job training and employment opportunities for economically disadvantaged, unemployed, or underemployed persons that will result in an increase in their earned income (Section 2). Persons over the age of 16 are eligible; youth of ages 14 and 15 are eligible with the approval of the secretary of labor. The CETA Amendments of 1978 provide both an opportunity and an incentive for cooperation and interaction between prime sponsors and local education agencies.

Title IV youth programs provide an opportunity for the LEAs to become involved with CETA. At least 22 percent of the funds for youth employment demonstration projects are to be used for programs for inschool youth that are carried out pursuant to agreements between prime sponsors and LEAs. Participants who are enrolled in or agree to enroll in a fulltime program leading to a high school diploma, a junior or community college degree, or a trade or technical school certificate of completion are eligible.[3]

Establish Policies

Policy making is a process that frequently grows like topsy. Policies are needed by schools to apply to similar situations as they occur. What may be good policy for regular students may not meet the special needs of handicapped and disadvantaged students. Also, the same policy may need to be implemented differently in different situations. Policies have to be developed and circulated so that all concerned know what is to take place and what the outcomes will be.

Policies may be defined as guides to action. While policies are generally broad and general, procedures are precise and mandatory and provide the sequence and manner in which tasks should be performed.

Initial thoughts on program policy should be transmitted for review by those with the primary interest in handicapped or disadvantaged programs, including the advisory committee and vocational education staff. After suggestions have been received from all parties having a primary interest in special need programs, a second policy draft should be developed. Finally, the policy should be reviewed again for minor changes, referred to the superintendent for appraisal, and ultimately submitted to the board of education for official sanction. Thus, the policy should be developed jointly by the district's vocational education teachers, advisory committee, and vocational education administrators and supervisors, then approved by the superintendent and the board of education.

Develop and Implement Policies

Philosophy and Objectives

The first step in developing policy for a handicapped or disadvantaged program is to delineate the objectives and underlying philosophy of the type of program desired. In policy development, the philosophy and objectives should reflect the thinking of the adult community, students, teachers, the administrative staff and board of education, and the director and supervisor who will make the program functional.

Program Emphasis

If the school has strong feelings about the goals of the program and the amount of emphasis being placed upon program objectives, these feelings should be included in the program policy. If this does not occur, the emphasis of the program will tend to follow the specific interests of the individual teachers in the schools, the school principals, or other staff members who are either directly or indirectly involved in the operation of the program. Some programs put major emphasis on orientation and exploration, while others concentrate on developing job-entry skills. Some programs grant credit toward graduation while others do not.

Organization, Staffing, and Limitation

An essential item of program policy for handicapped or disadvantaged students is program organization. This is concerned with answers to questions like these:

- In which schools will the program be operational?
- How many staff people will be assigned supportive roles in each school?
- If the program is to operate in more than one school, will there be a program director at the district level?
- If the number of students receiving services from the program increases or decreases, how will adjustments be made to ensure appropriate staffing for each program office? (This means that a staffing plan should be developed as part of the program policy.)[4]

Staff Relations

To avoid role conflicts, lines of responsibility and working relationships should be established and included in the program policy. In districts where programs are implemented in separate facilities, it is important that the lines of responsibility be a matter of written policy.

Criteria for Credit

A policy that explains course credits for participation in prevocational work experience and occupational education is essential. Only when program administrators have a written policy and adhere to it will students be treated fairly and equitably. The criteria should be appropriate, reasonable, and specific.

Program Evaluation

A person in a position of responsibility should be specified to provide the leadership and direction for program evaluation. If the program planners feel it is necessary to evaluate regularly, the intervals should be stated. Although it is not necessary to include methods of evaluation in program policy, guidelines for evaluation should be included.

Adhere to Established Mandates

The Vocational Education Amendments of 1976, Title II (Public Law 94-482), contain several mandates that must be adhered to in all programs operating under its provisions. Some of these mandates have been part of the vocational education scene for years; others are new in this act. The mandates concern advisory committees; sex equity; private, nonprofit school involvement; and vocational education data collection.

Advisory Committees

Advisory committees have been an important part of vocational education since 1917. The need for input from employers or vocational education students to keep the program current has been widely supported. This aspect of the program has now been made a requirement.

The requirement of a local advisory committee may be met by appointment of either a general advisory committee or individual program (craft) advisory committees, or both. A general advisory committee should be broadly representative. It can be established for all vocational education courses offered in the district and should consist of individuals who represent each vocational occupational area. A program (or craft) advisory committee should be representative of a specific occupational field and advise in that field's particular program. There may be separate committees for each vocational program offered in the district. Most separate, special, or alternate programs would warrant a program advisory committee, while the mainstream, prevocational, or tutoring models might be better off with a general committee.

The local advisory committee should be composed of representatives of the lay public, including persons from business, industry, and labor. It should also have an appropriate representation of both sexes and of racial and ethnic minorities in the school, community, or region that the committee serves. The committee members should be recognized for their occupational expertise, be representative of the community's employers, and be organized to advise school personnel on matters concerning the vocational education program. The advisory committee can provide assistance to the LEA by surveying current job needs, reviewing course outlines, determining community needs, providing inservice opportunities, providing financial and legislative support, performing public relations services, securing equipment, assisting student organizations, and so on.

The special needs advisory committee can be a valuable asset to the program if the administrator and teacher choose the members wisely and work with them effectively.

Sex Equity

Vocational programs must be free of sex bias, sex stereotyping, and sex discrimination. Students should be encouraged to enroll in programs that are nontraditional for their sex. Instructors are encouraged to use textbooks, curriculum, and lesson plans without discrimination as to sex.

Maintaining sex equity in special needs programs is primarily a matter of being aware of the situation and pitfalls and trying to avoid them.

Private, Nonprofit School Involvement

Private nonprofit schools must be given a chance to participate in vocational special needs programs. Letters from such schools, indicating their desire to participate or not to participate, should be included in the program proposal. These letters must be on file with the state board of vocational education. If such schools choose to be involved, space must be made available for their students.

Vocational Education Data Collection

The Vocational Education Data System (VEDS) was mandated in 1976 to collect data on every student enrolled in vocational education programs. The information collected includes not only the name and class enrolled in but also information regarding the student's disadvantagement and handicap. This information is collected for all students in vocational education classes, not only those enrolled in special needs programs.

The student's social security or identification number is used so that the student can be followed up in longitudinal studies after one or more years. This does not cause noncompliance with the Privacy Act because all information is grouped when reporting to the federal government or other interested parties. Information on individuals should not be given out by the state to any agency.

Provide for Program Planning Timeline

Planning for a new program and the first year's operation takes considerable time over an extended period. If the program is to be successful, this time must be spent dealing with the numerous situations that occur. Areas not previously examined that will need attention include staff development, schedule modifications, supplemental services, and community and business cooperation.

Staff Development

Since preservice programs to train personnel to serve the handicapped and disadvantaged are very limited, a well designed staff development program must be conceived that includes inservice training (for example, staff workshops, conferences, and seminars).

Schedule Modifications

In working with students with special needs, modified schedules are necessary to provide additional time for the faculty to assist students with special problems. Some of the schedule modifications might include extension of the school day, week, or year; instruction on an individual basis; or flexible scheduling to permit the open-entry, open-exit concept to be utilized.

Supplemental Services

Whether students are in regular or specialized vocational programs, supplemental educational services are necessary to assist them to achieve program objectives. These services may include guidance and counseling, tutorial services, and special aids for the handicapped, such as reader services for the visually handicapped, interpreter services for the deaf, and aide services to assist the physically handicapped.

Community and Business Cooperation

No matter how "effective" the process (the program) is, unless the product (the student) becomes employed, the objective of occupational training has not been achieved. To maximize the potential for success, the school should enlist the cooperation of the business and industrial community. Advisory committees can form an important link in this effort. Through such community support of vocational goals and job offers, the chances of success for disadvantaged or handicapped programs can be greatly enhanced.

The Table 12-2 chart provides an example of a timetable that can facilitate implementation of programs for handicapped and disadvantaged students.

ANNUAL PROGRAM REVIEW

A program's value rests on the degree to which it functionally prepares handicapped or disadvantaged students for independence in accord with that student's capabilities. One must have accurate data and efficient collection procedures to determine the effectiveness of the agency's processes and outcomes toward that end. Evaluation must be a built-in, cyclic component of the system. Its main function is continually to feed information back into the program.

Program evaluations are often better done by the persons who are responsible for a program and who are daily involved in implementation and ongoing revision. With the use of proper guidelines and instruments, a circumspect process of inhouse program assessment can offset the expertise and objectivity that are often assumed to accompany outside or third-party evaluations. In the absence of satisfactory internal procedures, data, or personnel, however, an agency may benefit from external evaluation. Still, the manager must be aware of the difficulties in interpretation of information derived from outside sources. External evaluation procedures may all too easily overlook, or fail to place emphasis on, forces operating on and the factors inherent in a program. Experts from different orientations and lacking important historical perspectives and knowledge sometimes fail to understand community, school-staff, or other significant sociopolitical realities.

One program self-evaluation guide suggests the following questions in evaluating major categories of a vocational program:

- How were vocational units selected?
- Will the unit enable the students to earn an adequate income?
- How are the students selected?
- Are the varieties of class content and methods satisfactory?
- How many students complete or drop out of the program?
- Are the teachers adequately prepared and qualified?
- Are employers adequately used?

Table 12-2 Timetable for Facilitating Programs

	PROGRAM TIMETABLE											
	July	Aug.	Sept.	Oct.	Nov.	Dec.	Jan.	Feb.	Mar.	April	May	June
Planning Year					Conceptualize program Survey agency and community		Submit proposal			Approval received	Initial identification of students Order supplies and equipment	Hire staff
Implementation Year		Staff inservice	Final student identification		Curriculum modification		Submit budget and program modifications First semester evaluation			Contact VR regarding probable clients	Program evaluation VEDS report	
Continuation Year				Follow up students completing program								

With respect to coordination with others, the same guide suggests the following evaluation questions:

- What coordination is maintained between special and vocational education?
- Is there evidence that the special needs program was planned jointly for handicapped students?
- Is there continuous joint evaluation of student progress?
- Is there a specific person designated to coordinate planning between academic and vocational training?
- What is done if the student succeeds in one area but is failing in another?
- Is there a systematic plan of parent involvement?
- Is there coordination between elementary special education teachers and secondary special needs teachers as to a logical curricular sequence?
- Is there frequent communication between the junior high prevocational teachers and high school special needs teachers?
- Is there evidence of coordination between high school special needs teachers and vocational rehabilitation personnel?
- Who is responsible for permanent job placement and followup?
- Is there an organizational chart and are there written job descriptions determining relationships and responsibilities among the personnel serving the handicapped and disadvantaged?
- Has the program received full positive sanction from the top administration regarding curricula, staffing, and scheduling arrangements?[5]

PERSONNEL FUNCTIONS

Managing

The quality of the staff determines the degree to which program aims are achieved. The hiring and supervision of the staff (if that is included in the duties of the manager of a special needs program) is one of the most important functions of program administration. The manager's role is usually to take personal responsibility to facilitate all or part of the program in the most efficient manner with the best personnel and resources available. This is the case regardless whether the title of the manager is director, coordinator, supervisor, or administrator. A strong argument can be made on practical grounds, however, that a "manager-educator" would better reflect the appropriate emphasis in special needs programming than an "educator-manager." Effective management requires persons who perceive themselves as administrators. Administrators should be prepared for their jobs prior to appointment and should continue to upgrade their management expertise. Having been an educator does not prepare one to manage a program, though it may be a logical prerequisite in terms of the credibility with which one is perceived. It is also of value to have had some role experiences similar to those being managed, particularly if the manager's role includes the provision of counseling or consulting with providers of direct service who are concerned with the problems of program implementation. At some level, managers must rise above specialized backgrounds and provide direction for a number of functional areas.

Hiring

The manager's role in the acquisition of capable special needs personnel usually encompasses the following recruiting activities:

Locating qualified teachers and support personnel (based on state standards and local policy). Teachers prepared for mainly traditional instruction are usually easier to find because of the larger numbers of graduates and higher educational preservice program content in that area. It is harder to find qualified vocational teachers who possess competencies that include substantial expertise in serving the handicapped and disadvantaged. Some states require a separate certification or endorsement for special needs teachers that combines special education with vocational education for secondary programming. We would strongly support that combination.

Attracting qualified personnel to your school and community. Inner-city and rural-isolated areas frequently have difficulty in attracting personnel. Special incentives, attractive salaries, and an energetic recruiting campaign may be necessary in these situations. One of the better aids to success in hiring needed personnel is a positive reputation for having developed a well-planned and effective program. Significant involvement in an extraordinary effort is very attractive to new personnel. It can also reduce turnover because of a greater probability of a sense of worthwhile personal investment.

Selection. A major problem arises in distinguishing between the "winners" and the "also-rans." In selecting personnel, most agencies must rely on the perceived potential for effective teaching or the support skills and abilities of the selected persons. Few managers know for certain how a particular choice will perform until they have the opportunity to observe the person in action. One possibility is to select someone who has demonstrated a capability elsewhere. However, timely data of dependable accuracy on such people are frequently unavailable. Tests, structured interviews, and a selection consensus from several interviewers are additional methods than can be used to assist in recruiting. No one, however, has invented a foolproof way of predicting success. No one source of information will provide conclusive answers; bits of information must be fitted together and judgment exercised to determine whether or not to hire the applicant. Whatever the procedure, the most objective and logically defensible method possible should be used.

Preparing Job Descriptions and Performance Reports

It is a worthwhile challenge to match persons to jobs so that all members of the service delivery team can perform their work competently and with a positive attitude and ability to get along well with others. Employees deserve to know exactly what is expected of them in job tasks that require specific knowledge, skills, and abilities. To achieve these ends, a well-stated job description is essential.

The hiring, firing, nonrenewal of "tenured" personnel contracts, layoff, transfer, promotion, demotion, compensation, and educational leave are all areas of risk in management decision making. Each decision raises the possibility of an EEO complaint from a member of a protected group or class based on race, religion, sex, national origin, age (40 to 65) or handicap. The complaint may cite probable adverse effects on a member of a protected group when the decision affects that person differently than it does members of another group. If it can be shown to have an adverse effect in any one of nine ways, the management decision or practice can be said to be discriminatory. The manager then must show that the adverse effect was based on a decision or practice that was job-related. If a manager can show job-relatedness in personnel decisions—even if there is an adverse effect—it may be possible to prove no unfair discrimination. A well-stated job description is thus essential in this area.

Because discrimination in personnel decisions is relatively easy to prove, because the time and expense of defending oneself in such cases can quickly become burdensome, and because members of protected groups are frequently affected by personnel decisions, managers must develop job related job descriptions (JRJD). Such descriptions are not only the basis of a good defense for having made a particular decision or choice, they are also very functional in selection interviews, in employees' orientation and understanding of their role, and in personnel evaluation. JRJDs are best constructed by the persons to be described in consultation with the manager. Evaluation of performance then becomes an assessment of the degree to which a teacher actually carries out the JRJD tasks at the necessary rate.

The following is an overview of a comprehensive JRJD that can be useful to a manager:

1. Describe the major function of the job in one or two sentences that state the overall purpose.
2. State the fiscal impact of the position in dollars and personnel terms.
   a. Number of persons supervised by position and annual payroll of persons supervised, if applicable.
   b. The dollar amount/revenue generated/annual budget that is affected or impacted by the position.

3. Specific duties starting with the most important (a task analysis of the job).
   a. List the major domains to be performed.
   b. List the typical tasks performed in each domain (as competencies to use in personnel selection or evaluation). How often are these tasks performed (hourly, daily, weekly, etc.)?
4. Describe the knowledges, skills, and abilities necessary to perform the tasks in each domain.
5. Accountability:
   a. From whom does one receive direction?
   b. How are assignments/instructions provided?
   c. Who reviews and approves performance?
   d. Who would one go to if a question arose about the work?
6. Decision making:
   a. What are the decisions to be made by a person in this position?
   b. Does the person or someone else carry out the action of the decision?
7. Report preparation: Name the reports to be completed (may be covered in No. 3).
8. Inter- and intra-agency: What persons in this and other agencies are contacted as a regular part of the job? How often and for what purpose are the contacts made?
9. Direction: List by title the type and number of personnel to be hired, supervised, assigned, or reviewed by this position.
10. Learning period: How long would it take a new employee with the minimum knowledge and abilities shown in No. 4 to handle the job satisfactorily? What inservice training will be provided to assist the employee if needed?
11. What additional information is not given already?

After completing a JRJD, the following questions developed by R.E. Biddle will help in reviewing it to be sure it includes critical components:

- Does the JRJD list the major job responsibilities?
- Are the domains listed in some kind of logical order, for example, natural order of progression, chronological order, professional discipline order, or order of importance?
- Are the most important tasks to achieve the goal or mission of the job depicted?
- Do the task statements indicate what is done, how it is done, and what is produced?
- Do the task statements describe the job how it actually is now, not how it was in the past or projected to be in the future?

- Do the task statements begin with an action verb or with a knowledge, skill, or ability?
- Does the JRJD give a good, understandable description of the complete job? If not, what additional information is needed to describe the job?
- Could each domain be backed up in court in terms of the general functions provided by others in the area or classification?
- Can each task statement be backed up with common examples of work performed?
- In an advertisement to fill the position, are all the critical knowledges, skills, and abilities listed, indicating appropriate levels and other requirements?
- Are the knowledges, skills, and abilities that are listed logical and realistic, that is, are they needed for success in the job?
- Does the JRJD list all the physical characteristics and other requirements of the job, for example, licensure, and certification or endorsement?[6]

Training

The most effective managers are those who have developed their intellectual abilities, special job skills and human relations abilities to a high degree. The aims of most preservice programs are directly concerned with these abilities. Development of managerial expertise is, of course, not limited by the degree or certification in programs at colleges and universities. The correlation between management expertise and preservice classroom success is far from perfect. Many managers appear to develop their knowledge and skill based on additional inservice training and experience. The same can probably be said of teachers and support personnel in special needs and other programs. Fundamentally, however, the benefits to society at large, to the school system and to the students in particular are best provided by sound preservice programs.

After the degree has been earned and certification acquired, many problems remain to be solved in increasing the competencies of teachers. There is general agreement among educators and other professionals that continuing education in most occupations is a necessity. Incentives are usually found in increased salaries, eligibility for advancement, and recertification based on additional training.

There is a basic interconnectedness between preservice and inservice. The growth and development of an organization is a dynamic aggregation of persons performing tasks and interrelating with students, parents, the community, and each other. A group is effective in delivering a service to the extent that the individuals comprising the group are also growing and developing in response to internal and external forces and problems. A group is never static. The training needs of teachers, administrators, and support personnel are never "finished," unless the system declines and ceases to exist. The role of the teacher, like that of the actor, requires continual development of knowledge and skill to deliver with maximal impact on the target audience. Increasingly, this fact is recognized and required in federal and state laws governing education for the handicapped. For example, a comprehensive system of development of personnel, including administrative, instructional and support personnel, is required by Public Law 94-142 as a condition of compliance. Regardless of what training opportunities may be provided by state, local, and university administrators and trainers, however, individuals must assume responsibility for their own training. Personnel development is for each of us ultimately self-development.

Teaming

An appropriate education for handicapped learners frequently involves several persons having a variety of role assignments and training in an increasingly broad array of professional and paraprofessional disciplines. The Education for All Handicapped Children Act, together with corresponding state and local laws or policies, mandates comprehensive evaluation, prescription, and programming. Under the act, a minimum team for making decisions on the eligibility, placement, prescription, and service delivery of special vocational education programs includes:

- An administrator, such as a director, supervisor, coordinator, principal, or superintendent.
- A teacher who may provide specialized instruction in special vocational needs or in special education (depending on state certification requirements).
- One or more regular education teachers, if the student spends a portion of the day in regular education. Only one teacher is required, however, even for secondary students. The best practice is to include teachers who must modify their curricula. Placement and goal setting decisions should involve the teachers and support personnel who will implement the program for a student through specific objectives to achieve long-range outcomes.
- The child's parents, guardian, or surrogate when the student is under 18 years of age. If the student has been adjudged "incompetent," the appointed guardian would continue involvement regardless of age (18 to 21 years).
- Persons qualified to conduct and interpret individual diagnostic examinations if the student is handicapped by learning disabilities. Inclusion of such persons is a good practice in making diagnostic and prescriptive decisions relative to any handicapping condition and its related services.
- The student, especially at the secondary level, as appropriate.

Team membership should be expanded by additional disciplines or agency representatives as appropriate for general or particular decisions. Such members might include psychologists, communication disorders specialists, nurses, other health-related disciplines, social workers, counselors, or staff members from mental health services, community developmental workshops, juvenile courts, youth rehabilitation agencies, crippled childrens' services, welfare departments, law enforcement agencies or vocational rehabilitation programs. The results of such teaming should be decisions made in the best interests of the student rather than the interests of the school system or a particular agency. In practice, team meetings are usually operated as efficiently as possible, due to the numbers of students involved and the time required.

A well-organized and effective team process does not just happen. Training in team work is necessary in each case. The process requires understanding and skill development in one's role as a member of the team and in the overall operation. A review of team concepts is usually a first step:

The *unidisciplinary* team is composed of one type of profession and typically concerns itself with only one aspect of a student's needs or strengths, such as academic achievement, socioemotional development, health problems, language development, or job-related skill acquisition.

The *multidisciplinary* team is composed of more than one profession or discipline and assumes that a student has needs and strengths requiring interventions that are best prescribed for the "whole person." Team members write separate implementation plans, which normally are not developed to complement other plans. The student is usually not involved in the team decision making.

The *interdisciplinary* team is composed of members of various disciplines who have systematically learned how to interact and work together in individualizing an overall coordinated program. The parts of the program that concern different disciplines are implemented in an integrated fashion. Goals and objectives are designed to fit together in a developmental and complimentary manner, each having an enhancing effect on the other. The team changes as the needs of the student change. Team activities are planned and carried out with frequent coordination and intercommunication by the people who have contact with the student. The time required for this type of teamwork is offset by the greater understanding, purposefulness, and efficiency with which an effective team can operate. Fragmentation is reduced, and student development and achievement are more effectively facilitated.

OUTLOOK FOR SPECIAL NEEDS PROGRAMMING

We are reaching "adolescence" in the growth of vocational training for handicapped students. These are exciting times in program development. We see the following developments as growing challenges in special needs programming:

- A downward extension to begin service delivery at earlier ages with more sophisticated methods and electromechanical instructional aids.

- An upward extension to include greater numbers of students by combining previously separate efforts of special education, vocational education, vocational rehabilitation, and adult education to properly evaluate, train, place, and followup with an intensive blending of job and "life" skills.
- Systematic instruction of individuals as persons with different requirements for learning and content, rather than teaching to categories of homogeneous groups.
- Increased advocacy for the disadvantaged, behavior-disordered, and socially maladjusted, with correlated programs of alternative educational approaches.
- More severely handicapped students deinstitutionalized or reared in group or parents' homes, requiring greatly modified prevocational and vocational approaches.
- More sophisticated program accounting and evaluation systems.
- Programming for longer than the usual nine-month school year.
- Increased use and effectiveness of paraprofessional instructors.
- Long-range multiagency planning, data collection systems, and tracking systems.

NOTES

1. Judy A. Schrag and Robert C. West, *Interagency Planning: Special Education and Related Services for Idaho's Handicapped/Exceptional Students* (Boise, Idaho: Idaho State Department of Education, 1978).
2. Jean J. Moore and Vance S. Engleman, eds., *Administrators Manual—Programing for Handicapped Students at the Secondary Level: Responding to Public Laws* (Salt Lake City, Utah: University of Utah, 1977) p. 22.
3. U.S. Public Law 95-93, Youth Employment and Development Act of 1977, Sec. 433 (d) (1) and (2).
4. Grady Kimbrell and Ben Vinyard, *Entering the World of Work* (Bloomington, Ill.: McKnight Publishing Co., 1978).
5. Judy Meyer, *Self Evaluation Guide for Local Districts for Vocational Education of Handicapped Students*, ED 974 275 (Houston, Texas: Houston University, Center for Human Resources, 1972).
6. R.E. Biddle, *A Plan to Implement Brief Guidelines Oriented Job Analysis* (Sacramento, Calif.: Biddle and Associates, Inc., 1977).

BIBLIOGRAPHY

Moore, Jean J., and Engleman, Vance S. eds. *Administrators Manual—Programming for Handicapped Students at the Secondary Level: Responding to Public Laws*. Salt Lake City, Utah: University of Utah, 1977.

Davis, Sharon, and Ward, Mike. *Vocational Education of Handicapped Students—A Guide for Policy Development*. Reston, Va.: Council for Exceptional Children 1978.

Idaho State Board for Vocational Education, Committee for Action. *A Handbook for Local Advisory Committees on Vocational Education*. Boise, Idaho: 1978.

———. *Planning Vocational Education Programs for the Disadvantaged and Handicapped, Competency-Based Administrator Education Module,* ED 145 123. Blacksburg, Va.: Virginia Polytechnic Institute, 1977.

———. *Policy and Procedures for the Use of Supplemental Services in Career/Vocational Education.* Boise, Idaho: Boise Independent School District #1, 1977.

Schwartz, Stuart E. *Another Step Forward: A System of Management.* Tallahassee, Fla.: Florida Department of Education, 1978.

Stevens, David W. *The Coordination of Vocational Education Programs with CETA,* Information Series #151. Columbus, Ohio: National Center for Research in Vocational Education, Ohio State University, 1979.

Chapter 13

Program Evaluation and Assessment

Jack Kaufman, Ed.D.

INTRODUCTION

The primary objectives of this chapter are to provide a brief overview of special vocational needs program evaluation and to present several steps necessary to conduct a meaningful program assessment. The chapter content was selected to serve as a first reference to special vocational needs teachers and administrators who find themselves charged with conducting, or having others conduct for them, an evaluation of the results of their teaching efforts.

EVALUATION DEFINED

In defining what we are talking about in program evaluation, we might take the obvious first step of consulting a dictionary. The *American Heritage Dictionary* defines evaluation as a process used to "ascertain or fix the value of worth."[1] While this definition is useful in establishing the concept, it provides very little pragmatic information to a teacher or administrator who wants to assess the value or worth of a specific special vocational needs program. Obviously, something beyond a dictionary definition is needed.

Rudyard Kipling provided us with a key for proceeding when he wrote:

> I keep six honest serving men
> (They taught me all I knew);
> Their names are What and Why and When
> And How and Where and Who.[2]

By looking at what the literature says to these six serving men, and by adding some thought of our own, we will arrive at an acceptable procedure for evaluating special vocational needs programs at the local level.

What

In describing the meaning of program evaluation, Arlene Fink and Jacqueline Kosecoff stated that "evaluation is a set of procedures to appraise a program's merit and to provide information about its goals, activities, outcomes, impacts, and costs."[3] Reflection on this very precise and definitive statement reveals that evaluation of a program will require a procedure, implying thereby that the results will be objective and capable of being replicated. Elaine R. Worthen was more specific in stating precisely the kinds of information programs evaluation should provide. She noted that, among other things, "evaluation includes (1) determining what measures and standards should be used to judge performance . . . (2) deciding whether the standards should be relative or absolute . . . (3) collecting the relevant information through measurement or other means, and (4) applying the standard in determining merit or effectiveness."[4]

We shall have occasion to study Worthen's statement in greater detail when we develop specific, detailed procedural steps to be used in conducting a special vocational needs program evaluation.

Why

In attempting to explain why program evaluation is necessary, Tim L. Wentling and Tom E. Lawson first alluded to the federal mandates and their subsequent requirements. They then went on to list more pragmatic and motivational reasons for program evaluations: as aids to planning and decision making, as a means of providing input for upgrading programs personnel, as a means of delineating improved programs for the students, and as a means of assuring accountability of expenditures.[5] Peter W. Airasian, further reinforcing the importance of adherence to federal mandates, described them as a primary cause of the demand for evaluation. He stated:

> At the local level, the demand for summative evaluation studies to assess the outcome of programs, policies, or practices arises from many sources. In cases where governmental funding provides the basis of support, the granting of funds is often contingent upon evaluation. When resources are in short supply and allocation or reallocation of limited funds, materials, or personnel is required, an evaluation study is often undertaken to determine where the resources should go . . . in contrast to many of the motives cited above, there are instances when a school board, administrator, or teacher engages in an evaluation study because there is a genuine interest in conserving something perceived as good, in building upon strategies which appear to work, or in learning about and improving school practices.[6]

It goes without saying that the latter rationale provides by far the most pleasant reasons to evaluate a program.

When

The answer to the question, When does program evaluation occur? is very likely to depend more upon the concept of the evaluation process by the person or persons conducting the evaluation and the authority to whom they report than upon any other single factor. Ideally, program evaluation should be an ongoing process that provides (as a minimum) continual monitoring of student achievement, ready identification of problems, a data base for realistic program-goal development and modification, and information for determining program cost-effectiveness.

Unfortunately, the idea of ongoing program evaluation rarely receives more than lip service. In the real world of education, evaluation is much more likely to occur as a point-in-time exercise in program parameter measurement. Without condoning the practice, it would seem that if program evaluation is to be a point-in-time affair instead of an ongoing process, the optimum points-in-time should be at the beginning of some chronological phase, for example, the beginning of a school year, and again at some point prior to completion of the period. Results of the first evaluation would provide a basis for planning, while results from the second would provide information which can, hopefully, be used to make proactive instead of reactive decisions about the program.

Where

The "where" of evaluation can be answered quite simply by responding: "Go where the action is." Program evaluations must focus on the students and their support services. Community programs and their representatives, such as those from business and industry, must be an integral part of the "where" process.

How

The "how" of evaluation will be dealt with in depth at a later point in this chapter. The reader should at this point simply keep in mind the need for a process when the question of "how" again surfaces.

Evaluation Resources

There is more to the decision about who should evaluate than merely settling on a person or persons to collect and analyze the data and report on the results. Since the idea of bias-free evaluation with purely objective results and conclusions exists more in theory than in reality, the question of who conducts the evaluation cannot help but enter into the outcome.

The normal procedure for selecting evaluators is to ask for and receive a list of individuals who have demonstrated their expertise at program evaluations. These evaluators could come from local, state, or national levels to evaluate the programs.

We sincerely believe that program evaluation results often have an excellent potential as means to justify program expansion and identify areas requiring more resources. Consequently, the program evaluators should be viewed as resources, and during the evaluative procedure their expertise should be solicited.

EVALUATION PROCEDURES

Common procedural elements of program evaluation are: (1) needs assessment, (2) program planning, and (3) student performance assessment.

Needs Assessment

A recent report by the National Association of State Boards of Education (NASBE) used a statement by Daniel L. Stufflebeam to help provide a definition of needs assessment. The report stated that "a needs assessment is the process of determining what things are needed to serve some worthy purpose."[7] The NASBE Report goes on to state that:

> more specifically, a needs assessment is . . . a process for identifying and examining the purposes against which needs are to be determined; getting these purposes modified if they are found improper or flawed; identifying the things that are requisite and useful for serving the validated purposes; assessing the extent that the identified needs are met or unmet; rating the importance of these met and unmet needs; and aiding the audience for the needs assessment to apply the findings in formulating goals, choosing procedures, and assessing progress.[8]

Stufflebeam's statement of what constitutes a needs assessment is overwhelming when viewed in its entirety; but when viewed item by item, it provides an excellent structure for presenting some of the practical steps necessary to conduct a needs assessment.

For purposes of the presentation, let us assume an ideal situation in which the needs assessment is being conducted prior to commencement of a special vocational needs program. The only difference in whether the program is in existence or is in the planning stage is in how the needs assessment results will be used. In the case of a new program, the results of the needs assessment will be used to establish objectives and procedures, whereas in an ongoing program the results will be used to modify and improve existing objectives and procedures.

The first requirement of a needs assessment is, according to Stufflebeam, to establish a process for identifying and examining the purposes against which needs are to be determined. There are several sources of purposes for special vocational needs programs but the three primary ones are federal legislation, the applicable state plan for vocational education, and the central administrative unit of the local school district (or districts) that will support the program.

Federal legislation. Public Law 94-482, and its accompanying rules and regulations, may be reviewed to obtain specific purposes for the establishment of special vocational needs programs, but the primary intent is embodied in the *Revised Edition: Suggested Utilization of Resources and Guide for Expenditures (RESURGE)*. Although this 1972 Bureau of Occupational and Adult Education (B.O.A.E.) publication addressed itself to the Vocational Education Amendments of 1968, its opening paragraph is still applicable to the 1976 amendments (Public Law 94-482). The paragraph states:

> The Vocational Education Amendments of 1968 (as continued in 1976) are restrictive in specifying eligibility for the disadvantaged or handicapped to avoid dissipation or commingling of earmarked funds in regular vocational education programs. However, once a person is identified as needing special help to succeed, the form or type of vocational education actions authorized to overcome the disadvantage or handicap is essentially unrestricted. Requirements of the statute specify (1) that the inability to succeed in a regular vocational program be the basis for identifying the disadvantaged and handicapped; (2) that individuals, not groups, be so identified; and (3) that the inability to succeed be a *result* of a condition and not a cause.[9]

The applicable state plan for vocational education. Requirements in state plans for vocational education can be expected to be in agreement with the program purposes contained in federal legislation and, in addition, to reflect state-level philosophy and policies regarding program expenditures. A brief excerpt from the *Idaho State Plan for the Administration of Vocational Education* regarding vocational education programs for handicapped students illustrates the state's expenditure philosophy and reiteration of federal purpose.

> Vocational programs, services and activities made available to handicapped persons, from federal funds set aside for this purpose, shall be developed in a manner that is consistent with the State Plan submitted for Education of the Handicapped Act of Idaho, and will implement Sections 613 (a) of the Education of the Handicapped Act, P.L. 94-142. These handicapped vocational programs, services, and activities shall include the following requirements: (1) Assure that all students served

> shall meet the (Idaho) definition of "handicapped" . . . (2) Assure that vocational teachers and support personnel shall be included in the team that develops and reviews the individual educational program plan required of each handicapped person receiving vocational educational services. (3) Designate what special services are to be provided that are not provided to nonhandicapped persons, or what modifications are made in the curriculum and instruction that are not available for nonhandicapped persons.[10]

Since Idaho's definition of handicapped closely parallels the federal definition contained in Public Law 94-482, items (1) and (3) in the above statement reiterate federal statements of purpose, while item (2) stipulates a state-level philosophy of expenditures.

The central administrative unit of the local school district. The third source of program purposes is the central authority of the local school district. Many times local school district officials are unsure as to what their specific program's purposes should be. This uncertainty results from the multitude of programs being proposed, financial considerations, and personnel needs. A good solution to this dilemma is to use the local advisory committee. This committee generally has a clear picture of training and employment needs and has the ear of the district administrators.

Based on the foregoing steps, a statement of program purpose can now be developed which will reflect a composite of local, state, and national requirements, thinking, and desires.

After the statement of purpose is in place, identification of needs becomes a relatively simple chore. The needs of the program are simply those things that are necessary to accomplish the program's purposes. For example, if the program purposes include the provision of cooperative employment experiences for special needs students in the junior and senior class, two very obvious questions about needs immediately arise. First, How many students are in the population? and, How many positions will local business and industry provide?

Notice that needs take the form of questions generated by the statement of purpose, and the needs assessment takes the form of a process or procedure to answer the generated questions. In our example, the question of population size can best be answered by interviewing (best practice) or surveying (last resort) vocational teachers, counselors, and high school principals. The answer to the second need will, of course, come from members of the business and industrial community. Here, the program developer will be well advised to recognize that conducting a survey rather than interviews is almost certain to lead to disappointment.

Stufflebeam's second requirement of a needs assessment is to get the previously developed purposes modified if they are found to be improper or flawed. The form for modifying the program purposes, and the procedure for assessing their flaws, depends almost totally on whether the program is in existence or is being developed. In the former case, the program purposes and characteristics can be compared and disparities can be identified. The procedure then consists simply of determining whether an identified disparity results from a program inadequacy, from an unrealistic statement of purpose, or both. In any case, the remedy is fairly obvious: change the offending element or elements so as to bring harmony between the purposes and the practices.

In the case of a program in the planning stage, the task is not quite so simple. There is no history of program achievement to review and no records of cooperative placements, achievement scores, or dropout rates that can be reviewed for assistance in developing a program performance rating. Only the statement of program purpose is in place, and it represents, at best, the potential for being tested and found lacking. Faced with this situation, the program developer has no alternative but to list the items of information that would prove most beneficial at this point in the decision-making process and to take steps to assure that the necessary data are collected in an ongoing manner when the program is implemented. If the frustration that results from a lack of hard data is a sufficient motivator to cause the collection of program performance data to be viewed as a high priority task, then the frustration will pay huge dividends later in the life of the program.

Stufflebeam's next charge is to identify the things that are requisite and useful to the validated purposes. Here, more than anywhere else in the entire needs assessment and evaluation process, the program director will have to face the basic question of economics. That question, simply stated, is, How can finite resources best be used to meet limitless desires? Procedures for developing "logical" answers to the question are almost as limitless as the desires themselves, but basically they all take the same form.

The general form for answering the basic economic question is the same whether the question is being applied to an individual, a family, a nation, or a special vocational needs program. The first step is to identify as many of the elements making up the desires as possible. In the case of a special needs program, the entire staff should, if possible, be brought into the process. The only ground rule necessary at this stage is that the items making up the desires be justifiable within the program's statement of purpose. The size and cost of the list of desires that will be developed will far exceed the resources available, but the list is only a starting point and should not be viewed as a limit on the process.

The next step will be to move the planning process to the issue of financing the proposed activities. Costs should be secured for each of the items on the list so that a ball park figure can be generated for the total proposed program.

The third step in the program planning procedure is to reduce the program activities back to a base that is both financially and programmatically feasible.

This activity reduction process could be conducted completely by the program administrator. But it is much more practical as well as palatable to involve the instructional staff. If the total staff is involved, more people will understand the final program that is developed and these individuals can do much to promote it within the general school setting.

Program Planning

It might seem that after the rather thorough treatment accorded the needs assessment, a formal program plan would be a redundancy. Actually, the needs assessment and program plan are elements of evaluation that are related but contain very different components. Perhaps an analogy will help to illustrate both the commonalities and the differences between the two.

Today, almost everyone is familiar with the term *game plan* as it is used in football. The statement of purpose developed in the needs assessment phase can be compared to a game plan. Game plans and statements of purpose both set forth the resources and strategies that will be used to achieve success. Both reflect the limitations imposed by the resources available, and both are based upon the assumption that they represent optimum utilization of the resources available.

Consider now the next step in the analogy. Even the most unrefined Monday morning quarterback recognizes that developing a winning team requires something beyond teaching the players the words to a new game plan each week; and indeed it does. Successful coaching requires development and practice in the specific plays necessary to implement the game plan. The analogous situation in special vocational needs is the development of a specific plan for implementing and achieving the program purpose. Let us now consider the specific steps of a program plan.

Program planning is primarily a refining process to develop a series of increasingly precise steps. These steps constitute the operational guidelines for the program and, when implemented, should result in achievement of the program goals.

Theoretically, it should make no difference whether the program plan under development will apply to a newly forming or to an existing program. Actually, however, there is a difference, and the difference is considerable. In developing the program plan for a new special vocational needs program, the validity of the plan's elements will be based on the level of expertise of the program developer and staff. In the case of an established program, the same holds true, but the planning staff has the benefit of experience that can help to indicate the validity and efficacy of elements of the plan. At all times, it should be clear to the planning staff that the reason for planning is to improve the operation and achievement of the program, and that the specific parts of the plan should be evaluated, discussed, and accepted or rejected on the basis of their contribution to overall program success.

Program Goals

The literature of evaluation and planning abounds with attempts to specify (usually once and for all) the difference between purposes, goals, and objectives, as these terms are used in education. No argument for a final definition of the terms will be presented here. Instead we will simply plead for the reader to view them as a series, ranging from general to specific. "Purpose" is the most general, "goal" is more specific, and "objective," with its several modifiers, is the most specific. Since, in our example, the purpose of the program was established in a previous step, the immediate task now is to develop the statement of program goals.

Program goals are transitional statements between purposes and objectives; they are thus generally worded in such a manner that their attainment is not immediately or easily measured. For example, in the case of a special vocational needs program, a goal "to provide a set of relevant vocational experiences to students with a high potential for leaving school in their junior or senior year" is much preferable to a goal "to provide relevant vocational experiences in the areas of welding, data processing, and office practices that will reduce the existing junior-senior dropout rate by 50 percent."

In the case of the first goal statement, the intent to offer courses to the potential dropout population is stated, with the desire to reduce the rate being implied. The second statement also expresses the intent to offer vocational instruction to the dropout population, but it has gone one step further; it has tied the perceived success of the program (and quite possibly its continued future operation) to a factor that is beyond the direct control of program personnel.

Consider for a moment the difference in outcomes if the program in the two cases could provide entry-level or higher skills for most of the students in their junior year. It is conceivable that many of the students might find the lure of an entry-level salary strong enough to preclude their returning to the program in their senior year. Such an outcome would be much more in keeping with the first goal statement than with the second. In fact, it could be argued that, under the first goal statement, such a program was a success in that it provided "a set of relevant vocational experiences" to the target population but that, in the second case, the same program would have failed because it did not "reduce the junior-senior dropout rate by fifty percent." Since the example assumes the same program in both cases, the fault of the second program obviously lies in the wording of its goal statement.

Several benefits accrue from developing program goals, but only two will be cited here. First, development of the program goals will help to identify weaknesses and strengths of the statement of purpose. The statement of purpose should be kept constantly available and referred to frequently during the program goal development phase of program planning. If a particular program goal seems highly desirable but cannot be justified in the light of the statement of purpose, the ramifications and consequences of expanding the statement of purpose should be considered.

The second major benefit accruing from program goal development is the increased ability of the staff (even a staff of one person) to see how their efforts contribute to the overall purposes of the program. Any special vocational needs program is sure to benefit from operation by a staff whose members are certain of the importance of their contribution to the total program.

Program Objectives

The next step in the refinement process called program planning is the development (or review, in the case of an ongoing program) of specific program objectives. These objectives will be suggested by the program goals. The major difference between the program goals and objectives will be in their degree of specificity. Where a program goal might be "to provide ancillary and vocationally related academic instruction to mainstreamed special vocational needs students," a resultant program objective would be "to provide tutorial or remedial instruction in mathematics to mainstreamed special vocational needs students; such instruction to continue with each student until the identified minimum competency necessary for successful performance in the course has been achieved." Note that the final part of the objective just stated implies that the minimum functional competency of a particular course has been established. Actually, so far in our plan it has not; and that fact brings us to the next step, the development of area or unit instructional objectives.

Instructional Objectives

The specific form taken by the instructional objectives will depend in part upon the size and goals of the program under development (or revision). In the case of a larger program with several staff members, the instructional objectives might be divided into two levels. Area instructional objectives could be developed for each vocational and academic area represented in the goals of the program. In addition, unit instructional objectives could be developed for each unit of instruction in each area.

In the case of a small program with only one area of vocational instruction represented, the instructional objectives for the vocational area may also serve as instructional objectives for the special vocational needs program. Even in the smallest program, however, the need for unit instructional objectives exists. The explicit need for unit instructional objectives will be more fully developed in the next section on assessing student performance.

In summary, area and unit instructional objectives should evolve from program objectives and should reflect, in measurable and observable terms, the intended consequences of instructional efforts. In the case of new programs, it should be anticipated that each unit objective will be susceptible to revision in the light of the realities of program operation. In the case of ongoing programs, it is important to review existing objectives in a challenge-justification atmosphere to ensure that instructional resources are not being expended on unnecessary or ineffective units.

Behavioral Objectives

The final phase of objective development, the establishment of behavioral objectives, is the most important and, at the same time, the most difficult phase. Behavioral objectives evolve from instructional objectives and should reflect, in measurable and observable terms, the desired outcome of a unit (or smaller element) of instruction. Behavioral objectives apply to individuals; they should state, as explicitly as possible, the student behavior required for successful mastery of an instructional unit.

The importance of behavioral objectives to special vocational needs programs becomes apparent when one observes that, unless behavioral objectives are tailored to individual students, individualized instruction and meaningful student performance evaluation become merely exercises in subjectivity. R.F. Mager has identified three things behavioral objectives should do. First, they should specify the desired terminal behavior by name. Second, they should try to define the desired behavior further by describing when or where it is expected to occur. Third, they should describe how well the student must perform to have the performance considered acceptable.[11]

Obviously, in most cases a single terminal behavior cannot be specified for all regular and special needs students in a class. In fact, it is very unlikely that a single terminal behavior will be generally applicable to all of the special needs students. One encounters the same problem in attempting to describe a universally applicable performance criterion. But this is as it should be, for certainly no thinking person would demand the same keypunch dexterity from a cerebral-palsied student that they would expect from a nonhandicapped student. Nevertheless, the example serves to illustrate the need for tailored behavioral objectives in special vocational needs programs.

Student Performance Assessment

There is an additional need for behavioral objectives in the evaluation of student performance. In this section we will examine first some of the elements in testing and measuring student performance. This will be followed by suggestions on how to use the program plan in developing test items for special vocational needs students. The section will conclude with a brief description of record keeping techniques.

Testing and Measuring

In the recent past, the entire concept of testing has come under fire by the press, television, civil rights groups, and members of Congress—to name only a few of the critics. In the aftermath of this barrage, many educators have lost sight of a very important fact: tests, when *properly used and interpreted* constitute one of the most, possibly the most, useful tools in the educator's inventory. Tests can be used to motivate, measure, and manipulate student performance. They can be used to alter, improve, and implement student behavior. They can be used to enrich, reward, and revitalize students' self-concepts. And certainly the list of benefits does not end there.

It is distressing to note that, because most of the criticism has been leveled at the invalidity of tests with disadvantaged and handicapped persons, and because these persons constitute the total population of special vocational needs students, special needs teachers are likely to feel more aversion to the use of testing as a valid teaching technique than their counterparts in regular classes. Certainly this is not the place to argue the merits of testing, but in order for what follows to have any value, the reader must assume at least an open, if not accepting, attitude toward the use of tests and measures.

Bennett Cerf has observed that there are only two categories of people in the world: those who put everything and everybody into one of two categories, and those who don't. Without admitting to either category, we suggest that all forms of tests and measures can, in fact, be classified into one of two categories, norm-referenced or criterion-referenced.

The persuasion of the norm-referenced theoretical camp is toward the use of standardized achievement tests. The argument here is that the norms represent real world performance against which students will compete and be judged.

Teachers in the criterion-referenced school are not as likely to use standardized tests. They argue that since their students have been identified as deviating from the norm in one or more areas, the comparative results of a standardized test are misleading at best. Teachers from the criterion-referenced camp are much more likely to administer unit tests that purport to assess the students' progress toward criterion-level performance.

As we shall see, these considerations, stemming from the two perspectives on testing, have obvious relevance to the next step in our process, the development of teacher-made tests.

Developing Test Items

Regarding the process of fitting present-purpose, teacher-made tests into the total program evaluation scheme, J.A. Green has noted:

> Teachers need several types of learning assessments as guide posts for instruction, notably: (1) initial assessment to determine the beginning

> level of instruction, (2) interim assessments to pace instruction and to provide feedback to the learners, and (3) terminal assessment to determine the ultimate achievement of the learners. The first two of these . . . are classed as *formative evaluation,* since their major objective is to help the learner . . . with feedback on his errors, his rate of progress, and his level of achievement related to the acceptable level of competence. . . . The third type of assessment, terminal assessment, is classed as *summative evaluation.* Summative evaluation has, as its purpose, a general assessment of pupils' achievement over an entire course or a large unit of a course.[12]

Upon analyzing Green's statement, one can hardly fail to recognize that the testing rationale he has offered is really a microcosm of the program evaluation model offered thus far. Green's allusion to an "initial assessment to determine the beginning level of instruction" corresponds precisely to the needs assessment phase of program evaluation.

Assuming that the analogy of initial evaluation (pretest) and needs assessment has allayed any concerns regarding the value of initial assessment, the problem of how to conduct the initial student assessment remains.

First, it is generally erroneous to believe that special needs students do not like to take tests. What they dislike is what most of us dislike, and that is failure. An astute special needs teacher will capitalize on that fact by using a battery or series of tests, rather than an individual instrument, and by assuring that the first tests used in the series meet the first requirement of motivation—early success. As a test series progresses, the items should be developed so as to reveal more and more information about the students' existing performance level. Most importantly, once the students' responses to an initial evaluation indicate a plateau of achievement, the teacher should not continue to belabor the issue by seeking additional proof that they do not have additional information.

Secondly, the question arises as to what form the test should take and what its content should be. First, regarding content, the initial assessment should address only those topics that can be logically identified as prerequisites for the goals and objectives, particularly the behavioral objectives, developed in the program design phase. Inability to derive prerequisite skills for a course from the course instructional and behavioral objectives indicates a weakness in the design phase.

With regard to forms, initial evaluation need not, indeed should not, be done only in the form of paper and pencil tests. All of the objections, mentioned earlier, to the use of a survey technique alone to conduct a needs assessment apply with equal force to the use of paper and pencil tests (surveys) to assess a student's development in an area. Much to be preferred are interviews and observation of performance on relevant tasks.

Finally, everything said about initial assessment holds true for interim and terminal assessments. The only arguments that can be made for the universal use of paper and pencil tests for any and all situations is the relative ease of administration and the seeming compatibility of the results obtained. While it is true that data from student assessments are indispensible to program evaluation, and while it is also true that test scores, since they usually assume a number value, provide desirable evaluation data, it is far from true that paper and pencil tests offer the only, or even the best, means of generating the data. The alternatives to paper and pencil tests will be examined further in the context of collecting student performance data.

Record Keeping

The following paragraphs provide a brief overview of the basic factors in the collection and maintenance of student performance data in program evaluation.

The first question to be addressed concerns the kinds of student performance data that should be collected. The answer is, simply stated, any data that (1) can be validly used to assess the degree of change in student performance and (2) can serve to identify the contribution made by the program in affecting the change. If one thinks of program evaluation as an attempt to assess the *amount* and also to identify the *cause* of change in students going through the program, the necessity for the two purposes of the data becomes obvious. It would be most unjust to laud a program staff whose students made remarkable positive progress if the cause of the progress was external to the program.

The specific data for ongoing collection should be readily identifiable by the information contained in the various levels of program objectives. If the objectives have been written to include observable results, it follows that records of those results constitute the primary items for collection. Student IEPs, if developed, would constitute another source of identified performance goals as the subject of data collection.

No discussion of data collection would be complete without at least acknowledging the different forms that data can take. The bulk of data collected for purposes of program evaluation will serve one of two general purposes. One is student performance and the other is program efficiency. A very basic discussion of general and specific requirements for the two data will now be presented.

If forms of data could be arranged on a spectrum, it could be thought of as extending from completely objective and numerical to completely subjective and verbal. This is not to say that objective data cannot be verbal or that numerical data is necessarily objective, but in practice it is often viewed in that light. When one considers that an important purpose of evaluation, particularly external evaluation, is to objectively assess program performance, usually in a limited amount of time, it follows that numerical data is most useful for this purpose. It also follows that if the program is being conducted by a parent or school board member whose interest is in an individual student, a case study of the student is apt to have much more impact than the more impersonal appearing numerical indicators of the student's performance.

Another important consideration is how the data are to be used. Since the major purpose of any educational undertaking is to produce change, it follows that data should be collected in a manner which will allow for comparison. For example, assume data were collected which indicated that students entering a small engine repair class could identify only ten percent of the parts of a particular engine. In addition, assume that a performance evaluation of the same group indicated an ability to find and repair 95 percent of the problems encountered in the same engine upon completion of the program. The results are interesting and perhaps intuitively helpful in assessing student change, but the data are not comparable. The first measure might be classed as a general or academic performance and the second a mechanical skill performance, and there is little to indicate that the two correlate well even though both are desirable skills.

A final suggestion on data collection that should prove useful concerns units of measure. Being alert to the units being measured will help to identify methods of presenting results in a meaningful manner. If an element of the evaluation is expenditure per student, or placements per teacher, the results will be a quotient obtained by dividing the term preceding the "per" by the term following it.

SUMMARY

This chapter has attempted to present some first steps in the evaluation of special vocational needs programs evaluation. Evaluation of any kind can take two forms, formative and summative. Formative evaluation implies an evaluation of a situation or environment and the collection of data for use in the required planning and decision making pertinent to the environment. Summative evaluation implies assessment of the effectiveness of efforts to change elements of the environment that have been identified in the formative evaluation.

A complete analysis of either of the two types is beyond the scope of this chapter. However, the most important elements of each can be subsumed under the headings of needs assessment (formative), program planning (formative), and student performance assessment (summative). Certain elements of evaluation require preplanning; at the same time, the necessity, or at least desirability, of considering program evaluation as an ongoing process should be kept in mind.

Many important topics in program evaluation are conspicuous by their absence in this chapter. One of the most important is longitudinal or followup evaluation. Special vocational teachers should always keep in mind the continuing effect their program has had on past students. Though followup evaluation is usually an expensive and frustrating undertaking and thus often not conducted, it is an evaluation component that should not be overlooked.

Finally, a brief epilogue. Evaluations should be viewed as essential program components that can be utilized to strengthen and expand the effectiveness of special needs programs. Through evaluations of both students and programs, special needs students will be more effectively served and special needs teachers will be able to better meet student training needs.

NOTES

1. *American Heritage Dictionary,* 1st ed., s.v. "evaluation."
2. Rudyard Kipling, "Just So Stories" in *The Writings in Prose and Verse* of Rudyard Kipling (New York: Scribner & Sons, 1920), vol. 20, p. 87.
3. Arlene Fink and Jacqueline Kosecoff, *An Evaluation Primer* (Washington, D.C.: Capitol Publications, Inc., 1978), p. 1.
4. E.R. Worthen, *A Look at the Mosaic of Education Evaluation and Accountability,* Northwest Regional Laboratory Working Paper No. 3 (Portland, Ore.: Northwest Regional Laboratory, 1974), p. 4.
5. Tim L. Wentling and Tom E. Lawson, *Evaluating Occupational Education and Training Programs* (Boston, Mass.: Allyn and Bacon, 1975), pp. 18-20.
6. Peter W. Airasian, "Designing Summative Evaluation Studies," in *Evaluation in Education: Current Applications,* ed. W.J. Popham (Berkeley, Calif.: McCutchan Publishing Corp., 1974), p. 152.
7. National Association of State Boards of Education, *Vocational Education of Handicapped Youth: State of the Art* (Washington, D.C.: National Association of State Boards of Education, 1979), p. 5.
8. Ibid.
9. U.S. Department of Health, Education and Welfare, Office of Education, Bureau of Occupational and Adult Education. Revised Edition. *Suggested Utilization of Resources and Guide for Expenditures: Resurge* (Washington, D.C.: Bureau of Occupational and Adult Education, 1972), p. 4.
10. State Board for Vocational Education, *Idaho State Plan for the Administration of Vocational Education* (Boise, Idaho: Idaho Department of Education, 1979), p. 27.
11. R.F. Mager, *Preparing Instructional Objectives* (Belmont, Calif.: Fearon Publishers, 1962), p. 12.
12. J.A. Green, *Teacher-Made Tests,* 2nd ed. (New York: Harper & Row, 1975), pp. 2-3.

ANNOTATED BIBLIOGRAPHY

Airasian, Peter W. "Designing Summative Evaluation Studies" In: *Evaluation in Education: Current Applications,* edited by W.J. Popham. Berkeley, Calif.: McCutchan Publishing Corporation, 1974.

This selection is from a major work in educational evaluation. The 585-page book contains a wealth of information, but it suffers greatly from lack of an index.

Fink, Arlene, and Kosecoff, Jacqueline. *An Evaluation Primer.* Washington, D.C.: Capitol Publications, Inc., 1978.

This is an excellent follow up to what has been presented in this chapter. The scope of the book allows for in-depth study of evaluation design and reporting of evaluation information. The book contains a good bibliography and an excellent annotated index. An entire chapter is devoted to "planning and conducting information analysis activities," which is the author's way of saying "statistical analysis."

Green, J.A. *Teacher-Made Tests.* 2nd ed. New York: Harper & Row, 1975.

This book is "must" reading for teachers who are interested in improving their student evaluation program. Green has chapters on construction and use of objective, performance, and essay tests and oral examination techniques. The final chapter deals with statistical treatment of test data from a very pragmatic, utilitarian point of view. The book is published in paperback format and should be a welcome addition to any special vocational needs teacher's professional library.

House, E.R., ed. *School Evaluation: The Politics and Process.* Berkeley, Calif.: McCutchan Publishing Corporation, 1973.

House has edited a collection of 24 articles addressed under the major headings of: Decision Making and Evaluation, Politics as Usual, Evaluating Teachers, If Everyone Agrees . . . and If Nobody Agrees. The epilogue, entitled "Can Public Schools Be Evaluated?" summarizes many of the problems associated with educational evaluation. It is interesting to note that, although some of the procedures are out of date, the observations on the politics of evaluations are as valid today as when they were written.

Mager, R.F. *Preparing Instructional Objectives.* Belmont, Calif.: Fearon Publishers, 1962.

A classic text that rates a place in every professional library.

National Association of State Boards of Education. *Vocational Education of Handicapped Youth: State of the Art.* Washington, D.C.: National Association of State Boards of Education, 1979.

Only a small part of this report addresses the subject of evaluation, but the topic of needs assessment is very effectively covered, and the balance of the writing is of immediate interest to vocational special needs teachers.

Welch, I.D.; Richards, F.; and Richards, A.C., eds. *Educational Accountability: A Humanistic Perspective*. Fort Collins, Colo.: Shields Publishing Co., 1973.
Evaluation and accountability seem to foster behaviorism. For those who would like to read another viewpoint, this book fills the bill.

Wentling, T.L., and Lawson, T.E. *Evaluating Occupational Education and Training Programs*. Boston, Mass.: Allyn and Bacon, 1975.
Wentling and Lawson have written one of the best books available on the subject of evaluating vocational and occupational programs. The book is well-written and well-illustrated with a wide range of forms to make the job of data collection easier. Although they provide excellent coverage of all aspects of evaluation, their treatment (in two chapters) of follow up of students and employers sets the book apart from the average text on evaluation. It is very unlikely that any text published in the near future will remove this book from its rightful place as a prime reference for vocational evaluation.

Worthen, E.R. *A Look at the Mosaic of Education Evaluation and Accountability*. Northwest Regional Laboratory Working Paper #3, Portland, Ore.: Northwest Regional Laboratory, August 1974.
Worthen bases the contexts of this working paper on the observation that "evaluation" and "accountability" are often used but little understood terms. She chooses the 1971 Colorado Accountability Act as a paradigm and discusses the pros and cons of evaluation in the light of the act's requirements for accountability. This working paper is one in a series of papers devoted to various aspects of educational evaluation. Information on the series can be obtained from the Office of Research and Evaluation Services, Northwest Regional Educational Laboratory, Portland, Ore.

Appendix A

Directory of Organizations, Advocacy Groups, and Curriculum Centers Related To Serving Special Needs Populations

AFL-CIO
Department of Civil Rights
815 16th Street N.W.
Washington, D.C. 20006

Alexander Graham Bell Association for the Deaf
3417 Volta Place, N.W.
Washington, D.C. 20007

American Association on Mental Deficiency
5201 Connecticut Ave., N.W.
Washington, D.C. 20015

American Association for Rehabilitation Therapy, Inc.
P.O. Box 93
North Little Rock, Ark.

American Association of Workers for the Blind, Inc.
1511 K Street, N.W.
Washington, D.C. 20005

American Cancer Society, Inc.
219 East 42nd Street
New York, N.Y. 10017

American Coalition for Citizens with Disabilities
1346 Connecticut Avenue N.W., #308
Washington, D.C. 20036

American Council for Nationalities Service
20 W. 40th St.
New York, N.Y. 10018

American Foundation for the Blind, Inc.
15 West 16th Street
New York, N.Y. 10011

American Lung Association
1740 Broadway
New York, N.Y. 10019

American Orthotic and Prosthetic Association
1440 N Street, N.W.
Washington, D.C. 20005

American Personnel and Guidance Association
1607 New Hampshire Avenue, N.W.
Washington, D.C. 20009

American Physical Therapy Association
1156 15th Street, N.W.
Washington, D.C. 20005

American Podiatry Association
20 Chevy Chase Circle
Washington, D.C. 20015

American Printing House for the Blind, Inc.
1839 Frankfort Avenue
Louisville, Ky. 40206

American Speech and Hearing Association
9030 Old Georgetown Rd.
Washington, D.C. 20014

American Vocational Association
2020 N. 14th
Arlington, Va. 22201

Arthritis Foundation
1212 Avenue of the Americas
New York, N.Y. 10036

Association for Children with Learning Disabilities
5225 Grace Street
Pittsburgh, Pa. 15236

Boy Scouts of America
Scouting for the Handicapped Division
North Brunswick, N.J. 08902

Bureau of Education for the Handicapped
U.S. Department of Education
400 Maryland Avenue, S.W.
Washington, D.C. 20202

Bureau of Occupational and Adult Education
(Disadvantaged and Handicapped Specialists)
7th and D Streets, S.W.
Washington, D.C. 20202

Center for Applied Linguistics
1611 North Kent Street
Arlington, Va. 22209

Center for Urban Education
105 Madison Avenue
New York, N.Y. 10016

The Clearinghouse on the Handicapped
Office for Handicapped Individuals
Room 338D, Hubert H. Humphrey Building
Washington, D.C. 20201

Council for Exceptional Children
1920 Association Drive
Reston, Va. 22091

Council of Organizations Serving the Deaf
P.O. Box 894
Columbia, Md. 21044

Division for Career Development
Council for Exceptional Children
1920 Association Drive
Reston, Va. 22091

EPI-HAB, L.A., Inc.
5533 S. Western Ave.
Los Angeles, Calif. 90062

Epilepsy Foundation of America
1828 L Street, N.W.
Washington, D.C. 20036

Federation Employment and Guidance Service
215 Park Avenue South
New York, N.Y. 10003

Federation of the Handicapped, Inc.
211 West 14th Street
New York, N.Y. 20014

Girl Scouts of the U.S.A.
Scouting for Handicapped Girls Program
830 Third Avenue
New York, N.Y. 10022

Human Resources Center
Willets Road
Albertson, N.Y. 11507

ICD Rehabilitation and Research Center
(Formerly Institute for the Crippled and Disabled)
340 East 24th Street
New York, N.Y. 10010

International Association of Laryngectomees
219 East 42nd Street
New York, N.Y. 10017

International Association of Rehabilitation Facilities, Inc.
5530 Wisconsin Avenue, #955
Washington, D.C. 20015

International Reading Association
800 Barksdale Road
Newark, Del. 19711

The Industrial Home for the Blind
57 Willoughby Street
Brooklyn, N.Y. 11201

Library of Congress
Division for the Blind and Physically Handicapped
Washington, D.C. 20542

Midwest Curriculum Coordination Center
State Department of Vocational and Technical Education
1515 West Sixth Avenue
Stillwater, Okla. 74074

Muscular Dystrophy Association of America
810 Seventh Avenue
New York, N.Y. 10019

National Association of the Deaf
814 Thayer Avenue
Silver Spring, Md. 20910

National Association of Hearing and Speech Agencies
814 Thayer Avenue
Silver Spring, Md. 20910

The National Association for Mental Health, Inc.
1800 North Kent Street
Arlington, Va. 22209

National Association for the Physically Handicapped, Inc.
6473 Grandville Avenue
Detroit, Mich. 48228

National Association for Retarded Citizens
2709 Ave. E. East, POB 6109
Arlington, Tex. 76011

National Association of Vocational Education
Special Needs Personnel
C/O American Vocational Association
2020 N. 14th
Arlington, Va. 22201

National Center for Audio Tapes
361 Stadium Building
University of Colorado
Boulder, Colo. 80309

National Center for a Barrier Free Environment
7315 Wisconsin Avenue
Washington, D.C. 20014

National Center for Research in Vocational Education
Ohio State University
1960 Kenny Road
Columbus, Ohio 43210

National Clearinghouse for Bilingual Education
Suite 802
1500 Wilson Blvd.
Rosslyn, Va. 22209

National Clearing House for Mental Health Information,
National Institute of Mental Health
5600 Fishers Lane
Rockville, Md. 20852

National Committee for Children and Youth
1145 19th St. N.W.
Washington, D.C. 20036

National Congress of Organizations of the Physically Handicapped, Inc.
7611 Oakland Avenue
Minneapolis, Minn. 55423

National Council for the Social Studies
Suite 400, 2030 M Street, N.W.
Washington, D.C. 20036

National Easter Seal Society for Crippled Children and Adults
2023 West Ogden Avenue
Chicago, Ill. 60612

National Education Association
Center for Human Relations
1201 16th St. N.W.
Washington, D.C. 20036

National Federation of the Blind
Suite 212, 1346 Connecticut Ave., N.W.
Washington, D.C. 20036

The National Foundation
March of Dimes
1275 Mamaroneck Ave.
White Plains, N.Y. 10605

The National Hemophilia Foundation
25 West 39th Street
New York, N.Y. 10018

National Inconvenienced Sportsmen's Association
3738 Walnut Avenue
Carmichael, Calif. 95608

National Industries for the Blind
1455 Broad Street
Bloomfield, N.J. 07003

National Information Center for the Handicapped
Closer Look
P.O. Box 1492
Washington, D.C. 20013

National Multiple Sclerosis Society
257 Park Avenue South
New York, N.Y. 10010

National Network for Curriculum Coordination in Vocational and Technical Education:

East Central Curriculum Management Center
100 North First St.
Springfield, Ill. 62777

Midwest Curriculum and Instructional Materials Center
1515 West 6th Avenue
Stillwater, Okla. 74074

Northeast Curriculum Center
Bureau of Occupational and Career Research Development
Division of Vocational Education
New Jersey Department of Education
225 West State Street
Trenton, N.J. 08625

Northwestern Curriculum Coordination Center
Building 17, Airdustrial Park
Olympia, Wash. 98504

Southeast Curriculum Coordination Center
College of Education
Mississippi State University
Box 5365
Starksville, Miss. 39762

Western Curriculum Coordination Center
College of Education
Wist Hall 216
University of Hawaii
1776 University Ave.
Honolulu, Hawaii 96822

National Paraplegia Foundation
333 North Michigan Avenue
Chicago, Ill. 60601

National Rehabilitation Association
1522 K Street, N.W.
Washington, D.C. 20005

National Rehabilitation Counseling Association
1522 K Street, N.W.
Washington, D.C. 20005

National Society for the Prevention of Blindness, Inc.
79 Madison Avenue
New York, N.Y. 10016

National Therapeutic Recreation Society
(A Branch of the National Recreation and Park Association)
1601 North Kent Street
Arlington, Va. 22209

National Urban League
55 E. 52nd St.
New York, N.Y. 10017

Paralyzed Veterans of America
7315 Wisconsin Ave., N.W.
Suite 301 W
Washington, D.C. 20014

President's Commission on Employment of the Handicapped
1111 Twentieth Street N.W.
Washington, D.C. 20210

President's Committee on Mental Retardation
7th and D Streets, S.W.
Washington, D.C. 20201

Professional Rehabilitation Workers with the Adult Deaf, Inc.
814 Thayer Avenue
Silver Spring, Md. 20910

Rehabilitation International USA
17 East 45th Street
New York, N.Y. 10017

Rehabilitation Services Administration
330 C Street, S.W.
Washington, D.C. 20201

Research and Information Services for Education
198 Allendale Road
King of Prussia, Pa. 19406

Sister Kenny Institute
1800 Chicago Avenue
Minneapolis, Minn. 55404

United Cerebral Palsy Association, Inc.
66 East 34th Street
New York, N.Y. 10016

United Ostomy Association, Inc.
1111 Wilshire Blvd.
Los Angeles, Calif. 90017

U.S. Civil Service Commission
1900 E Street, N.W.
Washington, D.C. 20415

U.S. Commission on Civil Rights
1121 Vermont Ave., N.W.
Washington, D.C. 20245

U.S. Department of Health and Human Services
Office of Human Development Services
Office for Handicapped Individuals
Washington, D.C. 20201

United States Employment Service
Washington, D.C. 20213

Urban Coalition
2100 M St. N.W.
Washington, D.C. 20037

Appendix B

Additional Special Needs Resources

The following resources will assist the reader in securing additional information and assistance in programming for special needs students. The list is in no way meant to be inclusive; the books and films included are, however, representative of the many resources currently available.

Books

Altfest, Myra. *Vocational Education for Students with Special Needs: A Teacher's Handbook*. Fort Collins, Colo.: Department of Vocational Education, Colorado State University, 1975.

Bailey, L.J., and Stadt, R.W. *Career Education: New Approaches to Human Development*. Bloomington, Ill.: McKnight Publishing Company, 1973

Barlow, M.L. *History of Industrial Education in the United States*. Peoria, Ill.· Chas. A. Bennett Company, Inc., 1967.

Bowe, Frank. *Handicapping America*. New York: Harper and Row, 1978.

Brolin, Donn. *Vocational Preparation of Retarded Citizens*. Columbus, Ohio· Charles Merrill Publishing Company, 1976.

Cruickshank, W.M. and Johnson, G.O., eds. *Education of Exceptional Children and Youth,* 2d ed. Englewood Cliffs, N.J.: Prentice-Hall, Inc., 1967

Dahl, Peter; Appleby, Judith A.; and Lipe, Dewey. *Mainstreaming Guidebook for Vocational Educators: Teaching the Handicapped*. Salt Lake City, Utah: Olympus Publishing Company, 1978.

Frierson, E.C., and Barbe, W.B., eds. *Educating Children with Learning Disabilities: Selected Readings*. New York: Appleton-Century-Crofts, 1967.

Gagne, R.M. *Learning and Individual Differences: A Symposium of the Learning and Research and Development Center, University of Pittsburgh*. Columbus Ohio: Charles E. Merrill Publishing Company, 1967.

Gardner, David C., and Warren, Sue Allen. *Careers and Disabilities*. Stamford, Conn.: Greylock Publishers, 1978.

Garton, M.D. *Teaching the Educable Mentally Retarded: Practical Methods*. Springfield, Ill.: Charles C. Thomas Publishers, 1970.

Gearheart, B.R. *Learning Disabilities: Educational Strategies*. St. Louis, Mo.: C.V. Mosby Publishing Company, 1973.

Gearheart, B.R. *Teaching the Learning Disabled: A Combined Task-Process Approach*. St. Louis, Mo.: C.V. Mosby Publishing Company, 1976.

Hammill, D.D., and Myers, P.L. *Methods for Learning Disorders*. New York: John Wiley and Sons, 1976.

Haring, N.G., and Schiefelbusch, R.L. *Teaching Special Children*. New York: McGraw-Hill Publishing Company, 1976.

Harkness, C.A. *Career Counseling*. Springfield, Ill.: Charles C. Thomas Publishers, 1976.

Hewett, F.M. *Education of Exceptional Learners*. Boston: Allyn & Bacon, 1974.

Industry-Labor Council of the White House Conference on Handicapped Individuals. *Steps: Handicapped Workers and Today's Labor Market*. Washington, D.C.: Industry-Labor Council, 1977.

Ingram, C.P. *Education of the Slow-Learning Child,* 3d ed. New York: Ronald Press, 1960.

Jones, R.L. *New Directions in Special Education*. Boston: Allyn & Bacon, 1970.

Kirk, S.A. *Educating Exceptional Children*. Boston: Houghton Mifflin, 1972.

Kolstoe, O.P. *Teaching Educable Mentally Retarded Children,* 2d ed. New York: Holt, Rinehart and Winston, Inc., 1976.

Koyloff, M.A. *Educating Children with Learning and Behavior Problems*. New York: John Wiley and Sons, 1974.

Mann, F.H., and Suiter, P. *Handbook in Diagnostic Teaching: A Learning Disabilities Approach*. Boston: Allyn & Bacon, 1974.

Meyan, E.L. *Developing Units of Instruction: For the Mentally Retarded and Other Children with Learning Problems*. Dubuque, Iowa: William C. Brown Publishers, 1972.

Meyan, E.L.; Vergason, G.A.; and Whelan, R.J. *Alternatives for Teaching Exceptional Children: Essays from Focus on Exceptional Children*. Denver, Colo.: Love Publishing Company, 1975.

Noar, G. *Individualized Instruction for the Mentally Retarded*. Glenn Ridge, N.J.: Exceptional Press, 1974.

Otto, W.; McMenemy, R.A.; and Smith, R.J. *Corrective and Remedial Teaching,* 2d ed. Boston: Houghton Mifflin, 1973.

Payne, J.S.; Polloway, E.A.; Smith, J.E.; and Payne, R.A. *Strategies for Teaching the Mentally Retarded.* Columbus, Ohio: Charles E. Merrill Publishing Company, 1977.

Peter L.J. *Individual Instruction.* New York: McGraw-Hill, 1972.

Peter, L.J. *Prescriptive Teaching.* New York: McGraw-Hill, 1965.

Phelps, L.A., and Lutz, R. *Career Exploration and Preparation for the Special Needs Learner.* Boston: Allyn & Bacon, Inc., 1977.

Pophan, W.J., and Baker, E.L. *Establishing Instructional Goals.* Engelwood Cliffs, N.J.: Prentice-Hall, 1970.

Pophan, W.J., and Baker, E.L. *Planning an Instructional Sequence.* Engelwood Cliffs, N.J.: Prentice-Hall, 1970.

Pophan, W.J., and Baker, E.L. *Systematic Instruction.* Engelwood Cliffs, N.J.: Prentice-Hall, 1970.

Rosenberg, M.B. *Diagnostic Teaching.* Seattle, Wash.: Special Child Publications, 1968.

Stellern, J.; Vasa, S.F.; and Little, J. *Introduction to Diagnostic-Prescriptive Teaching and Programming.* Glenn Ridge, N.J.: Exceptional Press, 1976.

Stephens, T.M. *Directive Teaching of Children with Learning and Behavior Handicaps* 2d ed. Columbus, Ohio: Charles E. Merrill Publishing Company, 1976.

Towenbraun, S., and Affleck, J.Q. *Teaching Mildly Handicapped Children in Regular Classes.* Columbus, Ohio: Charles E. Merrill Publishing Company, 1976.

U.S., Department of Health, Education, and Welfare, Office of Education. *A Primer for Career Education.* Washington, D.C.: Government Printing Office.

Weisgerber, Robert, ed. *Vocational Education: Teaching the Handicapped in Regular Classes.* Reston, Va.: Council for Exceptional Children, 1979.

U.S., Department of Health, Education, and Welfare, Office of Education. *Improving Occupational Programs in the Handicapped.* Washington, D.C.: Government Printing Office.

Films

(for information write to address listed)

A Different Approach

South Bay Mayor's Committee for the Employment
of the Handicapped
2409 North Sepulveda
Suite 202
Manhattan Beach, Calif. 90266

Cipher in the Snow

BYLL Press
Brigham Young Univ.
170 W. Stadium
Provo, Utah 84602

Count Me In

Stamfield House
12381 Wilshire
Suite 203
Los Angeles, Calif. 90025

Differences

A.C.I. Films, Inc.
Distribution Center
P.O. Box 1898
12 Jules Lane
New Brunswick, N.J. 08902

Getting It Together

FMS Films
1040 North Los Palmas
Los Angeles, Calif. 90038

If a Boy Can't Learn

Lawren Productions
P.O. Box 1542
Burlingame, Calif. 94010

Not Without Sight

American Foundation for the Blind
15 West 16th Street
New York, N.Y. 10011

The Reluctant Delinquent

Lawren Productions, Inc.
P.O. Box 666
Mendocino. Calif. 95460

To Live as Equals

London Films
52 Undercliff Terrace South
West Orange, N.J. 07502

Glossary of Special Needs Terms

This glossary was developed with the assistance of Stanley F. Vasa, Associate Professor of Special Education, University of Nebraska, Lincoln, Nebraska, and Judith Johnson, Montana Easter Seal Society, Helena, Montana.

Academic Aptitude: The combination of native and acquired abilities that is needed for school work; likelihood of success in mastering academic work, as estimated from measures of the necessary abilities. (Also called scholastic aptitude.)

Acoustics: The science of sound including the origin, transmission, and effects of mechanical vibrations in any medium, whether audible or not.

Acting-Out: Behavioral discharge of tension in response to a present situation or stimulus, as if it were the situation or stimulus that was originally associated with the tension. Often a chronic and habitual pattern of response to frustration and conflict.

Adaptive Behavior: That behavior that is considered appropriate for a given individual in a specific context. This term usually refers to behavior that is judged acceptable by authorities, such as teachers, and not in need of modification. These authorities are guided by developmental and societal norms in making such judgments.

Adjustment: The relation between the individual, his inner self and his environment.

Adventitiously Deaf: Those who become deaf from accident or disease after birth or lose hearing after acquisition of language.

Advisory Committee: A group of persons, usually outside the educational profession, selected for the purpose of offering advice and counsel to the school regarding the vocational program. Members are representatives of the people who are interested in the activities with which the vocational program is concerned.

Affect: Emotional feeling tone or mood.

Affective Disorder: Disorder of mood or feeling with resulting thought and behavioral disturbances.

Agriculture/Agribusiness Education: An occupation in agriculture/agribusiness is defined as an employment opportunity requiring competencies in one or more of the areas of plant science, animal science, soil science, management, mechanization, conservation, environmental quality, human relations, and leadership development needed to satisfactorily fulfill the employment needs in one or more of the functions of producing, processing, and/or distributing products and services related thereto.

Ambidextrous: Able to use either hand effectively.

Ambivalence: Simultaneous existence of conflicting feelings or attitudes toward an object or person. May be conscious or unconscious.

Ambulation: The art of walking without assistance from others. It may include the use of crutches, canes, or other mechanical aids.

Amnesia: A disorder characterized by partial or total inability to recall or to identify past experiences; lack or loss of memory.

Amplitude: Largeness; wideness; breadth of range or extent; the distance through space a vibrating body moves; directly related to intensity of sound and sometimes used synonymously with intensity and volume.

Anomaly: A structure or function that deviates from the normal.

Anoxia: Deficient amount of oxygen in the tissues of a part of the body or in the blood stream supplying such a part.

Anxiety Reaction: A neurotic reaction with diffuse anxiety and physiological anxiety indicators, such as sweating and palpitation based on an exaggerated state of fear or tension.

Apathy: Lack of feeling or response.

Aphasia: Loss or impairment of the ability to use or understand oral language. It is usually associated with an injury or abnormality of the speech centers of the brain. Several classifications are used, including expressive and receptive, congenital, and acquired aphasia.

Aptitude: A combination of abilities and other characteristics, whether native or acquired, known or believed to be indicative of an individual's ability to learn in some particular area. Thus, "musical aptitude" would refer broadly to that combination of physical and mental characteristics, motivational factors, and conceivably other characteristics, that is conducive to acquiring proficiency in the musical field.

Articulation: The enunciation of words and sentences.

Assimilation: The reception and correct interpretation of sensory impressions.

Ataxia: Condition in which there is no paralysis, but the motor activity cannot be coordinated normally. Seen as impulsive, jerky movements and tremors with disruptions in balance.

Athetoid Cerebral Palsy: Characterized by difficulty with voluntary movements, especially in controlling those movements in the desired direction (demonstrated by extra or purposeless movements).

Athetosis: A form of cerebral palsy marked by slow, recurring, weaving movement of the limbs.

Atrophy: A wasting away or diminution in the size of cell, tissue, organ, or part.

Attention Span: The length of time a person can concentrate on a single activity before losing interest.

Audiogram: A graphic summary of the measurements of hearing loss, showing number of decibels loss at each frequency tested.

Audiologist: A professional person who is engaged in the study of the hearing function; responsible for the evaluation of persons with hearing problems and for the planning of education programs for people with hearing impairments.

Auditory Discrimination: Ability to discriminate between sounds of different frequency, intensity, and pressure-pattern components; ability to distinguish one speech sound from another.

Aura: Premonitory sensations or hallucinations that may warn of an impending epileptic seizure.

Aural: Pertaining to the ear or to the sensation of hearing. Same as auditory.

Autism: A childhood disorder in which the child, responding to unknown inner stimuli, is rendered noncommunicative and withdrawn. Characterized by extreme withdrawal and inability to relate to other persons.

Baseline: Beginning observations prior to intervention; level of functioning established or measured without any active intervention from the observer.

Behavior Modification: A technique of changing human behavior based on the theory of operant behavior and conditioning. Careful observation of events preceding and following the behavior in question is required. The environment is manipulated to reinforce the desired responses, thereby bringing about the desired change in behavior.

Bilateral: Pertaining to the use of both sides of the body in a simultaneous and parallel fashion.

Bilingual: Using or able to use two languages.

Blind (Legally) (see also Visually Handicapped): Having central visual acuity of 20/200 or less in the better eye after correction, or visual acuity of more than 20/200 if there is a field defect in which the widest diameter of the visual field subtends an angle distance no greater than 20°.

Body Image: The concept and awareness of one's own body as it relates to orientation, movement, and other behavior.

Brain-Injured Child: A child who before, during, or after birth has received an injury to or suffered an infection of the brain. As a result of such organic impairments, there are disturbances that prevent or impede the normal learning process.

Business and Office Education: Business and office education is designated to meet the needs of persons enrolled in secondary, postsecondary and adult programs and has as its purpose initial preparation, the refreshing and/or upgrading of individuals leading to employment and advancement in business and office occupations.

Career Education: The totality of experiences through which one learns about and prepares to engage in work as part of a way of life.

Central Nervous System (C.N.S.): That portion of the nervous system to which the sensory impulses are delivered and from which the motor impulses pass out; in vertebrates, the spinal cord and brain.

Cerebral Dominance: The state in which one hemisphere of the brain is more involved in the mediation of various functions than the other hemisphere; a theory, expostulated largely by Orton, Delacato, and Travis, that one hemisphere is a dominant controller; right-hemisphere-dominant and ambidextrous people show mixed dominance.

Cerebral Palsy: Any one of a group of conditions in which motor control is affected because of lesions in various parts of the brain.

Channels of Communication: The sensory-motor pathways through which language is transmitted, e.g., auditory-vocal, visual-motor, and other possible combinations.

Cloze Procedure: A technique used in testing, teaching of reading comprehension, and determination of readability. Involves deletion of words from the text and leaving blank spaces.

Conceptual Disorders: Disturbances in the thinking process and in cognitive activities, or disturbances in the ability to formulate concepts.

Concrete Mode: One of the styles of cognitive functioning that describes the child's approach to problem-solving at a simple, elementary level. Also, the use of tangible objects in instruction, as opposed to purely verbal instruction.

Conductive Hearing Loss: A condition that reduces the intensity of the sound vibrations reaching the auditory nerve in the inner ear.

Congenital: Present at birth; usually a defect of either familial or exogenous origin that exists at the time of birth.

Consumer and Homemaking Education Programs: Education programs designed to help individuals and families improve home environments and the quality of personal and family life; includes instruction in food and nutrition, child development, textiles and clothing, housing, family relations, and management of resources, with emphasis on selection, use, and care of goods and services and on budgeting and other consumer responsibilities. Such programs are designed to meet the needs of persons who have entered or are preparing to enter useful employment in the home and are enrolled in secondary, postsecondary, or adult programs.

Continuum of Services: A full spectrum of services that are tailored to the individual needs of each student at any given time during the student's educational career.

Cooperative Vocational Education: A program of vocational education for persons who, through a cooperative arrangement between the school and employers, receive instruction, including required academic courses and related vocational instruction, by alternation of study in school with a job in any occupational field. The two experiences must be planned and supervised by the school and employers so that each contributes to the student's education and employability. Work periods and school attendance may be on alternate half-days, full-days, weeks, or other period of time in fulfilling the cooperative work-study (vocational education) program.

Coordinating Teacher (Teacher-Coordinator): A member of the school staff who teaches the related and technical subject matter involved in work experience programs and coordinates classroom instruction with on-the-job training.

Coordinator (Cooperative Education): A member of the school staff responsible for administering the school program and resolving all problems that arise between the school regulations and the on-the-job activities of the employed student. The coordinator acts as liaison between the school and employers in programs of cooperative education or other parttime job training.

Crisis or Helping Teacher: A teacher who provides temporary support and control to troubled students when they are unable or unwilling to cope with the demands of the regular classroom.

Cross-Modal: Including more than one sensory modality.

Curriculum: The organized content of a particular discipline with established parameters for instruction.

dB: Decibel.

Deaf: The child is impaired in processing linguistic information through hearing, with or without amplification, which adversely affects educational performance

Deaf-Blind: Concomitant hearing and visual impairments which cause severe communication and other developmental and educational problems that cannot be accommodated in special education programs solely for deaf or blind children.

Deafened: Pertaining to adventitious loss of all useable hearing.

Decibel: A unit of hearing or audition. One decibel is approximately equal to the smallest difference in loudness that the human ear can detect.

Desensitization: A therapeutic technique, based on learning theory, in which a client is first trained in muscle relaxation and then imagines a series of increasingly anxiety-provoking situations, until the person no longer experiences anxiety while thinking about the stimuli. The learning principle involved is reciprocal inhibition, according to which two incompatible responses cannot be made simultaneously by a person.

Directionality: Awareness of the up-and-down axis (verticality) and of the relative position of one side of the body versus the other (laterality).

Disadvantaged: Persons (other than handicapped) who have academic or economic handicaps or have limited English-speaking abilities, who require special services and assistance in order for them to be able to succeed in regular vocational education programs.

- Academic handicaps are determined by (1) instructor's records that indicate that the student cannot succeed in vocational education programs without special support services, or (2) information obtained from tests that indicates that the student needs help in one or more academic areas in order to be able to succeed in regular vocational education programs.
- Economic handicaps are determined on the basis of the family income-level standards established by the United States Department of Commerce and/or the United States Department of Agriculture for the issuance of free and reduced price meals, providing that the economic handicap is impairing the student's success in regular vocational education programs.
- Limited English-speaking ability. Persons who demonstrate minimal ability or lack the ability to express fundamental needs or thoughts lucidly, are unable to follow directions or react appropriately, and exhibit unnatural reticence in communicating with classmates may be considered to lack a functional command of the English language.

Distributive Education: Education that identifies a program of instruction designed to meet the needs of persons enrolled in secondary, postsecondary, and adult programs by:

- introducing and orienting each individual to the field of distribution,
- providing educational experiences that will enable the student to achieve career-level employment, and
- creating an occupational learning environment that will contribute to an increased awareness of career opportunities, advancement, and educational patterns for continued achievement.

Diversified Occupations Education Program: A program that provides an opportunity for schools in small communities to make available vocational education with supervised work experience in a variety of occupations. It can be utilized in communities that are not large enough to provide parttime jobs in sufficient quantity to support an occupational experience program in a particular area (e.g. agriculture, distributive, business, home economics, health, or trades and industries). If a program related to their vocational objectives is offered in the school, diversified occupations students should be enrolled in or have completed course work in this program. If it is not offered, the students could go directly into the diversified occupational education program in their senior year.

Due Process: The process through which the child and parents or surrogate parents are informed of the pending educational placement and either agree in writing or appeal the placement based upon their rights in Public Law 94-142 Subpart E.

Dyscalculia: Loss of ability to calculate, to manipulate number symbols, or to do simple arithmetic.

Dysgraphia: Impairment in spontaneous writing, the ability to copy being intact.

Dyslexia: A disorder of children who, despite conventional classroom experience, fail to learn to read. The term is most frequently used when neurological dysfunction is suspected as a cause of the reading disability.

Echolalia: Automatic reiteration of words or phrases, usually those which have just been heard.

Educable Mentally Retarded: Education terms used to describe retarded who can profit from academic education; mildly retarded—I.Q. generally from 50 to 75.

EEG: Electroencephalography.

Electroencephalograph: An instrument for graphically recording electrical currents developed in the cerebral cortex during brain function; often abbreviated EEG.

Electronic Mobility Devices: Devices to enhance hearing efficiency, detect obstacles, enable individuals to walk in a straight line, or reveal specific location of obstacles in the environment.

Epilepsy: A disturbance in the electrochemical activity of the discharging cells of the brain that is produced by a variety of neurological disorders. The causes are not clear. The electrochemical disturbances usually result in a seizure of some degree, i.e., in one of the following:

- petit mal—a mild seizure in which dizziness or staring into space takes place.
- grand mal—a seizure in which there are severe convulsions and loss of consciousness or a coma.
- Jacksonian—spasms limited mainly to one side of the body and often to one group of muscles.
- psychomotor—motor acts that the patient cannot remember performing.

Expressive Language: The ability to express or communicate verbal, written, or symbolic language.

Familial: Occurring in members of the same family; a familial disease.

Finger Spelling: The use of the manual alphabet to spell out words for the deaf.

Free Appropriate Public Education (FAPE): Special education and related services that are provided at public expense, including preschool, elementary school, or secondary school education.

General Education: Education that is concerned with the needs that are common to all members of society and that enable individuals to live with others, in order that they may be active in the social and democratic phases of life. Such education focuses upon knowledge, skills, and attitudes that are held useful for successful living, without reference or application to any particular vocation. General education fits people for life in general and acquaints them with the means of sustaining life.

Genetic: Pertaining to inherited factors.

Glaucoma: The intraocular pressure of the eye increases to such a level that the eye becomes damaged and sight is impaired.

Grand Mal Seizure: A type of epilepsy characterized by considerable neural discharge and usually lasting about five minutes. It begins with a severe contraction of the muscles and proceeds to rhythmic movements and tremors.

Handicap: A physical or mental impairment which substantially limits one or more major life activities.

Haptic: Pertaining to the sense of touch.

Hard-Of-Hearing: A hearing impairment, either permanent or fluctuating, which adversely affects educational performance but is not included under the definition of "deaf."

Health Occupations Education: Education designed for persons who are preparing to enter one of the health occupations and for persons who are, or have been, employed in such occupations in hospitals or institutions or establishments other than hospitals that provide patients with medical services.

Hearing Loss Degrees:

- Mild—27-40 dB: The person will have difficulty with faint or distant speech, may need favorable seating and may benefit from speech reading, vocabulary, and/or language instruction or may need speech therapy.
- Moderate—41-55 dB: The person can understand conversational speech at a distance of three to five feet; probably will need a hearing aid, auditory training, speech reading, favorable seating, speech conversation, or speech therapy.
- Moderately severe—56-70 dB: Conversation must be loud to be understood; speech will probably be defective; may have limited vocabulary; may have trouble in classroom discussions; services used are at moderate level, but specific assistance from the resource/itinerant teachers in the language area may be needed.
- Severe—71-90 dB: The person may hear loud voices at one foot; may have difficulty with vowel sounds but not necessarily consonants; will need all services mentioned and require many techniques used with the deaf.
- Profound—91+dB: The person may hear some sounds, but hearing is not the primary learning channel; needs all mentioned services with emphasis on speech, auditory training, and language; may be in regular class parttime or attend classes that do not require language skills.

Home Economics Related Occupations Programs: Vocational education designed to meet the needs of persons (enrolled in secondary, postsecondary, or adult programs) who have entered or who are preparing to enter gainful employment in an occupation involving knowledge and skills of home economics subjects.

Human Services: Consists of specialized assistance to individuals for the purpose of fulfilling their needs. These services are diverse in nature and deal with people-oriented projects that will realistically aid individuals who are unable to help themselves.

Hyperactivity (Hyperkinesis): A personality disorder of childhood or adolescence characterized by overactivity, restlessness, distractability, and limited attention span.

Hypokinesis: Absence of normal amount of bodily movement and motor activity.

IEP Planning Meeting: A group meeting in which the students and teachers develop the Individual Education Plan.

I.Q.: A numerical score used to indicate a person's relative standing on an intelligence test.

Individual Educational Program (IEP): The IEP is a written statement for a handicapped child that includes the present level of educational performance, a statement of annual goals, short-term objectives, specific and related services to be provided, projected dates for initiation of services, deliverers of the services, and the evaluation procedures to be used.

Inner Language: The process of internalizing and organizing experiences without the use of linguistic symbols.

Intelligence: A term used to describe a person's mental capacity; generally related to such things as problem-solving ability, ability to adapt to environment, or memory for learned material.

Itinerant Teacher: A teacher who travels from school to school helping children with special needs and acting as a consultant to the regular teacher.

Jacksonian Epilepsy: A form of epilepsy in which the seizure manifests no loss of awareness but involves a definite series of convulsions affecting a limited region of the body.

Lateral Dominance: The preferential use, in voluntary motor acts, of ipsilateral members of the different paired organs, such as the right ear, eye, hand, and leg, or the left ear, eye, hand, and leg.

Least Restrictive Environment: The environment in which handicapped students are educated with nonhandicapped students in public or private schools or care facilities to the maximum extent possible and appropriate to the needs of the students.

MR: Mentally retarded.

Mental Age (M.A.): An expression of the level of performance obtained on a standardized test. Compared with the performance of the average person of a given chronological age (C.A.).

Mentally Retarded: Significantly subaverage general intelligence functioning along with deficits in adaptive behavior and manifested during the developmental period, which adversely affects a child's educational performance.

Microcephaly: Abnormal smallness of the head.

Minimal Brain Damage: Early term for designating children with neurogenic learning and adjustment problems. The term is unsatisfactory because brain dysfunction is not necessarily due to damage. The term is often used and applied inaccurately for that reason.

Mobility Aides:

- Sighted guide: a sighted person who takes the blind person to a destination.
- Dog guide: A specifically trained dog used by a blind person to get to a destination.
- Cane: A white or silver cane often with a red tip used for getting to and from a destination.
- Electronic aides: Aides that are usually more successful when used as a companion with the cane. Two of the more acceptable ones are the Laser Cane and the Kaye Spectacles.

Modality: An avenue of acquiring sensation; the visual, auditory, tactile, kinesthetic, olfactory, and gustatory are the most common sense modalities.

Modeling: A procedure for learning in which the individual observes a model perform some task and then imitates the performance of the model. This form of learning accounts for much verbal and motor learning in young children.

Multihandicapped: Concomitant impairments (such as mentally retarded-blind, mentally retarded-orthopedically handicapped, etc.) which causes severe educational problems that cannot be accommodated in special education programs solely for one impairment. Does not include "deaf-blind."

Multiple Sclerosis: A disease marked by hardening in sporadic patches throughout the brain or spinal cord, or both. Among its symptoms are weakness, incoordination, strong jerking movements of the legs and arms, abnormal mental exaltation, scanning speech, and nystagmus.

Multisensory: Generally applied to training procedures that simultaneously utilize more than one sense modality.

Muscular Dystrophy: One of the more common primary diseases of the muscles. It is characterized by weakness and atrophy of the skeletal muscles with increasing disability and deformity.

Neurological Lag: Neurological or nervous system development that is slower than other physical development.

Norm: An average, common, or standard performance under specified conditions, e.g., the average achievement test score of nine-year-old children or the average birth weight of male children.

Ocular: Pertaining to the eye.

On-The-Job Training: Instruction in the performance of a job given to an employed worker by the employer during the usual working hours of the occupation. Usually the minimum or beginning wage is paid.

Ontogeny: The developmental history of the individual.

Ophthalmologist: A trained person with a medical degree who specializes in identification and treatment of eye discases and disorders.

Optometrist: A person who studies the measuring of visual acuity and grinds lenses for glasses, does not have a medical degree, and cannot prescribe medicines or treat eye diseases or disorders.

Oral Method: Method of teaching communication of language to deaf or hard-of-hearing patients by spoken words.

Orientation: An individual's use of relevant senses to establish a position and relationship to objects in the environment.

Orthopedically Impaired: Severe orthopedic impairment that adversely affects a child's educational performance. Includes impairments caused by: congenital anomaly, disease, amputation, fractures, burns, and cerebral palsy.

Other Health Impaired: Limited strength, vitality, or alertness due to chronic or acute health problems such as heart condition, tuberculosis, rheumatic fever, asthma, sickle cell anemia, epilepsy, etc., which adversely affects a child's educational performance.

Otitis Media: Inflammation of the middle ear.

Pathology: The study of the nature of disease and its resulting structural and functional changes.

Perceptual-Motor: A term describing the interaction of the various channels of perception with motor activity. The channels of perception include visual, auditory, tactual, and kinesthetic.

Perinatal: Occurring at or pertaining to time of birth.

Perseveration: The tendency for one to persist in a specific act or behavior after it is no longer appropriate.

Petit Mal Seizure: A type of epilepsy that is characterized by short lapses of consciousness; commonly begins in early childhood.

Phobia: Pathological fear of some specific stimulus or situation.

Physical Therapy: Helps overcome neuromuscular disability through exercise, massage, heat, water, light, sound, or electricity.

Postnatal: Occurring after birth.

Practical Arts Education: A type of functional education predominantly manipulative in nature that provides learning experiences in leisure-time interests, consumer knowledge, creative expression, family living, manual skills, technological development, and similar outcomes of value.

Prenatal: Existing or occurring prior to birth.

Prosthesis: The replacement of a part of the body by an artificial substitute.

Psychiatry: That branch of medicine that deals with mental disorders.

Psychomotor Seizure: A type of epilepsy characterized by automatisms that range from the unconscious continuing of normal activity to bizarre, inappropriate, or obsessive behavior.

Psychopathology: The study of the causes and nature of mental disease.

Psychosis: A severe emotional illness in which there is a departure from normal patterns of thinking, feeling, and actions. Commonly characterized by loss of contact with reality, distortion of perception, regressive behavior, and attitudes, diminished control of elementary impulses and desires, and abnormal mental content including delusions and hallucinations.

Psychosomatic Disorder: An ailment with organic symptoms attributable to emotional and other psychological causes. The disorder is aggravated by or results from continuous states of anxiety, stress, and emotional conflict.

Readability Level: An indication of the difficulty of reading material in terms of the grade level at which it might be expected to be read successfully.

Reauditorization: A term used to denote the retrieval of auditory images.

Receptive Language: Language that is spoken or written by others and received by the individual. The receptive language skills are listening and reading.

Resource Teacher: A specialist who works with children with special learning needs and acts as a consultant to other teachers, providing materials and methods to help children who are having difficulty within the regular classroom. The resource teacher may work from a centralized resource room in a school where appropriate materials are housed.

Seizures: Occur when there are excessive electrical discharges released in some nerve cells of the brain. The brain loses control over muscles, consciousness, senses, and thoughts.

Self-Care Skill: The ability to care for oneself; usually refers to basic habits of dressing, eating, and so on.

Sensory Perception: Direct awareness or acquaintance through the senses.

Seriously Emotionally Disturbed: Child exhibits one or more of the following characteristics over a long period of time and to a degree that adversely affects educational performance: inability to learn which can't be explained by intellectual, sensory or health factors; inability to build and maintain satisfactory interpersonal relationships; inappropriate behavior or feelings under normal circumstances; pervasive mood of unhappiness or depression, or a tendency to develop physical symptoms or fears associated with personal or school problems. Includes children who are schizophrenic or autistic. Not the socially maladjusted unless it is determined they are seriously emotionally disturbed.

Sheltered Workshop: A facility (usually in the community) that provides occupational training or protective employment of handicapped individuals.

Sign Language: A system of communication among the deaf through conventional hand or body movements that represent ideas, objects, and action; distinguished from finger spelling.

Special Class in a Regular School: Classes for students who receive their academic instruction from a special education teacher but may attend school-wide activities, such as assemblies and concerts, or nonacademic classes, such as physical education or industrial arts, with their peers.

Special Day Schools: Schools designed for students who have a serious handicap or are multihandicapped and need comprehensive special education services for their entire school day.

Special Education: A subsystem of the total educational system responsible for the joint provision of specialized or adapted programs and services (or for assisting others to provide such services) for exceptional children and youths.

Special Educator: One who has had special training or preparation for teaching the handicapped; may also work cooperatively with the regular classroom teacher by sharing unique skills and competencies.

Special Vocational Needs: Vocational education for disadvantaged or handicapped persons supported with funds under the Vocational Education Act of 1976 (Public Law 94-482) to include special educational programs and services designed to enable disadvantaged or handicapped persons to achieve vocational education objectives that would otherwise be beyond their reach as a result of their handicapping condition. These programs and services may take the form of modification of regular programs or be special vocational education programs designed only for disadvantaged or handicapped persons. Examples of such special educational programs and services include the following: special remedial instruction, guidance, counseling and testing services, employability skills training, communications skills training, special transportation facilities and services, special educational equipment, services, and devices, and reader and interpreter services. Such education includes working with those individuals in need of vocational training who cannot succeed in a regular vocational program due to a handicapping condition or the effects of disadvantagement.

Specific Learning Disabilities: Disorder in one or more of the basic psychological processes involved in understanding or using language, spoken or written. Problems in listening, thinking, speaking, reading, writing, spelling, or minimal brain dysfunction, dyslexia, and developmental aphasia. Does not include: problems which are a result of visual, hearing, or motor handicaps of mental retardation or of cultural, environmental or economic disadvantage.

Speech Impaired: Communication disorder such as stuttering, impaired articulation, language impairment, or voice impairment that adversely affects educational performance.

State Plan: An agreement between a state board for vocational education and the U.S. Office of Education describing the vocational education program developed by the state to meet its own purposes and conditions and the conditions under which the state will use federal vocational education funds (such conditions must conform to the federal acts and the official policies of the U.S. Office of Education before programs may be reimbursed from federal funds).

Task Analysis: The technique of carefully examining a particular task to discover the elements it comprises and the processes required to perform it.

Technical Education: Shall be designed to train persons for employment as highly skilled technicians in recognized technical occupations requiring scientific knowledge. Technical education should be conducted primarily on the post high school or adult level.

Trade and Industrial Education: Education to provide students with an understanding and the technical knowledge of our industrial society, to develop the necessary skills for employment in the skilled and semiskilled trades, crafts, or occupations that function directly in the designing, producing, processing, assembling, maintaining, servicing, or repairing of any manufactured product. Training in trade and industrial education enables young men and women to prepare for initial employment in trade, industrial, and technical operations. The basic principle of such education is learning by doing. The needs of the individual worker are the foundations upon which all instructional activity is based. Instructional objectives are tied to the skill or trade being pursued as a career.

Trauma: Any experience that inflicts serious damage to the organism; may refer to psychological as well as physiological insult.

Vakt: A multisensory teaching method involving visual, auditory, kinesthetic, and tactile sense modalities, e.g., the Fernald "hand-kinesthetic" method.

Visually Handicapped: Visual impairment that adversely affects educational performance, even with correction. Both partially-sighted and blind.

Vocational Education: Vocational or technical training or retraining that is given in schools or classes (including field or laboratory work and remedial or related academic and technical instruction incident thereto) under public supervision and control or under contract with a state board or local educational agency. The training or retraining is conducted as part of a program designed to prepare individuals for gainful employment as semiskilled or skilled workers or technicians or subprofessionals in recognized occupations in advanced technical education programs, but excluding any program to prepare individuals for employment in occupations generally considered professional or which require a baccalaureate or higher degree.

Vocational Educator: Persons who have had training or occupational experience in their chosen area of specialization.

Vocational School: A school that is organized separately under a principal or director for the purpose of offering training in one or more skilled or semiskilled trades or occupations. It is designed to meet the needs of high school students preparing for employment and to provide upgrading or extension courses for those who are employed.

Vocational Subject: Any school subject designed to develop specific skills, knowledge, and information to enable the learner to prepare for or to be more efficient in a chosen trade or occupation.

Work-Study Program: A program designed to provide parttime employment for youths who need the earnings from such employment to commence or continue a vocational education program.

Index

A

C

E

I

M

N

U

V